ALPHA BRAVO DELTA
GUIDE TO
THE U.S.
MARINE
CORPS

CLIFTON GANYARD, PH.D.

SERIES EDITOR
WALTER J. BOYNE, USAF (RET.)

ALPHA

A member of Penguin Group (USA) Inc.

CONTENTS

FOREWORD

The few ... the proud ...

The U.S. Marine Corps is a special breed—neither soldier nor sailor, Marines are amphibious warriors capable of operations on land or at sea. Established in the fires of the American Revolution, the Marine Corps is older than the United States, and every fresh-faced recruit sent to Parris Island knows it, too. New Marines are steeped in the Corps history, traditions, and *espirit de corps* from the moment they enter boot camp, and the Corps' future leaders—young officers trained at The Basic School at Quantico—are also educated in the customs of the Marine Corps even as they learn how to lead their troops into battle.

Over the past two centuries, Marines have been called upon to defend America's interests on hundreds of occasions, in places mostly forgotten by history. They have fought aboard ship, on far-flung beaches and shores, in jungles and deserts and, when necessary, on our own hallowed ground. During their long history, Marines have been hailed as heroes or vilified as interventionists, imperialists, and warmongers in equal measure. "From the Halls of Montezuma to the shores of Tripoli," the citizens of many nations first encountered the growing power and influence of the United States of America through these armed, green-clad "ambassadors."

You hold in your hand the remarkable history of this military institution. In lucid detail, Clifton Ganyard recounts the story of the U.S. Marines from their first beachhead assault on New Providence Island in the Bahamas in 1775, to their battles on smoldering deserts of Iraq in 1992, and on to Afghanistan in 2001. After reading this stirring narrative, you will better understand how the Marine Corps has evolved from a rag-tag group of revolutionary sharp-shooters firing from the tall masts of ships into the most elite fighting force on the face of the earth.

This book is also about American heroes—Marines who, through courage above and beyond the call of duty, have earned the highest honors our nation can bestow, and too often paid for that distinction with their own blood. Through his detailed and forceful narrative, Mr. Ganyard offers readers a fresh and much-needed new perspective on the Marine Corps, even as he remains "ever faithful" to the memory of those Marines whose stories he recounts. As Marine Corps Lieutenant General Alfred M. Gray once said, "[Marines go] where the sound of thunder is." Through his vivid narrative, Mr. Ganyard takes us there, too.

Marc Cerasini, author of *The Complete Idiot's Guide to the U.S. Special Ops Forces* and *Heroes: U.S. Marine Corps Medal of Honor Winners*

INTRODUCTION

NO BETTER FRIEND, NO WORSE ENEMY

On September 11, 2001, America came under attack. At 8:45 on that Tuesday morning, American Airlines Flight 11, hijacked by terrorists, slammed into the North Tower of the World Trade Center in New York City. Twenty-one minutes later, United Airlines Flight 175 slammed into the South Tower of the World Trade Center. At 9:40 American Airlines Flight 77 crashed into the Pentagon. At 9:50, the South Tower of the World Trade Center collapsed, and 40 minutes later the North Tower collapsed. A few minutes before the collapse of the North Tower, a fourth plane, United Airlines Flight 93, had crashed into a Pennsylvania field, its passengers having overcome the hijackers who had taken control of the plane. Two thousand eight hundred twenty-three people died in the World Trade Center attack and another one hundred twenty-five died in the Pentagon. Two hundred sixty-six people died aboard the four airliners that crashed.

The September 11 attacks were compared to the bombing of Pearl Harbor in 1941, and it was certain that the United States would go to war. But this war would be very different. In 1941, Japan had launched military strikes against American naval bases in the Pacific Ocean. That war would be exceedingly difficult, but America knew what had to be done. The enemy in America's War on Terrorism was an unconventional enemy, an elusive enemy who struck from the shadows against civilians and military alike before melting away. There was no country to attack, no army to fight.

Nevertheless, over the next few weeks, as President George W. Bush gathered evidence and international support for the War on Terrorism, the U.S. Marine Corps began preparing for battle, wherever that battle might be and against whomever the enemy might be. On September 28, the Marine Corps announced its intention to establish a brigade-size anti-terrorism unit to deal with foreign and domestic terrorist threats. One month later, the Corps announced the reactivation of the 4th Marine Expeditionary Brigade (Antiterrorism). The brigade includes an Antiterrorism

Battalion, the Chemical Biological Incident Response Force, the Marine Security Guard Battalion, and the Marine Corps Security Force Battalion. Emphasizing rapid response to terrorist threats, the Marine Corps would be prepared for any eventuality.

The Corps was also preparing for a conventional campaign. On September 20, President Bush outlined to Congress the objectives of Operation Enduring Freedom: the elimination of the terrorist infrastructure and activities in Afghanistan and the capture of al Qaeda leaders. The War on Terrorism would begin in Afghanistan. By September 28, the 15th Marine Expeditionary Unit (Special Operations Capable), consisting of some 2,200 Marines and embarked with the Peleliu Amphibious Ready Group, had arrived in the Arabian Sea. The 15th MEU had just completed a mission providing humanitarian assistance in the form of medical supplies, food, clothing, and construction materials to East Timor in Indonesia.

Operation Enduring Freedom began on October 7, 2001, with air strikes against Taliban and al Qaeda compounds in Afghanistan. The Marine Corps joined this battle on October 18, when Marine Fighter Attack Squadron 251 F/A-18s launched from the USS *Theodore Roosevelt* and flew several bombing missions inside Afghanistan. AV-8B Harrier jets from the 15th MEU joined them on November 3. In the meantime, the 15th MEU began preparations for establishing an advance base inside Afghanistan. Because Afghanistan is a land-locked country, it wasn't possible to simply storm ashore, as the Marines are so often depicted in films and novels. The ground campaign of Operation Enduring Freedom would require a complicated logistical plan to move the 15th MEU from the Arabian Sea more than 400 miles into Afghanistan for further operations.

On November 24, the 26th MEU(SOC), having completed Exercise Bright Star, an international military exercise with Spanish and Egyptian forces in Egypt, arrived in the Arabian Sea and embarked with the Bataan Amphibious Ready Group. In the wake of the September 11 attacks, someone had erected a sign outside their camp in Egypt that read, "United States Marines: No Better Friend, No Worse Enemy." There were now some 4,400 Marines in the region.

On the day after the 26th MEU arrived in the region, the 15th MEU initiated Operation Swift Freedom. Marine CH-53E Super Stallion helicopters carried the Marines several hundred miles and established an advance base at Camp Rhino in southern Afghanistan. The 15th MEU was the first American combat ground element in Afghanistan. On December 4, the 26th MEU's Task Force Sledgehammer, the Combined Anti-Armor Team and Light Armored Reconnaissance, arrived at Camp Rhino, and the following day the Marines set out across the brutally cold desert for Kandahar with the mission of cutting off supply and escape routes and allowing anti-Taliban forces to secure the city. By December 13, the Marines had secured Kandahar airport. Unfortunately, the Marines suffered their first casualty of the war when Corporal Chris Chandler stepped on a plastic mine. Corporal Chandler lost his foot in the explosion and two other Marines were injured. Corporal Chandler was the first Marine to earn the Purple Heart during Operation Enduring Freedom.

On December 17, an American flag—signed by rescue workers and friends and family members of the victims of the September 11 attacks—was raised over the airport in Kandahar. That same day, the U.S. Embassy in Kabul, which had been hastily evacuated in 1989 after the withdrawal of Soviet troops and the outbreak of civil war in Afghanistan, was reopened. Marines of the 26th MEU raised the American flag that the Embassy's Marine Guard had taken down 12 years earlier. On January 1, 2002, the Afghan national flag was raised over Kandahar for the first time since 1989.

By the end of January, the 15th MEU, relieved by the 13th MEU, would retire from the region for much deserved liberty in Australia. The 26th MEU and the 13th MEU would remain in the Arabian Sea to support the U.S. Army as it chased down the last Taliban soldiers and al Qaeda terrorists in Afghanistan. In March 2002, the 13th MEU provided vital support for Operation Anaconda, the most intense ground campaign of Operation Enduring Freedom. As the Army's 10th Mountain Division, with elements from the 101st Airborne and Special Operations Forces, searched through the mountains in Khowst and eastern Afghanistan's Shah-e-Kot Valley, the USS *Bonhomme Richard* Amphibious Ready Group in the Northern Arabian Sea launched Marine Harrier jets, Super Cobra and Super Stallion helicopters, and Hercules aircraft 800 miles into Afghanistan. The Marines flew more than 400 missions and provided close air support, airborne reconnaissance, and logistics support for the campaign, which was often conducted 10,000 feet above sea level. When the 13th MEU retired from the Arabian Sea on March 26, Major General F. L. Hagenbeck, the

Commander of Coalition Joint Task Force-Mountain, recognized 14 Marines for their exceptional meritorious achievement in combat: Lieutenant Colonel Gregg Sturdevant, commanding officer of Marine Medium Helicopter Squadron 165 (Reinforced), was awarded the Bronze Star, six Cobra pilots were awarded Air Medals with Combat "V," and seven support Marines were awarded Army Commendation Medals.

The Marine Corps had just completed the longest amphibious assault in its history, projecting its military force 400 to 800 miles inland.

★★★

The U.S. Marine Corps is one of the world's finest fighting forces. Lieutenant Colonel Jerome Lynes, commanding officer of Battalion Landing Team 3/6, 26th MEU during Operation Enduring Freedom, described the Marine Corps as "America's varsity," superbly talented individuals who work as a team to perform beyond the reach of the individual. Embracing the concept of *gung ho*, meaning to work together, the Marine Corps understands the importance of every aspect of warfare for the completion of its mission. An impressive military force, it is capable of conducting a variety of tasks anywhere, anytime. But it has not always been so.

The Corps was created 225 years ago during the American Revolution, and it served well in that conflict. For much of their existence, however, the Marines have been understood as soldiers of the sea, a small military force associated with the sea services. This perception has given the Marine Corps a unique role in American military history. Not exactly the Army, not exactly the Navy, the Marine Corps is something in between. The unique but sometimes ambiguous position has led to numerous downsizings and, whether motivated by jealousy or sincere criticism, multiple attempts to eliminate the Corps entirely. Its ambiguity has, however, opened the Corps to innovation as well, and throughout the late nineteenth and twentieth centuries, the Corps has been forced to redefine itself and its military mission, emphasizing its role as an amphibious assault force. Repeatedly, the U.S. Marine Corps has proven its worth.

The Marine Corps is a product of its amazingly rich history. Filled with tradition, with fighting, with humanitarian services, this history can show us not only who the Marines were, but who they are today—and, more important, what roles they are likely to play tomorrow.

The Marines have always been an elite group with a strong tradition of pride. Their slogan, "The few. The proud. The Marines," sums up their attitude, their *esprit de corps*, perfectly.

As of this writing, the war against terrorism continues. How this war will end, or where it will lead us next, is not known. Two things, however, are clear: The United States will not waver in its resolve to win this war; and, wherever the fighting occurs, against whatever enemy, the U.S. Marines will be there, *Semper Fidelis*—Always Faithful.

Acknowledgments

I would like to thank Jennifer Moore, Christy Wagner, Keith Cline, and Barrett Tillman for their thoughtful editing and suggestions. I would like also to thank John Helfers for his assistance with technical research, Larry Segriff, whose editing and friendship made this project much better than it otherwise would have been, and Marty Greenberg, without whom this project would not exist and whose constant encouragement has been much appreciated. Of course, any errors within are solely my own. Most of all, however, my wife, Paula, deserves recognition for her support.

CHAPTER 1

A FEW GOOD MEN: THE REVOLUTIONARY WAR

The development of modern marine forces was prompted by early European colonial expansion. As European countries began exploring the New World, Africa, and Asia, they became increasingly reliant on naval forces to retain contact between mother country and colony and to protect merchant ships carrying goods back and forth. This was particularly true of Britain and the Netherlands, both relatively small countries who depended to a great extent on their naval trade for prosperity.

During the Thirty Years' War, France's Cardinal Richelieu created the first regular marine unit of the modern era, the *Compagnie de al Mer*, in 1627. Their job was to protect France's ports, but they were really only sailors who were given additional training to fight on land.

By order of King Charles II, the Duke of York and Albany raised approximately 1,200 men and formed them into the first true unit of marines in 1664. His unit, officially named the Maritime Regiment of Foot, was better known as the Admiral's Regiment because the Duke was also the Lord High Admiral of England. The Admiral's Regiment was the first unit manned by soldiers trained for shipboard service rather than sailors trained to fight. The Netherlands followed suit the following year with the creation of the Royal Netherlands *Korps Mariniers.*

The Admiral's Regiment served in the Anglo-Dutch Wars, North Africa, and even the Virginia colony before being disbanded in 1690. Their creator, the Duke of York, ascended to the English throne in 1685 as King James II but was removed during the Glorious Revolution of 1688 and 1689. Fearing that the Admiral's Regiment would remain loyal to the deposed king, the new King and Queen, William and Mary, ordered them disbanded. The value of shipborne troops was not forgotten, however, and that same year Parliament commissioned the creation of the 1st and 2nd Regiments of Marines.

These new marine regiments served in the Grand Alliance against Louis XIV's expansive policies during the War of the League of Augsburg. Both regiments suffered heavy losses and, in 1698, they were consolidated into a single regiment. Three infantry units were converted into marine regiments as well.

In 1701, at the conclusion of hostilities, these units, too, were disbanded. A year later, however, in 1702, Louis XIV launched his final war of aggression, the War of the Spanish Succession, which would last until 1713, and Queen Anne called for the creation of six new regiments of marines. These regiments proved particularly useful for the British, who found themselves now in conflict with two continental powers, the French and the Spanish.

The British marines took part in several significant battles during this war, including the defeat of the Spanish at Vigo Bay, the capture of Gibraltar (which the British still hold), and the capture of Barcelona. They also assisted in an assault on Port Royal, Nova Scotia, in 1710. Fifteen hundred American militiamen and a unit of Indians joined 600 marines and 1,400 infantry for the assault. This was the first time American colonists served alongside British regulars in a conflict. The assault was successful, and the garrison at Port Royal surrendered on October 2. Due to military cutbacks in peacetime, however, the marines were again disbanded after the Peace of Utrecht in 1713.

Marine regiments did not appear again until 1739. With the outbreak of the War of Jenkins's Ear—which was caused by Captain Robert Jenkins's claim that a Spanish customs official had cut off his ear—new marine regiments were created and were retained throughout the War of the Austrian Succession, which began the following year and lasted through 1748. At the end of that conflict, the marines were disbanded once again, for what would prove to be the final time.

ANCIENT MARINES

The use of shipboard soldiers, or "marines," dates at least to the Greeks, whose galleys carried heavily armed soldiers called *epibatoe*. These infantrymen, armed with a short sword and a spear and wearing brass body armor, proved to be a superior fighting force for boarding actions, and were a decisive factor at the first recorded naval battle, Salamis in 480 B.C.E. during the Persian War. The heavily armed and armored troops easily defeated Persian shipboard troops who were usually archers wearing light armor.

The Romans, too, made use of shipboard troops, which they called *milites classiarii*, "soldiers of the fleet." During the first Punic War with Carthage, the Romans quickly learned that the Carthaginians were superior seamen. To counter the Carthaginian ramming tactics, the Romans developed the *corvus* ("raven"), a heavy gangway that could be dropped between ships, locking them together and allowing the Roman troops to storm across two abreast. The Carthaginian marines proved to be no match for the Romans, who were essentially highly disciplined seagoing legionnaires.

Seven years later, with renewed hostilities against France in the Seven Years' War, 50 independent companies of marines were again established. These marine companies were assigned to Royal Navy ships and were given distinct duties. Their primary duty was to shoot enemy officers and gun crews, repel boarders, and serve as back-up gun crews on their own ships during ship-to-ship combat. As a secondary duty, marines frequently enforced ship regulations for the officers and defended the ship from mutinous crews, a function the officers appreciated. These marine companies were not disbanded at the end of the Seven Years' War and mark the foundation of the Royal Marines, a title officially granted them in 1802.

★★★

American colonists frequently served with British regular forces during the mother country's conflicts. The War of Jenkins's Ear, for example, was largely comprised of British raids on Spanish possessions in the Americas. It was only natural that the British would enlist the colonists, who were already in the Americas and many of whom were already skilled mariners, in their conflict with the Spanish.

In 1740, General James Oglethorpe led American militia units from Georgia and South Carolina and Indians in an invasion of Florida. They captured two Spanish posts along the St. Johns River and laid siege to Castillo de San Marcos at St. Augustine. However, General Oglethorpe's forces were unable to seize the fortress, and two months later they were forced to withdraw.

At the same time, the British Parliament raised four battalions of marines in North America under the assumption that North American colonists were better suited to tropical campaigns. Thirty-six hundred men were recruited and formed into one large unit under the command of the lieutenant governor of Virginia, Colonel William Gooch. Gooch's Marines, as they were called, were commanded by officers drawn primarily from the elite of colonial society and a few British officers, but the rank and file were composed of the dregs of society, each of the colonies meeting its quota with debtors and criminals. These marines joined British troops in Jamaica in 1740. Early in 1741, the combined British and colonial forces set out in a fleet of 138 ships for an assault on Cartagena.

Initially, the Cartagena assault went very well. The marines established a beachhead on March 9 and captured two of the forts covering the channel on March 25. Shortly thereafter, on April 5, 1,500 troops landed for an assault of Fort St. Lazar. This initial success was fleeting, however, as cooperation between military branches broke down. Admiral Edward "Old Grog" Vernon and Brigadier General Thomas Wentworth, the commanders of the naval and land forces respectively, didn't see eye to eye on the progress of the operation. Vernon became convinced that the slow progress made by the land forces was due to the incompetence of Wentworth, and when the general requested additional troops, Vernon refused to provide them. Under continued pressure from Wentworth, Vernon eventually agreed to provide the support of the ships' guns, but he refused to enter the harbor itself.

Wentworth was equally thickheaded. He refused to emplace his own artillery for the assault on Fort St. Lazar. Because of this, the assault went forward primarily with infantry troops, with disastrous results: 43 officers and 600 men were killed or wounded. Colonel Gooch was one of the Americans wounded.

The expedition retired from Cartagena in August. The Americans did secure a landing base on Cuba at Walthenham Bay—now know as Guantanamo Bay—but by then disease had taken its toll on the troops. Only 2,700 of an original 11,600 men (3,600 colonists and 8,000 British troops) reached Cuba. Many of the losses came from disease in Cuba rather than from the conflict at Cartagena.

Three thousand British troops were sent to reinforce these troops in February 1742, but to little effect. Of Gooch's Marines, only about 10 percent survived the entire campaign. Clearly, the colonists were no more resistant to tropical conditions than regular British troops.

LAWRENCE'S LEGACY

One of those who survived the Cartagena campaign, at least for a short while, was Captain Lawrence Washington. His respect for the leader of the expedition, "Old Grog" Vernon, led Captain Washington to name his colonial estate after him: Mount Vernon. Captain Washington, however, soon died of disease he had contracted while on the expedition. His brother George inherited his estate.

American colonists also fought for the British during the War of the Austrian Succession, known in the colonies as King George's War. France entered the conflict in 1744 and quickly constructed a fortress at Louisbourg on Cape Breton Island to guard the St. Lawrence River. When a detachment of French troops from this fortress seized a fishing base at Canso, Nova Scotia, Governor William Shirley of Massachusetts proposed an assault on Louisbourg. The British government agreed to assist the expedition in the form of naval support, and 4,000 men from Massachusetts, New Hampshire, and Connecticut were recruited. The force was led by Colonel William Pepperell, and, sailing from Boston in its own transports, recaptured Canso on April 1, 1745. Three weeks later, with the Royal Navy having finally arrived to provide support, the force of New Englanders launched an assault on Louisbourg and captured the fortress on June 17.

Although amateur soldiers, the New Englanders had proven their mettle in seizing one of the largest fortresses in the colonies, a significant victory in the North American theater of King George's War. The fortress was returned to France in the Treaty of Aix-la-Chapelle (1748) that brought the war to an end.

Only a few years later, however, the Seven Years' War, or the French and Indian War as it was called in the colonies, broke out, and the colonists again found themselves facing a well-defended opponent when they launched amphibious assaults into French Canada. The colonists contributed troops to several British expeditions, and in 1755, 2,000 militiamen supported by 250 British regulars seized 2 French outposts. Five hundred New England rangers participated in the recapture of Louisbourg in 1758, and American troops also participated in the capture of Quebec in 1759.

In 1761, Spain entered the conflict on the side of France. Britain quickly organized an assault on Spanish possessions in the Americas and recruited 4,000 men from Connecticut, New Jersey, New York, and Rhode Island. Remembering the disastrous expedition led by Admiral Vernon and the effect that campaign had had on Gooch's Marines, the British didn't bother to mention that the target of the assault would be Havana, Cuba. Fourteen hundred colonials reinforced British troops already besieging Havana on July 28, 1762.

The British had nearly overcome the city's defenses by then, but malaria, yellow fever, and dysentery devastated the British force, killing nearly half its numbers. With the arrival of the American reinforcements, the British expedition was able to finish their assault, and Havana surrendered on August 11. Only seven American soldiers were killed or wounded in action. Nearly half of the rest, however, died from disease before their withdrawal in October.

★★★

The French and Indian War was the last conflict in which the colonists fought side by side with British regulars. After it ended, tensions began to rise between the American colonies and Great Britain. The colonists felt themselves to be British subjects, a feeling demonstrated by their willingness to support British military efforts in conflicts with France and Spain, and they expected to be governed as British citizens. The British didn't see it that way, however, and continued to view the colonies as a resource to be exploited. Throughout the 1760s and 1770s, they treated the colonies in exactly that manner.

The British believed that they had helped defend the colonists against the aggressions of the French. Because of this, they also believed that the colonists should help pay for the conflict. British officials enacted new trade regulations and instituted new taxes such as the Stamp Act of 1765. Such regulations outraged the colonists; pamphlets protesting the regulations were published, and newspaper headlines proclaimed, "No Taxation Without Representation!"

Because colonists had no representatives in the British Parliament, they had no voice on issues such as trade regulations or taxation. Furthermore, the colonies already taxed themselves, and much of the proceeds were used to pay for the administrative costs of the colonies and defense. Many colonists also pointed out that the colonies had not asked for British troops to be sent to the colonies in the first place, and the battles that were won at great cost in the colonies, such as the capture of the Louisbourg fortress during the King George's War, were simply thrown away during negotiations in Europe.

Radicals in Parliament eventually managed to repeal the Stamp Act, but Britain, still pressing for sovereignty in the colonies, continued to pass legislation regulating colonial trade. The colonists continued to protest. The final straw came in 1774, when Parliament taxed the most beloved of colonial luxuries: tea. Several colonists in Boston disguised themselves as Indians, crept aboard ships carrying British tea, and dumped the lot in Boston Harbor. In April of the following year, British troops and colonial militia confronted one another in battle at Lexington and Concord.

It was in this atmosphere of increasing violence that the Continental Congress, meeting in Philadelphia, began to take steps to defend the colonies it represented. Seeking munitions and supplies, a colonial militia expedition led by Ethan Allen and General Benedict Arnold, under the authority of the Connecticut Assembly and the Massachusetts Committee of Safety respectively, captured Fort Ticonderoga in the name of the Continental Congress on May 9, 1775. A few days later, the Continental Congress received word that the fort was in desperate need of men to reinforce the militiamen already there and money to outfit them. The Congress resolved to ask the governor of Connecticut, who had originally received the request, to send reinforcements to Ticonderoga. An expedition was immediately organized and soon left Hartford. Eight "well spirited and equipped" Marines accompanied the expedition, which had to travel through what at the time was still wild country, New York. The U.S. Marine Corps still reveres these eight men as the "Original Eight."

Similar requests poured into the Continental Congress over the next six months, and Congress responded by beginning to develop its own Continental forces to oppose and harass British forces. In October 1775, Congress authorized the refit of four ships to attack British supply ships, initiating the development of a Continental Navy.

The founding of the Continental Marines, however, which we would expect to be closely tied to the development of the Continental Navy given their traditional role as shipboard troops, was not related to the legislation passed in October. Instead, the Continental Marines were created in response to a request from the citizens of Passamaquoddy, Nova Scotia, who petitioned Congress to be included in the revolt of the North American colonies to preserve their rights and liberties.

Congress eagerly received this request because it offered the opportunity to extend liberty farther north to Nova Scotia, and, perhaps even more important, to establish a naval base at Halifax. Congress appointed a committee to consider the Passamaquoddy request. This committee recommended that two 550-man marine battalions be prepared for an expedition to Nova Scotia in December. The committee also recommended that these battalions be raised from the Continental Army outside Boston under the command of General George Washington, the brother of Captain Lawrence Washington who had served with Gooch's Marines on the disastrous Cartagena expedition.

On November 10, 1775, John Adams sponsored a resolution approved by the Continental Congress:

> ... that two Battalions of marines be raised, consisting of one Colonel, two Lieutenant Colonels, two Majors and other officers as usual in other regiments; and that they consist of an equal number of privates with other battalions; that particular care be taken, that no person be appointed to office, or enlisted into said Battalions, but

such as are good seamen, or so acquainted with maritime affairs as to be able to serve to advantage by sea when required: that they be enlisted and commissioned to serve for and during the present war between Great Britain and the colonies, unless dismissed by order of Congress: that they be distinguished by the names of the first and second battalions of American Marines ....

Although it would be another 10 months before the United States of America would be founded, November 10, 1775, is honored as the birth date of the U.S. Marine Corps. Congress quickly proposed the project to General Washington, but the battalions were never raised. Washington responded to Congress's proposals by remarking that weakening the Army currently besieging Boston by taking troops away from it for another project was unwise. Congress deferred to Washington's experience, but decided to raise the troops separately from the Army. Indeed, by this time, Congress had already begun appointing Marine officers.

Samuel Nicholas was the first officer commissioned in the American Marines. He was made captain on November 28. Although he never used the title himself, the U.S. Marine Corps honors Nicholas as its first commandant. Nine other officers were commissioned shortly after Nicholas received his captaincy.

The 10 officers' first job was recruiting men for 5 companies of Marines to serve in the fledgling Navy of converted merchantmen that Congress was creating. They organized parades to march through the streets, led by brightly dressed drummers playing drums painted with a coiled snake and the motto "Don't Tread on Me" to attract potential recruits. The parades usually ended at an agreed upon rendezvous, usually a tavern, where an officer waited to sign up for service the men who had followed the drummers. According to tradition, the principal rendezvous for these Marine battalions was Tun Tavern at the corner of Tun Alley and King Street in Philadelphia. Unfortunately, there is little evidence to support this legend, and it is more likely that the principal meeting place was the Conestoga Wagon, an inn owned by the Nicholas family. Robert Mullan, who received a commission as captain in the Marines in June 1776, might have been the proprietor of Tun Tavern, and it's possible that the tavern's association with the Marines began with him. Regardless of which inn or tavern served as the first recruiting center for the American Marines, Captain Nicholas and his fellow officers had successfully recruited five companies of Marines by the end of December.

THE FIRST COMMANDANT

Little is known about Samuel Nicholas. He was the son of a Philadelphia blacksmith and a Quaker. Nicholas had attended school at the Academy of Philadelphia, a forerunner to the University of Pennsylvania, and upon graduation he took his place in Philadelphia's elite circles and probably worked in his family's inn, the Conestoga Wagon. He was a member of two prestigious social clubs, the Schuykill Fishing Company and the Gloucester Fox Hunting Club, and apparently was fairly skilled as an outdoor sportsman. There is, however, little to suggest that he had any experience as a merchant or seaman, as was stipulated by the resolution passed by Congress, although he may have served as a shipowner's agent prior to the Revolution.

His lack of experience and his Quaker background make him an odd choice for a military commission in the Continental Marines. He may have been chosen mainly for his connections in Philadelphia's elite society, and his family's ownership of the Conestoga Wagon might have been seen as advantageous for recruiting purposes. Nicholas went on to serve courageously during the American Revolutionary War. After the war, he returned to Philadelphia and the Conestoga Wagon.

The small fleet to which the newly recruited Marines were assigned set sail on February 17, 1776, under the command of Commodore Esek Hopkins. Seven of the eight vessels in the fleet carried a detachment of Marines. The largest detachment, and the only one actually in uniform, was aboard Hopkins's flagship, the *Alfred*. This detachment numbered 62 Marines and was personally commanded by Captain Nicholas.

The newly formed American Marines had an inauspicious beginning at best: After only two days at sea there was a collision between two of the small fleet's ships, the *Hornet* and the *Fly*; the *Hornet* returned to port, and the *Fly* couldn't keep up with the rest of the fleet. This reduced Hopkins's fleet to 6 ships, manned by 580 men and carrying a mere 238 Marines, and posed a serious threat to his planned course of action. The orders he received from Congress had specified he clear the Chesapeake and central seaboard of British ships but were sufficiently lenient to allow the commodore to exercise his own discretion. He headed for the Bahamas with the purpose of seizing its capital, Nassau.

Nassau stands on the northern side of New Providence Island along a harbor separating New Providence Island from Paradise Island (which was known at the time as Hog Island). Fort Montagu protects it on one side and Fort Nassau on the other. A British garrison normally guarding Nassau had been withdrawn a few months earlier with the outbreak of hostilities, leaving Nassau guarded only by militiamen.

Hopkins's fleet reached the island on March 3 and anchored some six miles east of Nassau. Montfort Browne, the governor of the Bahamas, had known about the American fleet for two days but had done nothing to oppose the threat. As Nicholas's Marines disembarked and began marching toward Nassau, however, he decided that some defense was in order. Governor Browne sent a troop of militiamen to man Fort Montagu, but, as the Marines moved closer, he began to fear that they might move inland around the fort and attack Nassau directly.

Browne ordered his militiamen to fire three cannon shots as a warning and then to return to Nassau to help defend it against Nicholas's men. The American Marines, however, continued straight to Fort Montagu. Finding it deserted, they occupied it.

Captain Nicholas decided to allow his men to rest inside the fort for the night. He sent a message to Commodore Hopkins indicating the fort had fallen without any opposition. Encouraged by this news and believing now that the island could be taken without violence, Hopkins sent a proclamation to the citizens of New Providence stating that the objective of the American expedition was to take the powder and other British military supplies stored in Nassau. It was not his intention, he stated, to attack the citizens of New Providence or seize their property.

Hopkins's proclamation undermined any hope Browne had of resisting the American advance. At a council of war that evening, Browne's militia officers and the social elite of Nassau elected to surrender to the Americans. Browne ordered that some 162 barrels of powder be slipped out of Fort Nassau aboard merchant ships before the Americans could seize the fort but still left a fair amount of munitions behind when he withdrew.

The following morning, an emissary from the governor told Captain Nicholas that Fort Nassau would not be defended. The military stores remaining constituted a rich reward for seemingly little effort: 58 cannon, 15 mortars, 16,000 shot and shell, and various other equipment. It took two weeks for the crew to load this equipment aboard the fleet's ships, during which time Governor Browne was guarded by a detachment of Marines.

The governor and the citizens escaped unscathed—although Browne complained that the Marines helped themselves to his liquor—and the fleet sailed from Nassau on March 17. The first official action of the American Marines had been successful and had resulted in the first American invasion and seizure of foreign land.

LEATHERNECKS

When the American Marines first embarked on the ships of Hopkins's fleet few, if any, were properly equipped as professional soldiers. The Marines, outfitted in Philadelphia, were competing against the fledgling Pennsylvania State Navy and a Philadelphia militia unit known as the "Associators" for scarce weapons and equipment.

The Marines were able to scrounge together sufficient muskets to arm all five of the companies that had been recruited, but uniforms were unavailable. The Continental Army, arguably with greater need, had monopolized those stores. Not until September 1776 did the Naval Committee of the Continental Congress prescribe uniforms for the Marines.

That first official uniform was quite different from what we see today. The original Marines were outfitted in short green coats with white trim, a white waistcoat, white short breeches, woolen stockings, and short black gaiters. Officers wore small cocked hats, while enlisted men had round black hats with the brim pinned on one side. These green coats and round hats were probably a factor of availability—the Associators wore a similar uniform—and Marines probably did not appear in uniform in any significant numbers until 1777.

The uniform of the enlisted Marine, and several of the officers, included a stiff black leather collar adopted from the British marine uniform. This item, which was uncomfortable at best and hated by the Marines themselves, served two purposes: It improved posture while on parade, and more practically, it added some small protection against the cutlass during boarding actions. The Marines themselves probably thought that bayonets were better protection against a cutlass, but the leather collar remained a standard part of the uniform for the first 100 years of existence of the Marines. And it provided them with their oldest nickname: Leathernecks.

Hopkins's small fleet continued to have luck on its side for some short while. Most of the return voyage from the Bahamas was uneventful, but when the fleet reached the waters off the coast of Rhode Island, it encountered a myriad of British ships. Nevertheless, Hopkins's fleet managed to defeat two small naval vessels and captured a number of merchant ships.

On April 6, however, the fleet ran into the HMS *Glasgow*, a 20-gun frigate commanded by Captain Tyringham Howe. The encounter lasted three and a half hours with the *Glasgow* engaging first the *Cabot*, then Hopkins's flagship, the *Alfred*, and finally the *Columbus*. So completely outnumbered, the *Glasgow* should have been an easy target for the American fleet, but instead the British frigate held off each of the ships it engaged.

The *Glasgow* was heavily damaged in these battles but was eventually able to slip away, demonstrating Hopkins's lack of experience and inability to control a fleet in ship-to-ship combat. Nine Americans were killed in the conflict and 16 were wounded. Among these casualties were Marine Lieutenant John Fitzpatrick, the first Marine killed in action, and Lieutenant John Hood Wilson, who was mortally wounded. In return, however, Marine musketry killed one man and wounded two more, the only casualties suffered by the *Glasgow*.

Ultimately, there was an investigation into the liberties Hopkins had taken with his orders. He was censured and dismissed from service. Overall, however, the American Marines's first action was seen as a success. The Continental Congress was pleased with the Marine companies, which had performed as had been intended by the resolution of November 10, 1775, engaging in an amphibious assault on an enemy fortress as well as participating in ship-to-ship combat, although they did not have the opportunity to engage in a boarding action.

The expedition's shortcomings were not the fault of the Marines. Governor Browne had been able to spirit away much of the powder at Fort Nassau, but the Marines were in no position to prevent this, and it had been the unopposed advance of the Marines that caused Browne and his officers to waver in opposition to the American expedition. The escape of the *Glasgow* was the result of Hopkins's inability to control his fleet effectively, and the Marines performed well, inflicting the only casualties suffered on the British ship.

On June 25, 1776, Nicholas was promoted to major, and his pay was increased to $32 per month. He was also given orders to raise another four Marine companies for the frigates under construction in Philadelphia.

The organization and use of Continental Marines during the Revolutionary War was based upon the precedents set by the British Royal Navy. What knowledge the colonists had of military logistics, strategy, and tactics derived from their experience fighting with British regular forces against French and Spanish forces during King George's War and the French and Indian War. It was only natural that they would base their own organizations on these examples, including decentralizing the Marine companies by assigning them to individual vessels or joint service with one of the Continental Army units. Even if they had ignored the precedents set by the British forces, the conditions of the American Revolutionary War probably would have dictated such a strategy.

The newly created Continental Navy had great difficulty outfitting its ships. Although the colonies could boast a plenitude of experienced sailors, most of them preferred to serve aboard privateers, where the financial rewards were significantly higher. As a result, the Navy never had enough men to crew an entire fleet and had to rely on single-ship voyages as the rule.

The British Royal Navy was significantly larger than the little fleet the colonies managed to put together, consisting of more than 250 vessels at the beginning of the war and expanding beyond that during the war. Not all of these ships were committed to the American colonies, of course, as Britain had several other holdings, but the Continental Navy never had a chance to truly command the sea. It therefore came to rely primarily on commerce raiding or acting as escorts for convoys bringing supplies to the colonists.

In 1776, six Continental ships raided and captured a variety of British warships and merchants. In addition, two other vessels, the *Lexington* and the *Reprisal*, were converted from merchant ships and took part in raids as well. By the end of the year, there were 600 Marines in service, many serving on these eight ships. America's first African American Marine, John Martin, served aboard the *Reprisal* and went down with the ship off the coast of Newfoundland in September 1777. Marines were also serving alongside the Continental Army. The army had pushed into Canada in 1775 before being turned back at Quebec. A strong British army of 8,000 troops was able to push down the Richelieu River into New York. General Benedict Arnold, despite his later treason, proved himself to be an able commander. Arnold understood that the British advance relied upon water transportation, and so he began building a fleet of 17 ships manned by 900 sailors and Marines on Lake Champlain. Arnold's fleet was destroyed at the Battle of Valcour Island in October 1776, but it had delayed the advance of the British who decided to withdraw to Canada for the winter.

The British had also launched an assault on the central colonies in August 1776, capturing New York City and advancing as far as Delaware by winter. General Washington hoped to stall this campaign and revive the colonists' morale by undertaking a daring raid on a British outpost in New Jersey. Among the troops with Washington's army were three of the Marine companies raised by Major Nicholas for service in the frigates then under construction—the fourth company had already entered service aboard the *Randolph* under the command of Marine Captain Samuel Shaw. Captain Benjamin Dean, Captain Andrew Porter, and Captain Robert Mullan commanded the three companies in Washington's Continental Army.

The battalion as a whole numbered 141 men and officers fit for duty with another 36 listed as sick. Two of the men in Mullan's company, Isaac and Orange, were listed as "Negroes," two of the first African Americans to serve in the American Marines. Major Nicholas and his battalion of Marines were sent to reinforce Washington's troops in December, where they were incorporated into a Philadelphia militia brigade under Brigadier General John Cadwalader. Their main task was to provide both infantry and artillery support.

Cadwalader was unable to cross the Delaware and participate in the first battle of Trenton with Washington. On his own initiative, however, he crossed the Delaware on December 27 and took part in the second battle of Trenton on January 2, where his brigade, including Nicholas's Marines, defended a crucial bridge at Assunpink. On January 3, Cadwalader's brigade participated in Washington's assault on Princeton, supporting General Hugh Mercer's Continental Army brigade in one wing of the two-pronged attack. Mercer encountered two regiments of British regulars and, despite Cadwalader's reinforcement, both brigades were forced to withdraw.

Even so, the efforts of Cadwalader and Mercer and their men proved very valuable. Their support allowed Washington to attack the British flank, scattering the three British regiments there and taking Princeton. Nicholas's 3 Marine companies suffered heavy losses at Trenton and Princeton, losing 61 of their 141 men by the time the Army quartered for the winter at Morristown, New Jersey.

After they took Princeton, one company was assigned to escort British prisoners to Philadelphia in February. With no ship to board, however, the company disbanded. A second company returned to Philadelphia in April to return to naval duties aboard the frigates *Washington* and *Delaware*. The remaining Marines were either absorbed into Washington's Continental Army artillery or left service.

Many of the Marines who had returned to Philadelphia or who had been assimilated into Washington's Continental Army saw further action along the Delaware River at the end of 1777. The British captured Philadelphia in September of that year, and in an effort to hinder British control of the sea lanes, the Pennsylvania State Navy and six ships of the Continental Navy were detailed to defend the seaboard along the Delaware and Pennsylvania coasts.

Two of the Continental frigates, the *Andrew Doria*, which had sailed under Hopkins's command during the New Providence raid, and the newly finished frigate *Delaware*, carried detachments of Continental Marines. Three forts defended the Delaware River: Fort Mercer and Fort Mifflin just south of Philadelphia and Fort Billingsport farther south. Marines were stationed at Fort Mercer and Fort Mifflin, but the Continental Army could spare no forces for the defense of the Delaware River, and a mere 112 Pennsylvania militiamen under the command of Colonel William Bradford defended Billingsport.

While engaging a British artillery battery at Philadelphia, the *Delaware* ran aground and was captured. On September 28, two British regiments under the command of Lieutenant Colonel Thomas Stirling, the 10th and the 42nd, the infamous Black Watch, began to push up the Delaware River, first fighting off the New Jersey militia and then attacking Billingsport. Colonel Bradford's militiamen were no match for two regiments of British regulars.

The *Andrew Doria* and its detachment of Marines evacuated the militiamen from the garrison. The landing parties, led by Lieutenants Dennis

Leary and William Barney, also brought out most of the powder stored at Billingsport, spiked the five cannon there, set fire to the fort, and exchanged fire with the Black Watch before returning to the *Andrew Doria*.

The British, however, continued to press their way up the Delaware. The Marines garrisoned in Forts Mercer and Mifflin resisted the British pressure for seven weeks, but, ultimately, the British assault overwhelmed them. Fort Mifflin was evacuated on November 15 and Fort Mercer fell one week later. The British torched the American ships that had been assisting the defense of the Delaware.

The capture of Philadelphia and the Delaware River had a significant impact on the Revolutionary War effort; it meant that the British would spend the winter in the comfort of the city of Philadelphia while General Washington and his Continental Army would spend a torturous winter at Valley Forge.

★★★

One Marine company originally raised by Major Nicholas and commanded by Captain Samuel Shaw had been assigned to the *Randolph* under Captain Nicholas Biddle. The cruise of the *Randolph* seemed cursed. She lacked a full-crew complement and was confined by British ships to the Philadelphia harbor until December 1776. Her crew was finally filled with captured British seamen, however, and in January 1777 she put out to sea.

The *Randolph* had been assigned to cruise the coast of Virginia, searching for the HMS *Milford*, which had been raiding American shipping and generally proving itself a nuisance. But in March, before the *Randolph* was able to find the *Milford*, a storm caught the *Randolph* and snapped two of her masts in half. Furthermore, as Captain Biddle sailed toward Charleston for repairs, fever broke out and killed several members of the crew. The impressed British sailors decided to take advantage of the weakened crew and mutinied. Fortunately, Captain Shaw and his Marines were able to suppress the uprising, and the *Randolph* made it to Charleston.

She sailed again in June 1777, but her main mast was struck twice by lightning during the summer. The *Randolph*, repaired again and now equipped with Benjamin Franklin's new invention, the lightning rod, set sail once more in September 1777. This time, she was somewhat more fortunate.

Sailing south from Charleston, she encountered and engaged the British privateer *True Briton* and defeated it, taking a prize of rum from Jamaica intended for British troops in New York. The *Randolph* was able to take another three merchantmen, adding sugar, salt, ginger, and logwood to her holds, before she returned to Charleston.

In December 1777, with the aid of four smaller ships from the South Carolina Navy, the *Randolph* was able to break a blockade the British had placed around Charleston, and then, encountering no other British ships in the area, she set sail south for Barbados. This would prove to be the last cruise of the *Randolph*. On March 7, 1778, she met the HMS *Yarmouth*, an old British ship but heavily armed with 64 cannon, outgunning the *Randolph* two to one. The *Randolph* put up a very good fight for a ship so outgunned, and indeed, seemed to be getting the better of the *Yarmouth*, when, inexplicably, the *Randolph's* powder magazine exploded, tearing the ship apart. Only 4 of the crew of 305 men survived the blast.

★★★

The Marines remained involved in naval operations on the high seas and engaged in a variety of amphibious operations in 1778. One of these operations was a raid along the Mississippi River proposed by James Willing, the son of a prominent Philadelphia family who had failed in a business venture in Natchez, Mississippi.

Willing convinced the Continental Congress to give him command of an expedition to take control of the Mississippi River from Ohio to Louisiana. Congress gave him a commission in the Continental Navy and sent him to Fort Pitt, Ohio, where he raised a Marine detachment consisting of 36 Marines. Willing's troop of 36 Marines was assigned a river barge called the *Rattletrap*, equipped with a meager sail and 12 oars.

On January 10, 1778, the expedition set off from Fort Pitt. As the *Rattletrap* sailed down the Mississippi, Willing took the opportunity to raid any loyalist plantations he encountered. The farther along the Mississippi he traveled, the more damage Willing did. Homes and farms were burned, cattle were slaughtered, property was stolen, and slaves were carried off.

On February 20, Willing reached Natchez. The inhabitants capitulated to Willing, some joining his raiders, others accepting his guarantee of protection in return for neutrality. As his mob grew, Willing was even able to capture two British ships, the *Rebecca* and the *Neptune*.

But Willing walked a thin line down the Mississippi. Spain, which had remained neutral to that point, still controlled colonies to the west of the river and Oliver Pollock, the American agent in New Orleans, persuaded the Spanish governor, Bernardo de Gálvez, to allow Willing to set up a garrison at Manchac in Louisiana on the border with the Spanish colonies. Willing, however, proceeded to auction off the plunder his band had acquired along the Mississippi, to the chagrin of Bernardo de Gálvez, who now seemed to be supporting the colonies against Britain.

The British protested Willing's raids and profiteering, sent the HMS *Sylph* up the Mississippi, and captured the outpost at Manchac. Gálvez, hoping to avoid a conflict with Britain, decided to return most of the stolen property, including the *Neptune*. Pollock managed to buy the *Rebecca*, which was refit, renamed the *Morris*, and sailed in the Continental Navy for the next year.

Willing was cut off from Fort Pitt and was in no position to control the Mississippi River. Nevertheless, he continued to antagonize both Gálvez and Pollock, suggesting that he be allowed to travel north along the west bank of the Mississippi—controlled by the Spanish—under Spanish protection. Two of his lieutenants swore an oath to Gálvez not to bother the British, and they were allowed to lead the original Marine detachment back to Kaskaskia in present-day Illinois to join George Rogers Clark.

Willing left New Orleans in November as a courier to the Continental Congress. His ship was captured by a British privateer off the coast of Delaware, and he was later repatriated in New York in an exchange of prisoners. Willing's expedition had done nothing more than create numerous enemies along the river at great expense.

★★★

The Marines engaged in a second ambitious amphibious assault on New Providence Island. This assault was devised by John Peck Rathburn, captain of the *Providence*, who seems to have been motivated by vengeance against the British privateer *Mary*. The *Providence* had engaged the *Mary* in 1777, and Rathburn had lost his sailing master. The *Mary*, Rathburn had learned, was at Nassau for a refit.

Unlike Commodore Hopkins's assault 2 years earlier, Rathburn's expedition was composed only of his frigate and its 27-man Marine detachment commanded by Captain John Trevett, a veteran of the first New Providence assault. Landing on Hog Island at midnight on January 27, 1778, Trevett led his Marines to Fort Nassau, where, he recalled, one of the palisades was missing a stake. By luck, the militia of Nassau had never fixed the gap in the fort's defenses, or perhaps they simply never knew of it, and Trevett's Marines snuck into Fort Nassau, catching two night watchmen unaware and overpowering them before they could raise an alarm. At dawn, Trevett raised an American flag over the fort and announced to Nassau's citizens that no fewer than 30 Marine officers and more than 200 men had occupied Fort Nassau and that there was an American fleet just off Abaco Island.

Echoing Hopkins's 1776 announcement to the citizens of Nassau, Trevett declared that the sole purpose of the assault on Fort Nassau was the seizure of the *Mary* and other "warlike stores." The citizens and their property, of course, would remain untouched. The bluff worked like a charm. Stunned, and hoping to avoid an American assault on the town itself, the town council replied that the occupation of Fort Nassau and the seizure of the *Mary* would be unopposed. Trevett held the fort with his 27 Marines for 4 days while Rathburn prepared the *Mary* to sail along with 4 other American vessels they found in the harbor.

On February 1, Trevett and his Marines returned to the *Providence* and set sail for the colonies.

American forces were performing naval and marine operations on the other side of the Atlantic Ocean as well. France, which had no love for the British, favored the colonists during the American Revolution. They also assisted by occasionally providing ships for the Continental Navy and allowing American vessels to use French ports to launch raids on British shipping and even Britain itself.

The first of these raids was carried out by the *Reprisal* in January 1777, but the most audacious and colorful European raids were carried out in 1778 and 1779 under the command of John Paul Jones.

(Photo courtesy of U.S. Marine Corps Art Collection)

American Commissioner to France John Adams reviews Commodore John Paul Jones's Marines in spring of 1779. The painting, John Adams Reviews Jones's Marines, *is by Colonel Charles Waterhouse (Ret.).*

On November 1, 1778, John Paul Jones, commanding the *Ranger,* set sail from Portsmouth for Paris, France, bearing dispatches to Benjamin Franklin concerning the recent battle of Saratoga. The *Ranger,* carrying a small detachment of Marines under Captain Matthew Parke, reached France early in December. The Marines and their commander clashed on the voyage across the Atlantic, so Jones removed him from office and named Lieutenant Samuel Wallingford, the son of a New Hampshire Judge, to command the Marine detachment.

On April 10, 1778, Jones set sail from Brest, France, to the Irish Sea, planning to raid Britain. Over the course of the next 10 days, the *Ranger* captured 2 merchant ships and sank a Scots schooner and then turned toward the port at Whitehaven, from whence Jones had sailed to America as a boy. On the night of April 22, two boats set out from the *Ranger* to raid Whitehaven, one commanded by Jones and the other by Wallingford.

The raiding party was able to sneak into the town, taking several gunners prisoner and spiking their cannon before an alarm was raised. The raiding party managed to set fire to several of the ships docked there. The towns-people eventually extinguished the fires, but some damage had been done and, perhaps more important, the raid hurt British morale: It had been the first attack on British soil since 1667.

The following day, April 23, Jones continued to St. Mary's Isle, where he intended to kidnap the Earl of Selkirk and hold him hostage against the good treatment of American prisoners in British hands. The earl, however, wasn't at home that day. Jones's party looted Selkirk's silverware in reprisal for the looting the British had done to American homes in the colonies, though Jones later compensated Selkirk for the stolen silver. On April 24, on his return to Brest, France, Jones encountered the HMS *Drake*. After an hour-long engagement, the *Drake* was defeated and captured. The *Drake*'s commanding officer, Commander George Burden, was killed in action, shot in the head by an American Marine. On the American side, Lieutenant Wallingford was killed, likewise shot by an enemy marine. John Paul Jones was given command of a second ship in France in 1779, the *Bonhomme Richard*, a refitted East Indian merchant ship built in 1766. The *Bonhomme Richard* carried a detachment of 137 marines when it sailed in 1779, but these marines were not Americans; they were French marines of the *Infanterie Irlandaise, Regiment de Welsh-Serrant*, composed primarily Scots, Welsh, and Irishmen serving in the French army and assigned to the *Bonhomme Richard* for this expedition. The unit was nominally commanded by two French lieutenant colonels, but real leadership was provided by Lieutenants Edward Stack, Eugene McCarthy, and James O'Kelly, who were given commissions as Continental—that is American—Marines by Benjamin Franklin.

On August 14, 1779, the *Bonhomme Richard*, along with the American frigates *Alliance* and *Pallas*, set sail for a cruise around the British Isles. On September 23, 1779, the *Bonhomme Richard* encountered the HMS *Serapis* off Yorkshire's Flamborough Head and engaged it in battle. At one point, the *Bonhomme Richard*'s mast was splintered and the American colors lost. Captain Pearson, the commander of the *Serapis*, thought that the lack of colors indicated that the *Bonhomme Richard* was ready to surrender. Jones replied, "I have not yet begun to fight!"

Inspired by Jones's words, the crew of the *Bonhomme Richard* fought on. French marines climbed into the rigging and fired their muskets or threw grenades at the *Serapis*. A Scot by the name of William Hamilton crawled out on the yardarm and dropped grenades on the deck of the *Serapis*, one of which fell into an open hatch, igniting several sacks of powder on the gun deck and killing some 20 men. By the end of the battle, the *Bonhomme Richard* had lost 150 of 325 men, but the ship claimed victory in the end. Captain Pearson eventually surrendered the *Serapis*. The *Bonhomme Richard* sank the following morning, but with the help of some French Marines, Jones had recorded the first American defeat of a British naval vessel in British waters.

★★★

Despite the success of John Paul Jones's audacious expeditions, 1779 also witnessed a major defeat for the Continental Marines. On June 15, Brigadier General Francis McLean, leading a troop of 640 British regulars, occupied the Bagaduce Peninsula on Penobscot Bay in Maine, then a province of the Massachusetts colony. McLean's occupation was intended to provide a base from which to attack American privateers and to support loyalist forces in New England.

The government of Massachusetts resolved to launch an expedition against the British occupation of the peninsula before the troop could become entrenched. It assigned 4 of its state Navy's brigs and chartered another 12 privateers and 23 merchantmen as transports. In addition, the Continental Navy supported the Massachusetts expedition by assigning another three ships, the *Warren*, the *Diligent*, and the *Providence*, all of which carried Marine detachments. New Hampshire chartered one privateer in support of the expedition.

Fifteen hundred militiamen were assigned to the expedition, but only 873 actually participated. Still, this added substantially to the 227 Continental and Massachusetts Marines. The colonial forces were commanded by Captain Dudley Saltonstall of the Continental Navy and Brigadier General Solomon Lovell of the Massachusetts militia. Boston silversmith Lieutenant Colonel Paul Revere served as Lovell's chief of artillery.

The Bagaduce Peninsula, approximately 2 miles long and 1 mile wide, extends into the Bagaduce Harbor and is connected to the mainland by a narrow isthmus. When the American forces arrived in the harbor on July 24, the British had already established an artillery battery on Banks Island just off the peninsula and were busy building a log fort in the center of the peninsula (Fort George). The harbor entrance was, therefore, very well guarded, because it fell within the crossfire from Banks Island and the fort on the peninsula and was guarded by three British sloops as well.

On July 26, 1779, Captain John Welsh, the Marine commander aboard the *Warren,* led a unit of Marines in an amphibious assault on Banks Island, seized the small artillery battery there, and raised the Stars and Stripes. Revere turned the captured British cannon on the three British sloops defending the harbor entrance, which withdrew up the harbor to a position nearer the log fort.

After this initial success, however, the expedition quickly bogged down as the commanders of the force could not agree upon a course of action. Lovell wanted to land on the south side of the Bagaduce Peninsula, which offered the best landing site. In order for him to do so, however, Saltonstall would have to eliminate the three sloops remaining in the harbor, but Saltonstall refused to enter the harbor before Lovell had captured the fort on the peninsula. Saltonstall and Lovell compromised on a landing site on the western end of the peninsula, and on July 28, Captain Welsh led his Marines onto the peninsula.

They were met immediately by musket fire from British troops stationed on the headland and, once ashore, they found themselves struggling up a steep slope. Welsh, an Irishman who came to the colonies to fight the British, was killed immediately. His lieutenant, William Hamilton, fell mortally wounded. Another 13 Marines were killed and 20 more were wounded.

The Continental Marines pressed on, however, pushing the British troops back toward the fort. Massachusetts Marines followed the Continental Marines ashore and pressed up to the fort as well. General McLean stood in the center of his meager fort, ready to take down his colors as soon as his troops had made a token resistance, but the final assault never took place. General Lovell, to protect his men from British musket fire, called a halt to the advance and, during the next few days, began building earthworks and battery emplacements after the fashion of eighteenth-century siege craft against a fort with log walls barely reaching to shoulder height.

One of the Marines under his command later commented that Lovell was a very good sort of man, clearly one who cared about the well-being of his troops, but this sort of good man, the Marine continued, rarely made a good leader. Not wanting to expose his ships to cannonades from the fort, Saltonstall, too, hesitated to take action, and the entire assault bogged down for the next 16 days.

On August 14, the HMS *Raisonable* and seven other British ships entered Penobscot Bay. The Marines re-embarked on their ships and the small American fleet fled up the Penobscot River. Saltonstall beached the *Warren* and set her afire. The British pursued the rest of the fleet and over the course of the next two days captured two American vessels. Another 17 were abandoned and burned by their crews. Many of the sailors and Marines who made up the Penobscot Bay expedition were able to escape through the woods along the shore of the river, but casualty estimates run as high as 500 men lost. Saltonstall was brought before a court-martial and cashiered from service.

A FEW GOOD MEN

On March 20, 1779, Captain William Jones, commander of the Marine detachment aboard the *Providence,* placed an ad in the *Providence Gazette:* "The Continental ship Providence, now lying at Boston, is bound on a short cruise, immediately; a few good men are wanted to make up her complement." The famous phrase proved an effective recruiting slogan. The *Providence* set sail in June and, sailing east, encountered a convoy of British ships from Jamaica. The *Providence* took 11 prizes. After this cruise, Jones and his detachment were taken off the *Providence* in Charleston, South Carolina, in December 1779 to help man artillery batteries against an anticipated British assault on the city. Jones was captured in May 1780 when Charleston surrendered to the British and later paroled. He spent the final years of the American Revolution working in his family's hardware store in Providence, Rhode Island, but his advertisement had given the Marines one of their most famous descriptions.

The Penobscot Bay expedition was a disaster, one that would remain in Marine legend for some time, but it was followed quickly by another disaster in South Carolina. The British, having failed to pacify the central colonies, turned to a southern strategy, hoping to spark rebellion in the southern colonies where they thought loyalist sentiment was strongest. The Continental Congress, anticipating an assault on Charleston, sent four ships, the *Boston,* the *Providence,* the *Queen of France,* and the *Ranger,* each carrying a detachment of Marines, to South Carolina.

In February 1780, the British opened their campaign with an assault on Charleston. The Americans, though they anticipated the attack, were caught unprepared, and the larger British force was able to trap the small American force in Charleston's harbor and then drive it up the Cooper River and out of the battle. The *Queen of France* was scuttled, obstructing the river, and the Marines were assimilated into five Continental Army artillery units along the shore. The American forces at Charleston were outnumbered three to one and forced to surrender on May 12, 1780. It was the colonists' greatest defeat during the American Revolutionary War.

The defeat at Charleston also marked a low point for the Continental Navy. With the loss of the *Boston,* the *Providence,* the *Queen of France,* and the *Ranger,* the Continental Navy only had five ships left with Marine detachments, the *Alliance,* the *Confederacy,* the *Deane,* the *Saratoga,* and the *Trumbull.* When France entered the war on the side of the colonists, the Continental Navy became virtually superfluous as the French navy was much stronger and posed a much greater threat to the British navy than did the few ships the colonies could keep afloat. In addition, ships were expensive to build and too easily subject to loss, as had been made clear at the battle of Charleston. It was simply too expensive at that point in the war to continue building ships for a Continental Navy.

There were, however, a couple battles left in the small colonial fleet. In May 1780, the *Trumbull,* under the command of Captain James Nicholson, left New London, Connecticut, on its first cruise of the war. It carried on board a detachment of 30 Marines under the command of Captain Gilbert Saltonstall and Lieutenants Jabez Smith Jr. and David Starr. Two other marine officers, Captain John Trevett and Lieutenant David Bill, were on board serving as volunteers.

The *Trumbull* sailed south, and on June 1, just north of Bermuda, she encountered the British privateer *Watt*. The *Watt* attacked the *Trumbull* as soon as she spotted her, and the ensuing battle last for two and a half hours. As Captain Saltonstall later described, the *Watt* tore the *Trumbull* to pieces. The main topmast was shot away; the fore, main, mizzen, and jigger masts were also destroyed; two of her guns had been damaged; the sails had been cut to ribbons by cannon shot—62 through the ensign sail, 157 through the mizzen sail, 560 through the main sail, and 180 through the foresail, according to Saltonstall. Every yard of her hull had been shot through with cannon shot and much of the rest peppered by grapeshot or musket fire. After two and a half hours of such torture, Saltonstall managed to edge away from the *Watt* and, still under his command and able to sail, albeit limping, Saltonstall declared the battle a draw.

The *Trumbull* had suffered 13 dead and another 18 injured. Four Marines—three of the officers and Sergeant Ezekial Hyatt—were among the dead or mortally wounded. Lieutenant David Bill was killed early in the battle when scattershot shattered his skull. Lieutenant Starr, struck by grapeshot, lived until the following Monday. Lieutenant Smith lingered on until June 28, almost a month after the engagement. Captain Trevett had been wounded twice, once in the eye. Saltonstall recorded that he himself had been wounded 11 times by grapeshot or splinters.

The *Watt* fared no better than the *Trumbull*, however. According to Saltonstall's records, her sides had been equally as damaged as the *Trumbull*'s sails had been, and the *Watt*'s main topmast and mainmast were leaning to the side. In fact, at one point, so much water rushed through the holes in the *Watt*'s hull that it threatened to overwhelm her pumps. The *Watt*'s netting was also set on fire by the musket and cannon shot.

In all, the *Watt* lost 13 men, and 79 were wounded. The Marines aboard the *Trumbull* had played an important role in the battle, manning the cannon and firing muskets from the fighting tops of the masts.

Both ships managed to limp back to port. The *Watt* reached New York on June 11 and the *Trumbull* made it to Nantasket, Connecticut, on June 15. Saltonstall commented that it had been the bloodiest engagement of the entire Revolutionary War.

Almost a year after the bloody battle between the *Trumbull* and the *Watt*, on May 29, 1781, the *Alliance* engaged the *Atalanta* and the *Trepassey*. Caught in a lull, the *Alliance* was unable to maneuver while the two smaller British ships used oars to move to the bow and stern of the larger ship and, out of range of most of the *Alliance*'s cannon, and proceeded to fire on her at will. The battle went on for three hours before a breeze finally caught the *Alliance*'s sails, but in that time she had suffered numerous casualties. Among them were Lieutenant Samuel Pritchard, who had been hit by a six-pound shot, Lieutenant James Warren Jr., a Harvard graduate, who had been wounded in the leg, and Sergeant David Brewster, who had been shot in the head by a British marine. Once the *Alliance* could maneuver, however, she made quick work of the two smaller ships.

(Photo courtesy of U.S. Marine Corps Art Collection)

Marine topsmen take aim at British crewmen during the frigate Alliance*'s battle against both the HMS* Atalanta *and* Trepassey. *The painting,* Fighting Tops, *is by Colonel Charles Waterhouse (Ret.)*

Despite the *Alliance*'s narrow victory, the Continental Navy and the Continental Marines continued to suffer major losses in 1781, including three of the remaining five ships and their Marine detachments. The

Saratoga went down in a Caribbean storm in March, all hands lost. The *Confederacy* surrendered in April. The *Trumbull* was captured in August. Only the *Alliance* and the *Deane* remained in the Continental Navy, and the two detachments assigned to these two ships were the only units remaining in the Continental Marines.

By the end of 1781, the immediate need for the Continental Marines had ended. Britain's southern strategy was defeated in September 1781 when Continental and French forces under the command of Washington and Rochambeau encircled Cornwallis's army and defeated him at Yorktown, Virginia. The American Revolutionary War was essentially over, but fighting continued for the next year and a half as the two sides negotiated a peace.

Both the *Deane* and the *Alliance* launched successful cruises in 1782 and 1783. The final battle occurred on March 10, 1783, between the *Alliance* and the *Sybil*. At the end of the war, however, both the *Deane*, now named the *Hague*, and the *Alliance* were sold off in an effort to pay the debts that had been accumulated during the conflict. The last two detachments of Marines were disbanded as well. With the release of Lieutenant Thomas Elwood in September 1783, the Continental Marines ceased to exist.

Over the course of the American Revolutionary War, 131 officers and more than 2,000 noncommissioned officers and enlisted men had served as Continental Marines. Marine records indicate that 49 men were killed in action and another 70 were wounded in action. The Continental Marines, serving most often in conjunction with the Continental Navy but also alongside the Continental Army, had been a small force, but it had made significant contributions to the colonial war for independence. Perhaps more important, the Continental Marines had begun the traditions that would become the hallmark of the U.S. Marine Corps.

CHAPTER 2

TO THE SHORES OF TRIPOLI: BARBARY PIRATES, THE FRENCH QUASI WAR, AND THE WAR OF 1812

With the conclusion of hostilities in 1783, both the Continental Navy and the Continental Marines had been disbanded. The primary reason for this was financial. Maintaining a navy and a marine corps was expensive, and for some time after the end of the American Revolutionary War, the newly independent states were in no position to support a navy or a marine corps.

The Constitution of the United States, adopted in 1789, provided for the creation and support of a navy through the levying of new taxes, but disagreements between Federalist and Republican politicians in Congress prevented the actual creation of such a force. The Federalists argued in favor of a navy to protect maritime trade; the Republicans opposed it because they feared it would result in the financial ruin of the new country.

The Congressional deadlock came to an end in 1794. The "pirates" of the Barbary Coast—the coast of North Africa,

Morocco, Algiers, Tunis, and Tripoli—had for some time been demanding fees for safe passage from other seafaring nations. The United States had paid these fees until 1793, when Algiers, encouraged by renewed warfare in Europe, dramatically increased the fees it demanded of foreign shipping. The U.S. government took exception to this demand, and on March 27, 1794, Congress passed the Navy Act. This Act provided for the construction of six frigates with the stipulation that, should the United States and Algiers come to a compromise, the building program would be discontinued.

The United States and Algiers did ultimately reach a compromise settlement before construction was completed. The war between Britain and France in Europe severely limited available resources, and the construction of the planned frigates had proved to be much slower and more costly than Congress had expected. In the end, Congress realized that it would cost more to produce the six frigates than it would simply to pay Algiers the fees demanded, and the United States agreed to pay Algiers approximately $1 million. Nevertheless, the Federalists in Congress were able to reach a compromise on the construction of the fledgling American Navy, and three of the original six frigates, the *Constellation*, the *Constitution*, and the *United States*, were built in 1796 and launched in 1797. All three carried a Marine detachment. A Congressional Act of July 1, 1797, established the number of new Marines. There were to be 167: 140 privates, 8 corporals, 8 sergeants, 5 lieutenants, 3 drummers, and 3 fifers. These Marines were considered part of the ships' crews and were therefore part of the Navy. There was not yet a U.S. Marine Corps.

It was fortunate that Congress had approved even the small navy that it had, for new friction soon developed. This time it was between the United States and France.

★★★

War between Britain and France had been renewed in 1793 as the French Revolution took a radical turn and the conservative monarchies of Europe attempted to prevent the spread of revolutionary ideas. Both Britain and France claimed the right to interfere with ships trading with the enemy, which could become a serious problem for the American merchant marine. For some time France had elected not to interfere with American shipping, and the United States had reached an agreement with Great Britain in 1794 with the signing of the Jay Treaty, but in 1796, France announced that it would seize the ships of any nation that had been trading with Great Britain or that carried any article of British manufacture, including the United States. By the end of 1797, France had successfully seized more than 300 American merchantmen and privateers in the Caribbean.

The growing friction between the United States and France led the newly elected president of the United States, John Adams, a Federalist and a staunch supporter of both an American Navy and an American Marine Corps—he had introduced the resolution calling for the creation of a marine corps in 1775—to take action. The three frigates previously built were prepared for service, and Congress authorized the construction of several more vessels, which were built in the next several months. On April 30, the Navy Department was founded, and on May 28, 1798, the U.S. government instructed its naval vessels to attack any armed French naval vessels. The so-called Quasi War with France had begun. The *Delaware* was the first U.S. ship to see action when it defeated and captured the French privateer *Croyable* off the coast of New Jersey.

As the Quasi War with France took shape, Samuel Sewall, chairman of the House Naval Committee, introduced a resolution to Congress to establish a Marine Corps commanded by a major and including some 500 enlisted men. Congress passed Sewall's bill on July 11, 1798, four days after the *Delaware*'s victory over the *Croyable*. The newly created Marine Corps was placed initially under the direct command of the president of the United States, coming to be known as the "President's Troops," and were to serve either with the Army or the Navy, depending on the required service, which created something of an ambiguity as to the chain of command.

The Navy Act of 1794, in addition to authorizing the construction of the first U.S. frigates, authorized the attachment of a Marine Guard to each of the newly commissioned ships. On the 4 larger ships, these guards were to number 1 officer and 54 men; on the 2 smaller ships, it would consist of 1 officer and 44 men. Several officers had already received commissions as Marines.

In July 1798, Congress vastly increased these numbers. The new Marine Corps would number 33 officers—1 major, 4 captains, and 28 lieutenants—and 848 noncommissioned officers and enlisted men. In March 1799, its authorized size was increased to 41 officers and 1,044 men. But in reality, the Marine Corps remained small, numbering on average only about 600 men total, as the Corps was not authorized to offer enlistment bonuses like the Army and Navy. The new Marines were outfitted with leftover uniforms of blue with red facings.

President Adams selected William Ward Burrows, a wealthy Philadelphia lawyer and businessman, to be commandant of the new Marine Corps. Adams chose Burrows for his proven managerial skills as well as his political connections rather than any military proficiency. Commissioned with the rank of major, Burrows established the Marine Corps headquarters in what was at the time the national capital, Philadelphia, and a Marine camp was set up just outside the city.

Burrows set out an ambitious program for the small military force under his command. Many of the naval officers considered the Marine Corps as a supplementary military force to the navy, but Burrows hoped to establish it as a significant military force in its own right. Major Burrows provided unwavering support for his officers in opposing the misuse of the Marines. Ostensibly, the Marines were on board ship to protect the ship from mutiny and to provide musket fire during naval engagements. Ships' officers, however, frequently required Marines to perform sailors' duties such as rigging sails. Although Burrows allowed that Marines might voluntarily assist the sailors from time to time, he preferred that they maintain their equipment and drill in their free time.

Burrows also did what he could to ensure that his officers' authority was respected. In November 1799, Navy Lieutenant Allen McKenzie of the *Ganges* put a Marine in irons without consulting the Marine commander. Marine First Lieutenant Anthony Gale protested the action, and McKenzie responded by striking Gale. The ship's captain ignored the incident. At the end of the cruise, Gale challenged McKenzie to a duel. McKenzie chose pistols; Gale shot him dead. Burrows fully supported Gale's action, declaring that he hoped it would be a lesson to other naval officers to treat the Marines with respect. In August 1801, Secretary of the Navy Robert Smith issued a statement indicating that the Marines were not to be used for shipboard duties.

MARINE CORPS BAND

Major Burrows's main duties, of course, were to build the Marine Corps. But he was aware also of the importance of public relations. Among the 848 Marines authorized by Congress in 1798 were to be 32 drummers and fifers. Late in 1798, Burrows collected $10 from each of his officers, nearly half the monthly salary of a second lieutenant, and purchased the instruments for the fife and drum band. In January 1799, William Farr was appointed drum major. The Marine Corps Band made its debut in Philadelphia in 1800 for the Fourth of July celebration, and in March 1801, it performed for the inauguration of Thomas Jefferson as president, a function it has performed at every subsequent presidential inauguration, leading to its moniker as "President's Own" Marine Corps Band.

With one exception, all of the encounters between U.S. and French naval vessels resulted in the defeat and capture of the French vessels. Marines had been aboard the *Delaware* when it captured the *Croyable* in July 1798. The *Croyable* was quickly recommissioned in the U.S. Navy as the *Retaliation*, and a Marine Guard under the command of First Lieutenant Simon Geddis was attached to it. In November 1798, however, the *Retaliation* ran afoul of two French ships outgunning her by more than 5 to 1—the *Retaliation* mounted only 14 guns while the 2 French ships mounted 76 between them. The captain of the *Retaliation* surrendered, understandably, without resisting, and Geddis and his Marine Guard were the first U.S. Marines taken as prisoners of war.

Other naval encounters were more successful, and Marine Guard units frequently played important roles in them. The *Constellation*, for example, carried a Marine detachment under the command of First Lieutenant Bartholomew Clinch. On February 9, 1799, the *Constellation* captured the *Insurgente*, and on February 1, 1800, she defeated the *Vengeance*. Both encounters involved close combat, and the Marines on board the *Constellation* performed the traditional role of the shipboard marine, shooting at enemy personnel and throwing grenades. In the defeat of the *Vengeance*, a brutal night battle, Clinch's Marines successfully defended the *Constellation* and prevented the larger French vessel's crew from boarding her.

On January 1, 1800, 12 Haitian barge pirates led by a mulatto called Rigaud set upon a becalmed convoy of 4 American merchants and their 12-gun schooner escort, the *Experiment*, off the coast of Haiti. Rowing their barges, the Haitians were able to maneuver around the American vessels, attacked the convoy three times, and captured two of the merchantmen. For their part, the Americans managed to sink two of the Haitian barges, and Sheridine's steadfast Marine Guard had fought off every attempt by the Haitians to grapple and board the *Experiment*.

Marines also took part in two amphibious assaults during the Quasi War, the first at Puerto Plata, Santo Domingo, and the second at Willemstad, Curaçao. Commodore Silas Talbot, commanding the USS *Constitution*, was assigned to cooperate with the black Haitian general Toussaint L'Ouverture, a former slave who led a rebellion and overthrew French rule on the island. On May 12, 1800, Silas learned that the French privateer *Sandwich* was anchored at the Spanish fort of Puerto Plata loading coffee and sugar into its holds. Talbot sent the American merchantman *Sally* into the harbor with only a few men on deck. Below deck, however, the *Sally* was packed with 85 sailors and Marines led by First Lieutenant Isaac Hull. Captain Daniel Carmick and Second Lieutenant William Amory led the Marine detachment.

Captain Carmick later compared the daring raid to the Trojan horse, for the *Sally* sailed into the port of Puerto Plata unopposed, and the Americans easily boarded the *Sandwich* and captured her 23 crewmen. Carmick and Amory then led the Marines onto shore and captured the Spanish fort to prevent its cannon being turned on the *Sally* or the *Sandwich*. The raid was successful, and Talbot was very pleased with the performance of Hull, Carmick, and Amory.

The Dutch island of Curaçao had been invaded by French troops from Guadaloupe in September 1800. The American consul stationed on the island pleaded for help, and on September 22 two U.S. ships, the *Merrimack* and the *Patapsco*, responded. The Dutch residents and American merchantmen trapped by the French assault had retreated to Fort Amsterdam overlooking the harbor. The French invaders set up several artillery batteries in preparation for an assault on the fort, but on September 23 the *Patapsco* bombarded the French positions, destroying the gun emplacements, and on September 24, 70 American Marines and sailors landed to reinforce the defenders in the fort. The French withdrew that afternoon.

The Quasi War with France ended less than one week later with the Convention of Mortefontaine. The peace created by the convention didn't really represent a triumph for either side, but neither the United States nor France had been enthusiastic about the conflict in the first place.

Despite the rather neutral treaty, the United States had clearly won the conflict at sea. Eighty-five French privateers as well as two French frigates had been captured during the Quasi War. The United States lost only one small vessel, the *Retaliation*, which had been a captured French vessel. The Marine Guards attached to the American vessels had proven to be an invaluable asset, as demonstrated by the *Constellation*'s defeat of the *Vengeance* and the *Experiment*'s defense of the convoy off the coast of Haiti. The young U.S. Marine Corps suffered only 17 casualties, with 6 men dead and another 11 wounded. Second Lieutenant Dyre S. Wynkoop was the first U.S. Marine Corps officer to lose his life in the line of duty when the *Insurgente*, a captured French frigate, went down with all hands after sailing from Norfolk.

★★★

Commandant Burrows accepted a promotion to Lieutenant Colonel in April 1800 and moved the Marine Corps headquarters to the new national capital in Washington, D.C. In March 1801, the newly elected President Thomas Jefferson and Commandant Burrows, who were personal friends, selected the site for the Washington Marine Corps Barracks: the block between Eighth and Ninth and G and I Streets, Southeast. The Washington Barracks included the construction to the Marine Corps commandant's home, a small mansion in which every succeeding commandant has resided—Burrows's successor, Franklin Wharton, who became commandant in 1804, was the first to reside there. One year later, however, in 1802, President Jefferson, advocating a policy of economy, stopped construction on new vessels and ordered either the sale of naval vessels or their dismantling to reduce expenses. The Marine Corps itself was reduced to 450 men even though the United States found itself once again in conflict with the Barbary pirates of the North African coast.

This time the conflict was with Tripoli. Between 1795 and 1801, the United States had paid nearly $2 million—an astounding one fifth of its annual revenues—to the Barbary states, either through ransom for prisoners or for "permission" to sail the Mediterranean Sea. In May 1801, the

Pasha of Tripoli, Yusef Karamanli, declared that the United States hadn't paid him sufficient tribute and declared war on the new country. President Jefferson tested the powers of the American presidency by sending most of the U.S. Navy to the Mediterranean to protect American merchantmen and to blockade the port of Tripoli without a declaration of war.

The first ship reached the Mediterranean in July and conflict flared up in August when the *Enterprise* faced the *Tripoli*. The pirates on board the *Tripoli* tried repeatedly to board the *Enterprise*, but the American ship held off each of these attempts with its cannon and the musketry of the Marines. The *Tripoli* lost 50 of its 80 crewmen, but the *Enterprise* suffered not a single casualty.

The encounter between the *Enterprise* and the *Tripoli* was a rare one, however, as the American vessels weren't designed for shallow-water operations and the Navy lacked sufficient charts of the Barbary Coast. The blockade was never very effective, and the Tripolitan ships had never intended to seek ship-to-ship battle. There were, therefore, no other ship-to-ship battles and few other encounters until June 1803, when Lieutenant Lane, leading 50 sailors and Marines, attacked and burned several Triploitan vessels near shore.

Commodore Edward Preble assumed command of Mediterranean operations in September 1803 with the full intention of winning the war against Tripoli. But almost immediately the prospects of a quick victory were dashed when the *Philadelphia*, one of the two biggest ships Preble had at his disposal, ran aground while pursuing a blockade runner. Captain William Bainbridge tried to free the *Philadelphia* from the reef it had run aground on, even pushing his cannon overboard, but the *Philadelphia* was quickly surrounded by several small Tripolitan gunboats, and Captain Bainbridge, realizing the situation was hopeless, surrendered without resisting. First Lieutenant William Osborne and the 42 Marines under his command were among the 307 Americans taken prisoner. Two days later, the tides rose, allowing the Tripolitans to tow the *Philadelphia* into port.

The *Philadelphia* and her crew remained captives of Tripoli for several anxious months as the pasha used them as a negotiating tool, even threatening to burn them alive. On February 16, 1804, Navy Lieutenant Stephen Decatur led 74 volunteers, including Marine Sergeant Solomon Wren and 7 Marines, on a daring rescue mission.

On board a small coastal trader, Decatur and his volunteers slipped into the harbor where the *Philadelphia* was docked and were able to sneak aboard the *Philadelphia*. They easily overpowered the small crew set to guard it, set it on fire, and then escaped without losing a single man. But the 307 Americans remained prisoners of war in Tripoli.

Preble decided that the best way to persuade Pasha Karamanli to release the prisoners was to bombard the capital Tripoli. The American Navy at the time lacked the appropriate ships to conduct a shore bombardment, but Preble's flagship, the *Constitution*, and six smaller gunboats found an ally in the Kingdom of the Two Sicilies, which was also at war with Tripoli.

The Kingdom of the Two Sicilies supplied another six gunboats as well as two bomb ships. Preble began bombarding Tripoli on August 3, 1804. Immediately, a Tripolitan flotilla of 19 gunboats and 2 galleys set sail to drive off the assault. Lieutenant Decatur, commanding three of the American gunboats, engaged the Tripolitan flotilla, personally leading boarding parties that captured two of the enemy gunboats. Marine Sergeant Wren was one of the men injured during these actions.

Another Navy lieutenant, John Trippe, led Marine Sergeant Jonathan Meredith and a small boarding party on board one of the Tripolitan boats, but the 10 men soon found themselves stranded. The meager American boarding party held its own, however, and after a vicious melee, slew or wounded more than half of the Tripolitan crew. The rest surrendered. Trippe and three other boarders, two of whom were Marines, were wounded, the only American casualties of the engagement.

Preble began a second bombardment on August 7. The Tripolitans chose to attack the American ships from a distance, firing on them from shore-based cannon as well as from the gunboats. One of these shots ignited the magazine on Gunboat No. 9, killing 16 of the 28-man crew, including Sergeant Meredith.

Preble bombarded Tripoli three more times and attempted to blow up the harbor with a powder ship—which exploded prematurely—but the pasha held firm to his demands. In September 1804, Preble headed home under the impression that he had failed. As it would turn out, however, by the time Preble returned home, the American hostages would be free.

The year before Preble's bombardment of Tripoli, William Eaton, a 40-year-old Revolutionary War veteran, former U.S. Army captain, former schoolteacher, and then U.S. consul in Tunis, returned to the United States with an alternative solution to the Tripolitan situation. Eaton was familiar with Barbary politics and knew that Pasha Yusef Karamanli had seized power by assassinating one of his brothers, Hassan, and driving another, Hamet, into exile. Eaton eventually convinced the Jefferson administration that the ideal situation in Tripoli would be to return Hamet to power.

In July 1804, Eaton arrived in Egypt and convinced Hamet Karamanli to take up arms against his brother the Pasha. Preparation for the campaign against Yusef Karamanli was a lengthy affair, but "General" Eaton and Hamet Karamanli eventually assembled an army of approximately 400 men: 325 Arabs, a mercenary company of 35 Greeks, another mercenary company of 22 cannoneers, and 9 American Marines led by First Lieutenant Presley O'Bannon.

Eaton's army left Alexandria, Egypt, on March 8, 1805. The 600-mile march across the desert of North Africa proved difficult. Eaton's army was poorly provisioned, and O'Bannon's Marines and the mercenaries found themselves suppressing mutinies on several occasions. But by April 25, Eaton reached the Tripolitan frontier city of Derna. By then Eaton's army had been increased by nearly 200 Arab horsemen who had joined the expedition.

Although Eaton requested free passage by Derna, the city governor refused, and Eaton attacked two days later. Eaton launched a two-pronged assault, Hamet's cavalry attacking from the south of the city while the Marines and mercenaries, supported by fire from three of the Mediterranean Fleet's smaller ships, stormed the city's barricade to the east. The city's artillery proved too much for the initial assault, and Eaton decided that the only way to take the city was to charge.

O'Bannon led his Marines, the Greeks, and the Cannoneers—those not manning the army's single cannon—through a hail of musket fire, took possession of the city's artillery battery, and, raising the American flag over the ramparts, turned the cannon on the city. The defenders, demoralized by O'Bannon's bold assault and the loss of their cannon, retreated. Hamet Karamanli attacked and seized the castle. Within two hours, Eaton controlled the entire city, and most of its inhabitants quickly declared their allegiance to Hamet Karamanli. Eaton's army had lost 13 men, including Marine Private John Whitten, killed in action, and Marine Private Edward Steward, who died of his wounds.

Meanwhile, however, President Jefferson, frustrated by the 18-month hostage situation in Tripoli, sent Tobias Lear to negotiate with Pasha Yusef Karamanli, and on June 3, 1805, the United States and Tripoli signed a treaty ending the conflict. The pasha agreed to release the *Philadelphia*'s crew and, perhaps considering his brother's sizeable and successful army at Derna, waived all claims on future tribute in return for a one-time payment of $60,000.

Considering that 10 years earlier Congress had agreed to pay Algiers $1 million, this was indeed a bargain. Eaton felt betrayed by the treaty, having believed the United States intended to support Hamet Karamanli, but there was nothing either he or Hamet could do to prevent it, and Hamet and his troops, with the mercenaries and the American Marines, were evacuated from Derna aboard the *Constitution* on June 12.

Nevertheless, Eaton and O'Bannon returned home as heroes. Congress honored Eaton, O'Bannon, and the other American Marines who had fought at Derna with a resolution of thanks. Massachusetts honored its native son Eaton with a land grant. Virginia awarded O'Bannon the famous Mameluke sword, supposedly modeled on a sword presented to him by Hamet Karamanli. In later days, O'Bannon almost certainly would have received the additional reward of a promotion. Unfortunately, the Marine Corps of the early nineteenth century only had four captain's ranks among its officers, all of which were currently filled. O'Bannon resigned his commission in 1807, married, and settled in Kentucky, where he served several terms in the state legislature. First Lieutenant Presley O'Bannon had served only six years as a Marine, but his exploits in North Africa have made him one of the icons of the U.S. Marine Corps to this day.

THE MAMELUKE SWORD

The first Marine officer to carry the Mameluke sword was First Lieutenant Presley O'Bannon. He was given a jeweled scimitar by Hamet Karamanli for his actions during the Tripolitan War. Upon his returning to the United States, the state of Virginia presented O'Bannon a sword modeled on the jeweled scimitar, though they managed to misspell his name "Priestly"!

The Mameluke sword, named after a fierce tribe of desert warriors of North Africa, held a special attraction for Marine officers, many of whom began wearing similar swords themselves. By 1825, Marine Corps regulations mandated all Marine officers carry the distinctive Mameluke swords with their ivory grips, straight brass cross guard, gently curved blade, and silver scabbard. Except for a short period during the American Civil War, all Marine officers have since carried the Mameluke sword.

★★★

The Tripolitan War had come to an end under the leadership of a new commandant, Captain Franklin Wharton, who had been appointed to the office on March 7, 1804. Wharton had been given one of the original four captaincies of the Marine Corps in 1798 and had served afloat during the Quasi War with France. Subsequently, he had been given command of the Marine barracks in Philadelphia. Wharton proved to be a good commandant, demonstrating that he understood the importance of morale, public relations, and politics. He issued the first official uniform of the Marine Corps— blue coat and white pants with red facings and a tall hat with a red plume and a brass plate with the motto *Fortitudine*—meaning "with fortitude"— and he introduced the hand salute as well. He continued to support the Marine Corps Band and became one of Washington's civic leaders.

The early years of Wharton's command were relatively uneventful. In 1809, the possibility of war with Spain prompted Congress to increase the size of the Marine Corps to 46 officers and 1,823 men, but only 1,100 men were actually recruited. Marine Corps duties were also expanding. The Marines were now supplying guards to the Navy shipyards at Norfolk, Boston, Brooklyn, Charleston, and New Orleans in addition to those at Washington and Philadelphia. In 1811, the Marine Guard stationed at New Orleans under the command of Major Daniel Carmick engaged in the suppression of "Negro insurgents," probably escaped slaves most of whom fled into the bayou north of the city

In 1812, the so-called Patriot's War began. This was less a war than an underhanded attempt to seize eastern Florida from Spain. Due to the European conflict between Britain and France, which had caused the British to blockade the European continent and even seize American ships, the

United States had likewise put an embargo on British goods. Nevertheless, British goods were smuggled into Georgia through East Florida.

Based on the successful seizure of Baton Rouge from Spanish West Florida in 1811, a group of American "Patriots," promised land grants in compensation, were to seize the town of Fernandia, proclaim the "Republic of Florida," and then immediately cede the new republic to the United States of America. These Patriots would then push south, supported by American troops from Cumberland Island, Georgia, and seize St. Augustine.

Everything proceeded according to plan initially. The Patriots, assisted by American gunboats, under the command of Commodore Hugh Campbell as well as Army and Marine personnel, seized Fernandia and occupied Amelia Island on March 17, 1812. Less than a month later, they rendez-voused with the United States Regiment of Riflemen on the outskirts of St. Augustine, leaving the Marines to hold Amelia Island.

But the operation soon turned into a disaster. The American forces didn't have the artillery to properly assault the city, which was guarded by the impressive Castillo de San Marcos. In June, the Americans made the mistake of turning down an offer of alliance from the Seminole Indians. The Seminoles made the same offer to the Spanish, who quickly accepted, and the American lines were raided by Seminole war parties.

The following month, Captain John Williams was ordered to escort a supply train from Fernandia to St. Augustine. On September 12, Williams and 20 Marines and Patriots were ambushed by 60 Spanish and Seminole raiders while escorting the train. They beat off the assault but not before one Marine was killed and scalped, and eight more men were wounded. Captain Williams himself had been shot eight times; he died on September 29. Lieutenant Alexander Sevier took over Williams's command, and in February 1813 led a band of Marines on a raid against the Seminole Indians and burned their villages. By then it had become apparent that supplying the Patriots around St. Augustine was simply too difficult, and the Americans began to pull back from their positions. To make matters worse, the War of 1812 had begun.

War between France and Britain had erupted again in 1803. In an effort to force France into submission, the British had erected a blockade that eventually came to encompass the entire European continent. The British navy denied any trade with France, including that of neutrals such as the

United States, and not only seized American merchant ships but went so far as to impress Americans into British service. Indeed, it was said that there were more Americans serving in the British Royal Navy than there were in the U.S. Navy. The tensions created by such actions were intensified by the discovery in 1811 that British forces in Canada had been supplying Indian tribes resisting American settlements in the Ohio River Valley. In response, President James Madison asked Congress for a declaration of war against Great Britain, which it approved on June 18, 1812.

Many of the supporters of the War of 1812 had assumed that the defeat of the British and the annexation of Canada would be easy, but in 1812 the United States was ill prepared to conduct a war. The number of men serving in the U.S. military stood at only 12,631 total. The Marine Corps was composed of a mere 10 officers and 483 enlisted men. The U.S. Navy had only three first-class warships: the *President*, the *United States*, and the *Constitution*. In 1812, the United States met with defeat in three attempts to invade Canada.

The Madison administration soon realized that the losses were due largely to Britain's control of the Great Lakes, and that control of Lake Erie and Lake Ontario were essential to victory. To this end, during the summer of 1812, the Navy began rebuilding its fleet for use both on the Great Lakes and the open seas. Commodore Isaac Chauncey was given command of the naval forces on the Great Lakes, and naval bases were established on Lake Ontario and Lake Erie.

The U.S. Navy won important victories on inland waters at the Battle of Lake Erie and the Battle of Lake Champlain. Although no Marines served with Commodore Thomas Macdonough during the Battle of Lake Champlain, 34 served with Commodore Oliver Perry on Lake Erie. Perry's main goal was to harass British shipping in the area.

On September 10, 1813, Perry engaged the British fleet on Lake Erie and completely destroyed British capacity to control the Great Lake. Fourteen Marines were wounded during the battle, and four were killed in action, including the Marine commander, Second Lieutenant John Brooks, who was hit by a cannonball. By winning control of Lake Erie, Commodore Perry prevented the British from blocking American expansion into the Ohio River Valley.

On the open seas, the Navy was ordered to harass British shipping and to engage single British warships in combat when possible. In 1812, the U.S. Navy emerged victorious from three engagements with the Royal Navy. The Marines made substantial contributions to these victories. On August 19, 1812, the *Constitution* fought the *Guerrière*. Marines shot the British captain, his first lieutenant, and his second lieutenant. As the two ships came crashing together, Marine First Lieutenant William Bush, the commander of the *Constitution*'s Marine detachment, leapt to the railing, demanding of the *Constitution*'s captain whether he should lead his Marines in a boarding action. Lieutenant Bush was promptly shot in the head by one of the *Guerrière*'s Royal Marines, but the *Guerrière*'s decks were cleared by Marine musket fire. She was captured and burned.

On October 25, 1812, the *United States* captured the *Macedonian* off the Madeira Islands. On December 28, 1812, the *Constitution* clashed with the HMS *Java* off the coast of Brazil. As the captain of the *Java* attempted to lead a boarding party onto the *Constitution*, an American Marine marksman shot and mortally wounded him. The Marines had organized themselves into six-man teams, one marksman and five men reloading the muskets, which allowed for rapid, well-aimed fire. It proved invaluable. Other Marines firing from the rigging quickly picked off several other British officers, and the *Java* surrendered.

On June 1, 1813, Captain James Lawrence, new to command and with a green crew, sailed the *Chesapeake* from Boston harbor to engage the HMS *Shannon*, one of the Royal Navy's most formidable ships under the command of Captain Vere Broke. The battle was over in 15 minutes, resulting in the first loss of the war for the U.S. Navy. By the time the *Shannon* closed with the *Chesapeake* and Captain Broke led his Marines on board, the *Chesapeake* had been torn to pieces. Every officer on deck had been shot at least once, including the commander of the Marine detachment, First Lieutenant James Broome, who had been mortally wounded. As Captain James Lawrence was carried from the deck, however, he shouted, "Don't give up the ship!" The Marines stood firm, mustering the only resistance the British boarders faced, until they were overwhelmed. Fourteen of the *Chesapeake*'s 44 Marines were killed or died of their wounds. Another 20 were wounded, suffering a casualty rate of some 77 percent, more than twice the casualties of the ship's crew.

On June 28, 1814, the *Wasp* engaged the British brig *Reindeer.* During the battle, as the two ships came together, the *Reindeer's* captain, William Manners, already wounded twice, climbed into the rigging and called for his Marines to board the *Wasp.* Two American Marines shot him dead. The Americans seized the opportunity to board the *Reindeer* and captured her.

In one instance during the War of 1812, a Marine officer actually commanded a U.S. naval vessel. Captain David Porter, commanding the *Essex,* sailed around Cape Horn in February 1813 to attack the British whaling fleet. Off the coast of the Galapagos Islands, Porter captured three British whaling ships, refit them, and, having brought along extra crewmen, set prize crews to man them. One of the ships, the *Greenwhich,* was commanded to Marine First Lieutenant James Marshall Gamble. Porter assigned 14 men to crew the vessel, 2 of whom were expert seamen who could advise Gamble in running the ship. On July 14, the *Greenwhich,* commanded by Gamble, ran afoul of the *Seringapatam,* a notorious British warship that had harassed American whaling ships in the Pacific Ocean. After a nervous engagement, as Porter watched from the *Essex,* Gamble was able to defeat the *Seringapatam.*

During October 1813, Porter established a base at Nukuhiva in the Marquesa Islands, and, after resting and repairing his ships, he set sail to further harass the British Royal Navy. He left Gamble and several Marines and sailors to man the base. Porter never returned to Nukuhiva, however; he was defeated off the coast of Valparaiso, Chile, and taken prisoner. Gamble and his men didn't fare any better. Shortly after Porter set sail, the small base on Nukuhiva was attacked by hostile natives. Facing a mutiny among his own crew, Gamble was forced to give up the base, and with the few Marines under his command, he fled Nukuhiva aboard the *Sir Andrew Hammond.*

Gamble and his small crew managed to reach the Sandwich Islands after two weeks at sea. There they were greeted by friendly natives and traders who helped him refit the *Sir Andrew Hammond.* In return, Gamble agreed to transport several of the natives to a neighboring island where their king lived. Unfortunately, while en route, the *Sir Andrew Hammond* was attacked by the HMS *Cherub,* one of the ships that had earlier defeated Porter at Valparaiso. Escape was impossible, and the *Sir Andrew Hammond* and its crew were not prepared to resist. Gamble surrendered and was taken prisoner.

Gamble eventually made it back to the United States in August 1815, arriving at New York. He would later be promoted to major and then to lieutenant colonel for his service to the U.S. Marine Corps.

WEAPONS OF THE MARINES

The U.S. government established arsenals at Springfield, Massachusetts, in 1794 and at Harper's Ferry, Virginia, in 1799 to produce weapons for the U.S. Army. The Springfield arsenal began producing muskets modeled on the French .69-caliber Charleville musket in 1795 (M-1795). The American arsenals demonstrated little innovation during the first half of the nineteenth century, however, and simply copied the French models.

For the most part, the U.S. Marine Corps adopted the weapons used by the U.S. Army, and from its foundation through the War of 1812 and on into the Civil War, the Corps adopted various Springfield muskets as they became available.

The Marine Corps also experimented with a few other weapons. For example, in 1779, British inventor James Wilson proposed a multi-barreled musket for use by the Royal Marines. Based on Wilson's idea, London gunsmith Henry Nock built a flintlock musket with seven barrels arranged around a central axle (Nock's "volley gun" was adopted for use aboard British ships during the American Revolution). All seven barrels of the volley gun fired at once, providing impressive fire, and the U.S. Navy and Marine Corps later adopted the weapons for use by ship's Marine detachments. Firing from a ship's fighting platform, the volley gun could bring heavy fire down on enemy decks.

Like Nock's volley gun, many of the other weapons typically employed by the Marines were intended for ship-to-ship boarding actions. For some time, the brass-barreled blunderbuss, a short, heavy gun with a widely flared muzzle was also popular. Because of the flared muzzle, the gun could be loaded rapidly with a variety of ammunition ranging from buckshot to nails to stones. Marines also employed boarding pikes—short, spearlike weapons used during boarding actions—and cutlasses—short, heavy, curved, single-edge swords—as well as bayonets. Officers were typically armed with a brace of muzzle-loading .56-caliber flintlock pistols and a cutlass.

Marines also took part in defense of Washington. In 1814, as the war between France and Britain began to settle down—Napoleon Bonaparte having been defeated at the battle of Leipzig, captured in Paris, and exiled to the island of Elba, at least for the moment—Britain was able to muster a serious offensive against the United States. Commodore Thomas Macdonough's victory over the British invasion force from Canada at the Battle of Lake Champlain in September defeated one wing of this assault. But with the intention of raiding American cities and thereby diverting American troops, the British also launched a large-scale amphibious assault involving some 5,400 troops under the command of Major General Robert Ross. Ross's army was escorted by a convoy larger than the entire American Navy and successfully landed at Benedict, Maryland, on August 19. Ross immediately began the march northward toward Washington.

The British advance was challenged by Commodore Joshua Barney, the commander of the Chesapeake gunboat flotilla, who harassed General Ross's advance along the Patuxet River in vain. When Ross's force passed Barney, the commodore left his flotilla behind and traveled overland with the flotilla's 420 sailors and Marines, 5 cannon, and a detachment of 103 additional Marines under the command of Captain Samuel Miller, the Marine Corps's adjutant and inspector, whom Commandant Wharton had attached to the flotilla. Barney's force joined the force of 5,500 militia and one infantry regiment commanded by Brigadier General William Winder at Washington.

The first engagement between the two forces occurred on August 24 on the west bank of the eastern branch of the Potomac River across from the village of Bladensburg. Commodore Barney formed a line one mile behind the front line of the American militia on a ridge crossing the Washington Turnpike. Barney commanded a detachment of sailors and Marines operating two 18-pound cannon aimed straight down the turnpike. Captain Miller commanded three 12-pound cannon to the right of Barney. The sailors and Marines not detailed to the cannon batteries were formed into a firing line along the ridge, and a few other late-arriving units lined up on the units' flanks, militia men on the right, and an infantry unit, including another five cannon, on the left.

The first line of American militia was easily defeated by General Ross's troops, and, excited by the easy victory, the British forces charged straight down the turnpike. Barney's well-placed artillery and musketry caught the British by surprise and drove them back. They reformed and charged again only to be repulsed. A third time the British reformed and charged Barney's naval brigade. The charge stalled, and, seizing the moment, Barney ordered a counterattack. The sailors and Marines charged down the ridge shouting, "Board 'em! Board 'em!" and the battered British regiment began to give ground.

General Ross scrambled to the battlefield and ordered his troops to move around the flanks of the American troops. At the same time, however, in order to save the remnant of his army, General Winder ordered his troops to retire. Winder never notified Barney of the retreat, and Barney's naval brigade soon found itself facing the full force of Ross's troops and under fire from three sides. Barney was shot in the leg and Captain Miller was shot in the arm as he was exchanging musket fire with the British.

Barney finally gave the order to spike the cannons and retreat, but it was too late. Barney and Miller were both captured as the British advanced. The vast majority of the casualties at the Battle of Bladensburg—the British lost nearly 250 men, the Americans nearly 150—occurred during Barney's gallant stand against the British advance. The Marines suffered 8 dead and 14 wounded.

In one sense, Barney's stand had been in vain since there was never any realistic chance that Barney's small naval brigade could actually withstand the advance of Ross's army. Nevertheless, it did demonstrate the incredible valor of the American fighting man. On meeting Barney, General Ross complimented the commodore on his command and his brigade's gallant stand.

As the British army continued its advance toward Washington, Commandant Wharton gathered the Marine headquarters, records, and treasury as well as the Marine Corps Band and marched to the Washington Navy Yard. The Secretary of the Navy ordered Wharton to withdraw to Frederick, Maryland, the government's designated refuge in case of emergency.

Wharton initially volunteered to support Commodore Thomas Tingey in defending the Navy yard. Tingey declined Wharton's offer and then ordered the yard burned to prevent its capture. Wharton proceeded to Frederick, following the orders he had been given by the Secretary of the Navy. The British proceeded to burn Washington's public buildings but amazingly left Marine barracks and commandant's residence alone, perhaps out of respect for Barney's valiant naval brigade. General Ross's army embarked at Washington and sailed to raid and burn Baltimore. Landing there on September 12, Ross encountered a defending army 10,000 strong, most of whom were militiamen but also including a significant naval brigade made up in part of Marines who had fought at Bladensburg. The militia stood firm against the British advance, and General Ross was shot by a sniper. Cannon fire from the British ships failed to subdue Fort McHenry in Baltimore harbor, and the British withdrew two days later.

Despite the setback at Baltimore, the success of the raid on Washington encouraged the British to continue their strategy of raiding American cities. In December, Sir Edward Pakenham, brother-in-law of the soon-to-be famous Lord Wellington, assembled an amphibious force even larger than the one that landed in the Chesapeake for an assault on their next target, New Orleans.

The British arrived off the shore of Louisiana on December 8 and decided to attack the city through Lake Borgne, an arm of the Gulf of Mexico, rather than attempt to sail against the current of the Mississippi. They were met by 5 American gunboats manned by 147 sailors and 35 Marines. The American gunboats were no match for the vastly superior forces and on December 14, they were swept aside by boarding parties numbering nearly 1,000 men. But their loss provided Major General Andrew Jackson enough time to fortify New Orleans and assemble a rag-tag American force composed of frontiersmen, adventurers, and Jean Lafitte's pirates in addition to Jackson's army and a contingent of Marines led by Major Daniel Carmick.

The Marines fought in each of the battles for the defense of New Orleans, including a daring raid on the British advance guard led by Jackson on December 23, and the defense of the city against a preliminary British attack on December 28. At the battle on the twenty-eighth, Jackson placed Carmick at the head of a battalion of New Orleans volunteers. Carmick was killed by a rocket while leading a countercharge. The Marines finished the defense of New Orleans under the command of First Lieutenant F. B. De Bellevue and again defended the city on January 1, 1815. The British lost nearly 2,000 men in this engagement; the American losses were fewer than 100.

The War of 1812 continued at sea. On February 20, 1815, the *Constitution* fought two smaller British ships, the *Cyane* and the *Levant*. The Marines embarked on *Old Ironsides* were led by Captain Archibald Henderson, who at one point had threatened to resign his commission and join the Army if he didn't see action. The four-hour duel between *Old Ironsides* and the two smaller British ships gave Henderson the action he was looking for. The battle began at such close range that the *Constitution*'s Marines were engaged almost immediately. Thanks to the accuracy of Marine musketry, the *Constitution* proved victorious.

One month later, on March 23, 1815, the *Hornet* faced the HMS *Penguin*. As the *Penguin* closed with the *Hornet*, an American Marine shot the *Penguin*'s captain, killing him. His lieutenant was able to bring the *Penguin* alongside the *Hornet* and call for boarders, but the British sailors refused to board her. The *Penguin* surrendered shortly thereafter.

The battle for New Orleans and the victories of the *Constitution* and the *Hornet* proved belated, however. James Bayard, Albert Gallatin, Jonathan Russell, Henry Clay, and John Quincy Adams represented the United States during the peace negotiations held in Ghent, Belgium, in August 1814. The Treaty of Ghent was signed on December 24, 1814, ending the conflict.

The War of 1812 was significant for the development of the U.S. Marine Corps. It proved the value of such a fighting force and secured the reputation of the Marines. Although Marine losses were relatively small, consisting of only 46 dead and 33 wounded, they were in proportion to the losses of the Navy and the Army.

In recognition of the Corps's value, Congress passed two acts in 1814 strengthening it. The first raised the size of the Marine Corps to 93 officers and 2,622 enlisted men, a 60 percent increase over 1812. The second made Marine officers eligible for brevet promotions for meritorious conduct or having served 10 years in grade.

Six officers were given brevet promotions for their conduct during the War of 1812. Among them were Captain Samuel Miller, who had led the naval brigade at the Battle of Bladensburg, and Captain Archibald Henderson, who had commanded the Marine detachment aboard the USS *Constitution* in its engagement with the *Cyane* and the *Levant*.

★★★

The years following the War of 1812 were relatively quiet. During the war, the Barbary pirates again had demanded tribute from American merchantmen. Marines were embarked with two squadrons sent to the Mediterranean in 1815 to deal with the situation, and after four American vessels subdued an Algerian privateer, the other Barbary states acceded to American demands.

Marines also assisted with expeditions into Spanish East Florida to attack pirate lairs along the Apalachicola River in 1816 and on Amelia Island in 1817. Due to the relative inactivity of the Marine Corps, however, Congress decided to enact the first of what would be many peacetime cutbacks, the Peace Establishment Act, which reduced its size to 50 officers and 865 men only 3 years after its size had been increased to 93 officers and 2,622 men.

The U.S. Marine Corps went through some significant development in these years despite the lack of military action. In 1817, Brevet Major Archibald Henderson, disgusted with Commandant Wharton's perceived cowardice in failing to take a stand against General Ross's attack on Washington, brought charges against Wharton that resulted in a court-martial. Henderson accused Wharton of neglect of duty and conduct unbecoming an officer and a gentleman. The court acquitted Wharton of the charges, but his tenure as commandant didn't last much past his legal victory. He died on September 1, 1818, after a prolonged sickness.

Brevet Major Anthony Gale, whom Commandant Burrows had commended for his victorious duel against Navy Lieutenant Allen McKenzie, was selected to succeed Wharton. Gale had joined the Marine Corps in 1798, served during the Quasi War with France and the War with Tripoli, had commanded the Marine Corps barracks in Philadelphia, and had helped defend Baltimore against General Ross. He had been awarded his brevet rank in 1814 for 10 years of service in grade.

Given his long term of service, one would expect Gale to have succeeded immediately to the command of the Marine Corps. Instead, following the death of Commandant Wharton, Archibald Henderson served six months as acting commandant.

Both Henderson and Brevet Major Samuel Miller raised doubts about Gale's capacity to serve as commandant of the U.S. Marine Corps. Two charges in particular, both of which Gale had been cleared in 1816, were raised once again: misuse of government funds and conduct unbecoming an officer and a gentleman for intoxication while on duty. The reasons for rekindling the issues were clear: Henderson was second behind Gale in terms of seniority; and Miller, although sixth in terms of seniority, had Bladensburg in his background and had spent a great deal of time promoting his own candidacy, alienating Henderson but highly impressing at least one congressman. The accusations and confusion eventually led to a court of inquiry that convened in February 1819. The court once again cleared Gale of the charges, and on March 3, 1819, he was appointed commandant of the U.S. Marine Corps.

Despite Gale's vindication by the court of inquiry, Henderson's and Miller's doubts about Gale may not have been misplaced. In 1820, Gale came into conflict with Secretary of the Navy Smith Thompson. Thompson had essentially ignored the chain of command in granting furlough to several Marines and transferring others without consulting Gale. As at the beginning of his career, Gale challenged Thompson to clarify the command relationship between the Navy and the Marine Corps: Who had the authority to command the Marines? Thompson responded by removing two of Gale's personnel assignments, clearly stating that the Secretary of the Navy had the final say on command and could ignore the Marine Corps commandant if he so chose.

Gale, frustrated by the whole situation, set off on a wicked drinking spree that ended with his arrest, another court-martial, this one convicting him, and his dismissal from the Marine Corps. Ironically, the very characteristics that had earned First Lieutenant Anthony Gale commendation from Commandant Major William Ward Burrows in 1799 resulted in the expulsion of Commandant Brevet Major Anthony Gale 21 years later. Perhaps the Marine Corps had changed indeed.

CHAPTER 3

THE HALLS OF MONTEZUMA: THE MEXICAN AND INDIAN WARS

After the scandal involving Anthony Gale, Brevet Major Archibald Henderson was named the fifth commandant of the U.S. Marine Corps on October 17, 1820.

Henderson had been born in Colchester, Virginia, in 1783, just as the American Revolutionary War came to an end. He entered the Marine Corps in 1806 at the age of 23. He was an extremely ambitious young man even then, as demonstrated by his leadership of the Marine detachment aboard *Old Ironsides* during the War of 1812 and his apparent yearning for action. His efforts to oust Wharton from the command of the Corps and his subsequent challenge to Gale are also indicative of his ambition. No matter how one views Henderson's personal ambition, he was able at a crucial moment to supply the U.S. Marine Corps exactly what it needed: strong leadership.

Nevertheless, although the Corps had performed admirably during the War of 1812, the controversy surrounding the office of the commandant since the Battle of Bladensburg undermined what little support the Corps had left. In 1822, for example, Commandant Henderson assigned Brevet Major Samuel Miller, who never served afloat, to sea duty with the West India Squadron. There had been tension between Henderson and Miller since the two had sought the office of commandant in 1819 and 1820, and Henderson's maneuver may have been an effort to move Miller away from headquarters. Miller, however, went outside the chain of command and requested that President James Monroe countermand Henderson's order, which Monroe did. Henderson threatened to resign his office when the President intervened in the day-to-day business of the Marine Corps in this fashion, trying to maintain control of officer assignments. Monroe's intervention caused no end of trouble for the commandant as every officer of significant rank protested assignment to sea duty for the next decade.

Henderson worked hard to improve the quality of Marine Corps officers, however. Many officers had received their posts due to political patronage rather than military aptitude, which meant that they were perhaps not the best men to lead Marines into battle. Henderson knew that an easy solution would be to recruit officers from the U.S. Military Academy, but his requests for permission to do so were repeatedly denied. In response, Henderson required all new Marine Corps officers to report to the Washington Barracks for orientation, thereby creating a consistent regimen of officer training. He also watched carefully all civilian applicants for Marine Corps officer positions and was prepared to remove those he believed were not fit to act as Marine Corps officers. During the first two decades of the Corps's existence, officers had been dismissed from office on the average of once every four and a half years. Henderson doubled that rate.

Henderson even tried to improve life for enlisted Marines. He continually campaigned for increased recruitment allowances and gradually won some modest increases. By the time he died in 1859, the Corps stood at 63 officers and 2,010 enlisted men, still less than the size authorized in 1814, but certainly larger than when he took over as commandant. Henderson also initiated a number of reforms to correct abuses within the Corps and to improve recruiting and retention rates. Sunday was made a day of rest, flogging was abolished (20 years before the Navy abolished it), barrack living conditions were improved, pay raises were instituted, and allowances were made for food and clothing. Although the rank and file must have appreciated such reforms, Henderson was unable to improve either recruitment or retention to his satisfaction. The Corps was never able to fill its ranks to the full number of Marines authorized, and desertion remained high.

Like his predecessors, Henderson was keenly aware of importance of good public relations. The War of 1812 had demonstrated fairly conclusively that the nation needed an Army and a Navy ready to act in its defense. Yet although the Marines had fought valiantly when called upon, they weren't perceived as crucial to the defense of the nation. The Army and the Navy, many believed, were sufficient to defend the nation, and arguments were made for the absorption of the Marine Corps into one of these two armed forces. The continued existence of the U.S. Marine Corps, therefore, depended upon good public relations, especially with Congress and others who held political influence. Henderson, like Burrows before him, encouraged the ongoing performances of the Marine Corps Band, and its popularity continued to grow. This was especially true after the Neapolitan clarinetist Francis Marie Scala was appointed bandleader in 1845.

Ultimately, however, the performance that mattered most to the continued existence of the Corps was its performance in battle. The Marine Corps participated in two major wars, the Seminole War and the Mexican War, and made more than 40 additional landings under Henderson's tenure as commandant.

During the 1820s and 1830s, the main purpose of much naval and marine activity was to protect American lives and property. In the Caribbean and the Gulf of Mexico, for example, piracy had become rampant. In 1822, Commodore David Porter was given command of the newly created West India Squadron. He established a base at Key West and was assigned 300 Marines for use on expeditions.

Porter had been ordered to cooperate with Spanish officials in the area, but he actually found it more efficient to cooperate with the British instead. The British were far less scrupulous when it came to piracy and were not above simply hanging captured pirates without the benefit of legal courts.

Porter's Squadron and Marines attacked pirate outposts on Cuba and Santo Domingo and on Mexico's Yucatan Peninsula. In the end, the pirates were no match for a professionally trained Navy and Marine Corps. Porter also landed a Marine expeditionary force on Puerto Rico in 1824, apparently to avenge an insult given to the American flag. But this action went well beyond his orders and resulted in his recall and court-martial. He resigned his commission and wound up commanding the Mexican Navy.

Marines engaged in humanitarian operations as well, however. Marines from the Boston Navy Yard helped fight against the Boston fire of 1824, and Marines from the New York Barracks helped fight a large fire in New York City in 1835. Marines from the USS *Grampus* also landed in the Virgin Islands to fight a fire threatening St. Thomas in 1825.

In 1824, the Marine Corps was instrumental in suppressing a Massachusetts State Prison revolt. The prison administration sentenced 3 prisoners to be flogged for violating regulations, and 283 prisoners protested by seizing tools from the workshop, taking over the dining room, and declaring that they would not disperse until that order had been rescinded. The guards attempted to persuade the prisoners to return to work but to no avail, and the prison officials turned to Brevet Major Robert Wainwright, the commander of the Marine barracks at the Boston Navy Yard.

Wainwright, a 17-year veteran of the Corps, led a detachment of Marines to the prison to restore order. He led his Marines directly into the dining room and informed the prisoners that he had been assigned to end the insurrection and restore order. The prisoners replied that they were prepared to die where they stood. Upon hearing the prisoners' determination, Wainwright calmly ordered his Marines to load their muskets. The prisoners, however, believing that they could easily overwhelm the small Marine detachment with the weight of their numbers, remained determined.

The Marines were ordered to take aim but not to fire until they had been given the order. Wainwright stepped forward, repeated his declaration, and took out his pocket watch. He announced that the prisoners had three minutes to vacate the dining hall, after which he would order his men to open fire on any man still in the room. For two long minutes the standoff between desperate prisoners and disciplined Marines dragged on, until finally, a couple prisoners slipped quietly out the back door. They were followed a moment later by a few more, and then there was a rush toward the exit, and the hall was clear.

Wainwright's actions provided a positive image of the courageous and compassionate American Marine officer. Nevertheless, the continued existence of the U.S. Marine Corps remained in doubt, primarily due to financial reasons. President Andrew Jackson, in particular, was made aware of the high cost of maintaining the Marine Corps.

Although the entire Corps was approximately the size of one army infantry unit, it cost more than two and a half times as much money to maintain—an Army unit cost approximately $75,000 per year while the Marine Corps cost approximately $200,000 per year. Much of this difference was due to officer pay raises and allowances, as the Corps included five brevet lieutenant colonels by 1829.

Despite the obvious bravery of the Marines, such as Daniel Carmick, who had fought beside Jackson at New Orleans, or Robert Wainwright during the prison standoff, the president sent a message to the U.S. Congress in December 1829 suggesting that the Marine Corps should be merged with the Army. Such a merger would place the Marines under the command of Army officers, eliminating the high cost of maintaining additional Marine officers.

Jackson's proposal was brought to a congressional hearing the following year. The Secretary of the Navy, John Branch, presented to Congress an informal survey of naval officers, but the results were inconclusive: While several officers believed shipboard Marine detachments to be invaluable, others believed they had little or no value in ship-to-ship combat. Jackson's proposal died in committee, but in 1831, Branch, arguing that Marine guards were not necessary to safeguard command at sea, recommended the Marines should be either absorbed by one of the two branches or abolished entirely. Again, Congress decided not to take any action, and the Marine Corps remained independent for the time being.

Early in 1831, however, while the debate over the future of the Marines was under discussion in Congress, the Corps once again made its presence known. Malay pirates from Kuala Batu on Sumatra raided and plundered the U.S. merchant ship *Friendship*, killing three of her crew. Commodore John Downes, commanding the *Potomac*, a 44-gun frigate, was ordered to Sumatra. The *Potomac* set sail on August 27, news of the raid having taken some time to reach the United States, and arrived at Kuala Batu on February 5, 1832.

The following day, the *Potomac*'s executive officer, Lieutenant Irvine Shubrick, led a landing party of 286 men consisting of 3 divisions of sailors, each commanded by a Navy lieutenant, and the *Potomac*'s Marine Guard, commanded by First Lieutenant Alvin Edson and Second Lieutenant George Terrett. They also carried a six-pound cannon on shore.

The landing party set to attack three forts at the settlement. Lieutenant Shubrick led the first and third divisions of sailors against the largest of the three forts, while the second division and the Marine Guard each assaulted one of the other two. Despite staunch resistance from the native Malays, each of the two smaller forts soon fell. The second division of sailors and the Marine Guard joined Shubrick's efforts at the larger fort.

Many of the defenders were killed by grapeshot fired from the cannon, and the fort was overrun. A fourth fort, previously unseen on the edge of the jungle, opened fire on Shubrick's men, but it, too, was quickly overrun. Shubrick torched the forts and the village. Two members of the landing party had been killed and 11 more wounded, including 4 Marines. One hundred fifty Malays were killed in the assault, including Rajah Po Mahomet, the apparent leader of the Kuala Batu pirates. Downes bombarded what remained of Kuala Batu until a delegation of Malay natives paddled out to the *Potomac* to negotiate.

The extent of the influence the action at Kuala Batu had on Congress is difficult to estimate, of course, but by June 1834, Congress brought to an end the continued efforts of the Jackson administration to eliminate the Marine Corps. Until that point, the Marine Corps had operated either under the Army's Articles of War, while serving on land, or under Navy Regulations while shipboard. The act passed in 1834, an Act for the Better Organization of the Marine Corps, eliminated the ambiguous status of the Marine Corps by defining it as an independent sea service separate from the Navy but governed by the Navy Department and Navy regulations. In addition, the Act promoted the commandant of the Marine Corps to Colonel, and the authorized size of the Marine Corps was increased to 63 officers and 1,224 enlisted men. However, Marine officers were to be subordinate to Navy officers of the same rank, and brevet promotions for 10 years in grade were discontinued, allowing brevet promotions only for distinguished service. As a final point, the act reiterated the president's power to attach the Marine Corps to the Army in time of need.

Ironically, President Jackson made use of this latter clause during the Seminole War.

★★★

Congress had passed the Indian Removal Act in 1830. After the transfer of Florida to American control by the Transcontinental Treaty with Spain signed in 1819, emigrants from neighboring states, eager for land, began moving into Florida and encroaching upon lands claimed by Native Americans. Seminole Indians retaliated by attacking several of these new settlements. The U.S. government eventually came to an agreement with several of the Seminole chiefs and passed the Indian Removal Act, which called for the government to encourage and assist Indian tribes to move to reservations west of the Mississippi River.

The majority of Seminoles were strongly opposed to leaving Florida, and several Seminole chiefs later claimed that they had signed the treaty with the U.S. government under duress. Attempts to remove the Seminoles embittered them further, and in 1834, General Wiley Thompson was sent to Florida to negotiate with Osceola, one of the leading Seminole chiefs. During these "negotiations," Thompson clamped Osceola in irons and imprisoned him for a day. Enraged by this treatment of one of their chiefs, the Seminoles launched a war that would last for nearly seven years.

On December 28, 1835, Seminole warriors attacked 2 companies under the command of Major Francis Dade on a 100-mile march from Fort Brooke to Fort King, slaughtering both companies. The Seminoles proved to be superb tacticians and fighters, and assisted by escaped slaves and the difficult terrain, they turned the Seminole war into the deadliest of the Indian wars waged by the United States.

Marines attached to the West India Squadron frequently supported Army operations and protected Floridian settlements. After the assault on Major Dade's unit, a detachment of Marines from the *Constellation* and the *St. Louis* under the command of Lieutenant Nathaniel Waldron landed to reinforce Fort Brooke. Waldron's unit arrived at the fort in time to help defend it against a series of attacks in January 1836. Waldron's unit also fought under the command of General Winfield Scott along the Withlacoochie River in March 1836.

In spring 1836, three bands of Creek Indians rebelled in Georgia and Alabama. Commandant Henderson believed the Marine Corps could do more than patrol the coast of Florida, and in May he suggested to President Jackson that a regiment of Marines be raised to serve with the Army against the Creek Indians. Jackson accepted his offer.

Henderson assembled a 400-man battalion from the Marines stationed in Washington and set out for Georgia on June 1. Although probably apocryphal, Henderson is supposed to have posted a note on his office door that read, "Gone to fight the Indians. Will be back when the war is over." Brevet Lieutenant Colonel Samuel Miller was his second in command.

Henderson's battalion camped initially a few miles away from Columbus, Georgia, and began patrolling the area, but the Marines had no significant contact with the Creeks before they were subdued. A second Marine battalion of only 160 men, bound for Fort Mitchell in Alabama, had set out a few days after Henderson, but was soon transferred to northern Florida where it was joined by Henderson's battalion in August. The two battalions were consolidated into a single six-company regiment that was attached to Major General Thomas Jesup's Army of the South at Fort Brooke.

When Jesup marched into central Florida in January 1837, Henderson was placed in command of one of the Army's brigades, including a battalion of friendly Creek Indians, a mounted battalion of Alabama volunteers, and a mounted company of Marines, the so-called Horse Marines.

On January 27, scouts found evidence of Indians near Hatchelustee Creek, and Jesup ordered Henderson's brigade to advance and scout the area. Henderson soon found a Seminole village. The Seminole warriors, caught by surprise, fled the village, but Henderson's men captured 5 Indian women and children and 19 escaped slaves. Henderson pursued the Seminole warriors into the Big Cypress Swamp, and caught up to them at the Hatchelustee Creek, where they made a stand.

The creek was deep and approximately 25 yards across. It was bridged in two places by fallen trees. Henderson divided his troops into three units, two of which were deployed to set up crossfire on the opposite bank. Captain John Harris, commander of the Horse Marines, led the third unit across the fallen trees and the Seminoles fled farther into the swamp. Three times the Seminoles stopped to exchange fire with the Marines but continued to fall farther back, out of the swamp and into a stand of pines.

Late in the day, after the last of these brief stands, Henderson's men captured a family of three escaped slaves. The brigade had also passed one dead Seminole and two other escaped slaves during the day, but those were the only enemy casualties in evidence. Henderson lost six Marines, two killed outright and four more who were wounded and later died of their injuries.

Henderson's actions captured only a few Seminoles and killed even fewer, but seemed to have a strong impact nonetheless. The Seminole chief Abraham offered to negotiate with the Americans, and on March 6, 1837, the Seminoles signed a treaty agreeing to move their people to the reservations. Jesup and Henderson believed the war to be over, and Henderson requested leave to return to Washington. Jesup granted his leave with a commendation on his actions, for he had become the only serving Marine Corps commandant to exercise tactical command in the field. In May, Henderson returned to Washington with four of his six Marine companies. The other two Marine companies remained at Fort Brooke under Samuel Miller.

Jesup and Henderson had been mistaken, however. On June 2, a Seminole war party led by Osceola raided the detention center at Tampa, where some 700 Seminoles were awaiting transportation to the reservations, and freed them. In September, Osceola requested a truce to meet with Jesup. Jesup agreed to the meeting but then ignored the truce, arrested Osceola, and sent him off to prison at Fort Moultrie in South Carolina. Osceola died there in January 1838.

In 1839, although many Seminole warriors had been captured or killed, there were others who continued to raid settlements from the Florida Everglades. In April, the Navy assembled a rag-tag group of small craft and boats, dubbed the Mosquito Fleet, for "the suppression of Indian hostilities" in Florida. The fleet included two companies of Marines commanded first by Lieutenant George Terrett and then by Lieutenant Thomas Sloan.

In January 1840, command of the Mosquito Fleet was given to Navy Lieutenant John McLaughlin, who set out to invade the Seminole refuge. The Mosquito Fleet made several forays into the Everglades in 1840, and on December 31, 1840, McLaughlin personally led 150 sailors and Marines into the swamp. They emerged on the Gulf coast of Florida on January 19, 1841, becoming the first Caucasians to cross the Everglades. Another such expedition entered the swamp in November, and patrols continued from December 1841 until March 1842. They encountered few Indians on these missions, but McLaughlin's troops destroyed their crops, villages, and canoes. His troops likewise suffered few casualties from encounters with the Indians, but the heat and disease took their toll, often incapacitating as many as a quarter of the men on patrol.

The Seminole Indians never surrendered. However, by early 1842, it was apparent that few Seminole warriors remained to actively oppose the United States, and the government simply stopped chasing them. Three Marine officers were awarded brevet promotions for meritorious service, including Archibald Henderson, who was promoted to brigadier general, and John Harris, who was promoted to major. Brevet Lieutenant Colonel Samuel Miller retired after the Seminole War.

WEAPONS OF THE MARINE CORPS

Between the War of 1812 and the Civil War, the Marine Corps continued to experiment with new weapons. During the 1830s, the Corps tried out a variety of rifles. Among these was the Hall Breech-loading Rifle. Captain John Hancock Hall, who worked for a time at Harper's Ferry arsenal in Virginia, devised a system of loading a weapon at the base of its barrel rather than at its muzzle. Breech-loading rifles such as Hall's reduced the possibility of overloading the weapon with too much powder and threatening a catastrophic misfire, and because the rifled barrel—a barrel with grooves cut along it—actually spun the bullet, provided much greater range and accuracy in comparison to the musket. Unfortunately, because it was rifled, it was a fairly difficult weapon to load, and the musket retained a higher rate of fire. Although a few of Hall's rifles were used during the Seminole and Mexican Wars, the musket remained the primary weapon used by the Marine Corps.

Improvements were made to the musket during these years as well. In 1842, the Springfield arsenal produced a musket that employed a percussion cap rather than a flintlock. The percussion cap proved more efficient since the spark used to ignite the powder in the weapon was directed into the barrel rather than on an exposed flashpan, therefore offering a more reliable firing mechanism. In 1855, a .58-caliber rifled musket was produced at Springfield. Shorter than its companion, the .69-caliber M-1842 smoothbore musket, the M-1855 offered some of the advantages of the rifled barrel including greater range and accuracy. Ships' Marine Guards were frequently issued the rifled muskets while navy yard guard detachments were still issued smoothbore muskets. Both muskets were still in use by the Marine Corps at the beginning of the Civil War. In fact, the Marines who would quash John Browne's raid at Harper's Ferry carried M-1842 .69-caliber smoothbore muskets while some of the Marines who fought at the Battle of Bull Run would be equipped with M-1855 .58-caliber rifled muskets.

During the 1830s, the Marine Corps also experimented with Sam Colt's guns. Interested in overcoming the slow rate of fire of early nineteenth-century guns, Sam Colt invented a revolving cylinder that would allow a weapon to fire several times before being reloaded. Opening a plant in Paterson, New Jersey, in 1836, Colt produced a .55-caliber, 5-shot rifle and a .36-caliber, 5-shot pistol employing this new revolving cylinder. The Colt revolving rifle was issued to Marines at the beginning of the Seminole War, but the weapon had a tendency to misfire dramatically, resulting in a number of injuries, and the Marines took up their muskets once more. Colt did make a few sales to the emergent Republic of Texas, however, where a few of the revolving rifles and pistols were used by the Republic's armed forces, including its Navy and Marine Corps. The pistol proved particularly impressive during Texas' conflict with Mexico, and when the Mexican War began, Captain Samuel Walker asked Colt to produce a revolver for use by the U.S. Army. The 1847 model, dubbed the "Walker" by Colt, was a hefty .44-caliber, 6-shot pistol. The pistol proved so effective that the U.S. Navy adopted a version of the pistol in 1851 as did the Marine Corps.

★★★

Between 1835 and 1846, U.S. Marines engaged in several actions around the world. The U.S. Navy had by then established several overseas fleets: the Mediterranean Squadron, the African Squadron, the West India Squadron, the Pacific Squadron, the Brazil Squadron, and the East India Squadron. Although these squadrons were very small, they were able to offer some protection to American trade, property, and lives.

Marines embarked with these squadrons engaged in actions in South America (1835), the East Indies (1839), the South Pacific (two in 1840 and two in 1841), the Mexican province of California (1842), the west coast of Africa (1843), China (1844), and Vietnam (1845). Eleven of these operations were in support of American trade. The landing in Africa, however, was part of an effort to suppress the African slave trade.

The slave trade had been outlawed in Great Britain in 1772, in the United States in 1808, and in the British Empire in 1833, although it continued to be conducted by other states—and slavery remained legal in the United States—for some time. In 1842, the United States and Great Britain signed the Webster-Ashburton Treaty, which settled boundary disputes between the United States and Britain between Maine and New Brunswick and along the Canada–U.S. border among the Great Lakes. The Treaty also called for cooperation between the United States and Great Britain for the suppression of the slave trade along the west coast of Africa. The U.S. Navy maintained an African Squadron for this duty from 1843 until the beginning of the American Civil War in 1861.

In 1843, Commodore Perry, commander of the African Squadron, led a landing party of Marines and sailors into Liberia to investigate a report of the murder of Americans. At one point, Perry was attacked by one of the African chieftains. A Marine sergeant shot the chieftain, and a fight erupted. The Africans fled, and the Marines torched the village.

Marines performed similar duties for the African Squadron for the next 18 years. The last of these occurred in 1860 when the USS *Marion* sent ashore a detachment of Marines to protect American lives and property.

The year before Perry led his landing party ashore in Liberia, however, Commodore Thomas ap Catesby Jones seized Monterey, California, under the mistaken impression that the United States had gone to war with Mexico. It was a mistake that cost him his command. However, it turned out that Jones had only been a little early—three years later, the United States *was* at war with Mexico. The main cause of the Mexican War was the rather ambiguous status of Texas.

Although Texas and California were provinces of Mexico, many Americans had begun to settle there. As they did so, Mexican politics grew increasingly unstable. In 1834, Mexican President Antonio López de Santa Anna began restricting the freedoms and powers of the various Mexican provinces, igniting a series of rebellions throughout Mexico, the most important of which was in Texas.

Santa Anna invaded Texas with a strong army of more than 4,000 men and met with early victories, the most famous of which was the siege of the Alamo in San Antonio, where a mere 200 Texans and Americans, including Davy Crockett and Jim Bowie, inflicted massive casualties on Santa Anna's army before being wiped out on March 6, 1836.

The Texans declared their independence from Mexico and elected Sam Houston as their president. Houston retreated before Santa Anna's advance, but he recruited Americans as he went, and then suddenly turned, caught Santa Anna by surprise, and, shouting "Remember the Alamo!" defeated Santa Anna at the San Jacinto River in April. Having taken Santa Anna prisoner, Houston forced him to sign a treaty recognizing the independence of Texas. The Mexican government never ratified this treaty, however.

For the next decade, Mexico hoped to reclaim the Texan province. At the very least, the Mexican government wanted to maintain an independent Texas, for they feared that if the United States seized Texas, it might seize other Mexican provinces as well. The election of James Polk as president, however, ended any hopes that Mexico might have had.

Polk, a committed expansionist, had won the election at least partially on the merits of the annexation of Texas and soon after Polk's confirmation as president, Congress passed a resolution to annex the Republic of Texas. Polk sent agents to Texas to work toward the acceptance of such an annexation, but many Texans remained timid, fearing that American annexation would provoke an invasion by Mexico. Indeed, Mexico issued a statement to the effect that any incorporation of Texas into the territory of the United States would be the equivalent of a declaration of war against Mexico.

Polk supported the Texans' own claims that the Rio Grande was the southern border of the Texan republic. Mexico maintained that the Nueces River was the southern border of the province. The difference between the two rivers was significant, however, as the Rio Grande began about 100 miles to the southwest of the Nueces but then meandered northwest for some 2,000 miles. Polk was suggesting the annexation of land significantly larger than the small state that had won independence in 1836.

On July 4, 1845, Texas voted overwhelmingly to accept annexation. Mexico prepared for war, and Polk ordered General Zachary Taylor to the edge of the disputed territory. Taylor positioned his army at Corpus Christi just south of the Nueces River.

Polk's insistence on the Rio Grande as the southern border of Texas was motivated by his expansionist dreams: The president desired to annex

California—a Mexican province at the time—and gain the fine Pacific ports of San Diego and San Francisco. In October 1845, Polk received word from Thomas Larkin, U.S. consul at Monterey, California, that the British had designs on California for themselves. Furthermore, Larkin indicated that the Californians would prefer American rule to British rule. Polk believed that California might be acquired in the same way that Texas was being acquired: revolution and annexation.

Polk was faced, however, with the problem of conveying this plan to Larkin in Monterey. One route was by ship around Cape Horn of South America, but such a journey could take as long as nine months. A much faster route entailed sailing to the port city of Vera Cruz on the Gulf of Mexico, traveling overland to the Pacific port of Mazatlán, and taking ship from there up to Monterey. However, given that the particular message being born explicitly suggested open rebellion against the Mexican government, traveling through the heart of Mexico was not a journey to be taken lightly.

Marine First Lieutenant Archibald Gillespie set out on this assignment in November 1845.

Gillespie was 33 years old, having enlisted 13 years earlier as a private before being commissioned. Although Gillespie was fluent in Spanish, nine of his years in service had been spent afloat, not ideal preparation for a journey that would include a significant overland leg. Furthermore, he had not yet seen any action.

Nevertheless, having memorized and burned the secret instructions to be delivered to Consul Larkin, Gillespie began his journey under the guise of a traveling salesman for the MacDougal Distilleries, Ltd. of Edinburgh, Scotland. He successfully crossed Mexico without incident and reached Monterey on April 17, 1846, three months before the ship bearing identical instructions put into the Monterey harbor.

After discussing Polk's instructions with Larkin, Gillespie set out on the second leg of his mission. His road led north into Oregon country in search of Army Captain John Frémont, the "Great Pathfinder," a Georgia-born adventurer and the son-in-law of Senator Thomas Hart Benton, who managed to have Frémont's exploits published as government documents. Frémont had left St. Louis in 1845 with 60 men and traveled across the Salt Desert and the High Sierras and for some time had been moving back and forth between Oregon and California. Gillespie found Frémont, then on a mapping expedition, on May 9, at Klamath Lake, Oregon, and briefed him on Polk's instructions "to watch over the interests of the United States" in California. The next day, Frémont's 60-man unit turned south to return to California.

Frémont's return to California acted as a kind of catalyst among the American settlers there. Dissatisfied with Mexican rule, the Americans saw the return of Frémont's unit, which had been ordered out of California earlier that year, as a call to action. On July 4, 1846, a gathering of American settlers at Sonoma, taking advantage of the important symbolism of the day, proclaimed the independence of the "Bear Flag Republic"—the origin of the bear on present day California's state flag. Frémont in turn organized the "California Battalion," a 230-man strong volunteer battalion. Gillespie was appointed captain and second in command of the battalion.

At the same time that Gillespie set out for California, Polk sent John Slidell to Mexico City with instructions to gain Mexico's recognition of the annexation of Texas up to the Rio Grande border. Slidell was also authorized to offer Mexico $25 million for California and New Mexico, or, failing that, $5 million for just New Mexico. By the time Slidell arrived in Mexico City on December 6, 1845, however, the new Mexican president, José Herrera, had been backed into a corner by the threat of a military coup led by General Mariano Paredes.

In no position to negotiate concessions to the United States, Herrera refused to receive Slidell. Polk responded by ordering General Taylor to advance from his position at Corpus Christi to the northern bank of the Rio Grande, hoping that this advance would provoke a response from the Mexican government. It did. On May 9, 1846, the day Gillespie met Frémont, word arrived that a Mexican army had crossed the Rio Grande and ambushed two of Taylor's companies. One of Polk's supporters exclaimed, "American blood has been shed on American soil!"

This, of course, was an exaggeration, as a few of Polk's opponents pointed out; Taylor's men had been attacked in territory that no previous administration had claimed as U.S. soil. Nevertheless, Polk announced to Congress on May 11 that a state of war existed on account of Mexican actions and called for a $10-million appropriation to conduct the war.

Most Europeans expected the United States to lose the Mexican War. The Mexican army was about four times the size of the U.S. Army, and the last time the United States had attempted an invasion of a foreign country—Canada in 1812—it had failed miserably. The Mexicans, however, fought poorly for the most part. General Taylor, a 62-year-old veteran of the War of 1812, easily defeated the Mexicans at Palo Alto and Resaca de la Palma north of the Rio Grande. He then crossed into Mexico, defeated the Mexican army at Matamoras, and seized the capital of Nuevo León, Monterrey, in September.

In support of Taylor's campaign, the Navy blockaded the Mexican coast and launched a series of amphibious assaults on Mexico itself. Vice Commodore Matthew Perry, commander of the Gulf Coast Squadron, led an expedition including a 200-man unit of Marines under the command of Captain Alvin Edson, the Marine commander at Kuala Batu. The force captured Frontera and San Juan Bautista in October 1846, although it occupied neither city, and on November 14, it occupied Tampico unopposed.

The Mexican government knew that concession would almost certainly lead to revolution and refused to give in. Taylor's Army was unprepared to pursue the Mexican army across 400 miles of barren terrain to Mexico City, and the general agreed to a temporary armistice in which he pledged not to pursue the Mexicans. Polk then adopted a new strategy, proposed by General Winfield Scott, to conduct an amphibious assault on the port of Vera Cruz, which was only 200 miles east of Mexico City.

In the meantime, the declaration of the Bear Flag Republic in California and the formation of the California Battalion in July 1846 had acted as a catalyst for further hostilities. Commodore John Sloat, commander of the Pacific Squadron, had received reports that Mexicans and Americans were fighting in Texas. Cautious that he not repeat Commodore Jones's mistake a few years earlier, however, he had held off from actually landing troops in California. Frémont's obvious support of the Bear Flag revolt convinced him that it was time to invade California.

During the month between July 7 and August 6, 1846, the U.S. Navy peacefully occupied the cities of Monterey, San Francisco, Santa Barbara, and San Pedro. Leaving small Marine garrisons at each of these cities, the Pacific Squadron also delivered Frémont's California Battalion to San Diego, and on August 8, leaving Gillespie in San Diego with 50 men, Frémont marched at the head of a column of 120 men bound for Los Angeles, the provincial capital. On August 11, Commodore Stockton, having replaced the aging Sloat as commander of the Pacific Squadron, led a column of 360 sailors and Marines from San Pedro also bound for Los Angeles. Frémont and Stockton both entered Los Angeles on August 13 completely unopposed, and the remaining Mexican troops surrendered the next day. California had been conquered in just six weeks.

But it didn't last. Stockton, as ranking officer, decided to divide California into three military districts and appointed Gillespie as commander of the southern district, headquartered at Los Angeles. But the regulations and curfew Gillespie instituted and the arrests he made soon antagonized the Californians.

On September 23, several hundred Californians surrounded Gillespie and his men at their headquarters in Los Angeles and Gillespie was forced to evacuate his men from the city under the promise to leave California from the port city of San Pedro. During the siege in Los Angeles, however, one of Gillespie's men had managed to sneak through the lines and deliver a message to Captain William Mervine in Monterey. Mervine arrived in San Pedro aboard the *Savannah* on October 6, and on the following day he set out for Los Angeles at the head of 225 sailors and Marines with Gillespie and his Bear Flaggers.

On October 8, Mervine encountered 130 mounted Californians protecting a single cannon. Although the U.S. forces had no artillery of their own, Mervine attempted to seize the Californians' gun. The Californians, however, prudently withdrew the cannon upon each time the Americans charged. After three attempts, Mervine finally decided that the operation was a failure and called for a retreat, with Gillespie's men offering covering fire for the retiring sailors and Marines. Mervine's unit retired to San Diego.

Commodore Stockton had begun to lay plans for a renewed assault on Los Angeles involving the Pacific Squadron and Frémont's California Battalion when he received amazing news: Brigadier General Stephen Kearny, commander of the Army of the West, which had only recently occupied New Mexico, had marched into California with a small escort of 100 dragoons and four cannons under the impression that the province was at peace. Gillespie set out immediately with 39 men to meet Kearny and direct him to San Diego.

Gillespie reached Kearny's column on December 5 and learned that a Californian cavalry unit was camped nearby. Kearny decided to attack the next morning. The Californians were outnumbered by two to one, but the American assault was confused, and the Californians proved to be better fighters than expected. Armed with cavalry lances, the Californians charged into the melee and tore apart the American troops, who were armed with swords.

Gillespie was struck from behind and unhorsed. He was struck twice more before he was finally able to drag himself to his feet and struggle out of the combat. He scrambled to the cannon and was able to fire one of them, after which the Californians retired. Nineteen Americans were killed and 15 were wounded at the Battle of San Pascual. Only one Californian had been captured, and perhaps another dozen were wounded. Kearny sent a messenger to San Diego requesting aid, and a relief column found the struggling unit on December 10.

In San Diego, Kearny and Stockton assembled a rag-tag force of some 600 sailors, Marines, dragoons, California Battalion members, and other volunteers. The force was organized into four divisions, one of which was commanded by Gillespie, still recovering from the wounds he had sustained in battle with the Californians on December 5. On December 28, the force set out and on January 8, 1847, it encountered a mounted Californian army at the San Gabriel River.

The Americans organized themselves into a square formation, with each of the four units facing outward from one of the sides of the square—a standard formation for infantry facing cavalry in the early nineteenth century, allowing the infantry to guard against an attack from any direction—and began to ford the river. They immediately came under fire from two California cannon, and a unit of lancers began a charge at the left face of the American square.

The Americans struggled forward, and just beyond the river, set up their own cannon and returned fire. The more powerful American artillery stopped the lancers' charge, forcing the Californians to pull their own cannons back, and the American square resumed its advance. Most of the Californians pulled back with their guns, but the lancers made a wide circuit of the American square and attacked its rear face, where Gillespie's division was assigned. Gillespie's muskets stopped the lancers' second charge.

The Californians rallied their forces approximately one-half mile from their original position and brought their guns to bear upon the Americans once more. Again, however, the Americans' superior artillery forced the Californians to withdraw.

The next morning, the Americans resumed their march and soon encountered the remnant of the Californian army, which had suffered only about a dozen casualties during the engagement of the day before but which had been reduced to about 300 men by desertion. The Californians had deployed across La Mesa, a broad plain south of Los Angeles, in order to block the American advance.

The ensuing battle was to a large extent a replay of the previous encounters between the two armies: The lancers' charge was repulsed by musket fire, and the superior firepower of the American cannon forced the dwindling Californian army to retreat.

The American Army marched into Los Angeles on January 10, where Archibald Gillespie again raised the flag he had been forced to take down the previous September. Frémont arrived in Los Angeles four days later, having stopped to negotiate the surrender of the Californian army.

Sailors and Marines landed at San José del Cabo, San Lucas, and Loreto in Baja, and at Guaymas, San Blas, and Manzanillo in Mexico proper. Unopposed, each landing took just long enough to conclude conventions acknowledging American authority in those cities. In July, however, two companies of New York volunteers landed at and seized La Paz, the capital of the Baja province, and in November, the Navy seized Mazatlán, and two dozen Marines under the command of First Lieutenant Charles Heywood went ashore at San José. Although the Californians counterattacked three times at La Paz and twice at San José, the New Yorkers and Heywood's Marines were able to hold them off. Guaymas was assaulted four times between November 1847 and March 1848, but to no avail.

Despite the drama of the Californian campaign, the Mexican War was to be won in Mexico proper. Tampico, captured by Perry's expedition in November 1846, was selected as the base from which to launch Scott's assault on Vera Cruz. Scott's army of 8,600 men, including Edson's Marines, who were attached to the 3rd Artillery Regiment, landed south of Vera Cruz on March 9, 1847. The city surrendered on March 27.

The units serving in Scott's army, however, were largely composed of volunteers who had enlisted for one year, and that one-year enlistment was nearly up. To compensate for the impending reduction in forces, Congress authorized the raising of another 10 regiments and a wartime increase in the size of the Marine Corps of 12 officers and 1,000 men. Commandant Henderson, as he had done during the Creek uprising, again volunteered to raise a Marine regiment to serve alongside the Army. President Polk welcomed Henderson's offer, and the Secretary of the Navy approved its deployment on May 21, 1847. A new battalion of 22 officers and 324 enlisted men sailed for Mexico, where they would join the Marines embarked with the Navy in the Gulf of Mexico. Brevet Lieutenant Colonel Samuel Watson, a 35-year veteran, was chosen to lead the 6-company battalion. The Marines arrived in Vera Cruz on July 1.

AMPHIBIOUS ASSAULT

On March 9, 1847, the U.S. Navy conducted a massive amphibious assault for General Winfield Scott's attack on Vera Cruz, Mexico. Some 12,000 troops, including Marines, went ashore using surfboats under the command of Commodore Matthew Perry.

In contrast to the disastrous amphibious landing attempt at Penobscot Bay during the Revolutionary War, this assault came off nearly flawlessly. The Navy provided effective fire support, there were no quarrels among commanders, and the leadership remained bold. Perry, who took command of the Gulf Coast Fleet after this landing, conducted further amphibious assaults using Captain Alvin Edson's Marines as a core force at Alvarado, Tuxpan, Frontera, and San Juan Bautista. Although the U.S. Marine Corps wouldn't adopt the amphibious assault as its primary military tactic until the 1920s, it was clearly on its way to doing so.

In the meantime, Edson's unit of Marines, attached to Perry's squadron, continued to see action. On April 18, the squadron captured the port of Tuxpan. In May, the squadron occupied Coatzacoalcos and Carmen unopposed. And in June, Perry decided to seize San Juan Bautista again, because the Mexicans were receiving supplies from Central America through it.

Perry's expedition made an amphibious landing at Seven Palms a few miles south of San Juan Bautista. The Mexicans had reinforced San Juan Bautista since Perry's earlier visit, but the fortifications proved to be insufficient defense against Perry's 1,173 men, who managed to seize the city by mid-afternoon. Only five men were wounded.

Perry's success instilled in him a certain confidence at continuing such amphibious assaults. Indeed, his desire to conduct further amphibious assaults led him to refuse the release of Edson's Marines to the command of Brevet Lieutenant Colonel Samuel Watson, to the great frustration of Commandant Henderson. Nevertheless, Watson's battalion, meagerly reinforced as it was, set off on July 16 for Puebla, where Scott had been awaiting reinforcements since mid-May. Watson arrived in Puebla on August 6, and Scott assigned his battalion to the 4th Division and attached it to the 2nd Pennsylvania Volunteers, forming a brigade of which Watson was given command. Major Levi Twiggs, a veteran Marine who had fought in the War of 1812 and the Seminole War, was given command of the Marine detachment.

Scott's army marched from Puebla on August 7 and arrived just south of Mexico City 10 days later. The 4th Division was initially assigned to guard the baggage train and so saw no action in the first three assaults on the city. On September 10, however, Scott ordered a full-scale assault on Chapultepec Castle on the west side of Mexico City.

Chapultepec Castle was an impressive fortification. Originally, it had been designed to house the Spanish viceroys, but now was the site of the Mexican military academy. It sat atop a volcanic ridge some 200 feet high and 1,800 feet long. High stone walls enclosed the castle and the ridge. It was the key to the assault on Mexico City as it guarded two causeways that led to the city's San Cosmé and Belén gates. The assault would be a dangerous one. Scott's forces had been reduced by casualties to 7,200 men. General Santa Anna, commanding the defending forces, had approximately three times that many men at his disposal. But General Scott had planned well: In preparation for the assault, the American artillery would bombard the ridge for an entire day. The bombardment would be followed by a two-pronged assault. Brigadier General Gideon Pillow's 3rd Division would attack from the west while Brigadier General John Quitman's 4th Division attacked from the south. Major Levi Twiggs would lead the 4th Division accompanied by a 40-man storming party under Captain John Reynolds. The Marines would lead the assault on Chapultepec Castle.

The bombardment began on September 12, and at 8 the next morning, the American forces began their advance. Major Twiggs, armed with his favorite double-barreled shotgun, led the advance toward Chapultepec's outer wall, but the Marines encountered fire from one of the castle's cannon batteries and were forced to take cover in a ditch. Quitman ordered Watson's brigade to hold its position while a unit of Pennsylvania Volunteers veered off to the left and a brigade from the 2nd Division veered to the right. Twiggs's storming party and the Marines continued to exchange fire with the Mexican soldiers in the castle for some time, until Twiggs, frustrated by the stalled assault, climbed out of the ditch and was shot through the heart. Reynolds dragged the dead Twiggs behind a wall where he found Watson. Reynolds urged Watson to renew the advance.

In the meantime, however, the 3rd and 1st Divisions had made headway to the west and were assaulting Chapultepec Castle. Furthermore, the Pennsylvania Volunteers had advanced and were entering breaches in the outer wall of the castle, and the brigade on loan from the 2nd Division had made a sweep to the right and was threatening to envelop the Mexican artillery batteries to the south of the castle.

Quitman ordered the storming party to charge. Captain George Terrett, leading a company of Marines, heard the order intended for the storming party and ordered his own company to charge—while the rest of the Marine battalion maintained its position, offering covering fire as it had been ordered. Terret's company overran one of the artillery batteries, and the rest of the Marines stormed Chapultepec Castle.

Curiously, Scott had laid no plans for an attack on Mexico City proper after the capture of Chapultepec Castle, and it took some time for the American Army to prepare its assault on the city itself. Captain Terrett, however, had not waited for Scott and the rest of the American Army and had led his company of Marines, and a few other small Army units, on to the Calzada de la Verónica and began advancing toward Mexico City.

Two causeways ran from Chapultepec Castle to the city: the Calzada de Belén, which ran to the Garita de Belén, a fortified police and customs station; and the Calzada de la Verónica, which ran to the Garita de San Cosmé farther north. Eventually, Quitman's 4th Division, now expanded to include two regiments from the 3rd Division whose commander, Brigadier General Gideon Pillow, had been wounded during the assault on

Chapultepec, and which included the attached Marine battalion, advanced across the Calzada de Belén and attacked the Garita de Belén. The 1st Division, now also expanded to include a brigade from the 2nd Division, followed Terrett's advance along the Calzada de la Verónica.

After heavy fighting, the 4th Division was able to occupy the Garita de Belén in the early afternoon. Six Marines were killed and two were wounded during the occupation of the gate. On the Calzada de la Verónica, Terrett's company supported a small artillery unit in repulsing a Mexican counter-attack and then pushed forward until they were stopped at the San Cosmé road by Mexican cannon firing from rooftops. Some soldiers from the Army's 4th Infantry led by First Lieutenant Ulysses S. Grant joined them there.

Grant quickly realized that the American forces could outflank the Mexican emplacement by sweeping to the west around a small walled garden. Grant led the flanking maneuver while Terrett's Marines and soldiers led a charge to the front. The Mexicans retreated, and the Americans were able to push halfway down the San Cosmé road and overrun a barricade not far from the Garita de San Cosmé. According to Marine traditions, Terrett's company then attacked and occupied the Garita de San Cosmé, becoming the first Americans to set foot in Mexico City before the bugles sounded a withdrawal and the gate was abandoned. Unfortunately, this account is most likely exaggerated, and the Army's assault, including Terrett's company of Marines, probably advanced no farther than the barricade. At some point, possibly exacerbated by the quick withdrawal, the barricade must have been confused with the Garita de San Cosmé itself.

In any case, the 1st Division captured and occupied the Garita de San Cosmé later in the evening. The Mexican army withdrew that night, and the Americans occupied the city on September 14, 1847. General Quitman was appointed military governor. One of his first actions was to send the Marine battalion to restore order to the city, specifically to deal with looters raiding the Palacio Nacional. Thus, it was that Marine Second Lieutenant A. S. Nicholson became the first man to raise the American flag over the Halls of the Montezumas.

The Mexican War came to an end officially with the signing of the Treaty of Guadalupe Hidalgo on February 2, 1848. Mexico ceded Texas with the Rio Grande boundary, New Mexico, and California. The United States assumed the claims of American citizens against the Mexican government and paid Mexico an additional $15 million. From the land acquired after the Mexican War emerged the present-day states of California, Nevada, New Mexico, Utah, most of Arizona, and parts of Colorado and Wyoming. Nevertheless, some radical expansionists denounced the treaty because it had failed to secure all of Mexico.

On March 10, 1848, the U.S. Senate ratified the Treaty of Guadalupe Hidalgo as it was. The war had cost the U.S. Marine Corps 11 men dead and 47 wounded. More than half of these casualties had been suffered during the storming of Chapultepec Castle. Twenty-seven Marine officers were awarded brevet promotions, including fourteen for the storming of Chapultepec Castle. Archibald Gillespie received two such promotions for the defense of Los Angeles and San Gabriel. Upon their return, the citizenry of Washington presented the Marine Corps with a new flag bearing an eagle and an anchor and the motto, "From Tripoli to the Halls of the Montezumas."

"TO THE HALLS OF THE MONTEZUMAS"

The Marines have always carried a standard, although it is difficult to always know exactly what that standard was. During the American Revolutionary War, the Continental Marines probably carried the Grand Union flag into battle when Samuel Nicholas raided New Providence Island, March 3, 1776. It is also possible that they carried the Don't Tread On Me rattlesnake flag on this occasion and almost certainly used it during recruiting. During the 1830s and 1840s, the Marines carried a white flag with gold fringe and an anchor and eagle crest in the center. It bore the motto "To the shores of Tripoli," in honor of the role of the Marine Corps in the battle against the Barbary pirates. Shortly after the Mexican War, this motto was revised to read, "From Tripoli to the Halls of the Montezumas" in honor of the Marines' assault on Chapultepec Castle, the "Halls of the Montezumas."

★★★

In the decade after the Mexican War, the Marine Corps engaged in operations akin to those in which it had engaged before the war. Marines were involved in more than 20 landings between 1848 and 1859. Most of these occurred overseas, but one of them, in January 1856, occurred when the

American sloop *Decatur* sent its Marine Guard ashore to defend a small village in Oregon against a band of Native American Indians. The action was a minor one, but it turned out to be the last time the Marines engaged in fighting Native Americans.

Several of the overseas landings occurred in Central and South America, in Buenos Aires, Argentina (1852); Greytown, Nicaragua (1853); Montevideo, Uruguay (1855 and again in 1858); and Panama City (1856 and 1860) to defend the newly built Panama Railroad. Just as prior to the Mexican War, these operations were carried out to protect American lives and property. Most of the landings didn't require the use of force, but there were exceptions. In February 1852, for example, Marines attached to the *Congress* and the *Jamestown* landed in Buenos Aires to protect American lives and property against rioting Argentineans.

Several landings also occurred on the other side of the Pacific Ocean. Perhaps the most significant of these actions was Commodore Matthew Perry's expedition to Japan. Perry used Major Jacob Zeilin's 200-man Marine Guard of the East India Squadron, of which Perry was now the commander, to present an impressive show of military drill and precision in his meetings with Japanese officials at Uraga in July 1853 and Yokohama Bay in March 1854. Perry's expedition resulted in the signing of the Treaty of Kanagawa, which opened trade relations with Japan.

In addition to parade drills on diplomatic missions, Marines flexed their muscles in Asia. Marines made four landings in China during the Taiping Rebellion, for example. In April 1854, Chinese troops threatened the international settlements at Shanghai. The USS *Plymouth* landed some 60 Marines and sailors who joined with 150 British Marines and several American and British volunteers to defend the settlements and repel the Chinese forces.

A similar threat in May 1855 led to the landing of the USS *Powhatan*'s Marines, but in this instance, no fighting occurred. The *Powhatan* did collaborate with the HMS *Rattler* in August 1855 in an attack on a Chinese pirate fleet in Ty-Ho Bay near Hong Kong. Seventeen junks were captured, and the British and the Americans both lost two sailors and two Marines. The British and American troops were honored with a monument to their memory in Hong Kong's Happy Valley.

A final Marine landing was made during the Taiping Rebellion on November 15, 1856. In apparent reaction against British colonials, the four Barrier Forts on the Pearl River opened fire on the American East Indian Squadron. The USS *Plymouth* returned fire on the following day, and the captain of the *Plymouth*, Commander Andrew Hull Foote, attempted to open negotiations with the forces in control of the forts, but to no avail. Foote, as senior officer, decided that the only way to protect American lives and interests in the area was to occupy the forts.

On November 20, Foote led a landing party of 287 sailors and Marines from the *Plymouth*, the *Levant*, and the *San Jacinto* on shore under covering fire from the *Plymouth* and the *Levant*. Over the course of the next three days, the Americans captured all four Barrier Forts and held off three counterattacks made by Chinese forces from Canton province. The Marine contingent, led by Brevet Captain John Simms, led the assaults on the Barrier Forts—in two instances, Corporal William McDougal, the Marine standard bearer, was the first man to raise the American flag over the fortress—and held off two of the Chinese counterattacks. American casualties numbered 7 dead and 22 wounded, of whom 6 were Marines. The Chinese casualties numbered approximately 500.

Although 74 years old in 1857, Marine Commandant Archibald Henderson maintained a fiery spirit and made one more foray into "battle." During the election of 1857, the populist Know-Nothing Party made use of a Baltimore gang known as the Plug-Uglies to intimidate Washington's voters. The Plug-Uglies brought a brass cannon with them. Realizing that the Washington police were unprepared to deal with the riot that ensued, Mayor William Magruder asked President James Buchanan to send in the Marines.

Henderson, dressed in civilian clothes, accompanied two companies of Marines led by the Marine Corps adjutant officer, Captain Henry Tyler, as they marched to city hall. Rolling their cannon forward, the Plug-Uglies informed Tyler that they would open fire if the Marines did not withdraw immediately. Henderson stepped forward, stood in front of the cannon, and suggested that the rioters think twice about firing on U.S. Marines. But it soon became clear that the Plug-Uglies had no intention of withdrawing peacefully.

Under sporadic pistol fire from the Plug-Uglies, Henderson walked calmly over to Captain Tyler and informed him that the cannon needed to be seized immediately to protect the many bystanders in the area. One platoon of Marines charged the cannon and captured it. One Plug-Ugly leapt at Henderson, brandishing his pistol, only to have it knocked away by a Marine's well-placed musket swing. Henderson grabbed the rioter, marched him to the mayor, and placed him in his custody.

Despite the storm of pistol shot, Henderson and Tyler tried desperately to maintain the discipline of the Marines, most of whom were raw recruits. Thrown stones struck several Marines and one was severely wounded by a pistol shot to the face. Mayor Magruder, understandably upset by the riot surrounding him, shouted out, "Why don't you fire?"

In the din of the battle, several of the Marines apparently mistook Magruder's question for a command to fire and fired on the Plug-Uglies, who fled down the street. Tyler restored discipline to his troops, and the mob dispersed. The Marines remained on guard duty at the railroad station for a short time and then returned to the Marine barracks.

The dispersal of the Plug-Uglies was the last major action involving the Marine Corps during Henderson's tenure as commandant. Henderson died in his sleep on January 6, 1859. His tenure as commandant of the Marine Corps was one of the most important in the history of the Corps. Henderson didn't oversee the Corps during "important" conflicts such as the Revolutionary War, the Civil War, or the Second World War. Instead, he led it through a period of frequent small actions around the globe and through two lesser-known conflicts, the Seminole War and the Mexican War.

Nevertheless, his tenure was the longest in Marine Corps history, and his leadership proved invaluable in maintaining the existence and usefulness of the Corps during a period of doubt and in maintaining its independence from other branches of service. He also had built a reputation for the Marine Corps as an infantry force capable of amphibious landings. For this service, Henderson is remembered as the "grand old man of the Corps."

No struggle of succession followed Henderson's death as had followed Burrows's. Two days after Henderson's death, on January 8, 1859, Lieutenant Colonel John Harris was appointed commandant of the U.S. Marine Corps. At 68 years of age, Harris was the senior officer of the

Marine Corps, having enlisted in 1814 and having served in the War of 1812, 20 years at sea, and in the Mexican War.

Harris was a good officer and a good Marine who honored his duty to the Corps, but he didn't have the drive for leadership that would be required of him in two years' time. Indeed, by his own admission, Harris had lost that drive and fire by the end of the Mexican War. When Henderson had ordered Harris to Mexico in 1847, Harris replied that he had no desire to fight in the Mexican War but that he would, of course, go to war if that were what his service required of him.

CHAPTER 4

THE BLUE AND THE GRAY: THE CIVIL WAR

Before dawn on October 16, 1859, John Brown, a radical abolitionist, gathered 21 of his followers together and seized the arsenal
at Harper's Ferry, Virginia. Brown was hoping that the seizure of
the federal arsenal would spark a spontaneous uprising among the
slaves of Virginia and other southern states. Brown was mistaken;
the slaves didn't rise up in rebellion. The militia, on the other hand,
did take up their arms, and after an exchange of fire, they were
able to force Brown's raiders to take refuge in the arsenal's brick
firehouse. Brown took with him 11 hostages, including Colonel
Lewis Washington, the great-grandson of George Washington.

Governor John Letcher quickly requested the assistance of the
federal government. The nearest troops available were the Marines
stationed in Washington. That afternoon, First Lieutenant Israel
Greene led 86 Marines and 2 howitzers to Harper's Ferry. Accom-
panying Greene was Major William Russell, a veteran of the
Mexican War and now the Corps's paymaster, who as a staff officer
had no actual command authority but who could act as an advisor.

Greene's Marines reached Harper's Ferry at midnight and reported to the Army officers in command, Colonel Robert E. Lee

and his aide First Lieutenant J. E. B. Stuart. The next morning, Stuart approached the firehouse under the protection of a white flag with a note from Lee calling for Brown's surrender. Brown refused. Lee ordered Greene to storm the firehouse.

He and 12 Marines charged the firehouse and eventually knocked a hole in the double doors. Because there were hostages, Lee had ordered that no firearms could be used in the assault, and the Marines struggled inside armed only with their swords and bayonets. Greene was the first man through. Major Russell followed armed only with a rattan walking stick. The two Marines who entered after Russell were shot by Brown's men. Greene managed to make it to the back of the firehouse where the hostages were being held and found Colonel Washington, who pointed out Brown. Greene charged the kneeling man as he was reloading his carbine and cut at his head with his dress sword, knocking Brown unconscious.

The rest of the Marines followed Greene and Russell and killed two of Brown's group. The rest of Brown's men surrendered. No hostages had been harmed.

John Brown was tried and convicted of treason at Charleston, Virginia, and on December 2, 1859, he was hanged.

Brown's raid on Harper's Ferry didn't start the American Civil War, but it did dramatically illustrate the tensions growing between the North and the South over the question of slavery in the United States.

A HOUSE DIVIDED

There were several issues that divided the North and the South, most significantly differing economic systems and the question of states' rights in relation to the federal government, but slavery came to act as a focal point for many of these differences. The culture and economy of the southern states was based on cotton production, which had come to be dependent the exploitation of black slaves. In the northern states, however, the economy focused on the growth of industry. In addition, a strong abolitionist movement had arisen in the northern states. Many abolitionists, like John Brown, opposed slavery on moral grounds; others, however, opposed slavery because they believed that labor could not compete with slavery as slaves worked for nothing. The abolition of slavery, however, threatened the entire way of life in the South.

Tensions mounted with westward expansion. As new territories were acquired and new states were added to the Union, the question of whether these states would be free states or slave states arose. A few compromises were reached in which a slave state and a free state were each admitted into the Union at the same time to maintain the balance, but that only served to delay dealing with the real issue.

The election of Abraham Lincoln as president of the United States in November 1860 spurred the South to take action. Lincoln had opened his campaign in Illinois' Senatorial election of 1858 with the famous Divided House speech in which he claimed, "this nation cannot exist permanently half slave and half free." Most southerners took this remark to mean that Lincoln was in favor of the abolition of slavery. His election in 1860 as president was seen as an imminent threat to the livelihood of the South, and on December 20, 1860, South Carolina voted to repeal its ratification of the Constitution of the United Sates.

The election of Abraham Lincoln, a Republican and opponent of slavery sparked the Civil War. In an effort to defend itself against a perceived threat to its culture and economy, which was based upon slavery, South Carolina seceded from the Union on December 20, 1860, Mississippi, Florida, Alabama, Georgia, Louisiana, and Texas followed shortly thereafter and formed the Confederate States of America. On February 9, 1861, the Confederate Congress named Jefferson Davis as provisional president. He would be formally elected to that office on November 6, 1861.

Nevertheless, hostilities didn't break out immediately. President Lincoln, however, was willing to resort to force to preserve the Union, opposing the argument that states had the right to withdraw from it. In his inaugural address delivered in March 1861, Lincoln indicated that all federal property in those states that had seceded would be held and defended by the federal government of the United States of America. When the government of South Carolina learned that Lincoln intended to continue to supply Fort Sumter, the Confederate state launched an attack against the fort. Lincoln proclaimed an insurrection in the South and appealed to the remaining states to support the effort to maintain the Union. The threat of the use of military force pushed other states into secession, and Virginia, North Carolina, Arkansas, and Tennessee joined the Confederate States of America. All told, 11 states seceded from the United States of America to form the Confederate States of America. The Union had been divided.

Early in 1861, the Union Navy lost most of its bases in the southern states. Notably, Floridian authorities leading an Alabama militia unit took over the Pensacola Navy Yard in Florida on January 16 and forced Marine Captain Josiah Watson to sign a pledge not to bear arms against the state of Florida. Other Floridian troops took control of all of Pensacola's forts except Fort Pickens. In April 1861, Marine Lieutenant John Cash and 110 Union Marines and assorted Union Infantry occupied Fort Pickens and held it until a larger garrison could take control of it. The Union controlled Fort Pickens throughout the Civil War.

The secession of Virginia from the Union forced Marines from the *Cumberland*, the *Pawnee*, and the *Pennsylvania* to destroy the Norfolk Navy Yard. Other battalions were deployed quickly to the Brooklyn and Philadelphia Navy Yards for guard duty, and another battalion provided security for the recaptured Norfolk Navy Yard in May 1862.

The last such battalion, a small unit of only 112 men commanded by Major Addison Garland, suffered the most embarrassing Marine defeat during the Civil War. Sent to Mare Island Navy Yard near San Francisco, the entire unit was captured by Captain Raphael Semmes commanding the Confederate ship *Alabama* off the coast of Cuba on December 7, 1862. Semmes forced the Marines to sign promissory notes not to bear arms against the Confederacy and sent them on their way.

A MARINE CORPS DIVIDED

The U.S. Marine Corps had remained a relatively small force throughout the early history of the United States of America. By the outbreak of hostilities between Union and Confederacy in 1861, it numbered 1,892 men and officers, approximately one tenth the regular Army. As tensions increased and the South seceded from the Union, many Marine officers resigned their commissions and offered their services to the Confederate States of America. Approximately one half of the Marine captains, including George Terrett, one of the heroes of the Mexican War, resigned, and approximately two thirds of Marine lieutenants, including John D. Simms, who had earned a brevet promotion during the Mexican War and then fought at the Barrier Forts in China, resigned as well.

The relatively minor role the Union Marines played during the Civil War was partially due to the small size of the Corps. On January 1, 1861, the U.S. Marine Corps numbered only 1,892 officers and men. To compensate for various losses, 38 new officers were appointed early in 1861. In July, Congress increased the size of the Corps by another 28 officers and 750 men, and President Lincoln authorized two 500-man increases in 1861.

Commandant Harris understood the primary role of the Marine Corps to be shipboard service, much as it had done during the War of 1812. The main strategy of the Union was to force the surrender of the Confederacy by blockading the Atlantic coast, a task for which the Marine Corps would be well suited.

In addition, the Union sought to capture the Confederate capital, Richmond, Virginia. This task was given to Major General Irvin McDowell, who left Washington on July 16, 1861, at the head of some 35,000 troops. Included in this force was 1 small Marine battalion consisting of 12 officers and 336 men. Commandant Harris assigned Major John Reynolds, whose career stretched back to the Seminole War and who was one of the few veteran officers remaining in the Union Marine Corps, to command the battalion. Brevet Major Jacob Zeilin, another experienced commander, volunteered to command one of the battalion's four companies. The other officers and enlisted men in the battalion had little experience, however.

Five days later, on July 21, the Union Army was confronted by a Confederate brigade under the command of Thomas J. "Stonewall" Jackson. The Marines were assigned to support an artillery battery during the confrontation and soon found themselves caught in the midst of the Battle of Bull Run. The artillery battery the Marines were supporting changed hands three times during the battle until Confederate reinforcements appeared and tipped the battle in their favor. The Union Army, and the Marine battalion with it, dissolved.

Commandant Harris was understandably disappointed in the performance of his Marines, commenting to the Secretary of the Navy that this had been the only time in the history of the Marine Corps when any Marine had turned his back on the enemy. Reynolds, however, noted that the Marines had fought relatively well for a unit composed almost entirely of raw recruits.

Bull Run was the only land-based battle in which the Marines participated during the Civil War. For the rest of the conflict, the Marine Corps performed its traditional role of supporting naval actions and engaging in amphibious assaults. In August 1861, 200 Marines were attached to the Potomac Squadron assigned to search southern Maryland for Confederate arms. Also in August, Marines were assigned to the *Cumberland, Minnesota, Susquehanna,* and *Wabash* and established the first of the bases to be used by the Navy for their blockade efforts at Fort Hatteras in North Carolina.

Commandant Harris also composed a battalion under Major Reynolds for use as an expeditionary force for the establishment of advance bases farther south. The creation of such a brigade seemed to foretell a prominent role for the Marine Corps. Reynolds's battalion, though, seemed fated to misadventure. In October 1861, five days after leaving Hampton Roads, Virginia, bound for Port Royal Sound in South Carolina, the battalion's transport was caught in a storm and sank. The battalion lost only seven Marines, but it was unable to reach Port Royal Sound to aid in its capture, although the *Wabash*'s Marine detachment did land and occupy Fort Walker. Reynolds's battalion was sent to attack Fernandia, Florida, in March 1862, but the city surrendered before the Marines arrived. St. Augustine did the same two weeks later. Reynolds's battalion was disbanded at the end of March 1862.

Other Marine detachments proved more successful, however. In December 1861, Marines destroyed a Confederate headquarters near Charleston, North Carolina, after the *Dale* had bombarded it. In January 1862, the Marine detachment from the *Hatteras* landed and burned Confederate stores at Cedar Keys, Florida.

Marines continued to serve an important role aboard Navy ships as well. In September 1861, Union Marines attached to the *Colorado* boarded the *Judah* in Pensacola harbor and burned her. In November 1861, Marines from the *Santee* raided Galveston harbor and destroyed the Confederate ship *Royal Yacht*. The *San Jacinto*'s Marine detachment boarded the British ship the *Trent* and captured the Confederate diplomats James Mason and John Slidell, who had been sent to Britain and France to lobby for recognition of the Confederacy. The boarding of the *Trent* angered the British, but Lincoln released the two Confederate diplomats and avoided opening a second war with Britain.

CHAPTER 4: THE BLUE AND THE GRAY: THE CIVIL WAR

★★★

The Confederate Congress established its own Marine Corps on March 16, 1861. Initially, it was planned that the Confederate Marine Corps would consist of 6 companies, each of which would be made up of a captain, first and second lieutenants, 8 noncommissioned officers, 2 musicians, and 100 men. After Richmond became the capital of the Confederacy, the Confederate Corps was increased to 10 companies—46 officers and 944 men— and a headquarters unit consisting of a commandant with the rank of colonel, a lieutenant colonel, a major, an adjutant, a paymaster and quartermaster, a sergeant major, a quartermaster sergeant, and two musicians was established. The Confederate Corps never realized these authorized strengths, however.

Twenty U.S. Marine Corps officers left the Union and joined the Confederacy, 19 of whom accepted commissions in the Confederate States Marine Corps—the twentieth joined the Confederate Army. These men represented some of the most experienced officers then on active duty, including the adjutant officer and inspector of the Marine Corps, Major Henry Tyler, a 38-year veteran and commander of the Washington Barracks; Captain George Terrett, the hero of Chapultepec; Captains Algernon Taylor and Robert Tansill, who had been recognized for their valor during the Mexican War; Captain John Simms, who had led the assault on the Barrier Forts in China; and First Lieutenant Israel Greene, who had led the assault against John Brown's raiders at Harper's Ferry. Tyler was commissioned as the Confederate Corps's lieutenant colonel and Terrett as its major. Taylor was commissioned as quartermaster and Greene as the Corps's adjutant officer. Lloyd Beall was commissioned as Commandant Colonel of the Confederate Marine Corps. Beall probably owed this privilege to his acquaintance with Confederate President Jefferson Davis, whom he had met at West Point, the U.S. Military Academy, and with whom he served in the 2nd Dragoons before accepting a position as paymaster major, the post he resigned when the Civil War began.

The Confederate Marine Corps enlisted the first Marines in March 1861, and by July, three companies of Marines had been raised. Marine Guard detachments were raised for the CSS *Sumter* and the gunboat *McRae* as well. Confederate Marines saw their first action in July, occupying Ship Island off the coast from Biloxi, Mississippi.

Initially, most of the Marines raised between March and July 1861 were stationed at Pensacola, Florida, but they were soon reassigned: Company A was ordered to Savannah, Georgia, in September 1861, and Company B was ordered to Mobile, Alabama, in February 1862. In November 1861, Company C, under the command of Captain Reuben Thom, a former U.S. Infantry officer and veteran of the Mexican War, was assigned as a guard detachment to the CSS *Patrick Henry*, the CSS *Jamestown*, and the ironclad CSS *Virginia* (formerly known as the *Merrimac*) on the James River. Captain Thom commanded 54 Marines on board the *Virginia*, First Lieutenant Richard Henderson, Commandant Henderson's son, commanded 24 Marines on board the *Patrick Henry*, and First Lieutenant James Fendall commanded 20 Marines on board the *Jamestown*.

On March 8, 1862, the squadron ran into a blockade at Hampton Roads. The CSS *Virginia* rammed the USS *Cumberland* and shelled the USS *Congress*, sinking both ships. Marine Captain Charles Heywood fired the *Cumberland*'s final shot before the ship sank. Fourteen of his 44 Marines went down with the ship. For his valor, the Union Marine Corps awarded Heywood a brevet promotion to the rank of major.

On March 9, the Confederate squadron returned to Hampton Roads, intending to clear the blockade, and ran into the USS *Monitor*, another ironclad, resulting in the first battle between two ironclad battleships. Captain Thom commanded two of the *Virginia*'s guns during the battle. It's not clear what role the rest of the Marines played, but they may have manned other of the *Virginia*'s guns. Although the battle resulted in a draw, Franklin Buchanan, the *Virginia*'s commander, commended Thom on his service during the battle.

The Confederate squadron was unable to clear the blockade, and on May 9, the Confederacy evacuated Norfolk. The ironclad *Virginia* weighed too much to retreat up the James River with its wooden companions, and Buchanan opted to blow it up rather than allow it to fall into Union hands.

Confederate Marine Company C, now commanded by Captain Julius Meiere, another former U.S. Marine officer, joined up with Company B under the command of Captain Alfred Van Benthuysen, which had been transferred to Norfolk from Mobile in March. Meiere and Van Benthuysen led their companies in a retreat up the James River to a point about seven miles south of Richmond, Virginia. There, artillery captain Augustus Drewry had emplaced three cannons on a promontory on the south bank of the James River, where they commanded a field of fire straight down the meandering James River. The Confederate Marines set up alongside Drewry's guns, army engineers threw up earthworks, and several the *Jamestown*'s guns were wrestled up the slope to reinforce Drewry's firepower. The *Jamestown* was sunk to obstruct the river.

On May 15, the USS *Monitor* and another ironclad, the USS *Galena*, approached the Confederate positions up the James River. About 600 yards from Drewry's Bluff, the ironclads stopped and turned their broadsides to bombard the Confederate position. Confederate Marines led by Captain Simms occupying the banks along the James River fired at the ironclads and killed three of the *Galena*'s crew.

The ironclads maintained their bombardment of the Confederate position for four hours. The Union Marines assigned to the *Monitor* and the *Galena* demonstrated a great deal of bravery during the battle. After the *Galena* suffered an explosion, Corporal John Mackie rallied the *Galena*'s crew, carried the dead and wounded off deck, and managed to get three of the *Galena*'s guns firing again. Corporal Mackie was the first man awarded the Medal of Honor, which had been established in 1861 to reward enlisted men for their extraordinary heroism. Despite such determination, the *Galena* had taken more than 40 hits by 1 P.M., 13 of which actually pierced her armor, and 33 of her crew were dead or wounded. The Union ironclads withdrew.

Drewry's Bluff quickly became an important link in the defenses surrounding Richmond. Company A of the Confederate Marine Corps was ordered to join the other two companies at Drewry's Bluff, and Major Terrett was given command of the combined battalion at "Camp Beall." In 1863, the CSS *Patrick Henry* became the Confederate Naval Academy, and Drewry's Bluff soon developed into a full naval station, complete with log cabin quarters, a post office, a chapel, and a cemetery.

In 1862, the Union and Confederate navies and their respective Marine detachments confronted one another further south at the Battle of New Orleans, the war's most significant naval action. On the night of April 24, Union Flag Officer David Farragut's fleet fought its way up the Mississippi

River, past Fort Jackson and Fort St. Philip, and demolished several Confederate ships on the river. Twenty-six of the three hundred thirty-three Union Marines attached to Farragut's fleet were killed or wounded. A Confederate Marine Guard unit of about 20 men was taken prisoner when the CSS *McRae* sank.

Having breached the Confederacy's defenses, Farragut demanded that the city of New Orleans surrender on April 26. Negotiations went on for three days without any results. Farragut ordered Marine Captain John Broome to land a Marine battalion and occupy the city. Broome's Marines landed, occupied the U.S. mint, and raised the Union flag above it. On April 29, the rest of the squadron's Marine detachments landed, were organized into four companies under Broome's command, and occupied the customs house and city hall. General Benjamin Butler's army occupied the city on May 1, and the Marines returned to Farragut's squadron.

The Battle of New Orleans effectively ended Confederate Marine actions along the Mississippi River, but measures were soon adopted to strengthen other Confederate ports, and the activity of the Confederate Corps was soon expanded. Marine Guards were attached to the Confederate naval squadrons at Mobile, Alabama, and Charleston, South Carolina, in August 1862, and the new ironclad CSS *Atlanta* was assigned a guard unit in early 1863. The unit in Mobile was designated Company D and placed under Captain Meiere. Captain Tatnall began recruiting another company, Company E, at Savannah in January 1863, and Meiere raised yet another company the following April. Confederate Marines served aboard 25 ships and two floating artillery batteries as well as three commerce raiders.

The Union, however, soon turned its attention to Charleston, South Carolina. Capturing the capital of the first state to secede from the Union would be an important symbolic victory, and rumors that the Union would strike at Charleston prompted the Confederacy to send a 200-man battalion under the command of Captain Simms to help defend the city.

On April 7, 1863, eight Union ironclad war ships struck at Charleston harbor but were repulsed, and Simms's battalion soon returned to Camp Beall. But on July 10, 1863, approximately 3,000 Union troops landed on Morris Island off the south end of the Charleston harbor. A Confederate artillery battery emplaced on the north end of the island stopped their advance. Union troops attempted a second assault a week later, but it, too, was repulsed by the Confederate defenders.

Rear Admiral John Dahlgren, commander of the South Atlantic Blockade Squadron, landed his ships' Marine Guards to bolster the assault on Morris Island. Dahlgren requested additional Marines, which were placed at his disposal in the form of a new battalion of approximately 300 men commanded by Major Jacob Zeilin. This battalion landed on Morris Island on August 10 and was combined with Dahlgren's ships' guards to form a Marine regiment commanded by Zeilin.

Unfortunately, the new regiment was struck by disease, and Zeilin himself was taken ill. Lieutenant Colonel John Reynolds replaced Zeilin as commander and continued the assault on the Confederate emplacement, which was eventually taken on September 7 when the Confederates withdrew. Disease and combat continued to take their toll on the Marines, however, and by this time the regiment's strength had been reduced to a mere battalion.

From Morris Island, the Union forces planned to launch their attack on Fort Sumter guarding the mouth of the harbor. The Union ships had bombarded Fort Sumter, damaging several of the fort's walls and silencing the cannons emplaced there. Dahlgren knew that there were still Confederate soldiers in the fort, but he assumed that their number was small.

The night after the capture of Morris Island, five assault units, four composed of sailors and one composed of Marines from Morris Island, were to be towed close to Fort Sumter where they would begin to lay down covering fire for the Navy's ships to approach. Unfortunately, Dahlgren had grossly underestimated the Confederate strength in Fort Sumter, and he was unaware that the Confederates could read the naval code signals being used to relay orders between ships and assault units. In addition, the assault was hastily planned, resulting in miscommunication and misunderstanding among Dahlgren's subordinates.

Dahlgren had apparently planned to initiate the assault with a feint carried out by a single assault unit. This was meant to draw out the defenders and expose their strength and positioning. But when the order was given and one of the units began to move forward, the other four assault units mistook it as a general order to advance and rushed toward the fort.

Twenty minutes later, the assault was over, ending in confusion and failure. As the Union forces pressed forward, the Confederates in Fort Sumter shot off a signal rocket and artillery batteries emplaced on nearby James Island and Sullivan Island began bombarding the Union troops. The iron-clad CSS *Chicora* also began firing, and the Confederate troops in Fort Sumter appeared on the walls and began firing on the Union boats and those Marines and sailors who had already landed.

The assault on Fort Sumter was costly. The Union lost 124 men, most of whom were captured when their boats were shot out from underneath them and they found themselves trapped against the fort's walls. Two Marine officers and 39 enlisted men were among those captured. Six Union Marine officers were later given brevet promotions, however, for the gallantry they displayed during the ill-conceived attack. The Marine battalion that formed for the assault on Morris Island and Fort Sumter was withdrawn to Folly Island south of Charleston and was later disbanded.

WITH LINCOLN TO GETTYSBURG

In 1863, the governors of several Union states that had suffered losses at the Battle of Gettysburg arranged for the dedication of a National Cemetery there. Judge David Wills, who was organizing the dedication, asked Secretary of the Navy Gideon Welles if the Marine Corps Band might be able to perform at the dedication. Welles passed on the request to Commandant Harris, who directed the band to attend the ceremony. The band was accompanied by newly commissioned Second Lieutenant Henry Clay Cochrane.

On November 18, Cochrane and the Marine Corps Band accompanied President Lincoln by train to Gettysburg. The train was filled with cabinet members, politicians, and military officers as well as the band, but soon after the train had been boarded and had left the station, Cochrane was rather surprised to find himself sitting across from President Lincoln. Cochrane later wrote to his parents recounting the moment: "Ha!" remarked the president to the young Marine, "This is so much better," apparently relieved to have escaped the politicians in the other car.

In Baltimore, the president's party had to switch trains. While the trains were being prepared for departure, Lincoln shook a few hands and kissed a baby or two while the Marine Corps Band played a number of tunes, and then the journey continued. Lincoln talked with various dignitaries for some time, but when the train approached Hanover Junction, Cochrane heard him comment, "Gentlemen, this is all very pleasant, but the people will expect me to say something to them tomorrow, and I must give the matter some thought."

The train arrived at Gettysburg early that evening, and after a brief welcome from Judge Wills, the party retired to their respective lodgings. The next morning, the presidential party proceeded to the National Cemetery. Preceded by an honor guard of some 1,200 troops, President Lincoln rode out on horseback, followed closely by the rest of his party, including Lieutenant Cochrane and the Marine Corps Band. Cochrane was humbled by the destruction left by the battle five months earlier. The landscape was pitted and littered with shattered trees, broken weapons, and ripped uniforms.

The dedication ceremony was a lengthy affair, and the Marine Corps Band shared the stage with three other bands as well as a host of dignitaries. After a prayer offered by Dr. Thomas Stockton, Chaplain of the U.S. Senate, the Marine Corps Band played "Old Hundred," a favorite hymn of the time, and then the Honorable Edward Everett delivered the keynote speech of the day, which Cochrane described as a tedious speech in the manner of the Greek orators recounting the history of the conflict between North and South culminating in the Battle of Gettysburg. After nearly two hours, Everett finally finished his speech, and President Lincoln stood before the podium. Lincoln reached into his coat pocket and produced two or three pieces of paper and then donned his wire-rimmed glasses. "He began in a slow, solemn and deliberate manner," Cochrane wrote, "emphasizing nearly every word, and in two minutes sat down." That evening, they returned to Washington.

★★★

Confederate marines played more than a defensive role during the Civil War. In February 1864, the Confederates launched a combined assault on a Union base on the Neuse River near New Bern, North Carolina. The Confederate Navy and Marine Corps were responsible for dealing with any Union Navy ships that might come to the aid of the Union Army when the Confederate Army attacked.

John Taylor Wood, who held commissions as a colonel in the Confederate Army and as a commander in the Confederate Navy, commanded the Confederate naval forces for the assault on New Bern. His command consisted of 115 naval officers and men from the James River Squadron, 10 midshipmen from the Naval Academy, and 25 Marines from Company C stationed at Camp Beall.

The attack began on February 1, 1864, but the Confederate Army's assault broke down almost immediately. Wood decided to continue with the naval side of the operation and sought out Union gunboats. Very early on the morning of February 2, Wood's boats found the Union gunboat *Underwriter* and closed with it. The Confederate Marines exchanged heavy fire with the *Underwriter* and then boarded her and captured her after a vicious melee. Four Confederate sailors and one Marine were killed in the action, and another seven sailors and four Marines were wounded. Nine Union sailors were killed, another nineteen were wounded, and twenty-three managed to escape. Union forces on the shore began shelling the captured gunboat, and Wood decided to set the gunboat on fire and abandon it.

★★★

In May 1864, the Union again attacked Richmond. Union Major General Benjamin Butler landed with 30,000 troops at Bermuda Hundred on the James River about 10 miles south of Drewry's Bluff on May 5. By then, the Confederacy had been forced to withdraw many of the men stationed at Drewry's Bluff due to a shortage of troops. Approximately 4,000 troops guarded the southern approach to Richmond, and only about 350 artillerymen and Marines were actually stationed at Drewry's Bluff.

Butler should have been able to defeat the Confederate troops and take Richmond easily, but he had received his commission through political connections and was poorly qualified as a military leader. He was unable to take advantage of this overwhelming advantage. Butler didn't even attack Drewry's Bluff until a week after he landed. By then, the Confederacy had reinforced its position to nearly 20,000 men. The Union attack on Drewry's Bluff was repulsed, and the Confederacy counterattacked on May 16. Butler was driven all the way back to Bermuda Hundred, where he remained trapped until the end of the war.

Union Marine Corps Commandant Colonel John Harris died on May 12, 1864, the day of Butler's feeble attack on Drewry's Bluff. The man who most likely would have succeeded Harris was John Reynolds, one of the most senior Marine officers and an officer with a distinguished career. But Reynolds had embarrassed Harris, himself, and the Corps two years earlier when, suspecting that Harris had already chosen as his successor Major William Russell, the Union Marine Corps Paymaster, Reynolds had sent a letter to Harris criticizing the choice of Russell and demanding that Harris respect the traditions of the Corps. Harris was furious and court-martialed Reynolds on charges of drunkenness and disrespect. The court-martial acquitted Reynolds of both charges, and Reynolds retaliated by bringing charges against Harris.

Secretary of the Navy Gideon Welles, who was busy conducting a war at that moment, was exasperated and commanded both men to cease such behavior. Although Reynolds had been vindicated by the court-martial, his behavior was an embarrassment to the Marine Corps, and Welles didn't want to name him commandant. To solve the predicament, Welles ordered the retirement of the remaining 4 Union Marine Corps officers over the age of 60, including Reynolds, although these officers were allowed to continue their service until the war was concluded. That freed Welles to name the 57-year-old Major Jacob Zeilin as Marine Corps commandant.

While the Union Marine Corps was concerned about its future, the Confederate Marine Corps had little future left. Indeed, the Confederacy even considered merging the Confederate Marine Corps with the Confederate Army. A resolution calling for an investigation into the feasibility of the merger was introduced on February 6, 1865, but by then, the Confederacy had little use for the Marine Corps anyway.

By June 1864, the Confederacy controlled only four ports: Mobile, Savannah, Charleston, and Wilmington. On August 5, 1864, Farragut attacked Mobile with 4 ironclads, 14 wooden ships, and a gunboat. Farragut's fleet struggled through a narrow channel past Fort Gaines and Fort Morgan to engage Admiral Franklin Buchanan's Confederate fleet, the ironclad *Tennessee* and three gunboats. The Union fleet lost only one ship as it passed Fort Gaines and Fort Morgan, the ironclad *Tecumseh*, which wandered into a mine. With the approach of a vastly superior fleet, the Confederate Navy panicked: The *Gaines* ran aground, the *Selma* surrendered, and the *Morgan* retreated to Mobile. The *Tennessee*, left alone, put up a spirited fight but was eventually defeated and captured by Marines from the *Lackawana* and Farragut's flagship the *Hartford*. Although the city of Mobile remained under Confederate control, the Union controlled the harbor.

Several of the Union ships had carried Marine complements as had three of the four Confederate ships. Captain Meiere had collected a small unit of 27 Marines to reinforce Fort Gaines and Fort Morgan as well. The *Tennessee's* small Marine Guard was captured when she was. Captain Meiere's Marine unit was captured when Fort Gaines surrendered three days later. The Union fleet lost 315 men dead or wounded, 8 of whom were Marines. Marine Brevet Major Charles Heywood, who had fired the USS *Cumberland's* final shot in its engagement with the CSS *Virginia*, then under the command of Buchanan, was awarded a brevet promotion to lieutenant colonel. At only 24 years of age, Heywood was fated to bear the moniker of "boy colonel." Two other Marine officers were awarded brevets as well, and eight enlisted Marines were awarded the Medal of Honor.

On November 15, 1864, General William Tecumseh Sherman set out on his famous March to the Sea. The South Atlantic Blockade Squadron was ordered to assist in this campaign by pushing up the Broad River from Port Royal, South Carolina, in order to cut off the Savannah-Charleston railroad. A patchwork force of sailors, Marines, and a few Army units was organized for the expedition. The Marine unit consisted of 182 men from ships' guard units of the South Atlantic Squadron under the command of First Lieutenant George Stoddard.

Confederate forces prevented the patchwork force from completing its mission, although the Marines were commended for their actions, and Stoddard was awarded a brevet promotion to captain. The failure of the expedition turned out to be insignificant, however. Sherman reached Savannah on December 10, 1864, with 60,000 men. The Confederate forces, including Captain Tattnall's Marine Company E, consisted of barely one fourth that number. Confederate forces held out for 11 days before Savannah was evacuated on December 21. Captain Tattnall's company managed to escape: A small guard was attached to the ironclad *Macon* as it set out for Augusta, Georgia, while the rest of the Marines boarded a train bound for Charleston.

★★★

By the end of December, Wilmington was the Confederacy's only remaining Atlantic port. Wilmington itself was situated on the Cape Fear River some 10 miles inland. The mouth of the Cape Fear River was guarded by the impressive Fort Fisher situated on a peninsula. One wing of the fort bisected the peninsula while a second wing turned perpendicular to the first and stretched along the Atlantic face of the peninsula. The landward face of the fort, the face that bisected the peninsula, mounted some 20 cannons. Fifty feet in front of the gun emplacements was a palisade of sharply pointed logs driven into the earth, and 500 feet in front of the palisade was a minefield controlled by electric detonators. A small battery had been emplaced at the point of the peninsula to prevent enemy ships from entering the Cape Fear River and attacking the fort from behind.

Confederate Marines had been first assigned to Wilmington in January 1864 as ships' guards for the ironclads *North Carolina* and *Raleigh*. Captain Alfred Van Benthuysen assumed command of the Wilmington Marines in June 1864. At the end of December, when a Union fleet anchored off the coast, Van Benthuysen moved the Wilmington Marines to Fort Fisher, joining a small Marine Guard that had been attached to the gunnery battery in November.

The Union fleet, commanded by Rear Admiral David Porter, bombarded Fort Fisher for a day and a half but inflicted little damage. An expeditionary force led by Major General Benjamin Butler concluded that the fort had not been damaged enough to facilitate the assault, and the expeditionary force and fleet withdrew on December 26. A second fleet approached Fort Fisher on January 12, 1865, still commanded by Porter, but Butler had been replaced by Major General Alfred Terry. Again, Van Benthuysen's 70 Confederate Marines joined another 700 reinforcements sent to help defend Fort Fisher, bringing the total force up to about 1,500 men. Terry had 8,000 men at his disposal.

Union troops began landing on the peninsula on January 13 and started erecting gun emplacements. The next day, the fleet and the landed guns began bombarding Fort Fisher, and by mid-afternoon on January 15, all but one of the fort's guns had been disabled, the wires controlling the minefield had been severed, and the palisade had been breached.

Union forces launched two separate attacks against the landward face of Fort Fisher. General Terry led the Army Infantry along the riverbank while a naval brigade under Lieutenant Commander K. R. Breese, Porter's chief of staff, attacked along the seashore. The naval brigade included 1,600 sailors from the fleet led by their officers and a 400-man Marine battalion under the command of Captain Lucian Dawson. The Marine battalion advanced along the seashore with the intention of occupying successive trenches as it went and laying down covering fire for the advance of the sailors.

Dawson's battalion barely reached the second of three trenches when Breese sent him new orders, however. Believing that the slope of the beach provided sufficient cover, Breese joined Dawson there and then ordered the entire brigade, sailors and Marines both, to charge 600 yards down the beach at Fort Fisher. The Confederate defenders fired into the charging mass as quickly as they could and managed to break the rush about 50 yards from the fort.

Captain Dawson caught up to the leading Marine companies just as the charge faltered and ordered two companies to take cover and fire at the parapet as the rest of the brigade, including two Marine companies, fled. Once the rest of the naval brigade was out of range, Dawson and the remainder of his Marines withdrew. Breese later blamed the failure of the assault on the "absence" of the Marine battalion, though he was generous enough to comment that its absence was due to poor planning rather than cowardice. Nevertheless, although some of the Marines fled, Dawson had been able to rally many of his men and performed an important role in the withdrawal of the brigade. Of the 351 casualties suffered by the naval brigade, the Marine battalion lost 16 men killed or missing and 41 wounded. Dawson and seven other Marine officers received brevet promotions and seven enlisted men were awarded Medals of Honor.

The charge of the naval brigade was a disaster, but it had served as a significant distraction for Terry's assault along the riverbank. Five hundred of the defenders had repulsed the naval brigade's charge, and only two hundred fifty were left to defend the riverbank. In addition, Fort Fisher's commander, Colonel William Lamb, and the Wilmington district commander, Major General W. H. C. Whiting, had been occupied by the assault.

When Whiting realized that there was a Union flag waving along the riverbank, he called his soldiers to follow him and charged along the parapet to reinforce the meager forces there when he was mortally wounded. Fort Fisher was engulfed in fierce hand-to-hand combat as soldiers fought each other with swords, bayonets, and rifle butts among the traverses between the fort's guns. At one point, Colonel Lamb tried to organize a counterattack, but at the last moment, he was shot in the hip and went down before the attack could be launched.

The battle for Fort Fisher raged for five hours, until another Union brigade arrived to reinforce the assault, and the defense began to crumble. Captain Van Benthuysen, who had likewise been wounded, ordered the evacuation of Lamb and the dying Whiting, and with 400 men, retreated toward the gunnery battery on the promontory, where they learned that the battery's commander had already spiked the guns and withdrawn from the battle. The Union had captured Fort Fisher and with it control of the Cape Fear River, effectively isolating Wilmington.

WEAPONS OF THE MARINE CORPS

The war between the states acted as a catalyst for weapon development. The Marine Corps began the Civil War still using M-1842 .69-caliber smooth-bore muskets until enough M-1861 .58-caliber rifled muskets became available.

The conflict inspired the Navy and Marine Corps to experiment with breech-loading rifles in the hope that they might speed up the rate of fire. One of the first such weapons tested was the Sharps .52-caliber single-shot carbine. The Sharps rifle used a pre-measured linen cartridge of powder that reduced the danger of overloading the weapon. When the lock was closed, the end of the cartridge was cut off, exposing the powder. The Sharps carbine had an effective range of about 200 yards, and although it was only a single-shot weapon, its breech-loading mechanism allowed as many as 10 shots per minute, a significant improvement over the musket's 100-yard range and 3 shots per minute.

By the end of the war, a second breech-loading weapon was employed by the Navy and Marine Corps as well, the Spencer 7-shot repeating rifle. This weapon had been patented by Christopher Spencer in Hartford, Connecticut, in 1860 and was produced by the Spencer Repeating Rifle Company in Boston, Massachusetts. It fired a .52-caliber brass rimfire cartridge that prevented any gas leakage as the weapon was fired. Seven cartridges were loaded into a tube in the rifle stock. Working a lever on the weapon ejected a spent cartridge from the breech and automatically loaded the next cartridge, vastly improving rate of fire: The Spencer rifle could fire as many as 30 times per minute and had an effective range of 500 yards. The Spencer rifle also had the advantage that it could use standard Sharps rifle parts for repairs.

Some concern was expressed over the use of weapons with such high rates of fire. Critics were concerned that soldiers would simply fire blindly, wasting ammunition. Tests conducted by the Navy and Marine Corps suggested, however, that the tactical advantage offered by such weapons greatly outweighed the possible problem of wasted ammunition: The ease with which the weapon could be loaded meant that the soldier could pay greater attention to the enemy.

The Civil War also witnessed the first use of the Gatling Gun. Invented by Richard Gatling, the gun was composed of six barrels revolving around a central axis. A hand crank turned the barrels and loaded cartridges from a hopper mounted on top of the weapon. The Gatling could fire as many as 600 rounds per minute, each barrel firing 100 rounds. Despite the impressive rate of fire, however, the gun proved cumbersome and fragile, and the barrels didn't always align properly, reducing firepower and accuracy. Nevertheless, a few Gatling Guns were acquired by Union forces, at least one of which was used by Admiral David Porter. The weapon's potential inspired Gatling to make several improvements to the weapon, which was officially adopted in 1866.

Despite the vast advancements made in weaponry during the Civil War, muskets continued to see use in the Marine Corps after the end of the conflict, in part because muskets offered much greater firepower than the Sharps and Spencer rifles—.69- and .58-caliber as opposed to .52-caliber. A more important reason, however, was undoubtedly budget reductions, which severely limited the amount of money that could be expended on expensive breech-loading weapons and brass-encased cartridges.

The fall of Fort Fisher essentially ended the participation of Union Marines during the American Civil War, but the war was not yet over for the Confederate Marine Corps.

Charleston, South Carolina, finally gave in to Sherman's Army on February 17, 1865. Commodore John Tucker, the commander of the Charleston Squadron, scuttled his ships and led his sailors and Marines north to Richmond, where he incorporated the remaining Marines at Drewry's Bluff to form Tucker's Naval Brigade. Captain Tattnall led Marine Company E into North Carolina where it remained for the rest of the war.

On April 2, 1865, the Union Army broke through Confederate lines just south of Petersburg. Facing a two-to-one disadvantage, General Lee recommended to President Davis that Richmond be evacuated. Tucker's Naval Brigade joined Lee's Army as it marched south.

Union cavalry easily kept pace with the retreating Confederate Army, however, and attacked its flank and rear, slowing the Confederate column enough for Union Infantry to engage it in combat. Captain Terrett and a unit of Confederate Marines were captured in just such an engagement at Amelia Court House on April 5.

Union harassment compelled Lieutenant General Richard Ewell's Corps, including Tucker's Naval Brigade, to halt along Saylor's Creek. The Union artillery bombarded the ridge on which Ewell's troops were positioned, and then the Infantry advanced across the creek and up the slope. As the Union Army started up the slope, Ewell gave the command to counterattack, and the regiment, including Tucker's Naval Brigade with its Marine battalion, now commanded by Captain Simms, charged down the slope and pushed the Union Army back.

Despite such a heroic effort, Ewell's regiment was enveloped by two other Union divisions, and Ewell reluctantly surrendered. Tucker's Naval Brigade, unaware of the Union envelopment and Ewell's surrender, withdrew farther south, where it was able to secret itself in a densely wooded ravine. A Union general accidentally discovered the brigade that evening and returned under truce to inform Tucker of his situation. Tucker, too, reluctantly surrendered when he learned that he was surrounded by Union forces.

Captain Simms, 6 other Marine officers, and approximately 45 Marines were captured along with Tucker's Naval Brigade. A few Confederate Marines had managed to escape capture on April 6, and so 4 Marine officers and 25 Marines, including First Lieutenant Richard Henderson, accompanied General Lee when he signed the surrender at Appomattox Court House on April 6.

The remnant of the James River Squadron, too, had been ordered to join Lee's march south. Admiral Semmes, the commander of the squadron, scuttled his ships on April 2 and then led his 500 sailors and Marines to join Lee, only to find the Army had already left. Semmes organized a train at the railroad station in Richmond and proceeded to Danville, Virginia, arriving there on April 4 to find the Confederate government already established in the little town. On April 5, Semmes's men were organized into an artillery brigade, and Semmes was given command of it as a brigadier general of the Confederate Army. On April 10, however, news arrived that Lee had surrendered at Appomattox, and the Confederate government fled farther south. Semmes's brigade was attached to the Army of North Carolina for the rest of April, but surrendered at Greensboro on May 1.

Confederate Marine Company C had managed to survive the battle at Mobile Bay and continued to serve in the defense of the city of Mobile from March 27 until April 12, when the city fell to Union forces. It retreated up the Mobile River with the remnants of the Mobile Squadron to Nanna Hubba Bluff, where the squadron surrendered on May 10. The Civil War ended for the Confederate Marines with the surrender of the few Marines attached to the Mobile Squadron.

The Union Marine Corps had lost 77 men dead, 131 wounded, and 142 captured during the Civil War. Another 257 died of causes unrelated to combat. Two hundred fifty Confederate Marines are known to have been captured, but the lack of records prevents an estimation of other casualties on the Confederate side.

CHAPTER 5

SEMPER FIDELIS: REINVENTING THE CORPS

The U.S. Marine Corps survived the American Civil War, but the next 30 years were something of a low point in its existence. In June 1866, the U.S. Congress passed a resolution directing the House Naval Affairs Committee to investigate the possibility of disbanding the Corps. In response, Commandant Colonel Jacob Zeilin collected statements from high-ranking Naval officers, including Farragut, Porter, and Dahlgren, regarding the utility of the Corps. The Naval Affairs Committee concluded that there was "no good reason ... either for abolishing it, the Marine Corps, or transferring it to the Army; on the contrary, the Committee recommends that its organization as a separate Corps be preserved and strengthened." Furthermore, the committee recommended that the commandant of the Corps should hold the rank of brigadier general. Jacob Zeilin became the first Marine to hold the rank of brigadier general—Archibald Henderson had held the rank of brevet brigadier general, an honorific with no other privileges.

Initially, the Corps maintained its strength, having recruited enlisted men for four-year terms rather than for the duration of the war. However, over the course of the next decade, all the

American military services were cut, so that by the early 1870s, the number of active naval vessels available had plummeted from nearly 700 during the Civil War to only 50, the size of the Army was cut in half, and Marine Corps enlistment was reduced by one third and the officer corps limited to 75. Furthermore, the Marine Corps commandant's rank was again reduced to colonel, although Zeilin was allowed to keep the rank of brigadier general.

The limited number of officers meant that there were too few officers to adequately command the Corps and that promotions were stifled. Henry Clay Cochrane, for example, had been commissioned as a second lieutenant in 1861 and was promoted to first lieutenant in 1865. But he had to wait 14 years for his promotion to captain in 1879. And he would still hold the rank of captain 15 years later when he complained to Secretary of the Navy Hilary Herbert in 1894 that he was doing the same job then as he had been doing for 25 years.

Nevertheless, the Corps remained active, making nearly 30 landings during the last years of the nineteenth century. The Marines engaged in a variety of activities, including raids against illegal stills in Boston (1867, 1868, 1871), suppressing a labor riot during a railroad strike and safeguarding railroad property between Baltimore and Philadelphia and Baltimore and Washington (1877), guarding a quarantine camp during a cholera scare in New York City (1892), and protecting the U.S. mail during another railroad strike in California (1894). Furthermore, 13 foreign landings, including the only combat missions, occurred while General Zeilin was the Marine Corps commandant.

In March 1867, the American ship *Rover* was wrecked on the island of Formosa (Taiwan), and its crew was massacred by natives. In retaliation, Commander George Belknap, captain of the USS *Hartford*, the flagship of the U.S. Asiatic Squadron, led a force of 181 men on to the island on June 13. The force included 43 Marines under Captain James Forney. The Formosans proved elusive, however, ambushing Belknap's men and then withdrawing into the high grasses and jungle in guerilla war fashion. By 2 P.M., the men were exhausted by the heat, and Belknap, having only burned a few huts, called a halt. Shortly thereafter, a few shots were fired from the jungle, and Belknap assigned his second in command, Lieutenant Commander Alexander Mackenzie, to investigate. Mackenzie was killed.

Given the heat and the elusiveness of the Formosans, Belknap decided to return to the beach. The men were so exhausted by the time they reached their boats that Belknap ordered them to return to the ships. The Navy and the Marine Corps were clearly not prepared for guerrilla war, although Captain Forney was awarded a brevet promotion for his role in the expedition, the only Marine officer to be so recognized between 1865 and 1898.

A second action in which Marines engaged under the leadership of Zeilin proved more successful. In 1870, the *General Sherman* was stranded in the Han River in Korea. The Koreans used a raft to set fire to the ship, and when the crew of the *General Sherman* swam to shore, the Koreans massacred them.

Wishing to secure the safety of American lives and property, Frederick Low, the U.S. Minister to China, was assigned to open negotiations with Korea. Low arrived in Korea on May 23, 1871, escorted by five ships of the Asiatic Squadron led by Rear Admiral John Rodgers. Low soon made contact with the Koreans, and on May 31 a small delegation of low-ranking officials arrived to meet him.

Low dismissed the delegation on the pretense that he would only negotiate with first-rank officials. At the same time, the Koreans were informed that the Navy wished to chart part of the Han River Channel, the Salee River, between Kanghwa-do Island and the Kumpo Peninsula. The delegation was allowed one day to inform its superiors of the American charting expedition, and, assuming that the missive had been delivered to the appropriate officials, four launches and the gunboats *Monocacy* and *Palos* set out on June 1 to chart the river. As the boats entered the Salee River, Korean forts on Kanghwa-do Island fired on them. The Americans replied in kind, quickly silenced the forts' guns, and then returned to the squadron.

Admiral Rodgers waited 10 days for a Korean apology, but none was forthcoming. On June 10, therefore, he organized an expedition to capture the forts along the Salee River. Commander L. A. Kimberly was given command of 686 officers and men and a battery of seven 12-pound howitzers. They would be supported by the squadron's 2 gunboats and 12-pound howitzers mounted in the 4 launches. Included in this force were 109 Marines led by Captain McLane Tilton.

By this time, the Navy had adopted the Remington .50-caliber "rolling-block" breech-loading rifle. In fact, Tilton had served on the board that had made that adoption in 1869. Tilton's landing party, however, was armed with now antiquated .58-caliber muzzle-loading rifled muskets—"muzzle fuzzels" he disparagingly called them.

Three forts confronted the landing force on the island. The gunboat *Monocacy* began bombarding the first two of these forts at about noon on June 12. The *Palos*, towing the landing party in boats, arrived on the scene an hour later, by which time the guns of these two forts had been silenced.

The sailors and Marines landed on the island and began an arduous trek across the muddy terrain. The Marines deployed in a skirmish line and approached the first fort while the sailors pulled the howitzers from the mud. As the Marines advanced, the Korean defenders fled, and the Marines took the fort with relative ease. When Kimberly and the rest of the landing party reached the first fort, the Marines advanced toward the second fort but halted for the evening at a small wooded hill surrounded by rice fields. The next morning, the Marines found the second fort deserted. They spiked the fort's four main guns and rolled several of the smaller cannon off the bluff into the Salee River below.

The *Monocacy* began bombarding the third fort, a strong stone fortification on top of a steep hill on a peninsula stretching into the Salee River, at 11 A.M. on June 11. Some time after noon, having rested his men some 600 yards from the fort, Commander Kimberly instructed the *Monocacy* to cease its bombardment. A storming party of 350 sailors and Marines armed with muskets and fixed bayonets occupied a ridgeline about 120 yards from the fort.

The Marines quickly established fire superiority over the fort's defenders who were armed with obsolete matchlocks. At 12:30 P.M., Lieutenant Commander Silas Casey, commanding the battalion of sailors, gave the order to charge the fort. The Koreans courageously stood their ground, and the battle turned to hand-to-hand combat.

Clambering into the fort, Private James Dougherty engaged the man identified as the Korean commanding general and killed him, while Corporal Charles Brown and Private Hugh Purvis charged the Citadel's flagstaff and tore down the general's 12-foot banner. The defenders soon fled downhill toward the river, and the Americans took control of the fort. Approximately

250 Koreans were killed in the assault on the Citadel. Three Americans, including one Marine, were killed, and another ten, including one Marine, were wounded.

Admiral Rodgers was pleased with the operation, but, diplomatically, the operation left a great deal to be desired, and Low's mission was a failure. It would be another decade before the United States could successfully negotiate a treaty with Korea.

FORNEY'S REPORT

In 1872, Secretary of the Navy George Robeson sent Captain James Forney on a one-year tour of European Marine Corps as part of a reevaluation of the U.S. Marine Corps. Forney submitted a 400+ page report offering his evaluation of several of the corps he had observed.

Forney was particularly impressed by the British Royal Marines. The Royal Marines were a sizeable service numbering some 6,000 shipboard troops and another 8,000 designated to serve on shore. Those on shore were divided further into infantry and artillery, each with a distinctive uniform, red for the infantry and blue for the artillery. Perhaps most impressive, however, was the special depot set up at Deal for the training of all new recruits.

Forney was also impressed with the Imperial German Marine Corps, which he considered to be the second best. Forney commented on the sharp uniforms worn by the German marines—he even included several photographs in his report—a dark blue similar to what the U.S. Marines wore. More significantly, Forney suggested that the U.S. Marine Corps should be organized similarly to the Germans, in a three-regiment brigade with permanently designated regiments and companies.

Forney was less impressed with other marine services, such as those of France or Spain, but he noted that all of the European marine services spent a great deal of time at target shooting, whereas U.S. Marines rarely had opportunity to practice with their weapons, and, in Forney's opinion, were continually nervous about using or even carrying their weapons, even for ceremonial purposes.

Finally, Forney strongly urged that Marine Corps officers be trained at West Point rather than commissioned from civilian life. Forney's report and his comparisons between the United States and the European marine services made it clear that vast improvements were necessary to create a modern marine corps. Over the next 20 years, many of Forney's recommendations were adopted by the Corps.

★★★

The period between 1865 and 1898 also witnessed the institutional development of the Marine Corps. The budget constraints and the size restrictions of this era severely limited the usefulness of the Marine Corps. Many Marine officers realized that the continued existence of such a limited Marine Corps was doubtful.

Henry Clay Cochrane, whose advancement as an officer was frustrated by these limitations, was the most outspoken of the officers during this era. In 1875, Cochrane called for the reform of the Marine Corps. He argued that the Marine Corps needed a new mission to give its existence meaning and suggested that the Marines could be transformed into a U.S. Naval Artillery that could man the coastal defenses of the nation.

Few of his fellow officers liked the idea of a coastal defense force, but Cochrane further suggested improving the organization of the Corps, increasing its size, and improving the quality of both the officer corps and the enlisted men, essentially transforming the Marine Corps into an elite military service. This they found attractive.

He suggested that the quality of officers could be improved by restricting commissions to graduates of the military academies and requiring rigorous physical and professional examinations. These reforms would reduce the number of officers who received commissions for purely political reasons without any real military aptitude, and they should also improve the general fitness of the Corps. In addition, perhaps based on personal experience, he suggested that a mandatory retirement age of 62 be instituted. This would enable promotion and advancement. Selective recruiting of enlisted men should be instituted, and drills and training should be standardized as well, improving the quality, ability, and discipline of enlisted Marines. Desertions—at 20 percent per year, the highest among the U.S. armed forces—could be reduced by improving the quality of service and standardizing the system of promotion to noncommissioned officer ranks.

General Zeilin himself was interested in improving the quality of the Marine Corps. He adopted Major General Emory Upton's *Infantry Tactics*, which detailed the important military lessons learned during the American Civil War, for use by Marine Corps officers. Zeilin also updated the Marine uniform. In 1868, a board of officers adopted the familiar eagle, globe, and anchor for use as a cap badge, and in 1875 Zeilin approved the re-adoption of the Mameluke sword for use by officers—although NCOs continued to carry the straight Army sword. The annoying stock that gave the Marines the name "Leathernecks" was eliminated in 1875 as well.

These were fairly minor reforms, however, intended to keep the Corps up to operational standards. Zeilin was unsympathetic to the more significant reforms suggested by officers such as Cochrane and commented that the organization of the Marine Corps was the best that could be.

On November 1, 1876, at the age of 70, having spent 45 years in uniform, Jacob Zeilin retired. His successor was Charles McCawley, who became the eighth commandant of the U.S. Marine Corps. McCawley, the son of a Marine captain, had been commissioned in 1847 and served during the Mexican War. He was awarded a brevet promotion to first lieutenant after the battle of Chapultepec, and in the Civil War he was awarded a brevet promotion to major during the assault on Fort Sumter.

Zeilin had appointed McCawley as commander of the Washington Marine Barracks and director of recruiting in 1871. McCawley, like Zeilin, maintained a generally conservative outlook and had little in common with the reformers among the officer corps. However, his years as director of recruiting had made him aware of the need for improvement. Drills and training were standardized, recruits were required to read, write, and speak English, examinations were required for promotion to corporal and sergeant, and a pension was instituted after 30 years of service. McCawley hoped also to convince Congress to increase the size of the Corps and restore the rank of brigadier general, although he was unsuccessful in this effort.

McCawley was successful, however, in his petition to recruit officers from the military academies. On August 5, 1882, Congress finally passed a naval appropriations bill that included a clause authorizing the Marine Corps to recruit graduates of the Naval Academy. The measure was mutually beneficial to the Navy and the Marine Corps. As a result of the general cutbacks of the era, the Navy soon found that the Naval Academy was producing more officers than were needed, and Congress was planning to introduce a bill that would cap the number of officers allowed in the Navy. Allowing the Marine Corps to recruit officers from the Naval Academy, however, would eliminate this surplus without necessitating an officer cap and at the same time promote greater homogeneity between Naval and Marine Corps officers.

Between 1883 and 1897, 51 second lieutenants were commissioned in the Marine Corps, and every one of them was a graduate of the Naval Academy. Five of them, George Barnett (class of 1881), John Lejeune (class of 1888), Wendell Neville (class of 1889), Ben H. Fuller (class of 1892), and John Russell (class of 1892), were destined to be Marine Corps commandants.

SEMPER FIDELIS

The commandants of the U.S. Marine Corps were well aware of the importance of *esprit de corps,* the spirit that binds a group of soldiers together. Traditions play an important part in the creation of such a spirit, allowing troops to identify with those who have served before them, and helping define what it means to be a Marine. This is almost certainly one of the reasons Jacob Zeilin reinstated the Mameluke sword as part of the officers' uniform and adopted the eagle, globe, and anchor insignia, which reflected the Marine's origin as a soldier of the sea, global deployment, and, above all, national loyalty.

Mottoes—as much as uniforms and insignia—help define such a spirit, and the Marine Corps had used several in its early history. Zeilin, for example, replaced the motto *Fortitudine* with *Per Mare, Per Terram,* "By Sea, By Land," which he had borrowed from the British Royal Marines. In 1883, under the direction of Commandant Charles McCawley, the U.S. Marine Corps adopted a new motto: *Semper Fidelis,* "Always Faithful." The Marine Corps motto was added to the Marine Corps insignia on a ribbon held in the eagle's beak and helped bind the individual Marine to Corps and country. Today, "Semper Fi" is as well known a symbol for the Marine Corps as the eagle, globe, and anchor or the Mameluke sword.

★★★

Colonel Charles McCawley served as commandant of the Marine Corps for just over 14 years. He was able to accomplish a great deal institutionally, but the period of his tenure in office was also one of the quietest periods for the Marines. Only six landings were made in those years, and all but one of them were minor actions.

In 1882, a nationalist Arab pasha threatened revolution in Egypt, then a protectorate of Britain and France. On July 11, the British Mediterranean fleet, accompanied by three American ships, bombarded Alexandria, Egypt. U.S. Marines under Captain Henry Clay Cochrane landed in the burning, chaotic city with the purpose of protecting the American consulate there. The British army quickly occupied the city and restored order.

In January 1885, Colombia, too, experienced a revolution and withdrew its garrison from Panama. As the Colombians withdrew, two Panamanian leaders also launched revolutions, resulting in civil war for the small but significant province.

American attitudes toward the situation in Panama were mixed. Although the narrow isthmus was important to commerce and transportation, President Grover Cleveland initially desired to stay out of the civil war. The rebels seized Panama City, the western terminus of the American-owned Panama Railroad, and Colon, the eastern terminus. Finally, with American interests at stake, Cleveland decided to send in the Marines.

On April 2, 213 Marines sailed from the New York Navy Yard under the command of Brevet Lieutenant Colonel Charles Heywood bound for Panama. On April 7, the operation's commanding officer, Navy Commander Bowman "Billy Hell" McCalla, set sail with a second battalion of 250 men and 6 artillery pieces. Heywood's battalion arrived in Panama on April 11. Rear Admiral James Jouett, commander of the North Atlantic Station, ordered Heywood to secure Panama City.

McCalla and the second battalion arrived on April 15. McCalla kept the second battalion in Colon and ordered Heywood to organize the 2 battalions—796 men and officers—into a single brigade, the first brigade in Corps history. The Marines were responsible for maintaining security in Panama City and Colon as well as two villages along the railroad and on the trains themselves.

The intervention was a success. Order was maintained without any outbreak of violence, and Admiral Jouett could report that the trains continued to run on schedule. By the end of April, Colombian troops returned to Panama, and American troops were gradually withdrawn.

In 1888, a Haitian war vessel seized an American ship and took it to Port au Prince. Rear Admiral Stephen Luce was assigned to recover the ship and given command of the *Galena*, the *Yantic*, and their Marine detachments. The Haitian authorities, however, were sufficiently cowed by the show of force, and when Luce informed them of his intention to retake the vessel, it was returned without resistance.

WEAPONS OF THE MARINE CORPS

The advent of breech-loading rifles during the Civil War was a tremendous leap forward in firearm technology. American rifle manufacturers were quick to incorporate this innovation into their weapons, and developed some of the most robust and reliable rifles in the world.

However, the end of the Civil War brought with it budget cuts, and the new weapons proved too expensive to purchase so muskets continued to be the standard issue weapon for some time following the end of the Civil War. Erskine Allin, an armorer at the Springfield armory, was able to convert the .58-caliber muzzle-loading rifled musket to a .45-caliber "trapdoor" breech-loading rifle. On the Allin conversion rifle, a small plate could be lifted on top of the barrel allowing the rifle to be loaded at its base. In 1868, a new rifle modeled on Allin's conversion was introduced and remained in use until the Spanish-American War.

Other breech-loading rifles were soon developed and eventually adopted. One of these was the Remington rolling-block rifle in both .46- and .50-caliber. Using a revolutionary breech block that could be rolled back to expose the chamber once the hammer had been cocked, Remington made the feature an integral part of the rifle, and engineered the hammer and the breech block to work against each other for an unbreakable breech. With a range of up to 1,000 yards, the rifle was accurate and tough enough to weather all kinds of hardships and still fire.

During the 1870s, the .45-caliber Remington-Lee bolt-action rifle was adopted for use by some ships' guard units. A detachable vertical box magazine that held five rounds, invented by James Paris Lee, was attached to the underside of the weapon, vastly improving reloading and firing rates. A similar weapon, the Winchester-Lee straight-pull rifle, was adopted by the Navy and Marine Corps in 1895. The Winchester-Lee was likewise a five-shot rifle using a box magazine but used 6mm rounds. The Winchester-Lee rifle was used during the Spanish-American War and the Boxer Rebellion. It is also the weapon featured on the Marine Corps Good Conduct Medal.

★★★

Colonel Charles McCawley left the office of commandant in January 1891 at the age of 64, having reached the mandatory age for retirement in the Marine Corps. His successor was Charles Heywood, who at the age of 51 was no longer the "boy colonel" he had been dubbed during the American Civil War, but who still bore a striking martial bearing.

Heywood was very sympathetic to the reformers in the officer corps and set out immediately to make changes. Only four months after his assumption of office, he had already convinced Secretary of the Navy Benjamin Tracy to establish a School of Application at the Washington Marine Barracks. Captain Daniel Mannix, a Civil War veteran who had spent four years on detached duty teaching at the Chinese Naval Academy, organized the school. The school offered training and instruction to newly commissioned second lieutenants and NCOs in infantry, artillery, military art, engineering, torpedoes, administration, and law. Heywood was also able to improve the quality of his officers by requiring all Marine commanders to submit an annual fitness report on each of their officers, and in 1892 Congress approved the requirement that officers pass a physical examination and a professional examination prior to promotion.

By the end of the century, the U.S. Navy was also undergoing a revolution of sorts. This was in part inspired by renewed national aspirations to international power and the adoption of a military strategy based on Alfred Thayer Mahan's famous assertion that naval power was the determining factor in national power. In 1884, the U.S. Navy embarked on a new naval building program resulting in the first modern ships built since the American Civil War. At the same time, the second industrial revolution was introducing profound changes in military hardware.

The new ships built at the end of the nineteenth and the beginning of the twentieth centuries were heavily armored, steam-driven battleships that carried centerline turrets with breach-loading, rifled guns. These ships ushered in a new form of naval warfare, one in which ships rarely closed to a distance where sharp shooting or boarding could have any effect.

With this new model of naval warfare, the role the Marine Corps was questioned. Reformers suggested that one role the Marines could play aboard ships would be to man several of the smaller guns mounted on these new battleships.

Ironically, the Navy had a different role in mind for the Marine Corps. The new steam-driven Navy, reliant on coal depots, would need to be able to seize and defend bases to ensure a supply of fuel for their ships in foreign waters. The Marine Corps, the Navy suggested, should be transformed into a specialized expeditionary force that could be deployed quickly for the seizure and defense of coastal bases.

Although the Marine Corps maintained a great deal of pride in its readiness and rapid deployment, even the reformers in its ranks were wary about abandoning the role of the Marine Corps as ships' guards. This role had been the traditional reason for the existence of the Corps, but now many Navy officers found the idea of a ships' guard to be anachronistic.

Back in 1889, Commandant McCawley had proposed that guard detachments be assigned to secondary batteries on Navy ships. But Commodore James Greer, the head of the Navy Board of Organization, Tactics, and Drill, rejected the proposal. Furthermore, Greer again recommended the removal of the Marines from the Navy's ships entirely and their use as a specialized expeditionary force only. Many other Navy officers supported Greer's suggestions, some demonstrating outright antipathy toward the Marines. Fortunately, Commandant Heywood retained the support of the Secretary of the Navy, and in the summer of 1896 Navy regulations were amended so that Marine Guards were to be assigned to man secondary batteries on Navy ships. Indeed, Heywood enjoyed such strong support from the Secretary and Congress both that an enlistment increase of 500 men was approved shortly after the naval regulations had been amended.

Other than the struggle for existence as an institution, operations remained relatively quiet under Heywood's leadership. Only 10 landings were made between 1891 and 1898, and for the most part they were fairly minor incidents. Five of the landings were in the Caribbean and Central America, one in South America, three in Asia, and one in the Pacific. Four had been to protect American diplomatic offices during war or revolution and the rest to protect American lives and property. For the most part the Marine Corps continued to do the same job it had done during periods of relative peace throughout the nineteenth century. In one instance, however, during April through October 1891, Captain Henry Clay Cochrane led 43 Marines to the Bering Sea to enforce international agreements limiting the hunting and killing of fur seals.

★★★

In 1895, Cuban patriots launched a revolution against Spanish rule. Although many Americans were sympathetic toward the Cubans, neither

President Grover Cleveland, who was leaving office, nor President William McKinley, who had just been elected, believed that the United States should become involved in the revolution. McKinley even urged the Spanish to come to some kind of accommodation with their Cuban colony. But by 1898, "yellow" journalism, such as that published in William Randolph Hearst's *New York Journal,* had fired American national opinion.

On February 9, Hearst published in his *Journal* a letter written by the Spanish minister in Washington, Dupuy de Lome, which had been stolen from the U.S. mail. In the letter, de Lome depicted McKinley as a spineless, double-dealing politician. McKinley didn't take Hearst's bait, however, and in an effort to defuse increasing tensions and maintain good relations between the United States and Spain, he organized a series of naval exchanges between the two countries.

In 1898, the United States sent the battleship *Maine* to Havana, Cuba, while Spain sent the *Vizcaya* to New York City. The *Vizcaya* was still on its way to New York when disaster struck the *Maine* on the evening of February 15: There was a sudden explosion, and the ship's forward magazine exploded. The explosion punched a hole in the hull of the *Maine* and killed 266 of her crew, including 28 Marines. A fire in the adjacent coal storage caused the explosion, but that wasn't evident at the time, and Americans quickly jumped to the conclusion that the *Maine* had been sabotaged. A naval inquiry blamed the explosion on an underwater mine, and newspaper headlines proclaimed accusations about the "Spanish Mine."

The American temper flared, and cries of "Remember the *Maine!* To Hell with Spain!" were soon heard. President McKinley was genuinely anguished both by the tragedy and the prospect of war, but he wasn't willing to risk his popular support by opposing the American mood. On April 11, he asked Congress to declare war on Spain. On April 19, Congress passed a resolution recognizing Cuban independence and authorizing the use of force to expel Spanish forces from Cuba. Colorado Senator Henry Teller introduced an amendment to the resolution declaring that the United States had no interest in "sovereignty, jurisdiction, or control" of Cuba and that the United States would leave Cuba once independence was assured. Spain declared war on the United States on April 24. Congress reciprocated the following day.

The United States won an important early victory in the Spanish-American War when Commodore George Dewey's Asiatic Squadron struck the Spanish fleet at Manila Bay in the Philippines on May 1 and destroyed or captured all 10 Spanish ships. Dewey landed Marines at Cavite near Manila on May 3, the first to raise the American flag on Spanish territory, and shortly thereafter Marines occupied the pacific island of Guam unopposed. But the main theater of action for the Marine Corps would be on Cuba itself.

Rear Admiral William Simpson requested that two Marine battalions be assigned to the North Atlantic Squadron. Colonel Heywood mustered a battalion of 450 Marines at New York City by April 20. A second 200-man "battalion" was mustered and attached to the first battalion 2 days later. The battalion, which represented nearly a quarter of the Marine Corps in 1898, was organized into five companies, four infantry, and one artillery. It was commanded by Lieutenant Colonel Robert Huntington, a veteran of the Battle of Bull Run. Henry Clay Cochrane, who had finally been promoted to major the previous February, was named second in command. "Huntington's Battalion" arrived in Key West, Florida, on April 29.

In an effort to isolate Cuba, Marines and sailors from the USS *Marblehead* set out in boats on May 11 to cut the transoceanic cable off the shore of Cienfuegos. Spaniards along the shore quickly opened fire, and the party was forced to withdraw with seven casualties. Despite this setback, Admiral Sampson hoped to intercept Spanish Admiral Pascual Cervera's fleet, which had left the Cape Verde Islands on April 29, after its long voyage across the Atlantic. Unfortunately, he missed the fleet, and by May 28, Cervera's fleet had made port in Santiago de Cuba.

Sampson decided to blockade the port and ordered Huntington's Battalion to secure Guantanamo Bay, 40 miles east of Santiago, as a coaling station for the North Atlantic Squadron. War correspondent Stephen Crane, author of *The Red Badge of Courage*, accompanied Huntington's Battalion to Guantanamo Bay. On June 7, the *Marblehead*, the *Yankee*, and the *St. Louis* steamed into Guantanamo Bay and drove the lone Spanish gunboat *Sandoval* away. The Marines cut the transatlantic cable at Playa del Este.

Three days later, "Billy Hell" McCalla landed unopposed on the western side of Guantanamo Bay and established a small camp that came to be called Camp McCalla. The following afternoon, however, two Marines were ambushed while on guard duty, and that evening the Spanish attacked Camp McCalla. The Spanish were never able to penetrate the camp's perimeter, but the battalion's surgeon and a sergeant were both killed and two more Marines were wounded. Huntington moved the camp to a more defensible position, but by then the strain was beginning to have an effect on many of the commanding officers, none of whom was under 50 years of age. Some of the aged commanders even suggested withdrawing altogether, though McCalla and Cochrane both argued for maintaining their position. The Spanish attacked again that night.

Huntington learned from Cuban patriots that there was a Spanish camp only two miles away at Cuzco Well, the area's only source of fresh water. On June 14, Huntington ordered Captain W. F. Spicer to attack Cuzco Well with Companies C and D supported by 50 Cuban patriots. En route to Cuzco Well, however, Captain Spicer succumbed to sunstroke, and 51-year-old Captain George Elliott took command.

Elliott ordered Lieutenant Louis Magill to lead his company around Cuzco Well and behind the enemy in order to cut off any retreat, and then arranged the remaining company along a ridgeline overlooking the Spanish camp. The ensuing firefight resulted in a stalemate, and when Captain Elliott wished to order fire support from the nearby *Dolphin*, he realized that he had forgotten his signal flag. One of his Marines, Private John Fitzgerald, tied his neckerchief to his rifle and bravely stood to give the signal to the *Dolphin*. The *Dolphin* complied but overshot the Spanish camp, and unfortunately bombarded Magill's Marines on the other side of the camp.

On three occasions Sergeant John Quick tied his own neckerchief to a stick and stood to signal corrections to the *Dolphin*. Stephen Crane, describing the scene for his readers in the States, wrote, "I watched his face, and it was grave and serene as that of a man writing in his own library ...." There was not a single trace of nervousness or haste ...." The *Dolphin's* guns, brought on target by the heroic work of Fitzgerald and Quick, soon broke the Spanish who fled to the east. The Marines destroyed the camp and wrecked the well. Only one Marine had been hit; miraculously, neither Fitzgerald nor Quick were injured. Approximately 5 Spaniards were killed or wounded, and 18 were captured by Cuban patriots.

With a secure coaling station, Admiral Sampson set about attacking Santiago, only to find that the channel had been mined and that the minefield was protected by a series of artillery batteries along the shore. He requested assistance from the Army, which landed 17,000 men under the command of Major General William Shafter.

On July 1, American forces captured two important Spanish garrisons at El Caney Hill and San Juan Hill overlooking Santiago de Cuba, the latter of which was captured by Theodore Roosevelt's "Rough Riders." The governor-general of Cuba panicked and ordered Cervera to attack the American fleet. On July 3, Sampson's North Atlantic Squadron destroyed Cervera's fleet.

Santiago surrendered on July 17, and an armistice soon followed. The Marine Corps suffered 6 dead and 16 wounded during the whole of the Spanish-American War. Fifteen Marines, including Private Fitzgerald and Sergeant Quick, were awarded the Medal of Honor, and thirteen officers were awarded brevet promotions. Huntington's Battalion returned home as heroes. Stephen Crane's stories from Guantanamo Bay and the stories of other war correspondents had been printed in numerous newspapers, and the average American, probably for the first time, became aware that the United States had a Marine Corps and that it was filled with the likes of Private Fitzgerald and Sergeant Quick.

Four hundred years of Spanish colonial rule had come crashing down in just 114 days. Americans might be expected to learn a cautionary lesson from such events, but few held such somber reflections on July 4, 1898. It had been, John Hay commented in a letter to Theodore Roosevelt, "a splendid little war." It had not been really. Relatively few Americans were killed in action—379—but, more significantly, nearly 5,000 had died of food poisoning, malaria, and yellow fever.

But the United States had been victorious. In December, a treaty between the United States and Spain was signed in Paris officially ending the Spanish-American War. Spain recognized Cuba's independence and paid her $20 million. In addition, Spain ceded the Philippines, Puerto Rico, and Guam, and the United States suddenly had an overseas empire. The *Washington Post* summarized the American mood when it observed that "[a] new consciousness seems to have come upon us—the consciousness of strength— and with it a new appetite ... [t]he taste of empire."

CHAPTER 6

THE MARINES HAVE LANDED: THE AGE OF U.S. IMPERIALISM

The United States emerged from the Spanish-American War as an imperial power. The Treaty of Paris, which ended the war and recognized Cuba as an independent nation, also granted the United States control of several former Spanish colonies: Guam, Puerto Rico, and the Philippines. In addition, the United States, in its support of the Cuban revolution, had essentially established itself as the protector of the small island nation. By the end of the year, the United States would add Hawaii to the list of small islands around the world that it controlled.

Suddenly, the United States had great need of a strong Navy to protect this far-flung empire. During the nineteenth century, the Navy and the Marine Corps had frequently been involved in foreign landings to protect American lives and property. Now, however, there was the additional need to protect actual territory. Alfred Thayer Mahan, the former head of the Navy War College in Newport, Rhode Island, suggested in *The Influence of Sea Power upon History* that national power was dependent upon naval force. His thesis had a powerful influence upon all imperial nations at the end of the nineteenth century, and the United States was no exception. The naval building program suddenly surged forward, and over the next decade, the U.S. Navy commissioned an average of two battleships per year.

The imperial commitments the United States had acquired and the sudden expansion of the Navy to protect those commitments also promised the expansion of the Marine Corps. Indeed, even as the United States was fighting Spain, Congress approved the permanent expansion of the Corps to a total strength of 3,073 men, and the temporary addition, for the duration of the Spanish-American War, of some 1,580 men.

Commandant Heywood understood, however, that such temporary increases were insufficient for the rapidly expanding responsibilities of the Corps. After the conclusion of the Spanish-American War, Heywood proposed the permanent expansion of the Marine Corps to almost double its current size. Congress, caught up in the exuberance of the victory over Spain and the prospects of imperial expansion, agreed. It passed the Naval Act of 1899, which expanded the Marine Corps to 201 officers and 6,062 men. The office of the commandant was again raised to the rank of brigadier general, and there were now to be five colonels and five lieutenant colonels in the Corps. Henry Clay Cochrane, who had been promoted to captain after 14 years of service, and to major after another 19 years of service, was rapidly promoted to lieutenant colonel and then to colonel in only two years.

Furthermore, the Marine Corps took up the responsibilities of establishing advance bases for the Navy and serving as a kind of colonial infantry. The Navy had desired the development of expeditionary advance bases for some time, but disagreements between Navy officers and Army officers caused several Navy officers to doubt the reliability of the Army in establishing such advance bases. The Marine Corps, however, which was strongly connected to the Navy and which had clearly demonstrated its ability to establish such bases at Guantanamo Bay, was ideal for this mission.

Commandant Heywood was skeptical, however. He did agree to instruct Marines in the construction of field fortifications and the emplacement of artillery, fundamental aspects of advance base establishment, and by 1902 one Marine battalion had undergone such training and was available to participate in the Navy's maneuvers. But Heywood refused to provide the greater number of units the Navy's General Board requested for this purpose. By then, too many Marine forces were serving as colonial infantry.

Although the Marine Corps had been assigned the task of developing advance base capabilities, its traditional service continued. Marine Guards were still assigned to the Navy's ships, and the Corps participated in a number of landings to protect American lives and property. However, the Navy had need of ready force to protect the fledgling American empire. Deployment as colonial infantry could absorb a sizeable force and last for several months, which would naturally limit the ability of the Marine Corps to develop advance bases. Although it might have been possible to meet both missions by eliminating ships' guard units, the Marine Corps desired to maintain this traditional role, and so found itself incapable of completing all three missions.

Acting as a colonial infantry, an extension of the traditional role of the Corps as shipboard troops and expeditionary force, became the primary role of the U.S. Marines Corps at the turn of the century. Indeed, it quickly became apparent that maintaining an empire was going to require a great deal of effort, and the Marines were called upon almost immediately to maintain order in America's new empire.

In March 1899, natives in the Samoan Islands (jointly administered by British, American, and German authorities) rebelled against European and American rule, and Marines from the USS *Philadelphia* were sent ashore with Royal Marines to restore order. It was not an easy task. The Samoans proved to be tenacious, and on April 1, they attacked a patrol of American and British troops on Upolu Island. Both the British and the American commanders were killed in the ambush, and a small unit of U.S. Marines under First Lieutenant Constantine Perkins had to cover the retreat of the British seamen. Despite such setbacks, order was restored by the end of April. In 1904, a naval station was set up in American Samoa, and the Fita-Fita Guard, a native guard trained and commanded by Marines, was created.

KRAG-JORGENSEN MODEL 1898 .30-CALIBER RIFLE

The U.S. government had desired a rifle equipped with a magazine since the late 1870s and had experimented with a number of possible models over the last two decades of the nineteenth century. Eventually, the Navy had adopted the Winchester-Lee 6mm straight-pull rifle, which was used by the Marine Corps during the Spanish-American War.

In 1892, however, the U.S. Army adopted a rifle designed by Ole Krag and Erik Jorgensen at the Konigsberg Arms Factory in Norway. The Krag-Jorgensen rifle had several advantages over the "trapdoor" still in use by U.S. armed forces at the beginning of the 1890s: It used smokeless powder, which made it more difficult to spot the shooter; the 5-shot magazine increased rate of fire significantly; the smaller .30-caliber ammunition weighed less, so a soldier could carry more—100 .30 rounds compared to only 60 .45 rounds; and the rifle had better accuracy.

The first M-1892 Krag-Jorgensen rifles were produced in 1894, and after several modifications, an improved M-1896 was produced between 1897 and 1899. Further improvements were made on the M-1898 rifle. The U.S Army, New York volunteer units, and Teddy Roosevelt's Rough Riders were armed with the M-1896 Krag-Jorgensen rifles during the Spanish-American War. The Marine Corps adopted the M-1898 rifle in 1900 primarily because its adoption by the Army meant that the weapon was in ready supply.

Unfortunately, the Krag-Jorgensen had a relatively lower muzzle velocity and less stopping power than higher caliber weapons. The Marines were equipped with Krags for only a few years, but they were used extensively in the Philippines and China. Indeed, adapting to their new role as colonial infantry, the Marines adopted the motto "Civilize 'em with a Krag!"

In February 1899, Filipino patriots led by Emilio Aguinaldo began a revolutionary war against American rule in the Philippine Islands. Three years earlier, Aguinaldo had led a revolt against Spanish imperial rule. Defeat had led to Aguinaldo's exile in Hong Kong, but after the defeat of the Spanish fleet at the Battle of Manila Bay in 1898, Commodore George Dewey returned Aguinaldo to the Philippines, where he cooperated with American forces during the siege of Manila.

On June 12, 1898, Aguinaldo had declared an independent Philippine republic with himself as president, as he expected that the Philippine government would be turned over to Filipino rule after the ultimate defeat of the Spanish. On August 13, 1898, Manila fell, and Aguinaldo, his Filipino rebels, and the U.S. Army entered the city. Aguinaldo was promptly told, however, to leave the city. The United States evidently had no intention of turning the Philippines over to the Filipinos. Aguinaldo's new revolution began on February 4.

Dewey, recently promoted to admiral, requested a Marine battalion to garrison Cavite Peninsula in Manila Bay, and the "First Battalion of

Marines," composed of 15 officers and 260 men equipped with two Colt machine guns and four 3-inch guns under Colonel Percival Pope, arrived in May. Two more battalions would be sent to the Philippines by the end of 1899. Most of the Marine Corps actions in the Philippines involved small skirmishes with the revolutionaries. On October 8, 1899, however, a 400-man battalion under Lieutenant Colonel George Elliott assisted the Army in an attack against Filipino revolutionaries in a village on Novaleta. The Marines were assigned the actual assault on the village while the Army took up positions to cut off any escape. With the support of the U.S. Navy gunboat *Petrel*, the Marines waded through the hot marshes and rice paddies and into the village. Excitement gripped the men as they raced chaotically through the village firing at will. Nevertheless, the Marines captured the village, losing only three men killed and another nine wounded.

Most of Aguinaldo's conventional forces were dispersed relatively quickly, but a guerilla war dragged on for some time. Over the next year and a half, the Marines chased revolutionaries, supervised public works projects, built schools, and supervised elections. The Army eventually gained control of the conflict, however, and captured Aguinaldo in March 1901. President Theodore Roosevelt declared that the war was over in July 1901 after many of Aguinaldo's followers voluntarily surrendered at his urging. Nevertheless, although the Christian Tagalogs who lived in the Philippines seemed to accept American rule, the Muslim Moros who also inhabited the islands did not, and two areas of violent resistance remained: Luzon and Samar.

On September 28, on the island of Samar, rebels and townspeople attacked the Army's 9th Infantry garrison at Balangiga in a surprise Sunday-morning assault. Nearly all the soldiers were killed. The massacre at Balangiga provoked a severe response from American forces. Brigadier General Jacob "Hell-Roaring" Smith was ordered to pacify the island of Samar, and the Navy assigned Major Waller's battalion of Marines to assist him. Major Littleton Waller, a fiery Virginian, had entered the Corps in 1880. He had served with Cochrane in Alexandria, Egypt, and as commander of the *Indiana*'s Marine Guard at the battle of Santiago during the Spanish-American War. He had been assigned originally to organize a Marine barracks on the Pacific island of Guam.

Smith's orders to Waller were brutal; Smith supposedly told him, "I want no prisoners. I wish you to burn and kill. The more you burn and kill, the better it will please me." Essentially, anyone who was capable of bearing arms was to be slaughtered and their villages burned to the ground. To his credit, Waller was appalled by such orders. Although he reveled in the experience of combat, he saw no need to make war on women and children, and although he repeated Smith's orders to his men, he urged them to remember his own opinion on the matter.

Waller was given an area of 600 square miles of unmapped jungle to control. He established a base at the coastal town of Basey with two companies of Marines and sent another two companies to Balangiga. Waller's Marines set up regular patrols and pushed into the jungle, and by November 12, they had burned 255 huts, destroyed a ton of rice, and killed 39 revolutionaries and captured another 18. On November 17, the Marines attacked a supposedly impregnable stronghold at Sohoton Cliffs. While Major Waller paddled up the Cadacan River with 75 Marines and a 3-inch field gun lashed to a raft, Captain David Porter approached the cliffs overland with 125 Marines. Upon reaching his position, however, Porter realized that Waller's unit could be cut to pieces as it approached the stronghold. He decided to move ahead without waiting for Waller and ordered Gunnery Sergeant John Quick to take command of the unit's machine gun and establish covering fire. Corporal Robert Leckie bravely swam across the Cadacan to secure a boat that Porter's unit then used to cross the river.

Stunned by the audacity of the American Marines, the Filipinos forgot to pull up the ladders they used to climb into their cliffside stronghold, and Porter led his men up those same ladders while Quick kept up a pattern of covering fire. The Marines killed 30 Filipinos in fierce hand-to-hand combat and captured 40 cannon as well as gunpowder and foodstuffs. Not one Marine was injured in the operation. By the time Waller's unit arrived at Sohoton Cliffs, Porter had the situation well in hand. He was later awarded the Medal of Honor. Samar seemed essentially pacified after the victory at Sohoton Cliffs, but tragedy soon struck Waller and his battalion. Ordered to map a path through the jungle for a telegraph line to Basey, Waller set out from Lanang on the east coast on December 28, 1902, with 55 Marines, 33 Filipino bearers, and 2 Filipino scouts. The expedition found it nearly impossible to advance and struggled up the Sohoton Mountains during the monsoon season. Drenched and tired, making little progress, it soon became apparent that Waller had miscalculated the time it would take to cross the mountains and reach Basey.

Having brought with them rations for only four days, the Marines were forced to reduce rations, and the men's health deteriorated quickly. Waller finally ordered the most fit men of the expedition go for help, and one unit, led by Waller himself, continued on to Basey while a second, led by Captain Porter, returned to Lanang. First Lieutenant Alexander Williams remained in command of the 33 Marines who were too weak to make the journey. Ten of these Marines died by the time relief arrived on January 18, and the others were only barely alive.

As the Marines' health deteriorated, the Filipino bearers became increasingly uncontrollable, apparently even plotting to kill the Americans as they grew weaker. On one occasion, Lieutenant Williams drew his sidearm to enforce an order, but was attacked by a Filipino and struck several times before the Filipino could be subdued. Waller, now suffering from fever himself and perhaps remembering the Balangiga massacre, ordered that 10 of the bearers and 1 of the scouts be executed. Their executions were carried out on January 20.

Waller dutifully reported the unfortunate actions to his superior officer, General Jacob Smith. But the commander of the American forces in the Philippines, Major General Adna Chafee, soon learned of the executions, and, embarrassed by reports of American atrocities, ordered both Smith and Waller court-martialed. Anti-imperialists in the United States saw him as an example of all that was evil with American imperialism, labeling him the "Butcher of Samar." Waller was acquitted on the grounds that the executions were justified by the situation. Smith's original orders to kill and burn everyone also came out during the hearings, however, and he was forced into retirement. The Marines saw the actions of their men on Samar as honorable, and those officers and men who survived Samar were customarily honored with a tribute when they entered the mess hall: "Stand, gentlemen, he served on Samar."

Both Luzon and Samar were finally pacified by April 1902. The Philippine Insurrection had lasted 3 years and involved more than 125,000 troops, 4,200 of whom were killed in action. Twenty-six Marines were killed or wounded during the revolution; six earned Medals of Honor. Marines occupied the Philippines until 1914.

COLT-BROWNING M-1895 MACHINE GUN

One of the first true machine guns—as opposed to the Gatling gun with multiple barrels that rotated around a central axis—was invented in 1890 by John Moses Browning. While on a hunting trip, Browning noticed the effect that gas released from the muzzle had on surrounding foliage and surmised that this released gas could be harnessed to drive an automatic weapon. In Browning's design, gas released from the .30-caliber cartridge when it was fired was diverted to operate a piston, ejecting the spent round and loading a new one. As the piston operated, a lever located underneath the barrel swung back and forth. If the weapon were set up too close to the ground, the lever would dig up the dirt as it swung back and forth, giving the weapon its nickname, "potato digger." The weapon was manufactured by Colt, and in 1895, the U.S. Navy and Marine Corps adopted it for use. It proved invaluable throughout the early years of the twentieth century, especially during the Philippine Insurrection and the 55-day siege of Peking during the Boxer Rebellion.

★★★

Rebellion against western imperialism spread quickly throughout the Far East. In 1898, a grass-roots peasant rebellion adopting the name the Fists of Righteous Harmony began to spread throughout the countryside of China. The goal of the Fists of Righteous Harmony was the removal of all foreign influences in China, and by 1900 the "Boxer Rebellion" had spread far enough to threaten Peking, the seat of the Manchu court and 11 foreign diplomatic missions.

As the rebellion spread into Peking, the diplomats in Peking began to worry about their safety and the safety of numerous Chinese Christians in the city. On May 28, all 11 foreign diplomats requested protection, and a multinational force entered Peking on May 31. Captain John T. "Handsome Jack" Myers commanded a Guard of 49 Marines and 5 sailors at the U.S. diplomatic headquarters in Peking. His small guard unit had left their baggage behind in order to carry as much ammunition as they could: 20,000 rounds for their rifles and another 8,000 rounds for their Colt machine gun.

Myers's Marines patrolled the diplomatic quarter near the Imperial city for the next three weeks, occasionally fighting small bands of Boxers and rescuing refugees. But the Boxers continued to swarm into the city, burning churches and the homes and shops of Chinese Christians. The foreign diplomatic missions asked for more protection from the Chinese Imperial Army, but the Chinese became belligerent when they learned that British Admiral Sir Edward Seymour had landed at Tientsin with a force of 2,130 British, American, Russian, and Japanese troops and had set out to relieve Peking on June 10. The Manchu Court declared war and ordered its soldiers to side with the Boxers.

Myers's Marines played an important role in defending the foreign diplomatic missions in Peking, frequently taking defensive positions along the Tartar Wall that ran along the south edge of the foreign diplomatic quarter. The defense of the quarter was a grueling ordeal. The Chinese continually bombarded the quarter and gradually built barricades that approached the Tartar Wall. The expert marksmanship of the Marines and the Colt machine gun served to keep the Chinese under cover most of the time. By July 1, however, the Chinese barricades had come within a few feet of the Marine position, and the Chinese were in the process of building a tall stone tower. On July 3, Myers led 30 American Marines, 26 Royal Marines, and 15 Russian sailors in a surprise assault that captured the tower and killed 30 of its garrison. Two American Marines were killed, and several others, including Myers, were wounded.

Myers's assault helped secure the southwestern quadrant of the diplomatic quarter. In the following days, Marines reinforced French and Italian forces on the eastern side of the quarters. Private Dan Daly won his first Medal of Honor for holding off several Chinese attacks with the Colt machine gun. By July 16, the diplomatic quarter was secure, although the Marines would have to endure shelling, sniping, sickness, and fatigue for nearly a month longer.

In the meantime Admiral Seymour's expedition, which included 112 American sailors and Marines commanded by Navy Captain Bowman McCalla, was attempting to reach Peking and relieve the besieged foreign missions. The expedition was attacked several times by Boxers and the Chinese army but pressed on toward Peking even though the Boxers captured the railroad. At that point, the expedition had been hurt badly, having suffered nearly a 20 percent casualty rate, and Seymour was forced to turn back. His expedition found refuge in the Hsiku Arsenal just north of Tientsin on June 22.

One week earlier the Chinese army attacked the foreign settlements at Tientsin. The allied western forces were able to capture several forts guarding the mouth of the Pei-Ho River, however, ensuring a bridgehead into China. Major Tony Waller was ordered from the Philippines and landed with 138 Marines at Tangku on June 20.

As the Chinese assault continued on the foreign diplomatic quarter in Peking, Waller's Marines marched toward Tientsin to recapture the foreign settlements there. On the way, Waller encountered a force of approximately 440 Russian soldiers, whom he managed to convince to join him in an assault on the Chinese position on June 22. Waller's force encountered several thousand Chinese soldiers heavily entrenched in Tientsin, however, and the assault failed. With reluctance, Waller gave the order to retire, and the Marines, having suffered 13 casualties, slowly withdrew to Tangku. British and Russian reinforcements arrived at Tangku that night, raising their strength to 2,300 men, and on June 24, this force captured the Tientsin foreign settlement.

On June 25, a courier from Seymour's expedition miraculously appeared in Tientsin. A relief column including Waller's battalion was assembled quickly. Fortunately, there was little opposition, and the remnant of Seymour's battered expedition was escorted back to Tientsin on June 26.

For the next two weeks, the allied forces remained in the foreign settlements at Tientsin and awaited reinforcements. To the American contingent were added two battalions from the Army's 9th Infantry stationed in the Philippines as well as another Marine battalion, bringing their force up to regiment size of nearly 1,000 men. The makeshift regiment was commanded by the aging Colonel Robert Meade, who had participated in the assault on Fort Sumter during the American Civil War.

The allied forces, now 6,800 strong and under the command of British Brigadier General A.R.F. Dorward, attacked Tientsin proper on July 13. A Marine artillery battery under the command of Captain Ben Fuller bombarded the city's walls as Colonel Meade, despite his rheumatism, led the American forces during the assault. The Marines clambered over the outer mud wall and struggled across rice paddies toward the city. Unfortunately, they were stopped some 200 yards from the city's inner walls by a canal, and the assault bogged down.

Japanese soldiers eventually destroyed the gates to the city at 3 A.M. on July 14, and the allies stormed into the city, burning and looting as they went.

... AND SAINT DAVID

Throughout the assault on Tientsin, Meade's Marines served next to the Royal Welch Fusiliers, and as a result, a close bond developed between the Welshmen and the Americans. To this day, on March 1, Wales's national holiday, St. David's Day, and on November 10, the birthday of the Marine Corps, the colonel of the Fusiliers and the commandant of the Marine Corps exchange the traditional watchword from their service in China: "... and Saint David."

Again, the allies recovered and waited for reinforcements before beginning an advance on Peking. Another Marine battalion under the command of Major William Biddle and another Army infantry regiment under the command of Major General Adna Chafee arrived at the end of July. Biddle took command of the Marines as Meade was too sick and returned to the United States, and Chafee became commander of the American forces.

The allied forces, having by then amassed 18,600 men, began the long march to Peking on August 4, 1900. Only Waller's battalion accompanied Chafee's 2,500-man force, the other 2 battalions having been assigned to guard Tientsin. The exhausted allied forces arrived in Peking on August 14 to find to their relief that the foreign delegations were still holding out after 55 days of siege. Seventeen Marines had been wounded or killed during the siege of Peking, and another thirty-four Marines were wounded or killed during the city's relief. Thirty-three Marines were awarded the Medal of Honor. Ten officers, including Waller, Meade, and Myers, were awarded the last brevet promotions before its discontinuation.

BREVET PROMOTIONS

A brevet promotion was awarded to an officer for valor in combat before it became common to award medals. It was a purely honorary award, recognizing the officer's actions but carrying with it no monetary rewards or increased authority.

The award of brevet promotions was authorized in the U.S. Army in 1806, and the U.S. Marine Corps was authorized to award brevet promotions beginning in 1814. Initially, the Marine Corps was authorized to award brevet promotions not only for gallant conduct on the field of battle but for 10 years of service as well. Congress modified the original standards for brevet promotions in 1834, however, eliminating brevet promotions for service and restricting the award to meritorious conduct. A brevet promotion for meritorious conduct would remain the highest award a Marine could earn for more than 80 years.

Anthony Gale was the first Marine awarded a brevet promotion in 1814 for having served 10 years in service. Brevet promotions remained relatively rare, no more than seven being granted within the Marine Corps in any one year. Over 86 years, from 1814 until 1900, 100 Marines were awarded a total of 121 brevet promotions, 82 officers receiving one such award, 15 officers—including John Harris, Charles Heywood, Charles McCawley, Robert Meade, Samuel Miller, and Robert Wainwright—receiving two brevet promotions, and three officers—William Dulaney, James Forney, and Archibald Henderson—receiving three brevet promotions.

The relative peace following the Civil War led to a sharp decline in brevet promotions—only three brevet promotions were awarded to Marine officers between 1866 and 1897, two of which were awarded to James Forney. Brevet promotions were awarded again during the Spanish American War and for service in the Philippines and in China; Smedley Butler, Robert Meade, John Myers, and Tony Waller were among the last Marine officers to earn brevets. Although the Marine Corps remained active during the next two decades, there were no major conflicts such as the Spanish-American War or the Boxer Rebellion that provided opportunities for such gallantry as warrants a brevet promotion. In addition, the practice of awarding medals—such as the Navy Cross and the Distinguished Service Medal—for service and gallant conduct gradually replaced the brevet.

In 1921, however, Commandant John Lejeune issued Marine Corps Order Number 26, which awarded a Brevet Medal to active Marine officers who had been previously awarded brevet promotions and recognizing their unique contributions. Only 20 officers were awarded Brevet Medals, including Wendell Neville and Charles McCawley for service during the Spanish-American War, David Porter for service during the Philippine Insurrection, and Tony Waller, Smedley Butler, and John Myers for service during the Boxer Rebellion. Percival Pope was awarded the Brevet Medal in recognition of a brevet promotion he had earned during the American Civil War.

In addition to landings in the Philippines and China, the U.S. Marine Corps made several minor landings to protect American lives and property, including six in Panama, two in Honduras, one in Santo Domingo, and one in Beirut. Additional major landings would soon follow in Panama, Cuba, Nicaragua, Mexico, Haiti, and Santo Domingo.

ROOSEVELT COROLLARY

In 1902, three European countries, Britain, Germany, and Italy, blockaded and bombarded the Republic of Venezuela. These countries claimed that their interests and property had been damaged during a recent revolution in Venezuela, and they demanded appropriate compensation. President Theodore Roosevelt eventually became tired of this rather familiar treatment of a country in the backyard of the United States and recommended to Kaiser Wilhelm that the three countries submit their grievances to The Hague for arbitration. If they didn't, he would send the Atlantic Fleet to break the blockade. The United States would not interfere with the just claims of European countries against countries in the U.S. sphere of influence, Roosevelt told Congress, but only so long as the actions of the claimant countries did not "take the form of acquisition of territory." When Latin American countries were found guilty of "chronic wrongdoing," the United States would act as an "international police power." This statement came to be known as the "Roosevelt Corollary" to the Monroe Doctrine, and it was the basis for many U.S. interventions in Latin American countries during the first two decades of the twentieth century.

★★★

In 1879, a French company had secured a 25-year concession to build a canal across Panama, then controlled by Colombia, that would allow easier passage between the Atlantic and Pacific Oceans. Unfortunately, poor management and yellow fever plagued the project, and by 1889 the French company had gone bankrupt. The French company offered the concession it had acquired from Colombia to the United States, originally asking $109 million in order to recoup its losses. Eventually, the French lowered the price to a mere $40 million, and Congress jumped at the opportunity.

Early in 1903, the United States signed a treaty with Colombia for a 99-year lease to finish and operate the Panama Canal in exchange for $10 million plus $250,000 annually. Declaring that the payment was insufficient, however, the Colombian Senate rejected the treaty in August 1903. President Roosevelt was outraged by the unexpected failure of the treaty, and, determined to have his canal, he arranged for Philippe Bunau-Varilla, an official of the bankrupt French company, to use his connections in Panama to orchestrate a revolution led by the Panama City Fire Department.

The revolution began on November 3, 1903, and Colombia quickly landed 500 troops at Colon. An American gunboat, the *Nashville*, conveniently waiting off the coast of Colombia, landed 50 sailors and Marines to prevent the Colombians from using the Panama railroad, which was still under American control, to reach Panama City. The sailors and Marines weren't needed, however; Bunau-Varilla bribed the Colombian commander, and the Colombians set off for home on November 4.

On the following day, a Marine battalion under the command of Major John Lejeune landed at Colon. The United States recognized Panama's independence on November 6, and Philippe Bunau-Varilla quickly declared himself Panama's first ambassador to the United States. Three more Marine battalions were sent to Panama over the next two months. Fortunately, the crisis passed without further conflict, and construction on the canal began in May 1904. A Marine battalion remained in Panama until 1914.

Cuba continued to be another area of concern for the United States. After the Spanish-American War, the Cubans had adopted a constitution very similar to the U.S. Constitution—except for the Platt Amendment, which gave the United States the right to intervene to preserve Cuban independence and maintain its government. In August 1906, however, the Cuban Liberal Party was defeated in an election. Believing that the election had been manipulated, the Liberals revolted against the Conservative government, and President Tomás Estrada Palma requested American help. President Roosevelt, concerned about American interests in sugar plantations on the island, agreed to help Palma.

On September 13, 130 Marines and sailors landed at Havana and moved to protect the president's residence. Three days later, a second battalion under the command of Major Albertus Catlin joined them. Additional Marine detachments also went ashore to protect sugar plantations owned by Americans, and on September 19, Secretary of War William Howard Taft led a special commission to Cuba.

Palma resigned on September 28, and President Roosevelt ordered Taft to form a provisional government. Shortly thereafter, two more Marine battalions were put ashore to form the 1st Regiment of Marines under Lieutenant Colonel George Barnett, while a second regiment was created from the ships' detachments of the Atlantic Fleet and placed under the command of Lieutenant Colonel Franklin Moses. Colonel Tony Waller arrived on October 1 to assume command of the new Marine brigade, consisting of 97 officers and 2,795 men.

By October 10, a more permanent U.S. Army of Cuban Occupation was being put into place, lessening the need for the Marine brigade. It was disbanded, and Waller returned to Norfolk at the beginning of November, though the 1st Marine Regiment remained intact and on duty with the Army of Occupation. The Marines who remained on duty in Cuba saw no combat action but were kept busy with weapon collection and guard duty. They remained on duty there until January 23, 1909.

★★★

Commandant Heywood retired in October 1903, and President Roosevelt appointed George Elliott commandant of the Marine Corps. Elliot continued Heywood's efforts to grow the Corps, and by 1908, Congress twice had approved expansions, increasing the size of the U.S. Marine Corps to 10,000 men. But the debate over the future of the Marine Corps continued.

Commandant Elliott also continued to struggle for the independence and recognition of the U.S. Marine Corps. He was offered a promotion to major general twice but on both occasions refused, arguing that the rank of major general should be attached to the office of commandant rather than an individual. Eventually, the office of commandant was given a rank of major general, and in May 1908, Elliott was promoted to major general.

Later that same year, Rear Admiral John Pillsbury recommended once more that the Marine Guards should be withdrawn from Navy ships. Secretary of the Navy Victor Metcalf agreed with Pillsbury's recommendation, and on November 12, 1908, despite Elliott's protests, President Roosevelt signed Executive Order 969, which stated that the duties of the Marine Corps were to garrison Navy yards and stations, to provide defense of naval bases and stations outside of the continental United States, to garrison the Panama Canal Zone, and to provide defensive expeditionary forces. No mention was made of shipboard service.

Roosevelt wished to do more than remove Marines from Navy ships, however; he wished to merge the Corps with the Army. Elliott sought support from Congress, which he found in the person of Congressman Thomas Butler, the father of Marine Major Smedley Butler, and on March 3, the so-called Butler Rider was attached to the Naval Appropriations Bill stating that appropriations for the Marine Corps could only be made so long as Marines continued to serve on board Navy ships. Thanks to Butler's amendment, the traditional Marine role as soldiers of the sea would continue.

Elliott also sought to improve Marine training by insisting on a three-month training period. He improved the organization of Marine bases by dividing the Marines stationed at the bases into barracks detachments, which were not intended for rapid deployment, and one or two companies specifically prepared for rapid deployment as expeditionary forces.

Several minor landings took place during Elliott's tenure. Marines under the command of Captain George Thorpe escorted a diplomatic mission to Emperor Menelik II of Ethiopia in 1903 and 1904; Marines landed in Seoul, Korea, in January 1904 to guard the U.S. diplomatic mission during an outbreak of anti-American demonstrations; and Handsome Jack Myers led the USS *Brooklyn*'s Marine Guard ashore at Tangiers, Morocco, to secure the safety of naturalized American citizen Ion Perdicaris who had been kidnapped by the bandit Raisouli.

In 1909, Nicaragua was under the control of José Santos Zelaya, an anti-clerical dictator who was heavily in debt to Europe and the United States. Juan Estrada, the leader of the Catholic conservatives, led a revolution against Zelaya's dictatorship. The United States decided to support Estrada's faction and broke off diplomatic relations with Zelaya. In December, Major Smedley Butler, only recently assigned to Panama, led a Marine battalion into Nicaragua, and Colonel James Mahoney led a small 750-Marine regiment down from Philadelphia. Estrada's conservatives seemed in control by March 1910, and Mahoney returned to Philadelphia while Butler returned to Panama. But the conservatives lost their hold on their positions, and in mid-May the USS *Paducah* landed its Marine detachment, and by the end of the month, Major Butler had to return as well. With this impressive support and encouragement, Estrada returned to the offensive, and the conservatives gained control of the capital city of Managua by September. Butler once again returned to Panama.

★★★

On November 30, 1910, Major General Commandant Elliott retired. William Biddle took over as acting commandant until a new commandant could be determined. Tony Waller seemed to be the ideal candidate except for his tarnished record as the "Butcher of Samar." The Republicans were able to persuade President Taft that Biddle, who came from a respectable Philadelphia family, was the better man for the job, and on February 13, 1911, Biddle was named the eleventh commandant of the U.S. Marine Corps.

Biddle, although not the most vigorous commandant of the Marine Corps, had been a Marine for 36 years and had served at the Battle of Manila Bay during the Spanish-American War, had commanded the Marines on their march to Peking, and had served in the Philippines. He worked hard to expand the Marine Corps. He set up recruiting depots at Philadelphia, Port Royal, Mare Island, and Puget Sound, and by the time he retired in 1914, the Marine Corps had grown to 10,000 men.

In addition, Biddle activated the Marine Advance Base Force. Twelve years earlier, Major Henry Haines had been directed to develop advance base operations for the Marine Corps. With 44 Marines, Haines carried out a series of small-scale landing exercises at Newport, Rhode Island. The need for rapid deployment and the establishment of advance bases had become evident over the course of the first decade of the twentieth century, especially in places such as Panama, Cuba, and Nicaragua. In 1910, the Advanced Base School was created at New London, Connecticut, but relocated to Philadelphia the following year. By the end of 1912, nearly one fifth of the Corps had passed through it.

The Marine Advance Base Brigade was activated on December 23, 1913, and placed under the command Colonel George Barnett. It was composed of three detachments. The 1st Regiment was a "fixed-defense regiment," charged with manning the base's guns and fortifications. The 2nd Regiment was organized as a mobile infantry unit, composed of four rifle companies, a machine-gun company, and a battery of landing guns.

The third and final detachment was an aviation detachment of two officers, seven enlisted men, and two flying boats.

This last detachment was a brand new addition. First Lieutenant Alfred Cunningham demonstrated an enthusiasm for the new technology of flight that quickly led his superiors to order him to attend the new aviation camp at Annapolis. His training took place at Marblehead, Massachusetts, however, where after two and a half hours of instruction, Cunningham flew a Curtiss seaplane. He became the first Marine pilot. The next Marine to qualify as a pilot was Lieutenant Bernard Smith, who was placed in command of the Aviation Detachment, Advance Base Force in 1913.

The first Advance Base Force exercise was held in January 1914. Colonel Barnett and the Advance Base Brigade were ordered to hold the island of Culebra near Puerto Rico and set about fortifying it with entrenchments, gun emplacements, and minefields. The "Black" Fleet assigned to conduct the mock assault of the island began a "bombardment" of the island on January 19 and then landed an assault force on January 21. After only a few hours, the Black Fleet's assault was declared a failure, and the exercise was considered a success.

COLT GOVERNMENT MODEL 1911A1 .45-CALIBER PISTOL

At the end of the nineteenth century, U.S. armed forces were armed with .38-caliber revolvers. After the campaign in the Philippines, however, the U.S. Army came to the conclusion that the .38-caliber pistol lacked sufficient stopping power—reports indicated that some Filipinos had been shot six times and still kept attacking. The Army, therefore, began reviewing replacement pistols in 1906.

The U.S. military chose a giant .45-caliber automatic pistol designed by John Moses Browning and manufactured by Colt in 1907. The Army was not entirely happy with the M-1907 pistol and requested further tests. The pistol performed remarkably well, however, and on March 29, 1911, the Browning-Colt M-1911 .45 became the official sidearm of the U.S. military.

The pistol was very reliable and packed significant stopping power. Nicknamed "Old Slab-Sides" for its broad, flat handle, the venerable pistol received an overhaul and became the A1 model. The changes were primarily cosmetic, with alterations to the handle, trigger, and frame, none of which changed the overall excellent performance of the pistol. Holding seven .45-caliber rounds in its magazine, the gun was most effective at close range, within about 30 feet.

The 1911A1 model was so popular that it remained in service into the 1980s. Even then, efforts to change the armed services standard sidearm were resisted by the top brass, who had gone through their own service with the .45 and felt there was no need for a new weapon. Even Congress spoke out against replacing the pistol, and it wasn't until the 1980s that the .45 was replaced with the M-9 Beretta 9mm pistol.

But old habits die hard, particularly in the Marine Corps. In 1986 a limited number of M-1911 MEU (SOC) .45-caliber pistols were re-engineered to make them more user friendly with an ambidextrous safety, rubber grips, high-profile combat sights, and stainless-steel magazines with an extended floor plate.

★★★

Cuba and Nicaragua continued to pose problems during Biddle's tenure. In 1912, the Marines found themselves once more in Cuba. Slavery had been abolished on the island in 1886, but racism and discrimination continued long after that. In 1912, the Negro Revolution began, and again, Marines were called upon for the maintenance of the Cuban government.

The 1st Provisional Marine Regiment was mustered at Philadelphia under Colonel Lincoln Karmany. A second regiment was mustered in Key West under the command of Colonel Mahoney. When the two regiments arrived in Cuba, they were combined into a brigade under the command of Karmany. Despite the ostensible reason for the presence of the Marines in Cuba, the prime concern during this intervention, as during the 1906 intervention, was the protection of American-owned sugar plantations and mines. The Marines stationed platoons or companies in or near 26 towns and railroads. By July, the Cuban government seemed to have things under control once more, and the Marines pulled back to Guantanamo Bay. By the end of the month they returned to the United States.

Problems persisted in Nicaragua as well. In July 1912, General Luis Mena, the minister of war, launched a revolution against the conservative government of President Adolfo Díaz. The U.S. diplomatic mission at Managua soon called for help. One hundred sailors and Marines from the USS *Annapolis* landed at Managua on August 4, and Butler's Panama Battalion arrived at Corinto 10 days later. On September 4, the 1st Provisional

Marine Regiment under the command of Colonel Joseph "Uncle Joe" Pendleton landed at Corinto to support Butler's battalion. Pendleton assumed command of the Marine forces.

Butler's battalion was given the assignment of opening the railroad to Granada. This turned out to be a difficult task as the battalion ran into stiff resistance. Near Masaya, two forts overlooking the railway, Coyotepe and Barranca, bombarded Butler's battalion. Butler decided to press ahead with the intention of returning to Masaya, but even so, it took his battalion 5 days to cover the last 15 miles to Granada. By that time, heat, exhaustion, and disease were beginning to take their toll on the battalion, and Butler himself was suffering from a fever of 104 degrees; his men began calling him "Old Gimlet Eye."

Butler managed to convince Mena to surrender, but the rebellion continued under the leadership of General Benjamin Zeledón. Butler and Pendleton met at Masaya at the beginning of October to deal with Coyotepe and Barranca, which were still held by the rebels. On October 2, Pendleton ordered Zeledón to surrender. Zeledón refused, and the following day, Pendleton bombarded the forts.

On the morning of October 4, before the sun came up, 850 Marines and sailors launched an attack on the forts. It was over in 37 minutes. Twenty-seven rebels had been killed and another nine captured. The Marines suffered 4 dead and 14 wounded. The Nicaraguan Army captured Massaya that same day, and two days later another American force occupied León. In November, Pendleton returned to the United States, and Butler, once again, returned to Panama. The Marines suffered 37 casualties during the Nicaraguan intervention.

General Biddle retired from the office of commandant on February 24, 1914. Two days later, George Barnett was named major general commandant. Barnett, the first graduate of the U.S. Naval Academy to serve as commandant, was appointed to the office for a fixed four-year term with the possibility of a second four-year extension, a new policy legislated by Congress in 1913. Marine recruiting continued apace under Barnett's tenure, and the Naval Station at Port Royal, South Carolina, was renamed Paris Island and received recruits from east of the Mississippi. Mare Island in California received recruits from west of the Mississippi.

CHAPTER 6: THE MARINES HAVE LANDED: THE AGE OF U.S. IMPERIALISM

★★★

Revolution swept into Mexico in 1910. The government of General Porfiro Díaz, which had been in power since 1876, was essentially a dictatorship that, although it had brought greater stability to Mexico, had placed heavy burdens upon the Mexican people. In 1910, the liberal leader Francisco Madero launched a revolution to remove Díaz from office. Madero earned significant support from the Mexican people, and in 1911, Díaz was forced to resign from the presidential office. Madero was elected president shortly thereafter.

Unfortunately, Madero was unable to bring stability to Mexico. Emiliano Zapata, for example, denounced Madero, called for sweeping agrarian reform, and led a peasant uprising in Morelos. At the same time, Profirist generals led a counterrevolution against Madero's government. Madero was assassinated in 1913, and General Victoriano Huerta seized control of the government. Zapata continued to resist Huerta's government as did Francisco "Pancho" Villa, who had supported Madero's revolution in 1910.

American businessmen had invested heavily in Mexico during Porfiro Díaz's long presidency. Although Huerta ordered his forces to protect American lives and property, newly elected President Woodrow Wilson seemed to take the assassination of Madero personally. An idealist and staunch defender of democratic ideals, Wilson refused to recognize Huerta's government and lifted an arms embargo to Mexico, tacitly supporting Zapata and Villa's opposition to Huerta. In addition, Wilson ordered the Navy to patrol the Mexican coast.

On April 9, 1914, the USS *Dolphin* put into port at Tampico, Mexico, to buy gasoline. The paymaster and crew went ashore and were promptly arrested and thrown in jail. General Huerta immediately ordered their release and issued an apology for the misunderstanding. Rear Admiral Henry Mayo, however, felt the apology was insufficient and demanded a 21-gun salute to the American flag. This Huerta refused, and Wilson, justifying intervention with ideas such as democracy and justice, ordered the Army to prepare a land invasion of Mexico, ordered the Navy to blockade Mexico's ports, and ordered Colonel John Lejeune to prepare his Marine expeditionary brigade to land at Tampico.

However, President Woodrow Wilson soon learned that a German merchant ship was bound for Veracruz with a shipment of weapons. Wilson ordered Rear Admiral Frank Fletcher to seize Veracruz immediately. Fletcher notified the military commander of Veracruz, General Gustavo Maass, of his orders and requested that he offer no resistance. President Huerta eventually ordered Maass to withdraw, but the order arrived too late, and Maass prepared to repel the invasion.

Lieutenant Colonel Wendell "Buck" Neville's 2nd Regiment of Marines and Lieutenant Colonel Albertus Catlin's 3rd Provisional Regiment of Marines, which was mustered from the fleet, some 600 Marines in all, landed at Veracruz on the morning of April 21. Initially, the landing was unopposed, and the Marines quickly seized the cable station and the power plant, but by midday Neville's regiment had become caught up in a fire-fight over the rail yard. By evening, Butler's Panama Battalion arrived to support Neville and Catlin.

The next day, the fighting degenerated into house-to-house combat, with the Marines sometimes literally breaking though the walls of one house into the next. By noon, Veracruz, for the most part, had been secured, though sniping would continue for some time. American casualties numbered 17 dead, including 4 Marines, and 63 wounded, including 13 Marines. Nine Marines were awarded the Medal of Honor for their service in Mexico. Among them was Major Smedley Butler, who initially refused the honor, claiming that he had not done anything particularly heroic, but was told to keep it and wear it.

Colonel Lejeune led the new Marine Advance Base Force on shore and took command of the 3,141 Marines on shore. By April 24, Veracruz had been pacified, and on April 29, Army Brigadier General Frederick Funston assumed command of operations. On May 1, Colonel Tony Waller arrived and, as senior Marine officer, took command of the Marine brigade. The Marines remained in Veracruz until November 23, 1914. Although there was some consideration of continuing with an invasion of Mexico, General Huerta resigned and fled Mexico in July. If the political situation in Mexico was a mess, the situation in Haiti had reached nightmarish proportions. Between 1908 and 1915, seven presidents had been assassinated or overthrown. In 1914, Haiti's finances collapsed, and several foreign banks, including British, French, German, and American institutions, wished to retrieve the money they had loaned the country. The United States offered to indemnify the country's debt, but the offer was refused. In

December 1914, a Marine detachment landed at Port-au-Prince and seized the $500,000 remaining in Haiti's treasury for safekeeping.

In March 1915, Vilbrun Guillaume Sam took the president's office, but he failed to maintain order. In July 1915, a violent riot in Port-au-Prince led Sam to order the execution of 167 political prisoners. Facing an enraged mob, Sam sought refuge with the French Embassy, but the mob found him and killed him, making him the eighth president overthrown by Haiti's "revolutionary habit." On July 28, Captain George Van Orden led an improvised Marine regiment from the armored cruiser *Washington* into Port-au-Prince and restored order. Colonel Eli Cole arrived in Port-au-Prince on August 4 with the 2nd Regiment of Marines, and Colonel Waller arrived on August 15 with the 1st Regiment.

Rear Admiral William Caperton supervised the election of a new president and the signing of a treaty placing Haiti under American protection. In the meantime, Waller took control of several customs houses and garrisoned several towns. The Haitian insurgents, who called themselves *cacos* after a red-plumed bird of prey, had proven to be one of the biggest problems for Haitian politics. Essentially bandits who exploited the peasantry, they frequently played kingmaker for ambitious politicians and offered their machetes to the highest bidder. Waller initially offered a subsidy worth $20 to *caco* chiefs and $10 to other *caco* bandits if they would turn in their weapons. He also initiated patrols into the interior of the island and gave Smedley Butler, who had been brought over from Panama to act as executive officer, the assignment of hunting down the remaining *cacos*.

Butler caught up with the *caco* leader, "General" Rameau, on September 18 and captured him. He then moved to scout out the *caco* mountain stronghold Fort Capois. Butler's patrol of 26 Marines was ambushed on October 24. Their pack horses were scattered; the horse carrying the unit's machine gun was killed, and the weapon sank to the bottom of a stream. As a firefight erupted, Sergeant Dan Daly volunteered to retrieve the sunken machine gun, for which he was awarded a second Medal of Honor. By morning, the firefight ended, leaving some 18 *cacos* dead and only 2 Marines wounded. The rest of the *cacos* fled, allowing Butler's Marines to capture their base, Fort Dipitié. Waller assigned five companies to assist Butler, and on November 5, Butler captured the Fort Capois.

Finally, Butler moved against an old French bastion, Fort Rivière on the 4,000-foot-high Montagne Noir, a supposedly impregnable *caco* fortress. Butler led three companies of Marines and one company of sailors for his assault, which began on November 17, 1915. He reached the wall of the fortress with 24 Marines only to find that the main gate had been bricked up. Butler found an open drain, however, and as bullets flew around them, Sergeant Ross Iams dashed through the drain. Private Samuel Gross pushed past Butler to follow Iams, and Butler quickly led the rest of his Marines in as well. A fierce bayonet and machete melee ensued, but the Marines emerged victorious. Fifty *cacos*, including the last of the *caco* generals, "General" Josefette, were killed. Butler, Iams, and Gross were awarded the Medal of Honor for the capture of Fort Rivière, Butler's second, which he accepted without complaint this time.

By the time the *cacos* had been defeated, a new Haitian government had been created at Port-au-Prince. A Haitian constabulary was created as well, and the new Haitian government agreed to allow American officers to lead it. The first commandant of the *Gendarmerie d'Haiti* was Lieutenant Colonel Smedley Butler. Initially composed of 55 Marine officers and 1,530 gendarmes, the *Gendarmerie* proved quite successful, maintaining order and improving the infrastructure of the country by building roads, improving water supply and sanitation, refurbishing lighthouses, and acting as fire fighters. In February 1916, the *Gendarmerie* became Haiti's official police force.

In the following year, however, civil war broke out across the border in the Dominican Republic. President Juan Isidro Jiménez dismissed General Desiderio Arias, his chief political rival, from his post as minister of war. Arias seized control of the capital Santo Domingo, and by April 1916, the situation had become completely chaotic. On May 5, Marine Captain Frederic Wise landed at Port-au-Prince with the 6th and 9th Marine companies and then moved to Fort Geronimo just outside Santo Domingo. Arias agreed to evacuate Santo Domingo nine days later and withdrew to Santiago de los Caballeros in the mountains.

By April 15, a Marine battalion had been assembled under Major Newt Hall, and Santo Domingo was captured without any resistance. President Jiménez refused to aid the Americans against his fellow countrymen and resigned his office. The United States had no intention of allowing Arias's revolution to succeed, however. On May 26, Wise landed at Monte Cristi, where he encountered 150 rebels, whom he defeated easily, primarily with the use of a single machine gun. Another detachment of Marines landed at Puerto Plata on June 1, and pushed the rebels into the hills.

General Pendleton landed at Monte Cristi with the 4th Regiment on June 18, where he left a garrison of 235 Marines while he proceeded with the remainder of his regiment—833 officers and men—toward Santiago de los Caballeros. Pendleton encountered a rebel force at Las Trencheras, a ridgeline crossing the road to Santiago. Pendleton bombarded the ridge with his artillery while his machine guns fired on the rebel positions.

On June 27, the Marines charged the ridge and cleared it. The rebels counterattacked the next night, but were shredded by Pendleton's machine guns, and on July 3, Pendleton cleared the road to Santiago, defeating the last rebels at Guyacanas. On July 4, Major Hiram Bearss, who had landed at Puerto Plata with a battalion, marched into Santiago without resistance.

As in Haiti, Pendleton paid the citizens of the Dominican Republic for their firearms and collected some 53,000 guns, but problems persisted. The governor of Pacifcador Province, Juan Perez, refused to recognize American authority. Fearing that Perez would free and arm the prisoners being held in the *fortaleza* at San Francisco de Macorís, Marine First Lieutenant Ernest Williams led a dozen men to take custody of the prisoners. They were greeted by gunfire that wounded eight of Williams's men, but Williams and the others managed to gain entry to the fort. After two Dominicans were killed at point-blank range, the rest of the garrison laid down their arms. Williams was awarded the Medal of Honor. Perez fled into the countryside with his loyal followers, but Marines from La Vega and Sanchez pursued him until his following had been dispersed.

In November, Navy Captain Harry Knapp was named military governor and given the assignment of pacifying the Republic. The 2nd Marine Brigade occupied 10 towns on the island, and the *Guardia Nacional Dominicana*, modeled on the *Gendarmerie d'Haiti*, was activated in April 1917. The various Latin American entanglements in which the Marines became involved throughout the first two decades of the twentieth century were relatively minor, however, when compared with the threat looming on the horizon. By 1917, the First World War had been underway in Europe for three years. President Woodrow Wilson, elected initially in 1912, was re-elected in 1916 on a platform that promised to keep the United States out of the European conflict. But Wilson believed that the First World War was largely a struggle against German imperialism to make the world "safe for democracy."

Despite the irony of such an attitude, Wilson began preparing for what he viewed to be inevitable: American entry into the Great War. In 1916, Congress approved a naval construction plan intended to make the U.S. Navy "second to none." One hundred fifty-seven ships were approved for construction as was an increase of 25,000 naval personnel. The Naval Act of 1916 also approved a proportional increase in the size of the U.S. Marine Corps, authorizing 597 officers and 14,981 enlisted men. The officer corps was expanded to include seven brigadier generals. Three staff positions—adjutant, quartermaster general, and paymaster general—received promotions to brigadier general, as did four line officers, Cole, Lejeune, Pendleton, and Waller. In addition, a small Marine Corps Reserve was created, and the president was given the authority to increase the size of the Corps by 2,515 officers and men during wartime.

CHAPTER 7

RETREAT, HELL! WE JUST GOT HERE!: WORLD WAR I

The Great War began in August 1914. At the outbreak of hostilities in Europe, President Woodrow Wilson immediately announced American neutrality, reflecting the prevailing American mood that the Great War was a European affair, not an American one. Indeed, he campaigned in and won the election of 1916 with the slogan "We didn't go to war."

But despite Wilson's admonitions to Americans to remain neutral "in thought as well as in action," his own beliefs created bias regarding the conflict. Wilson envisioned a world made "safe for democracy" and based upon the American values of democracy, freedom, and capitalism. A German victory would ensure the dominance of autocracy and imperialism. Indeed, even should the Allies—Great Britain, France, and Russia—prove victorious, a liberal, democratic future was not ensured; Britain and France both had extensive colonial empires and Russia was still ruled by the tsars, who were little better than Germany's Kaiser.

Wilson's fears were justified as Great Britain imposed a naval blockade around Germany, declaring the North Sea a war zone and lacing it with mines. American merchant ships were intercepted and their cargoes confiscated as contraband. Wilson protested such actions, but Great Britain was determined to exploit its naval advantage.

Germany likewise took actions that affected neutral countries. While Britain controlled the surface of the seas, Germany had gained control of its depths through the use of submarines. From the ocean depths, however, it was difficult to determine the nationality of vessels in war zones. Germany declared a policy of unrestricted submarine warfare in an effort to break Britain's blockade and warned American citizens against travel on British or French vessels.

Unfortunately, that policy brought Germany into conflict with the United States in a much more dramatic fashion than did British infringements on the rights of neutral countries. On May 7, 1915, a German U-boat sank the British ocean liner *Lusitania* off the coast of Ireland. Of the 1,198 people who died in the attack, 128 were Americans. The tragedy sharply turned American opinion against Germany. The German government backed away from the policy of unrestricted warfare for a time, and the United States remained neutral for a while longer.

Trade with Germany and the other Central Powers—Germany, Austria-Hungary, the Ottoman Empire, and Bulgaria—dropped precipitously as the British blockade continued. Germany initially had demanded that if the United States intended to remain neutral, it must persuade Britain to follow "the rules of international law." Wilson's sympathies clearly lay with the Allies, however, and he conveniently ignored this demand. Furthermore, it quickly became apparent that American financial well-being was dependent on trade with the Allies. Wilson allowed American banks to make several loans to the British and the French in their war effort against Germany—these loans totaled $2.3 billion by 1917. In comparison, American banks only loaned $23 million to Germany. These dealings greatly strengthened the U.S. economic position in the world, but it also made the Allies economically dependent on the United States.

On January 31, 1917, facing the stiff British blockade, Germany announced that it would resume its policy of unrestricted submarine warfare.

Some within the German government, including Chancellor Bethmann-Hollweg, had argued against the resumption of this policy, but the military leaders maintained that the United States was already involved in the war financially and that an actual declaration of war would have little military impact on the conflict in Europe. Three days after the formal declaration of the resumption of unrestricted submarine warfare, President Woodrow Wilson broke off diplomatic relations with Germany.

In February and March, five American ships were sunk by German U-boats. On February 24, the United States learned of the infamous Zimmerman telegram sent from Germany to Mexico suggesting a military alliance between Germany, Japan, and Mexico should the United States declare war on Germany; Mexico was promised the return of territories lost during the Mexican War (see Chapter 3). With such a threat to the freedom of the seas and to American lives and property, President Wilson asked Congress to declare war on Germany, which it did on April 6, 1917.

★★★

Major General Commandant George Barnett was determined to see the Marine Corps at the forefront of the American Expeditionary Force (AEF) to be sent to France, and on May 29, President Wilson approved the inclusion of a Marine regiment as an infantry unit in the AEF. By the time of the American entrance into the First World War, Marine Corps strength had risen to 511 officers and 13,214 enlisted men. Even so, Marine regiments tended to be undermanned by regular Army standards and numbered perhaps 800 to 1,000 men each. They were generally organized into rifle companies of about 100 men each, but companies and regiments were scattered throughout the world, in keeping with their most recent missions as colonial infantry units.

For service in Europe, the Marine regiment to be included in the AEF needed to be organized and equipped according to the current standards of the U.S. Army, which meant that unit strength would need to be increased to 250 men per company, and those units would then need to be organized into battalions and regiments. Modern combat units, such as machine gun companies, would need to be added as well. As a first step, Commandant Barnett recalled Marine companies from Norfolk, Cuba,

Haiti, and other stations around the world to fill out existing companies and create the 5th Regiment of Marines, which consisted of 70 officers and 2,689 enlisted men.

Barnett also initiated an aggressive recruiting campaign based on the slogan "First to Fight." Three officers and 33 enlisted men from the new Marine Corps Reserve joined regular Marine units almost immediately. Recruiting depots at Parris Island and Mare Island and temporary recruiting centers at the Philadelphia Navy Yard, the Brooklyn Navy Yard, and the Norfolk Navy Yard were soon flooded with volunteers. Parris Island, South Carolina, became the center of Marine Corps training and quickly earned a reputation for military toughness. Furthermore, Barnett established an advanced combat-training program at the recently acquired base at Quantico, Virginia. There, Marines destined for service in Europe received specialized training in modern warfare from veteran British and French officers. Those recruits who wished to be commissioned as officers were required to complete the rigorous program of instruction at the officer candidate school. By December 1918, the Marine Corps had grown to peak strength of 78,839 officers and enlisted men.

PARRIS ISLAND

For more than 135 years, the Marine Corps had no organized instruction program for its recruits. For the most part, any instruction Marines received was conducted at the posts to which the Marines were assigned or on board ship. The need for structured training was recognized early in Marine Corps history by Commandant Franklin Wharton early in the nineteenth century, and it was reiterated later that century by James Forney's reports on European Marine forces. Unfortunately, frequent budget cuts and the perpetually small size of the Marine Corps prevented the development of a centralized, structured training program.

In 1911, Commandant William Biddle instituted a number of reforms including an organized training program. Recruits were required to complete two months of rigorous training at one of four training depots: Philadelphia (PA), Norfolk (VA), Puget Sound (WA), and Mare Island (CA). In 1912, Mare Island became the sole west coast training depot, and in 1915, east coast training was shifted to Parris Island, South Carolina, the site that would become synonymous with Marine recruit training.

For a short time, Parris Island was designated "Paris Island." This was due in part to the First World War. In 1917, before the United States entered the war, there were only 835 recruits at the depot. The enormous expansion of the Marine Corps to meet its duties in Europe increased the number of recruits training at the depot to 13,286 at the peak of the war. More than 46,000 Marines were trained at Parris Island over the course of 18 months.

An enormous increase in mail accompanied the expansion of Marine training. Initially, mail sent to recruits training in South Carolina was sent to Port Royal, the nearest town to the Marine base. The number of letters received by the Port Royal post office caused a great deal of confusion, however, and the Postmaster General directed that the official designation of the Marine Corps post at Port Royal, South Carolina, be changed to Marine Barracks, "Paris Island," South Carolina. This spelling remained the official spelling until 1919, when Brigadier General Joseph Pendleton, commander of the depot, learned that the historical spelling of the island was "Parris" and requested a change in the designation.

The new recruit's experience at Parris Island came as a shock. The recruit was stripped of his civilian clothes, shaved and numbered, lectured on patriotism and Marine heroism, and given a complete physical examination. The training course lasted eight weeks. During the first three weeks, recruits engaged in intense physical conditioning, forced marches, swimming, and other physical training as well as drilled and practiced personal combat and bayonet combat. When they weren't training, the recruits were busy building barracks. The fourth and fifth weeks were dedicated to continue drilling and guard training as well as boxing and wrestling. The last three weeks were devoted to marksmanship. The instruction at Parris Island was grueling. One recruit remarked, "The first day I was at camp, I was afraid I was going to die. The next two weeks my sole fear was that I wasn't going to die. After that I knew I'd never die because I became so hard that nothing could kill me."

This regimen of training would continue largely unchanged into the 1950s. After the German invasion of Poland in 1939, the training program was reduced to a mere four weeks to train as many recruits as rapidly as possible. The result was very low scores in marksmanship, and the training period was restored to an eight-week program to properly train recruits. Although the Second World War would bring an incredible influx of new recruits, requiring Parris Island to produce some 6,800 Marines every month from December 1941 through February 1942, the regimen of training remained largely the same as it had during the First World War.

★★★

The 5th Regiment of Marines under Colonel Charles Doyen sailed on June 14, 1917, and arrived at Saint-Nazaire on June 27. General "Black Jack" Pershing, commander of the AEF, spread the 5th Regiment along the front to act as line-of-communication troops and military police. A second regiment, the 6th, commanded by Colonel Albertus Catlin, and the 6th Machine Gun Battalion, led by Major Edward Cole, reached France by February 1918, and by early 1918, the 5th and 6th Regiments were consolidated as the 4th Brigade, 2nd U.S. Division.

Doyen was promoted to the rank of brigadier general and given command of the brigade, which numbered 280 officers and 9,164 enlisted men, rivaling the size of some of the battered British and French divisions at the front. Although the Matrines who made up the majority of the brigade were new recruits, a substantial percentage of their numbers were "old-timers," men with at least one year of service in the Corps. Twenty percent of the 5th and 6th Regiments were such "old-timers," significantly more than regular Army units, of which experienced soldiers made up only about 5 percent.

SPRINGFIELD "03" 30-06 RIFLE

After the U.S. military equipped its soldiers with the Krag-Jorgensen rifle, interest began to rise in an American rifle for the infantry soldier and Marine. The Krag-Jorgensen worked well, but was a bit unwieldy in restricted combat zones, such as the jungle. In 1906, the Springfield Model 1903 (originally commissioned with a 30-inch barrel, which was reduced to 24 inches for the final version) was adopted for general use. Chambered for .30-caliber ammunition, it was a well-made, reliable rifle whose only disadvantage was its small magazine, which held only five bullets.

The Springfield 1903 was eventually replaced by the Garand M-1, but not before it underwent several modifications, including an attachment which allowed it to be fired as a fully automatic rifle in 1918. It remained in use well into World War II, where it was equipped with a scope and used as a sniper rifle.

General Pershing tried to remove all officers he considered too old or infirm to command units in the field, and General Doyen was among those who returned to the United States. Marine Colonel "Buck" Neville, now commander of the 5th Marines, should have been given command of the Marine brigade, but Pershing chose Army Brigadier General James Harbord as its commander. Neville couldn't have been happy about being passed over for an officer who, although he held a higher rank, probably had less experience. When Harbord arrived at the Marine camp, Neville presented him with a pair of Marine Corps insignia. To his credit, Harbord pinned them to his collar.

HOTCHKISS MACHINE GUN

Early twentieth-century light and heavy machine guns suffered from over-heating problems. A partial solution was to use water jackets to surround part of the barrel, like on one of the first true machine guns, the Maxim gun. But the liquid-cooled guns limited their usefulness in the field, as the need for water often reduced the weapon's effectiveness. (Stories were told of soldiers urinating into the water jackets to supply liquid.)

One of the first practical air-cooled guns was the Hotchkiss Modèle 1914, an 8mm heavy machine gun that used a series of broad metal discs to increase the radiation area, drawing heat away from the barrel. The Army tested one of these machine guns in 1900 against a water-cooled machine gun, and found its service to be comparable. With a 2,600-yard range and a cyclic rate of 500 rounds per minute, the Hotchkiss was mounted on a tripod, which made it fairly portable for a 3-man crew despite its 115-pound total weight.

The Hotchkiss gun proved its worth in World War I, when the French army used it in several battles, including one where 2 machine guns fired more than 150,000 rounds over 10 days with ease. The AEF adopted the Hotchkiss machine gun when it arrived in France.

★★★

The Germans began their spring offensive along the Chemin des Dames north of the Aisne River on March 21, 1918. The staggering assault drove the British back some 40 miles. The British were able to contain the German offensive, however, and after a second assault on April 9 failed, the German High Command turned its attention to the French. On May 27, General Erich Ludendorff, commanding the German forces, launched an offensive that opened a four-kilometer gap in the front, surprising the French and sending them reeling backward.

The Germans had achieved a stunning breakthrough. General Pershing initially desired to keep all U.S. forces separate from British or French units, but the German breakthrough convinced him that American forces were needed immediately. One infantry regiment from the 1st Division and the entire 2nd Division, including the 4th Marine Brigade, moved forward on May 28 to the Marne River to block the German advance.

On May 31, the Marine Brigade was assigned to the Paris-Meux sector of the front, to a place called Château-Thierry. The demoralized French 43rd Division retreated before Ludendorff's assault, and one French major, upon encountering them, informed the Americans that they should retreat quickly as the Germans were advancing on their position. Captain Lloyd Williams is credited with replying to the stunned French officer, "Retreat, hell! We just got here!" On June 1, the U.S. 2nd Division formed a line along the Paris-Metz road, the 5th and 6th Marine Regiments holding the center, flanked by the 23rd Infantry on the left and the 9th Infantry on the right. The next day, the German 28th Division, driving toward Paris, assaulted the Marine center. With deadly accuracy, the Marines began to fire at the German division as it advanced, shooting enemy soldiers at an astonishing 800 yards, three times standard combat range. The Germans faltered under the Marine fire and then dove for cover.

The Germans attacked several times over the next couple of days, but the Marines held their position. By June 5, the Germans fell back. This was as close as the Germans came to Paris, only 25 miles away.

It seemed that the Germans had underestimated the military impact of the American forces. General Ludendorff knew that the United States, eventually, would be able to field an enormous army. Germany's only hope was to demoralize the Americans before that could happen by hurting them so badly that President Wilson would have second thoughts about sending more Americans to die in a foreign land. Ludendorff ordered his forces to hit American units particularly hard.

The 461st Imperial German Infantry, a 1,200-man regiment reinforced with Maxim machine guns, took up defensive positions in Belleau Wood. Standing on a small hillock of rocky ground, Belleau Wood stretched about a mile and a half north and south and about half a mile east and west. The trees were tall, relatively narrow in diameter, but so closely spaced together that visibility was limited to about 20 feet. The Wood itself had little strategic significance for the German High Command, but, determined to wound the Americans severely, the Germans prepared for a fierce battle.

On June 6, the 1st Battalion, 5th Marines advanced across a field splattered with blood-red poppies toward Hill 142 west of Belleau Wood. The Germans waited for the Americans to approach across the field before firing on them, but the Marines were able to take the hill by noon. With Hill 142 under control, the 2nd Battalion, 5th Marines and the 2nd and 3rd Battalions, 6th Marines advanced into Belleau Wood itself.

The Marines were armed relatively poorly. They were equipped with Springfield rifles and bayonets as well as automatic pistols and were supported by Hotchkiss machine guns, but they had few grenades, no artillery—not even mortars—and no signal flares. The German machine gunners would have to be shot or stabbed, and the attack quickly became fragmented and confused as the Americans discarded the obsolete tactics they had learned from the French and improvised.

Floyd Gibbons, a war correspondent, was a stunned witness as First Sergeant Daniel Daly, a Medal of Honor recipient during the Boxer Rebellion and in Haiti, encouraged his platoon by leaping forward and yelling, "Come on, you sons of bitches—do you want to live forever?"

An apt summary. The Marines took two thirds of Belleau Wood by the end of the day but lost more men in a single day than it had in its 143 year history: 1,087 dead and wounded. Many companies reported that all of their officers had died in the assault and that NCOs had to take their place.

One of the few Marines who escaped the battle unscathed was John Quick, the sergeant, now a major, who had stood in front of enemy fire at Cuzco Well in Cuba and who had fought at Sohoton Cliffs in the Philippines. Learning that Lieutenant Clifford Cates needed ammunition at the village of Bouresches, Quick commandeered a truckload of ammunition and grenades and drove it under constant fire to Cates. Miraculously, he made it to the village, and wisely, he decided to stay there rather than risk a return trip.

The following day, the Marines reinforced their position, digging a number of shallow pits that someone dubbed "foxholes." The Germans counterattacked on June 8, and the Marines attacked again on June 9. After several days of bloody hand-to-hand combat, the Marines finally managed to control the northern tip of Belleau Wood by June 12. On June 13, the Germans launched a counterattack led off by an artillery barrage and mustard gas and followed by a fresh wave of storm troopers.

John "Johnny the Hard" Hughes's 1st Battalion, 6th Marines withstood the terrifying cloud of gas and the shattering artillery barrage and managed to rise to meet the German assault. The Marines held their positions. Major Hughes quipped, "Have had terrific bombardment and attack .... Everything is okay .... Can't you get hot coffee to me?"

Hughes's desire for coffee was a light-hearted comment on the status of his men; the Marine brigade was beaten and exhausted. Some of the battalions had been reduced to one third strength, and Hughes's battalion alone had suffered 450 casualties. General Harbord demanded that the Marines be relieved. The Army's 7th Infantry replaced the Marine Brigade on June 16, and the Marines went into reserve. The Army fared no better than the Marines had in clearing the Wood, and by June 23, the Marines were again in Belleau Wood.

Three days later, General Harbord could report that the Marines controlled the entire Wood. The 4th Marine Brigade had lost more than 5,183 men killed or wounded in the battle for Belleau Wood, more than half their initial strength. Captain Williams, who had so defiantly retorted "Retreat, hell!" to the retreating French officer before the battle, was among the dead. General Degoutte, commander of the French Sixth Army, declared that Belleau Wood would officially bear the designation, *Bois de la Brigade de Marine*, the Marine Brigade's Wood.

★★★

By this time, Brigadier General John Archer Lejeune had arrived in France and extended Commandant Barnett's offer of an additional Marine brigade and a Marine artillery regiment to General Pershing. Lejeune assumed that he would be placed in command of the Marine division that would be created by these additions, but Pershing, although he admired the excellence of Marines as soldiers, opposed their independent operation. He did accept the new Marine brigade as well as several Marine artillery officers, although not the whole regiment, and Lejeune was given command of a National Guard unit.

On July 14, General Harbord replaced General Bundy as commander of the 2nd Division, and Colonel Buck Neville took command of the Marine brigade. The following day, the Germans launched their last offensive of the war. The 2nd Division was sent to the southeast of Soissons to launch a counterattack, and on July 17 the Marines moved to positions in the Forest of Retz. The counterattack began the next day. By the end of the day, the 5th Marines had captured Vierzy, and on the following day, the 6th Marines passed Vierzy and advanced another mile before a German counterattack stopped them.

The fighting around Soissons was brutal. First Lieutenant Cliff Cates issued the legendary report, "I have only 2 out of my company and 20 out of some other company. We need support, but it is almost suicide to try to get it here as we are swept by machine gun fire and a constant barrage is on us. I have no one on my left and only a few on my right. I will hold."

As it turns out, Americans were not the only U.S. Marines to demonstrate their bravery. Two central Europeans serving with the 5th Marines were awarded the Medal of Honor for their bravery during the battle for the Forest of Retz. Sergeant Matej Kocak, an Austrian, single-handedly captured a German machine gun nest and then led 25 French Moroccan troops to capture another one. Louis Cukela, a Serb who had joined the U.S. Army in 1914, learned that the Germans had overrun his village. He bought his discharge from the Army, and, returning to the United States, joined the U.S. Marine Corps in 1917. When his unit was pinned down, Cukela maneuvered behind the German positions, assaulted and captured one German machine gun nest, bombed the German line with captured grenades, and captured two more guns and four enemy soldiers.

By July 19, the Germans had withdrawn across the Marne River. After only 2 days of fighting at Soissons, the Marines had 1,972 dead and wounded. In the seven weeks between their baptism by fire along the Paris-Metz road and the battle for Soissons, the 4th Marine Brigade had lost nearly its entire original strength.

LEWIS .303 MACHINE GUN

The Lewis machine gun was designed and built by Colonel Isaac Newton Lewis of the U.S. Coast Artillery, who offered it to the U.S. Army, but was turned down. He then operated a factory in Belgium and began manufacturing the gun, which was unusual in that it used a top-mounted, 47-round or 94-round circular magazine to hold the .303 rounds it fired. The gun only had one setting, full automatic, but a good machine gunner could fire single rounds, and a two-round "double-tap" was also possible. Although at 27 pounds it was too heavy for a true light machine gun, it was used by the Allies as an infantry support firearm throughout World War I and into World War II. It also proved to be an effective antiaircraft weapon, especially when placed into triple and quad mounts.

The Marine brigade was relieved on the night of July 19, and the 2nd Division was ordered on July 23 to retire to Nanteuil-le-Haudoin for rest before moving on to Nancy to receive reinforcements and training. On July 29, General Harbord was assigned to oversee the AEF's confused supply system, and Lejeune, who had just taken command of the 4th Marine Brigade a few days earlier, was given command of the 2nd Division. Neville resumed command of the Marine brigade.

Secretary of the Navy Franklin Delano Roosevelt, who had just visited Belleau Wood, inspected the brigade on August 5. He was so impressed by the performance of the Marines that he immediately authorized enlisted men to wear the Marine Corps insignia on their collars, a privilege that previously had been reserved for officers.

★★★

On August 6, the 2nd Division moved to Marbache, a relatively quiet sector along the Saint-Mihiel salient, where they remained for 10 days. The salient was a 16-mile deep, 25-mile wide indentation into the Allied front that the Germans had occupied since 1914. A successful campaign against Saint-Mihiel would open up important rail lines and communications for Allied forces. The American assault began with a four-hour artillery bombardment on September 12. The Army's 3rd Infantry led the assault through the pouring rain and slick mud. The 5th Marines, now under Colonel Logan Feland, and the 6th Marines, now led by Colonel Harry Lee, followed the infantry on the following day. As luck would have it, the Germans were already in the process of withdrawing, and by mid-September, Pershing's First Army captured its objectives, along with some 16,000 prisoners and

443 guns, with relative ease—relative ease compared to Belleau Wood and Soissons at any rate. The First Army suffered some 7,000 casualties during the assault; the Marines lost 132 dead and 574 wounded.

In addition, in September 1918, Brigadier General Eli Cole led the 5th Marine Brigade, consisting of the 11th and 13th Marines and the 5th Machine Gun Battalion, to Europe where it was placed under General Pershing's command to do with as he saw fit. Command of the brigade was given to Brigadier General Smedley Butler, who was disappointed to learn that the 5th brigade had been assigned to the supply service at headquarters in Brest. Butler and many other Marine officers had hoped that this new brigade would be combined with the 4th Marine Brigade to form a Marine division.

Indeed, there was some discussion of an amphibious landing by a Marine division in the Adriatic in an effort to flank the Austro-Hungarian Empire. Proper preparation of such a division, supplemented by the appropriate artillery and engineering units, would have required some time, however, almost certainly longer than the war lasted, but at the time, expectations were that hostilities would continue into 1919. The 5th Marine Brigade was broken up instead and supplied rear area duties.

★★★

Pershing's First Army moved some 40 miles west of Saint-Mihiel to relieve battered French troops in preparation for an Allied offensive along the Meuse-Argonne scheduled for September 25. In the meantime, the U.S. 2nd Division, with its Marines, and the U.S. 36th Division were attached to General Henri Gouraud's French Fourth Army for an offensive in Champagne between the Argonne Forest and Reims.

The Germans had stopped the French advance at Somme-Py in Champagne at Mont Blanc, the "White Mountain," which the Germans had held since 1914. General Lejeune proposed a plan of attack on Mont Blanc in which the Marines would make a frontal assault while the Army 3rd Infantry and French would attack from the right and left respectively.

The 6th Marines launched the attack on October 3 after a brief, 5-minute, 200-gun artillery bombardment of the German positions around the mountain. The French fell behind quickly, however, and were unable to get past the Essen Hook, an entrenched German position filled with machine guns and snipers. The 5th Marines came to their assistance, taking the Essen Hook position in a maneuver Gouraud would later characterize as remarkable.

On October 4, the 5th Marines returned to the frontal assault, passing through the 6th Marines and driving forward another 3 miles toward Saint-Étienne. Although the Germans launched a counterattack, they were unable to stop the advance of the Marines, and on October 6 the Marines captured Saint-Étienne. The 3-day battle had cost another 2,538 Marine casualties. In recognition of their accomplishments at Mont Blanc, the 5th and 6th Marines were awarded the Croix de Guerre by the French government, and General Lejeune was appointed a Commander of the Legion of Honor.

The Marine accomplishments at Mont Blanc were impressive, but they also revealed the exhaustion of the German army. Lejeune had been opposed by 11 German divisions, but only 2 were truly combat ready.

The Central Powers were crumbling. Bulgaria surrendered on September 29. In October, Germany began diplomatic inquiries based on Woodrow Wilson's 14 Points. Turkey withdrew from the conflict on October 31, as did Austria-Hungary on November 3. The German High Command's order for one last suicidal naval battle sparked a mutiny at Wilhelmshaven on October 28 that spread to Kiel by November 3 and threatened revolution in Berlin by November 9. While these events unfolded, however, the battles continued to rage along the front.

The U.S. 2nd Division was subsequently reassigned to the American First Army. During the final offensive of the war, the division was placed in the center of the First Army line and given the assignment of driving a wedge into the "Hindenburg Line." On November 1, the Marine Brigade led the 2nd Division's attack and advanced some 5 miles, capturing 1,700 prisoners.

The Germans pulled back behind the Meuse. On the night of November 3, the 9th and 23rd Infantry and the 5th Marines marched through the darkness and rain to surprise the Germans behind the front lines and just missed capturing a general. Rations dwindled, and the Marines were forced to scavenge discarded German supplies and food from French civilians, but by November 6 they had reached the Meuse River. The next day the division began preparations to cross the river and seize the east bank.

In a bloody battle, the 2nd Division crossed the Meuse River on the night of November 10, the 143rd birthday of the Marine Corps, and by morning on November 11, two battalions of the 5th Marines, with one battalion from the 9th Infantry, had managed to cross the river as well and secured a position with part of the 89th Division. At 11 that morning, an armistice was signed, ending the conflict. The bloody crossing, it seemed, had been unnecessary. The Meuse-Argonne offensive cost the Marines 273 men killed and 1,363 wounded.

CHAUCHAT AUTOMATIC RIFLE

The French-made Chauchat light machine gun was hastily designed and poorly made, and certainly fired like it. First created in 1907, it was modified in 1915 and was one of the few light machine guns available at the beginning of World War I. The Allies, however, might have been better off with nothing at all. The Chauchat was crudely stamped and its recoil stroke was so long that it was almost impossible to aim. Its oddly shaped semicircular 20-round magazine fitted into the bottom of the gun. When reloading the gun, the first round would have to be manually loaded using the cocking handle. The U.S. Army was stuck with 34,000 of these inferior guns, but used them along with the Lewis gun and Browning machine guns at the end of the war.

★★★

By the time the United States entered the First World War, the U.S. Marine Corps had established a small Marine Aeronautical Section at the Naval Aeronautical Station in Pensacola, Florida. Under the command of Captain Alfred Cunningham, the Marine Aeronautical Section consisted of 7 officers and 45 enlisted men. It had a total of five airplanes and two kite balloons at its disposal.

Shortly after Congress declared war on Germany, the Marine Aeronautical Section was moved to the Philadelphia Naval Yard. In October, it was split into two companies, the 1st Marine Aviation Squadron and the 1st Marine Aeronautic Company.

From October through December 1917, the 1st Marine Aeronautic Company flew antisubmarine patrols from Cape May, New Jersey, and in

January 1918 it was transferred to the Azores, where it continued its anti-submarine patrol missions in the eastern Atlantic, although no U-boats were spotted.

In April 1918, the 1st Marine Aviation Squadron was transferred to Curtiss Field in Miami, Florida, where it was expanded into the Marine Aviation Force in preparation for use in the Navy Northern Bombing Group to be stationed near Calais, France. Many of the pilots in the Marine Aviation Force were eager Navy pilots who accepted commissions in the Corps in order to join the fight in Europe.

Three squadrons of the Marine Aviation Force, consisting of 101 officers and 657 enlisted men were sent to France under the command of Captain Cunningham and arrived at Calais at the end of July 1918. Awaiting the arrival of the new De Havilland-4 (DH-4) bombers, the Marine aviators were assigned first to serve with Royal Air Force Squadrons equipped with De Havilland bombers. On September 28, 1918, Lieutenant Everett Brewer and Gunnery Sergeant Harry Wersheimer became the first Marines to shoot down an enemy plane.

AIRCO DH-4

Nicknamed the "flaming coffin" by its pilots, the DH-4 was designed by Geoffrey de Havilland of Great Britain. Of the 6,295 planes manufactured, 4,846 were built in the United States. The biplane was fast, with a 12-cylinder engine and a top speed of 143 miles per hour, and heavily armed, with 2 to 4 machine guns and 460 pounds of bombs. However, it had a serious design flaw in that the large gas tank was placed between the pilot and observer, which also hampered communication between the two. The DH-4 was widely used by the U.S. Air Service with many planes modified for service after World War I.

The Marine aviators were finally able to take flight in their own planes in October 1918. By that time, however the German submarine bases were no longer in use, and the Marine aviators were assigned to support the British advance. On October 14, 12 German fighters attacked an American squadron of 8 bombers over Thielt, Belgium. Lieutenant Ralph Talbot and observer Corporal Robert Robinson managed to shoot down one of the German planes, but Robinson was seriously wounded as the other German pilots shot up their DH-4. Amazingly, their "flaming coffin" didn't explode as it was wont to do, and Talbot shot down a second, stunned German pilot. Having downed two German planes, Talbot dove toward the ground, swooped over the German front lines, and landed in Belgium. Talbot died in a crash a few days later.

The Marine Aviation Force also performed its first aerial resupply mission, dropping supplies to French troops along the western front when their supply lines had been cut. From its inception, Marine aviation had always held as its first duty the support of ground troops, unlike their comrades in other branches of the service who were often individual glory seekers.

By the time of the armistice on November 11, the Marine Aviation Force had flown 57 bombing missions and dropped nearly 34,000 pounds of bombs. Marine pilots scored confirmed kills of four German planes and claimed another eight. Four Marines were killed in action. Three Marines were awarded the Distinguished Service Medal, and their observers were awarded the Navy Cross for the aerial resupply missions they flew. Second Lieutenant Ralph Talbot and Corporal Robert Robinson were awarded the Medal of Honor for their incredible performance against overwhelming odds.

Although the Marine aviators saw a very brief period of action, Marine aviation in general had been expanded vastly. By the end of the war, there were 280 officers, 2,200 enlisted men, and 340 aircraft. In February 1919, however, the Marine Aviation Force was dissolved, as was the Marine Aeronautic Company in March. Marine aviation, reduced to a mere 67 pilots, was transferred from Pensacola, Florida, to Parris Island and Quantico that summer.

MARINETTES

The Marine Women's Auxiliary was originally organized as part of the build up for the First World War. Olpha Johnson was the first woman to sign up in August 1918, and 305 more women joined the Corps during the last years of the war. The Marinettes, as they came to be called, performed several important support services during the war, mostly in clerical jobs at headquarters. The primary purpose of the Marinettes was to release men from clerical jobs so that they could fight. Nevertheless, Marinettes received instruction in drill and ceremony, served under military discipline, and wore a simple, long-skirted version of the green uniform of the Marines. Such austerity and discipline was in stark contrast to their sisters in the Navy, who, although they had been recruited earlier, still wore open collars and lace, which the Marinettes viewed as overly feminine for military service.

★★★

A few days after the armistice, the 4th Marine Brigade marched into Germany with the 2nd Division for occupation duty. Lejeune's men marched more than 200 miles through France, Belgium, and Luxembourg to the Rhine River, reaching Koblenz on December 31, 1918. The 5th Marines occupied the Wied Valley while the 6th Marines occupied several towns along the river. Ridiculously, an inspection by General Headquarters, somehow ignoring the incredible nature of the First World War, found Lejeune's troops to be in shabby condition. But the war was over, and the civilian population accepted the occupation as inevitable. The Marines turned into bored tourists rather than toughened fighting men.

The 2nd Division returned to the United States in mid-summer 1919. On August 9, 1919, the division paraded through New York City, and, three days later, the 4th Marine Brigade paraded past the White House. The brigade was demobilized at Quantico the following day, and most of the men who served in it went home carrying their gas masks as souvenirs.

By June 30, 1920, most of the Marines who had served during the First World War had been demobilized, and the strength of the Corps had been reduced to 17,165 officers and enlisted men from its peak of 78,839 men. Some 32,000 Marines had served in the AEF during the 19 months the United States participated in the First World War—2,459 of them were killed and another 8,907, 1 out of every 6 Marines who served in France, were wounded. Only 25 Marines had been taken prisoner. The 5th and 6th Regiments of Marines had been cited three times by the French government, for their achievements at Château-Thierry (Belleau Wood), the Aisne-Marne (Soissons), and the Meuse-Argonne offensive.

In January 1920, the U.S. War Department accepted the French *fourragère* in the red and green of the Croix de Guerre, an award given only to units who had been awarded three citations, for three battalions of the 4th Marine Brigade. The 4th Brigade as a whole was also cited for its actions at Château-Thierry, and the 6th Machine Gun Battalion was cited for its actions at Château-Thierry and the Aisne-Marne. Eight Marines were awarded 13 Medals of Honor, 6 by the Army and 7 by the Navy. Five Marines, including Louis Cukela and Matej Kocak, thus received two Medals of Honor for bravery, one each from the Army and the Navy.

CHAPTER 8

SEND IN THE MARINES: BETWEEN THE WARS

Some 32,000 Marines had served in Europe during the First World War, but that wasn't even half the number of Marines enlisted in the Corps in 1917 and 1918. When Commandant George Barnett offered to raise Marine units for service with the American Expeditionary Force, he had promised that the Corps would continue to meet its other obligations. During and after the First World War, therefore, the Marines continued to provide the services they had previously, serving on Navy ships and guarding naval stations. In addition, three small brigades remained in Cuba, the Dominican Republic, and Haiti, and a small Advance Base Force remained in the United States. For a brief time, the Marines also became engaged in the Russian Revolution.

In 1918, the new Communist government under Lenin freed many of the POWs captured by the Russians during the First World War. Most soldiers were of German, Austrian, or Eastern European origin, and many from the lands that would become Czechoslovakia after the end of the war. Upon their release, these men formed the Czech Legion, an anti-Communist, Czech nationalist force.

Under the belief that Britain and France would transport them back to Europe where they could fight against Austria for Czech independence—many of them had been drafted into the Austrian army against their will—the Czech Legion boarded the Trans-Siberian Railroad and traveled east to Vladivostock, a Russian Pacific port. Marines and sailors from the *Brooklyn* landed in Vladivostock, along with British, French, and Japanese forces, to maintain order in the port. The ostensible reason for the landing was to prevent any chaos the legion might raise in Vladivostock, or, more probably, to raise anti-Communist agitation. Most of the Marines were withdrawn, but a guard unit was left in Vladivostock to maintain a radio station there until 1922.

The Caribbean continued to be an important area for Marine action as well. There was a revolt in Cuba early in 1917, and the Wilson administration felt compelled to invoke the Platt Amendment, by which the United States reserved the right to maintain a naval base at Guantanamo Bay and to intervene in Cuba as it saw fit. A few Marines from the Atlantic Fleet landed in February, but with the declaration of war against Germany, they were withdrawn for service overseas. The 7th and 9th Marines and the 3rd Marine Brigade Headquarters landed on Cuba later in 1917, however. Continued Marine involvement in Cuba despite European commitments demonstrated the importance of the small island, primarily for its sugar production. The 1st Marines joined the 7th Marines in Cuba in December 1918, but by August 1919 most of the Marines had been withdrawn. One battalion remained near Guantanamo Bay until 1922.

The 9th Marines and the 3rd Marine Brigade Headquarters were transferred to Texas in July 1918, where they joined the 8th Marines. The infamous Zimmerman Telegram, a communiqué from Germany to Mexico urging the Mexican government to attack the United States should it declare war on Germany, had been intercepted in 1917, and the 8th and 9th Marines were charged with border patrol along the Texas-Mexico border.

As it turned out, Mexico didn't pose a threat, but trouble erupted once again in Haiti. Charlemagne Masséna Peralte had become chieftain of the *cacos* and had begun agitation against the island's government. Charlemagne, a member of a prominent Haitian family, had just managed to escape from a five-year sentence of hard labor for attempting to rob the *Gendarmerie d'Haiti*'s payroll. Charlemagne's sentence had been part of a system of forced labor imposed by the American government in Haiti several years earlier, a policy native Haitians despised and believed was merely a precursor to the reintroduction of slavery. Charlemagne received broad support in his opposition to American rule.

On October 17, 1918, Charlemagne attacked the *Gendarmerie* post at Hinche. Marine Colonel Alexander Williams, commandant of the *Gendarmerie d'Haiti*, requested assistance in controlling the *cacos*, and a reinforced 1st Marine Brigade was sent to Haiti. In July, Lieutenant Colonel Frederick Wise relieved Williams as commandant of the *Gendarmerie*. Over the next six months, the Marines and the Haitian *gendarmes* fought more than 130 engagements with the *cacos*, but Charlemagne's followers continued their rebellion. On October 7, Charlemagne led 300 *cacos* and stormed into Port-au-Prince itself. They were driven off by the police and Marines, leaving 30 dead behind them, but Wise realized that the rebellion would continue as long as Charlemagne was their chieftain.

The Marines laid a trap for Charlemagne near Grande Riviere, but the rebel leader never appeared. Frustrated, Marine Sergeant Hermann Hanneken, who held the rank of captain in the *Gendarmerie*, and Marine Corporal William Button, who held the rank of First Lieutenant in the *Gendarmerie d'Haiti*, decided to go after Charlemagne themselves. Disguised as *cacos*—they had colored their skin with burnt cork—and assisted by a *gendarme* "deserter," the pair bluffed its way past six *caco* checkpoints under the premise of offering Charlemagne a "captured" Browning automatic rifle (BAR). They were led before Charlemagne and the chieftain was pointed out to Hanneken, who drew his Colt .45 and shot Charlemagne twice. Corporal Button proceeded to shoot down the chieftain's bodyguard with the BAR. Charlemagne's body was carried back to Cap Haitien where it was photographed. Prints of the photograph were spread throughout the country in an effort to demoralize the *cacos*. Button and Hanneken were awarded the Medal of Honor.

BROWNING AUTOMATIC RIFLE 1918A2 .30-CALIBER LIGHT MACHINE GUN

Few weapons are more synonymous with the Marines than the .30-caliber Browning automatic rifle. Although technically a machine gun, it was classified as a rifle because it looked like one, albeit one that was four feet long. Developed by John M. Browning in 1917 and weighing just 19.5 pounds fully loaded, the BAR could be carried by one man, and today would be classified as a squad automatic weapon. The A2 model, developed in 1940, could fire single rounds or two different rates of automatic fire: 350 rounds per minute and 600 rounds per minute.

With a 20-round box magazine, the BAR was eagerly sought by nations around the world. (France alone ordered 15,000 of them.) Production began in 1918, and the gun saw heavy action in World War II, especially by the Marines in the Pacific theater, and in the Korean War.

Unfortunately, Button and Hanneken's heroic act didn't end the problems in Haiti as another *caco* chieftain, Benoit Batraville, soon emerged. The 8th Marines reinforced Colonel John Russell's 1st Marine Brigade in December 1919, and Russell set about patrolling the island looking for the *caco* chieftain. Although some 3,500 *cacos* surrendered in January and February 1920, Batraville continued to fight, and on January 14, 1920, he struck at Port-au-Prince with some 300 *cacos*. Once again, the Marines and *gendarmes* drove them off.

In the meantime, Marine pilot Lieutenant Lawson Sanderson began experimenting with dive-bombing, pushing his biplane into a steep, 45-degree dive and releasing his bombs just before flying over the target. This technique allowed Marine aviators to strike precisely the small clearings in the jungles of Hispaniola. In March, Sanderson's pilots used the technique to good effect, coordinating their efforts with Russell's patrols and devastating Batraville's *cacos*.

Batraville took his revenge on the Marines by ambushing a small patrol on April 4, 1920, and capturing Marine Sergeant Lawrence Muth (a lieutenant in the *Gendarmerie d'Haiti*). After killing Muth, the *caco* chieftain followed a voodoo ritual and ate his heart and liver, hoping to acquire his courage. Batraville was finally caught by a Marine patrol six weeks later. The Marines, enraged by the ghastly treatment Sergeant Muth had received, charged from the bush as Batraville fired on them wildly. Sergeant William

Passmore blasted the *caco* chieftain with his BAR. Amazingly, Batraville began to rise to his feet. Had Batraville actually been granted some special power from Muth's heart? Sergeant Albert Taubert shot him in the head.

The *caco* revolt came to an end with the death of Batraville. Some 2,000 *cacos* had been killed during the three years of the rebellion, while the *Gendarmerie d'Haiti* suffered approximately 75 casualties. The 1st Marine Brigade sustained only 23 casualties.

★★★

In the wake of the *caco* rebellion, American "bayonet rule" was severely criticized. Colonel Russell had court-martialed three of his Marines for killing Haitian prisoners for sport. All three were found guilty. Commandant Barnett, shocked by Russell's report, demanded that the "indiscriminate killing" of natives be stopped immediately. When the press reported Barnett's orders to Russell in 1920, Secretary of the Navy Josephus Daniels ordered Major General John Lejeune and Brigadier General Smedley Butler to investigate Marine actions in Haiti. Lejeune and Butler concluded, however, that there had been relatively few cases of Marine misconduct and all the culprits had been punished accordingly.

The Dominican Republic, across the border from Haiti, had been placed under a military government headed by Rear Admiral Harry Knapp, while Marine General "Uncle Joe" Pendleton oversaw the departments of War and Navy, the Interior, and the Police. As in Haiti, many Dominicans didn't accept American rule, and resistance built up over the next few years. In response to this persistent rebellion, the Marines instituted a series of courts and collected some 53,000 firearms in 1917 and 1918.

No big battles took place in the Dominican Republic, but there were frequent firefights. In January 1917, Lieutenant Colonel Hiram Bearss captured the bandit "Chacha" at the Consuelo sugar plantation near San Pedro de Macorís, and another bandit, Vincento Evangelista, was killed near El Seibo. In 1918, the 2nd Brigade fought 44 skirmishes, losing 5 men and wounding 13. Opposition increased in 1919, however, and Briga-dier General Ben Fuller, who had replaced Pendleton, requested additional troops. The 15th Marines arrived in February, and shortly thereafter six DH-4 aircraft arrived as well, forming the first task-organized Marine air-ground unit. As in Haiti, the aircraft proved invaluable as spotters and dive-bombers. Marines fought more than 150 skirmishes in 1919; fortunately, their casualties were low—only 3 dead and 4 wounded.

Nevertheless, opposition continued to rise in the Dominican Republic. The Wilson administration began to regret the increasing violence, and by the end of 1919, the president had decided to begin withdrawing the Marines from the small country, though they would remain for several years yet. In response, the military government of the Dominican Republic provided improved training to the new *Policia Nacional* (formerly known as the *Guardia Nacional*) and took more extensive measures to pacify the rebels. Beginning in 1920, the Marines increased their efforts to end the rebellion before they were withdrawn. They began a systematic cordon-and-search in the districts of Macorés and Seibo, and an offer of amnesty was extended to those who turned in their weapons. By May 1922, virtually all banditry had been eliminated. A new constitutional government was sworn in on July 12, 1924, and the Marines began leaving the country the following month, the last departing on September 16.

STATE DEPARTMENT TROOPS

The "limited wars" the Marine Corps conducted in the Caribbean soon earned it a reputation. It was quickly understood that if "banana republic" countries didn't act according to American wishes, the U.S. government would "send in the Marines." Whereas an Army landing might be perceived as an "invasion," and, thus, invite international criticism, the lower profile of the Marine Corps suggested a limited "intervention." For better or worse, the Marine Corps soon came to be known as the "State Department Troops."

In an article published in *Common Sense* in 1935, Smedley Butler, by then retired, commented critically on his own Marine career:

> Thus, I helped make Mexico and especially Tampico safe for American oil interests in 1914. I helped make Haiti and Cuba a decent place for the National City Bank boys to collect revenues in. I helped in the raping of half a dozen Central American republics for the benefit of Wall Street. The record of racketeering is long. I helped purify Nicaragua for the international banking house of Brown Brothers 1909–12. I brought light to the Dominican Republic for American sugar interests in 1916. I helped make Honduras "right" for American fruit companies in 1903. In China in 1927 I helped see to it that Standard Oil went its way unmolested.

> During those years, I had, as the boys in the back room would say, a swell racket. I was rewarded with honors, medals, promotion. Looking back on it, I feel I might have given Al Capone a few hints. The best he could do was to operate his racket in three city districts. We Marines operated on three *continents*.

★★★

In 1918, Secretary of the Navy Josephus Daniels named General George Barnett to a second term as Marine commandant. Unfortunately, Daniels and Barnett didn't get along well. In 1920, Daniels demanded Barnett's immediate resignation from the post of commandant, arguing that Barnett had promised to step down after the end of the First World War. Barnett claimed that no such promise had been made, but eventually he did step down, accepting a post at the new Department of the Pacific in San Francisco. On June 30, 1920, Daniels named General John Archer Lejeune Marine Corps commandant.

Lejeune had an incredible impact on the development of the U.S. Marine Corps, even though he was faced with shrinking Corps strength during peacetime. In 1919, Congress again reduced the Marine Corps to 1,093 officers and 27,400 men, a little more than a third of its wartime strength. The Corps was reduced even further during the first 2 years of Lejeune's commandancy, sinking to 962 officers and a mere 16,085 men, and Lejeune promised to cut expenses by as much as half in 1921 and 1922.

Nevertheless, Lejeune expected a high standard of duty and conduct from his Marines, and sought to improve the quality and spirit of officers and men. Hoping to replace the traditional system of promotions based on seniority, he sought the institution of an examination board to review promotions. He was unsuccessful, but his efforts demonstrated a concern with the quality of Marine leadership. He was more successful in the improvement of Marine Corps training. Lejeune expanded the Planning Section of the Marine Corps, which he had helped found, into the Division of Operations and Training in 1920 and consolidated the various Marine schools at Quantico in 1921.

One of Lejeune's principal goals in improving training and planning was preparation of the Marine Corps for amphibious warfare. He believed that the Corps had lost this focus during the First World War, becoming, in essence, a second land army. Under Lejeune's direction, the Marine Corps began preparing its amphibious assault mission. One of the planners involved in this development was Lieutenant Colonel Earl Ellis.

Ellis had enlisted in the Marine Corps in 1900 and had served as an instructor at the Naval War College. He had also served in the Philippines— where he had met Lejeune—and in France during the First World War. He was a remarkably intelligent and capable soldier and officer. Unfortunately, he was also an alcoholic. Nevertheless, or perhaps overlooking this flaw, Lejeune asked Ellis to examine possible strategies for dealing with a war in the Pacific Ocean against Japan. Japan had exploded on to the international scene during the first two decades of the twentieth century. In 1905, Japan had defeated Russia, a European great power, in a short war; in 1915, Japan's "Twenty-one Demands" successfully extorted territorial and economic concessions from China; between 1918 and 1922, Japan participated in the Siberia intervention with Britain, France, and the United States; as one of the victors during the First World War, Japan was a signatory to the Treaty of Versailles that ended the war, essentially recognizing her as a world power; in 1920, Japan was granted permanent membership on the League of Nations League Council; and in 1922, Japan was acknowledged as a major naval power at the Washington Naval Conference, which established a ratio of 5:5:3:1:1 for naval ships between Great Britain, the United States, Japan, France, and Italy, placing Japan behind Britain and the United States but before France and Italy. Because the United States governed several colonies in the Pacific, most notably the Philippines and Guam, it seemed prudent to prepare for a possible war that with Japan.

Ellis submitted an extensive report titled "Advance Base Operations in Micronesia, 1921." In considering a war in the Pacific, Ellis predicted that should war break out, Japan would strike first. As a strategy for conducting a war in the Pacific, Ellis proposed a series of amphibious assaults against Japanese-held islands in the central Pacific, beginning with the Marshall Islands. Ellis's prescription for a war against Japan involving amphibious assault forces and coordinated naval and aerial support proved prescient, and many of his recommendations became the basis for Pacific operations during the Second World War.

CHAPTER 8: SEND IN THE MARINES: BETWEEN THE WARS

In the summer of 1921, Ellis, with Lejeune's permission, set out on a clandestine tour of the Pacific islands to investigate Japanese strengths in the Pacific. Ellis wished to substantiate his suspicions that the Japanese were already developing bases on those islands. No concrete evidence was ever collected, but on May 12, 1923, Ellis died at Koror in the Palau Islands. Reports indicated that the Japanese had become aware that Ellis was a spy, and for some time many suspected that he had been killed by the Japanese secret police. After the Second World War, however, an investigation was conducted that indicated that the Japanese did not kill Ellis. Unfortunately, his efficiency and professional success had caused his superiors, including Lejeune, to overlook his serious problem with alcohol, and it's quite possible that he simply drank himself to death.

Despite the loss of Ellis, Lejeune was determined to carry forward the Marine Corps strategic goal of amphibious warfare. In 1922, the Advanced Base Force conducted exercises at Guantanamo Bay, Cuba, and Culebra, Puerto Rico. The following year Lejeune changed the name of the Advanced Base Force to Expeditionary Force, and Brigadier General Eli Cole conducted significant amphibious exercises in the Caribbean with 3,300 Marines. These exercises were fraught with problems as naval support was inadequate and troops landed on the wrong beaches, but Cole learned a great deal from the exercises. Another exercise, conducted in Hawaii in 1925, showed signs of improvement over the Caribbean exercise, but problems with air support, ship-to-shore movement, and communications persisted. Commitments abroad forced the Marine Corps to curtail amphibious exercises, but Lejeune's commitment to the development of an amphibious strategy forced the Army and the Navy to recognize that amphibious warfare was the purview of the Marine Corps.

Lejeune also supported Marine aviation. Although Marine aviation had grown remarkably during the First World War, and by 1918 consisted of some 280 officers and 2,180 men, many had become disillusioned by its actual deployment during the war. Marine aircraft had not been used to support Marine ground forces, as had been originally envisioned by early proponents such as Alfred Cunningham, and several officers suggested that the air program be discontinued. Lejeune, however, disagreed with such objections and supported Cunningham's continued efforts to expand Marine aviation. Lejeune's support convinced Congress to authorize a

Marine aviation force in 1920, and four squadrons were established. Two of those squadrons proved invaluable in Haiti and the Dominican Republic.

★★★

Lejeune's leadership and the success of Marine operations in Latin America helped the U.S. Marine Corps develop a reputation for getting the job done. When a number of railway mail cars were robbed in 1921, Postmaster General Will Harp asked President Harding for help. Harding ordered Secretary of the Navy Edwin Denby to "send in the Marines." Some 2,200 Marines took posts guarding the railcars on November 11 with Denby's orders, "If attacked, shoot, and shoot to kill." The robberies ended abruptly, and the Marines were withdrawn from their posts after only four months.

Railway mail robberies would increase again in 1926, and the Marines once again would be sent in to guard the mail. As in 1921, the robberies would end abruptly once the Marines were posted.

WHAT PRICE GLORY?

Because the U.S. Marine Corps remained a relatively small unit in comparison with the Army and the Navy, and because it was frequently targeted for dissolution by either the Army or the Navy or anti-imperialists, it was important that the Corps try to maintain a positive—and impressive—public image. Indeed, Marine Corps commandants had frequently attempted to present just such an image to politicians and citizens alike. The Marine Corps Band is a good example of such public relations, as is the remarkable press the Corps received during the First World War.

Similar efforts and developments continued during the 1920s. Commandant Lejeune made sure that the public was aware of the military prowess of the Marine Corps. Immediately after the end of the First World War, the Marine Corps came to dominate the interservice rifle and pistol shooting competitions. In addition, Smedley Butler sponsored impressive Marine football and baseball teams at Quantico. Butler also led his Marines to reenact Civil War battles, including Chancellorsville, Gettysburg, and Antietem, in which southern Marines played the role of Confederate soldiers and northern Marines played the role of Union soldiers. The reenactments were very popular events, and even President Harding attended on occasion.

Furthermore, amid the outpouring of war literature that followed the First World War—the likes of Ernst Jünger's *Storm of Steel* or Erich Maria Remarque's *All Quiet on the Western Front* (and the Academy Award–winning film), Robert Graves's *Goodbye to All That,* or the poetry of Wilfrid Owen or Siegfried Sassoon—there were a few pieces reflecting the Marine experience. Captain John Thomason Jr. wrote the popular book *Fix Bayonets!* narrating the exploits of the 4th Brigade's battles in World War I. Captain Lawrence Stallings, who had served with the 5th Marines at Belleau Wood and had been crippled when he attacked a German machine gun nest, co-authored the popular 1924 Broadway play *What Price Glory?,* which depicted two Marines competing for the love of a French woman during the First World War. Despite the romantic overtones, the play's realistic portrayal of the western front during the First World War caused some controversy at the time, and the play was banned in Boston for its language.

What Price Glory? was made into a movie in 1926 starring Victor McLaglen and Edmund Lowe and again in 1952 starring James Cagney and Dan Dailey. Smedley Butler acted as a technical consultant for *Tell It to the Marines* (1926), which starred Lon Chaney as hard-nosed Marine Sergeant O'Hara. The film presented the Marine Corps as a loyal fraternity defending American interests around the globe, following new recruit Skeet Burns (William Haines) through boot camp to the Philippines—where the Marines dutifully put down a rebellion—and to China—where the Marines fight against a warlord. Such images helped define the American Marine as tough, loyal, and proud.

★★★

Civil war in China throughout the 1920s demanded the gradual strengthening of the American Diplomatic Mission Guard stationed in Peking. When Chiang Kai-shek's Chinese nationalist party, the *Kuomintang*, marched north into the Yangtze River Valley in July 1926, Marines landed to protect American lives and property as well as foreign missionaries who requested protection. In January 1927, President Calvin Coolidge authorized the activation of the 4th Regiment of Marines, and it arrived in China that February. Brigadier General Smedley Butler was given command of the 3rd Marine Brigade, including the 4th Marines, and arrived at Shanghai on May 2, 1927. In addition to the 4th Marines, Butler's Brigade included the 6th Marines, an artillery battalion—the 1st Battalion, 10th Marines, equipped with 75mm field guns—a tank platoon, and an aviation squadron.

The 4th Marines remained in Shanghai while the rest of the brigade traveled the familiar railway up to Tientsin. By summer 1928, Chiang Kai-shek had control of Peking, but fortunately the American diplomatic mission was not accosted, and the Marines did not see any action. Marine duties under Butler's command in China focused on the demonstration of Marine presence to instill a sense of order. Butler went out of his way to make his Marines look as imposing as possible, putting on a continuous military pageant exhibiting American military strength, including the impressive "Horse Marines."

HORSE MARINES

Originally, the term "Horse Marine" was derisory. After all, Marines were supposed to be soldiers from the sea not cavalry. But in 1907, the Marine guard stationed in Peking, China, organized a mounted platoon called the Horse Marines. The platoon was intended primarily to assist with crowd control, but over the years, it became something of an elite unit. Armed with straight-blade sabers, the Marines presented a very sharp appearance in their dress blue uniforms and jauntily cocked hats, and they soon earned a reputation for their swagger and arrogance as well. While Smedley Butler commanded the 3rd Marine Brigade during the late 1920s, the Horse Marines participated in frequent patrols and parades to demonstrate the American presence in China, and for a time during the 1930s, the legendary Chesty Puller commanded the platoon. Although Marines occasionally made use of horses in other parts of the world—notably in Nicaragua—the Peking guard's mounted platoon was the only regularly constituted Marine "cavalry" unit. The Horse Marines would remain on duty in Peking until 1941, when the last of the 4th Marines were withdrawn from China.

In January 1929, the 3rd Brigade, with the exception of the 4th Marines, returned to the United States. The 4th Marines remained on duty in Shanghai, a post it would hold until just before the bombing of Pearl Harbor in 1941.

★★★

Problems also persisted in Latin America, and the Marines were sent to restore order. The government of Nicaragua was unstable, the Liberals and the Conservatives continuing to struggle for control of the government, and the order the Marines had helped to restore in 1913 began to disintegrate. In 1922, the presence of a Marine Guard helped suppress a bubbling Liberal revolution, and in 1924 American mediators witnessed an election that installed the Conservative Carlos Solarzano as president and the Liberal Juan Sacasa as vice president. With a legally elected coalition government in place, the Marines returned to the States on August 4, 1925.

Unfortunately, many Nicaraguans found such a compromise unacceptable. In October 1925, Conservative General Emiliano Chamorro launched his own revolution to overthrow the government. Solarzano and Sacasa fled the country, and Chamorro named himself president in January 1926. The Liberals struck back. General José Maréa Moncado led a Liberal army against Conservative forces at Bluefields. As violence between the two parties increased, the USS *Cleveland* landed Marines and sailors at Bluefields and declared it a neutral zone to protect American property. The United States sponsored a meeting between Liberal and Conservatives at Corinto in October, and another Marine detachment landed to provide security. Chamorro became suspicious of the conference, however, and resigned the presidency on October 30. The conference elected the Conservative Adolfo Díaz president, and the United States quickly recognized him as the legitimate leader of Nicaragua.

The civil war continued, however. General Moncado didn't approve of Díaz's presidency and remained in the field with his army. Furthermore, Sacasa, with Mexican support and claiming to be the legitimate president, returned to Nicaragua in December 1926. Sacasa and Moncado began a new rebellion, raiding coastal towns and stealing American property for supplies, while Díaz requested American help in restoring order and maintaining his government. When the Liberal forces killed an American citizen, Marines from the Special Services Squadron landed and established neutral zones at Puerta Cabeza, Prinzapolca, and Río Grande. The 2nd Battalion, 5th Marines landed at Bluefields on January 10, 1927.

Moncado marched west toward Managua. Lieutenant Colonel James Meade, commanding the 2nd Battalion, left one company to guard Bluefields and sailed with the rest of the battalion through the Panama Canal, landing at Corinto and taking the train the rest of the way to Managua. There, he assumed the defense of the capital and Díaz's government. In February, the remainder of the 5th Marines and Major Ross Rowell's

Marine Observation Squadron One—equipped with six DH-4s—landed in Nicaragua. At the end of March, the 2,000 Marines now in Nicaragua were designated the 2nd Marine Brigade and placed under the command of Brigadier General Logan Feland.

In April 1927, Coolidge assigned former Secretary of War Henry Stimson to negotiate a settlement between the Nicaraguan Conservatives and Liberals. The Peace of Tipitapa was concluded on May 4, 1927. By this agreement, the Conservatives would remain in power for the moment, both sides would lay down their weapons and disband their forces, and a United States–supervised election was scheduled for November 1928. The 2nd Marine Brigade would maintain law and order in the country and begin training the newly created *Guardia Nacional de Nicaragua*.

Unfortunately, Liberal Augusto César Sandino did not accept the disarmament order. Sandino was a *mestizo* who had a wry sense of humor and a keen awareness of public opinion. In an interview with American journalist Carleton Beals, Sandino compared himself with George Washington, and the charismatic leader quickly came to represent opposition to imperialism for many throughout Nicaragua and the rest of the world; he received support from Mexico and fundraisers were held in his honor in the United States. Sandino led his followers into the jungles of Nueva Segovia province along the Honduran border.

On July 16, 1927, Sandino led some 800 men—called Sandinistas after their leader—in an assault on a garrison of 37 Marines and 48 *guardias* at Ocotal. The battle began at 1 A.M. and raged throughout the morning and into the afternoon. At about 2:30 P.M., Major Rowell flew over the town leading four DH-4s and proceeded to strafe and dive-bomb the Sandinistas. They were routed. Fifty-six Sandinistas were killed in the battle, and approximately 110 were wounded. The Marines lost one man dead and five more wounded.

Sandino proved tenacious, however. He attacked again on September 19, at Telepaneca. The Marines and *guardias* repulsed the Sandinistas, losing two Marines and one *guardia* in the process. The Sandinistas suffered about 50 casualties. Sandino had learned an important lesson from this second defeat, however, and from that point on, the Sandinistas employed ambush tactics rather than facing the Marines in open combat.

Some 225 Marines and *guardias* were detailed to hunt down Sandino in Nueva Segovia, but he remained elusive. On October 8, a Marine reconnaissance plane was forced to land along the Sapotilla ridge north of Telepaneca. A small patrol was sent out to find the pilot and observer but was ambushed by the Sandinistas and forced to fall back, losing three men. A larger patrol set out and fought their way through the Sandinistas to the ridge by the end of the month. By then, however, it was too late; Sandino had hanged the pilot and observer.

The Marines continued to hunt down Sandino, and on November 23, Rowell's Observation Squadron spotted Sandino's fortified mountain stronghold, El Chipote. Some 200 Marines and *guardias* set out to attack it. On December 30, the Marines and *guardias* were ambushed by 1,000 Sandinistas and suffered the loss of 8 men dead and 30 wounded. The Marines and *guardias* were driven back to the village of Quilali, where the Sandinistas surrounded them. On January 6, however, salvation arrived in the form of First Lieutenant Christian Schilt and his 02U-1 Vought Corsair biplane. Under fire from the Sandinistas, Schilt landed his plane on the improvised airstrip of Quilali's main street. Over the next 2 days, Schilt flew in 1,400 pounds of supplies and flew out 18 of the seriously wounded men. Schilt was awarded the Medal of Honor.

THOMPSON M-1A1 .45-CALIBER SUBMACHINE GUN

Today, the Thompson submachine gun is remembered for its starring role in countless gangster films and for its use in the infamous "St. Valentine's Day Massacre" of 1929. But its origins stem from the U.S. military's need for a light automatic machine gun to effectively fight trench warfare.

At the end of World War I, U.S. Army general John Thompson designed a "trench broom" for clearing enemy forces out of the trenches. As the weapon would be used at short range, pistol ammunition was deemed acceptable. The classic model, the M-1928A1, came out too late for use in the war and was sold to police forces and, unfortunately, also wound up in the hands of mobsters and other underworld figures, which gave it much of its notoriety.

Public image aside, the first model of the Thompson was an overall solid gun, but it had a few problems. Able to take a 20-round box magazine, the "Tommy" gun could also handle a 50-round drum magazine, but the military passed on that idea due to the weight and complexity of the drum. There was also a fluted device on the muzzle to divert escaping gases upward to keep the gun from rising due to recoil, but that was later removed. It was capable of firing a single shot or fully automatic with a cyclic rate of 600 or 725 rounds per minute

The early version of the Thompson submachine gun, produced by Colt in 1921, was widely used by the Marine Corps in "limited wars" such as the one conducted in Nicaragua. The Navy was so impressed by its effectiveness in the hands of Marines that it adopted the later Colt M-1928A1 model in 1932, and in 1938 the U.S. Army adopted the Thompson, and modified it into the M-1A1, removing the bulky and ineffective Cutts Compensator on the muzzle, the complex rear sight, and the famous forward pistol grip (replacing it with a simple straight forehand stock). A 30-round magazine was introduced, and the Thompson saw service not only with the U.S. military, but several foreign services as well, all of whom were desperate for reliable automatic weapons. The Thompson M-1A1 saw wide use throughout the Second World War, by the Marines in the Pacific as well as the Army in Europe.

In January 1928, the 11th Regiment of Marines was assigned to the hunt. Rowell's DH-4s pummeled El Chipote on January 14, and Marines arrived there on January 26 to find it already abandoned, Sandino having escaped into Honduras. Sandino returned, however, at the end of February.

In April 1928, Captain Merritt "Red Mike" Edson set out after Sandino. The red-bearded Vermonter led several patrols along the Coco River in paddleboats. Paddling up 350 miles of river through unmapped territory was tortuous work; boats capsized, torrential rains drenched the men, malaria struck, and rations ran short. Fortunately, Edson's patrols were supported by Rowell's Marine observation squadron, which frequently dropped supplies to the Marines on the ground and acted as scouts whenever possible. Edson finally caught up to the Sandinistas in early August, fought three skirmishes with them on August 4, 6, and 14, and still Sandino escaped.

On November 4, 1928, the elections agreed upon at the Peace of Tipitapa were held under the watchful eyes of some 900 Marines. General Moncado won the election on a Liberal platform, but the Sandinistas, opposing the American presence in Nicaragua, continued their rebellion. The Marines caught up to the Sandinistas again in 1929, this time capturing one of Sandino's lieutenants, Manuel Jirón, but Sandino again escaped, this time to

Mexico. By then, more than 5,000 Marines, one third of the entire Corps, had been assigned to Nicaragua.

Secretary Stimson, now serving as Secretary of State in the Hoover administration, realized that the U.S. commitment to Nicaragua was excessive and announced that Marine forces had to be reduced. Few Marines objected to Stimson's decision. The conflict in Nicaragua had essentially come to a stalemate with the Marines chasing but never catching Sandino, and Sandino's followers remaining few in number. Furthermore, the Marines had no influence with the native population and found it impossible to control the countryside. By the end of the year, only 1,800 Marines remained in the country.

The hunt for Sandino was handed over to the *Guardia Nacional*, which remained under Marine leadership for some time. One officer in particular, *Guardia* Captain Lewis "Chesty" Puller—a First Lieutenant in the Marine Corps—continued the pursuit of Sandino. Puller served 2 tours as a *Guardia* company commander, fought 60 engagements, and was awarded 2 Navy Crosses for his service in Nicaragua. Puller would use the vast experience he earned chasing Sandino in the Pacific campaign during the Second World War, where he would earn a reputation as the toughest Marine alive.

By 1932, however, the *Guardia Nacional* had assumed responsibility of patrolling the countryside, and in November 1932, Liberal Juan Sacasa was elected president. He was peacefully inaugurated on January 1, 1933, and the next day the last of the 2nd Marine Brigade left the country. During the 6-year campaign, 47 Marines had been killed and 67 had been wounded. Duty in Nicaragua had been grueling, and the search for Sandino must have been frustrating, but the Corps learned valuable lessons about jungle fighting in Nicaragua, which they would apply to the jungles of the South Pacific in the Second World War. With the departure of the Marines, Sandino accepted the Liberal government and its offer of amnesty. *Guardia* General Anastasio Somoza had Sandino assassinated in 1934. Somoza overthrew Sacasa's government and found a dictatorship that lasted nearly 50 years.

★★★

Major General John Lejeune remained commandant through the end of the 1920s, being re-appointed first by President Harding and then by President

Coolidge. Having served nine years as commandant, Lejeune retired in 1929 and accepted a position as superintendent of the Virginia Military Institute. Wendell Neville was appointed Lejeune's successor as commandant, but he died on July 8, 1930, after having served only one year of his appointment.

Smedley Butler seemed the logical choice to pick up the mantle of commandant, but President Hoover selected Brigadier General Ben Fuller instead. Fuller more clearly represented the future of the Marine Corps. Butler vehemently hated everything—and everyone—related to the Navy, whether they were simply Naval Academy graduates or full admirals. Fuller, on the other hand, had graduated from the Naval Academy the same year as Admiral Veazie Pratt, who was then chief of naval operations. President Hoover undoubtedly hoped Fuller and Pratt would work together to promote interservice cooperation. Butler was disappointed by this decision, and one year later, flamboyant as ever and amid controversy over a public indiscretion, retired from the Corps.

"Uncle Ben" Fuller was a kind and gentle leader whose commandancy was relatively quiet. He spent most of his energy trying to protect the Corps from the impact of the Great Depression, and when the authorized Corps strength was reduced from 18,000 to 15,350, Fuller's testimony before Congress was instrumental in preventing further cuts.

Perhaps Fuller's most important contribution, however, was the appointment of Major General John Russell as assistant commandant in February 1933. Russell had served as the high commissioner of Haiti for eight years before returning to duty in 1930, and he would be appointed commandant of the U.S. Marine Corps on March 1, 1934, after Fuller's retirement. During his tenure as assistant commandant and commandant, Russell initiated a number of institutional changes that helped propel the U.S. Marine Corps into the future.

First, disliking the designation "expeditionary" that had been attached to the East and West Coast Marine units, Russell suggested that these two units be renamed the Fleet Marine Force (FMF), a suggestion that was approved by Navy Department Order 241 on December 7, 1933. The new designation made these Marine units integral parts of the U.S. Navy with the primary responsibility of establishing advance bases. One FMF would be headquartered at San Diego and the other would be headquartered at Quantico.

Second, Russell promoted the creation of the Marine Corps Equipment Board in 1933. The board's primary responsibility was the testing of landing vehicles for amphibious assaults and advance base establishment.

After 1935, annual fleet landing exercises were held once again. With the practical knowledge gathered from the exercises, it became evident that the biggest problem in conducting amphibious assaults was the movement of men and vehicles from ship to shore. (There were other problems, of course, such as the importance of the control of the sea, unity of command, and good communications, all demonstrated by the exercises conducted under Lejeune's commandancy, but these required less innovation on the part of the Marine Corps. The Navy, after all, had the responsibility of establishing control of the sea, and the importance of command and communication seemed obvious.) Frustrated by the sluggish pace with which the Navy developed new landing craft, the Marine Corps Equipment Board sought alternatives.

Andrew Higgins solved the problem. Higgins was a New Orleans boat maker who had developed the flat-bottomed Eureka boat for use in Louisiana's swamps and marshes. The Eureka boat was adopted by the Marine Corps Equipment Board and was designated the Landing Craft, Vehicle and Personnel (LCVP). Higgins went on to develop several variations of the Eureka for military use, including a boat, designated the Landing Craft, Mechanized (LCM) by the Marine Corps Equipment Board, which was capable of transporting light tanks.

Another vehicle, invented by Donald Roebling, also caught the attention of the Marine Corps. Roebling's "Alligator," an amphibious tracked vehicle invented for rescue missions in the Florida Everglades and capable of crawling over coral and onto beaches, was also adopted and was designated the Landing Vehicle, Tracked (LVT).

Russell was also instrumental in the preparation of the *Tentative Manual for Landing Operations* in 1934. The Navy published a revised edition of this manual in 1938 under the title FTP-167, *Landing Operations Doctrine, U.S. Navy.* The Army adopted a nearly identical document, FM 31-5, *Landing Operations on Hostile Shores,* in 1941.

Russell's final achievement was gaining authorization from Congress to promote officers based on merit through the use of a review board rather than based on seniority. He retired in 1936, and President Roosevelt named a relatively junior officer, Brigadier General Thomas Holcomb, as his successor. Holcomb would be appointed to a second term as commandant in 1940.

★★★

When Japan attacked China in 1937, Brigadier General John Beaumont led the 2nd Marine Brigade and the 6th Marines back to China, where they deployed to Shanghai and Tientsin to reinforce the 4th Marines. The Japanese were determined to break the western hold on the old international settlements in the Shanghai-Tientsin area. Although the 4th Marines resisted Japanese pressures for several years, relations with the Japanese worsened, and the position of the Marines in China became precarious as the Japanese became more belligerent. Concluding that U.S. armed forces would not be able to support the distant Marine position and fearing Japanese designs on the Philippines, President Franklin Delano Roosevelt decided to withdraw the Marines from China. The 4th Marines left on November 28, 1941, bound for Corregidor.

When Germany invaded Poland on September 1, 1939, the U.S. Marine Corps had strength of 18,052 men. One week after the invasion, the Corps was authorized to increase its enlisted strength to 25,000 men, recalling retired and volunteer officers if need be. On October 5, 1940, the Marine Corps Reserve—comprised of 232 officers and 5,009 enlisted men—was reactivated, and reservists were used to fill in the ranks of regular Corps units. Defense battalions were dispatched to several Pacific islands, including Johnston, Midway, Samoa, and the Palmyra Islands.

In February 1941, while participating in Fleet Landing Exercise 7, the 1st Marine Brigade was redesignated the 1st Marine Division and placed under the command of Major General Holland "Howlin' Mad" Smith. By May 1941, the division was composed of the 1st, 5th, and 7th Marines and stationed at Quantico and Parris Island until a new amphibious base was built at New River, North Carolina. In September, the 1st Marine

Division relocated to that camp, which later would be known as Camp Lejeune.

The 2nd Marine Brigade, stationed on the West Coast, was likewise expanded in 1941 to comprise the 2nd, 8th, and 9th Marines. Marine aviation was finally expanded to fulfill the goal stated in 1939 that aircraft should be used primarily to support the Fleet Marine Force. The 1st Marine Aircraft Wing was activated on July 7, 1941, and the 2nd Marine Aircraft Wing was activated three days later.

★★★

As the war in Europe progressively declined for the Allies, the British began recalling various units from overseas. In May 1941, Winston Churchill recalled the 25,000 British soldiers stationed in Iceland for service in Britain. Churchill suggested to President Roosevelt that the United States might take up the defense of Iceland as a kind of extension of the Monroe Doctrine. Thus, on June 22, 1941, the 1st Provisional Marine Brigade, formed around the 6th Marines, set sail from Charleston for Iceland, where it landed on July 7.

From the outbreak of war in 1939, President Roosevelt had been convinced that the United States and Great Britain were natural allies against the aggression of Adolf Hitler. Should Great Britain fall to German expansion, it would only be a matter of time before German expansion began to spread across the Atlantic. In this sense, it's easy to see the Marine garrison at Reykjavik, Iceland, as a part of Roosevelt's general support for Great Britain, including the lend-lease policy, by which the president could "lend" military supplies to countries whose security was vital to the United States, namely Britain.

Elements of the 1st Marine Division remained at Reykjavik for the next 10 months, but on March 8, 1942, a U.S. Army brigade replaced them. Although service in Reykjavik was short and relatively uneventful, it left a lasting impression on the Marines who served there. The brigade adopted the polar bear shoulder patch that had been worn by the British soldiers they replaced, and as they did with many of their tours, they added an unofficial verse to the Marine Hymn:

Again in nineteen forty-one
We sailed a north'ard course
And found beneath the midnight sun,
The Viking and the Norse.
The Iceland girls were slim and fair,
And fair the Iceland scenes,
And the Army found in landing there,
The United States Marines.

CHAPTER 9

ISSUE IN DOUBT: THE SECOND WORLD WAR, 1941–1943

The Second World War began in 1939 when Adolf Hitler ordered the invasion of Poland, ostensibly to reclaim German lands lost at the end of the First World War, most notably the so-called Danzig Corridor. The invasion of Poland, however, would have a much greater impact on world history than the mere reconquest of lost land. Initially, President Franklin Delano Roosevelt, like Wilson in 1914, remained neutral. The United States, still struggling to overcome the Great Depression of the 1930s, had no desire to become embroiled in another European conflict. It was clear, however, that Roosevelt thought the United States should become involved in the war, as exemplified by the lend-lease agreement he arranged with Great Britain.

Two years into the war, fate beckoned Roosevelt and the United States to take action. On the morning of December 7, 1941, Marine Aircraft Group (MAG) 21 watched spellbound as Japanese fighters flew over Ewa Mooring Mast Field in Hawaii on their way to attack Pearl Harbor. Before the Marines could scramble in pursuit of the Japanese bombers, a wave of Japanese Zeros strafed the field, destroying or disabling every Marine aircraft while they were still on the ground.

As the Japanese bombed the ships in Pearl Harbor, the 3rd Marine Defense Battalion scrambled for battle stations, but, taken by surprise, proved ineffectual, having only small arms to hand. The battalion claimed a mere three enemy aircraft shot down with machine guns. At Camp Catlin just outside Pearl Harbor, the 4th Marine Defense Battalion worked desperately to bring antiaircraft guns to bear on the Japanese planes. At the end of the nearly 2-hour attack, 4 battleships had been sunk and 2,403 Americans had lost their lives. Marine losses numbered 108 killed and another 49 wounded.

At the same time the Japanese attacked Pearl Harbor—although across the dateline and so technically December 8—the Japanese attacked the American islands of Guam, Wake, and Midway. After 2 days of bombardment, the meager garrison of 153 Marines, 277 sailors, and 326 native policemen on Guam found themselves overwhelmed by more than 6,000 Japanese soldiers and surrendered on December 10.

On Wake Island, Major James Devereux's 1st Defense Battalion, supported by Major Paul Putnam's Marine Fighter Squadron (VMF) 211 (which had arrived on the island only four days earlier), was able to hold out for a few days. The Japanese bombing raid destroyed 7 of Putnam's 12 brand-new F4F-3 Grumman Wildcats. The remaining Wildcats continued to fly missions.

On December 11, the Japanese attempted to land on the small island, but the defense battalion's artillery batteries sank one destroyer and several transports. In 1946, Captain Harry Elrod was awarded the Medal of Honor for sinking the Japanese destroyer *Kisagari*, technically the first Medal of Honor awarded to a Marine for service during the Second World War. Putnam's pilots managed to sink a second destroyer and shoot down four enemy planes. By December 22, however, all the Wildcats had been destroyed. Just before dawn on December 23, Navy Commander Winfred Cunningham reported, "Enemy on island; issue in doubt."

The Japanese landed 1,000 men on the island that day. Realizing the futility of resistance, Cunningham sent Major Devereux to parley with the Japanese under a white flag of truce. The Japanese suffered 820 men dead and 330 wounded in capturing Wake Island. American casualties numbered

3 sailors and 49 Marines as well as 70 civilians. The survivors, 1,146 civilians, 470 Marines, and 5 sailors, were taken to Shanghai and imprisoned.

★★★

The 4th Marines, under Colonel Samuel Howard, had transferred to Corregidor in the Philippines, leaving Shanghai only days before the Japanese bombed Pearl Harbor. On December 20, General Douglas MacArthur, the commander of U.S. Army Forces in the Far East and soon to be Supreme Allied Commander in the Pacific theater, requested that Howard's Marines be added to his command for the defense of the islands. MacArthur's defense of the Philippines proved ineffectual, however, and after five months of combat he ordered his forces withdrawal to Bataan. The 4th Marines were given the sad duty of burning the naval bases at Olongapo and Cavite before they withdrew.

Howard assigned one battalion to defend the Mariveles base on Bataan while the rest of the 4th Marines were stationed on Corregidor, the small, fortified island guarding Manila Bay. On March 12, however, President Roosevelt ordered MacArthur to withdraw from the Philippines. Japanese forces launched an attack on Bataan and the island fell three days later. There were 105 Marines among the 75,000 captured GIs and Filipinos who were marched along the infamous Bataan Death March.

The 11,000 Americans and Filipinos clustered on Corregidor suffered through 27 days of bombardment before the Japanese launched their final assault on May 5. On May 6, Army Major General Jonathan Wainwright, commanding officer after the departure of MacArthur, sent a Marine captain under white flag to parley with the Japanese. Colonel Howard ordered the colors of the 4th Marines burned. The Marines suffered nearly 700 casualties on Corregidor, and 1,282 were taken prisoner.

President Roosevelt didn't wait for these developments, however. On December 8, the day after the Japanese attack on Pearl Harbor, in his famous "Day of Infamy" speech, he asked Congress to declare war on Japan. Three days later, Adolf Hitler, remarkably honoring the agreements of the so-called Rome-Berlin-Tokyo Axis, declared war on the United States, and Benito Mussolini followed suit. Congress returned the favor that afternoon. The United States was fully embroiled in a world war once more.

★★★

American strategists believed that Japan would strike at Samoa next. On January 6, therefore, the 2nd Marine Brigade sailed from San Diego for American Samoa while the 3rd Marine Brigade, pulled from the East Coast, was sent to Western (British) Samoa. The 4th Marine Defense Battalion was assigned to New Hebrides at the end of March, and by April 30 the Efate airstrip had been constructed from crushed coral and was ready to receive MAG-24. Furthermore, in May the 1st Marine Division under the command of Major General Alexander Vandegrift was sent to New Zealand.

The American strategists guessed wrong: The next target of the Japanese was Midway, where the 6th Marine Defense Battalion and MAG-22 continued to hold out. Fortunately, the U.S. Navy had intercepted and broken the Japanese code and were warned of the impending attack. On June 4, MAG-22 took off to intercept the Japanese. Major Floyd Parks's fighter squadron of obsolete F2A Brewster Buffaloes engaged 108 enemy aircraft and lost 15 fighters. Major Lofton Henderson's bomber squadron of equally obsolete SB2U-3 Vought Vindicators attacked the Japanese carriers *Akagi* and *Soryu*. Eleven bombers were lost. Both Parks and Henderson were killed in the battle. Captain Richard Fleming, who reportedly crashed his burning plane into the Japanese cruiser *Mikuma*, was awarded the Medal of Honor. Nevertheless, the heroic defense offered by MAG-22 bought enough time for the U.S. Navy to reach Midway. The Navy lost the *Yorktown* and 98 aircraft but sank 4 Japanese carriers and saved Midway.

By mid-May, the Japanese had captured the Solomon Islands, were building an airbase at Rabaul on the island of New Britain, and were threatening New Guinea. Although the Allies had agreed upon a "Germany first" strategy, Admiral Ernest King argued that the momentum gained against the Japanese at the Battle of Midway and the Battle of the Coral Sea should not be abandoned. Reports that the Japanese were constructing an airfield on Guadalcanal in the Solomon Islands convinced the Joint Chiefs of Staff to launch a major assault against Guadalcanal and the nearby island of Tulagi in August. It was clear that the campaign against the Japanese in the Pacific would require frequent island landings, as Colonel Ellis had forecast 20 years earlier, and the Marine Corps, which had spent so much of its time preparing for just such a campaign, was obviously best suited for this kind of warfare.

The Pacific campaign would be long and arduous, however, and military leaders desired a more immediate victory. A Marine expedition was therefore set the objective of raiding the Makin Atoll in the British Gilbert Islands. The mission was assigned to Lieutenant Colonel Evans Carlson's 2nd Marine Raider Battalion.

RAIDERS

The Marine Corps had considered creating an elite unit based on the British commandos throughout the 1930s. During the first two years of the Second World War, before the United States entered the conflict, the performance of the British commandos in raids against German bases in Europe and Africa reinforced this idea. In January 1942, Captain James Roosevelt, USMCR, the president's son, suggested to Commandant Holcomb that Marines take the initiative in forming a commando unit with the purpose of spearheading amphibious landings, conducting raids against enemy positions, and conducting guerilla warfare. The Japanese lines in the Pacific were extended and seemed particularly susceptible to this kind of attack.

Holcomb and many other senior Marine officers, including Major General Holland Smith, commanding officer of the Amphibious Force, Atlantic, and Major General Alexander Vandegrift, commanding officer of the 1st Marine Division, both of whom would play major roles in the Pacific theater, were opposed to the idea of forming "elite" units. Efforts to man, equip, and train such specialized units would drain desperately needed resources from the 1st and 2nd Marine Divisions. In addition, senior officers considered all Marines "elite." Any Marine unit, they suggested, should be able to carry out the kinds of assignments intended for such commando units.

Despite such opposition, however, "very high authority" determined that such units would be created. The 1st Raider Battalion was formed on February 16, 1942, and the 2nd Raider Battalion was formed three days later. Lieutenant Colonel Merritt Edson and Lieutenant Colonel Evans Carlson were given command of these units respectively. James Roosevelt, recently promoted to Major, was named Carlson's executive officer.

Initial battalion organization followed standard Marine battalion organization, but training and experience soon led to an emphasis on flexibility. Carlson's 2nd Raider Battalion became the model. The battalion was divided into six rifle companies and a headquarters company. Each company was further divided into two rifle platoons and a weapons platoon. The weapons platoon was organized into two light machine gun squads with two machine guns each and a light mortar squad. Each rifle squad was divided into three squads, each commanded by a corporal leading three three-man teams. Each team was equipped with a BAR, and M-1 Garand rifle, and a Thompson submachine gun. In addition, the headquarters company included a 14-man unit composed of snipers and demolitions specialists. Two more Raider battalions, the 3rd and the 4th, would be formed in September and October 1942. The 1st Marine Raider Regiment, composed of the first four Raider battalions, would be formed in March 1943, and the 2nd Provisional Raider Regiment would be formed in September 1943. The Raiders served throughout the Solomon Islands campaign, including on Guadalcanal, New Georgia, and Bougainville. In addition, elements of the 2nd Raider Battalion participated in the defense of Midway Island and in the raid on Makin Atoll. Despite proven effectiveness, opposition to "elite of the elite" Marine units continued, and based on the argument that the nature of the war in the Pacific had changed, the Raider program was discontinued at the end of 1943. Most of the Raider units were redesignated as elements of the reconstituted 4th Marines in January and February 1944.

Two Navy submarines, the *Nautilus* and the *Argonaut*, departed Pearl Harbor on August 8, 1942, and arrived at Makin Atoll on the night of August 16. Lieutenant Colonel Evans Carlson, Major James Roosevelt, and 219 officers and men rowed ashore in rubber boats. The landing was unopposed, but at dawn, the Raiders encountered a unit of Japanese soldiers, including machine guns and snipers, entrenched along the coastal road. A firefight ensued, but the Raiders broke through the enemy line around 11:30 A.M. At about the same time, the *Nautilus* and the *Argonaut* sank a patrol boat and a transport as they entered the atoll's lagoon.

Around noon, two Japanese scout planes flew overhead. Twelve more flew over a little while later and strafed and bombed the Marines throughout the day. The Japanese attacked the American positions three times that afternoon, and Carlson came to believe that his force was greatly outnumbered. He decided to withdraw and rendezvous with the submarines, even though the Raiders had not destroyed any of the Japanese facilities or taken any hostages. Unfortunately, the surf at Makin Atoll proved intense. Several of the boats capsized, and much equipment was lost. Approximately one third of the Raider's boats were able to make it through the surf and rendezvous with the *Nautilus* and the *Argonaut*. The remainder of the Raiders were stranded on the atoll for another day.

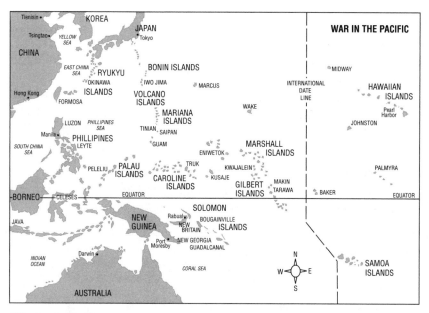

War in the Pacific.

With the battalion exhausted and facing an entrenched enemy, Carlson decided to surrender. He sent two Marines to parley with the Japanese, but they reported that they had not encountered anyone on the island. In truth, there had been only about 70 Japanese on Makin Atoll. Carlson's Raiders set out to scour the island and found only two more Japanese soldiers, whom they shot. Carlson destroyed the radio station and supplies he found, and then called the submarines to pick up the battalion and return to Pearl Harbor. The Raiders suffered 30 dead, 14 of whom were killed in action and another 7 of whom drowned. Tragically, nine Raiders were left on the atoll. It is not clear how these men were left behind, but it might be that their boat was unable to break through the surf and drifted down shore unseen by the Carlson and the rest of the Raiders. They were later captured and executed by the Japanese. Their tragic fate would be revealed only after the end of the war. Both Carlson and Roosevelt were awarded the Navy Cross, Carlson's second, for leadership and heroism.

Meanwhile, Operation Watchtower, the assault on Guadalcanal and Tulagi in the Solomon Islands, had been placed under the command of Major General Alexander Vandegrift, commander of the 1st Marine Division. Vandegrift was informed on June 26 that the assault was to commence on

August 1. The stunned Vandegrift asked for another six months to prepare properly, but received only one more week. Colonel Frank Goettge, the 1st Marine Division's intelligence officer, went to work quickly, gathering information from British Colonial Office files, while Lieutenant Colonel Gerald Thomas, the operations officer, and Lieutenant Colonel Randolph Pate, the logistics officer, began planning the assault. On July 17, Guadalcanal was photographed by a B-17 and a sketchy photomap of the island was pieced together. It appeared that the Japanese had congregated around Lunga Point and that they were indeed building an airfield there. Colonel Goettge guessed that a Japanese infantry regiment, approximately 5,000 men, must be present at Lunga Point, with perhaps another 1,500 on nearby Tulagi.

On the morning of August 7, 1942, the 1st Marine Raider Battalion under Lieutenant Colonel Merritt "Red Mike" Edson and the 2nd Battalion, 5th Marines under Lieutenant Colonel Harold Rosecrans landed on Tulagi, a small, 3-mile-long island just off the coast of Florida Island, 20 miles north of Guadalcanal. The Marines encountered increasing resistance throughout the day, but by evening Edson had pushed the Japanese defenders back into a ravine. Rosecrans secured the northern end of the island and then moved to support Edson's position along the ridge that ran the length of the island. The Japanese counterattacked throughout the night, but Edson's Raiders held. There were only been about 500 Japanese on the island, and the Marines secured the island by the afternoon of August 8.

The 1st Marine Parachute Battalion landed on two nearby smaller islands, Gavutu and Tanambogo, about four hours after the assault on Tulagi began. Japanese resistance was strong, however, and the 3rd Battalion, 2nd Marines were called in to help the light parachute battalion take the islands. Colonel LeRoy Hunt led the 5th Marines onto Guadalcanal about 5 miles east of Lunga Point, and the 1st Marines under Colonel Clifton Cates followed about 2 hours later. They met no resistance during their landing. As it turned out, there were only about 2,230 Japanese on Guadalcanal, rather than the anticipated 5,000, and most of them were construction workers.

On the next morning, the 1st and 5th Marines executed a pincer maneuver against the airfield at Lunga Point, the 5th Marines attacking the airfield directly while the 1st Marines circled around to the south and attacked the airfield from the jungle. They captured the airfield with little difficulty, driving the 430 Japanese troops and 1,700 Korean laborers into the jungle.

It seemed the Marines had the situation well in hand. Unfortunately, a Japanese air raid hit Lunga Point that afternoon, raising serious concerns among the Naval officers about their position in the Solomon Islands. Still recovering from the initial Japanese victories in 1942, the Navy could ill afford the loss of more ships. Rear Admiral Frank Fletcher, who had lost one aircraft carrier at Midway and another at the Battle of the Coral Sea, didn't want to lose a third at Guadalcanal. In addition, Australian Rear Admiral V. A. C. Crutchley, commanding the screening force, was concerned that his fleet might get trapped in the channel between Tulagi and Guadalcanal. Rear Admiral Richmond Turner, the task force commander, informed General Vandegrift that he could not afford to keep unprotected Navy ships, whether carriers, cruisers, or transports, in the area and that Operation Watchtower's naval support would withdraw from the Solomons only 72 hours after the assault had commenced.

General Vandegrift was understandably stunned by this decision, but even before the withdrawal could begin, Turner's fears seemed justified. On the night of August 8, the Japanese launched a massive counterattack. A Japanese task force sailed into the channel between Guadalcanal and Tulagi and destroyed nearly all of Crutchley's fleet at Savo Island. Four heavy cruisers were sunk at the Battle of Savo Island and another was seriously damaged. The fleet retreated on August 9, stranding 11,145 Marines on Guadalcanal and another 6,805 on Tulagi, Gavutu, and Tanambogo with few supplies. Vandegrift dug in, setting up a defensive perimeter along the coast, and ordered his engineers to build an airfield, which they had completed by August 12. The airstrip, named Henderson Field in honor of Major Lofton Henderson, killed at the Battle of Midway, was the key to Vandegrift's defense of the island. As long as Henderson Field remained operational, supplies could be delivered, wounded could be evacuated, and the Marines would have at least some air support.

The Japanese Imperial Staff assigned Lieutenant General Haruyoshi Hyakutake the mission of retaking Guadalcanal. Hyakutake had at his disposal an impressive force, the 17th Army, including the 35th Brigade under Colonel Ichiki Kiyono, the 2nd Sendai Division under Lieutenant General Maruyama Masao, and the Kawaguchi Detachment, as well as the 38th Division, the 8th Tank Regiment, and an artillery group, nearly 50,000 men in all.

The Imperial Staff and Hyakutake had underestimated the Marine force on Guadalcanal and Tulagi, however, believing that only 2,000 Marines had landed in the Solomons instead of the nearly 19,000 actually there. Hyakutake assigned Ichiki, then at Guam, to begin the assault. Colonel Ichiki planned to land and strike quickly across the Tenaru River at the airfield, catching the Americans by surprise. Ichiki's brigade had landed on Guadalcanal by August 18.

On August 19, Jacob Vouza, a native scout, encountered Ichiki's brigade and was captured. Tortured and left for dead, Vouza survived and struggled to the Marines to report the Japanese troops. The next night, Ichiki attacked the Marine perimeter across the Tenaru River, but Lieutenant Colonel Edwin Pollock's 2nd Battalion, 1st Marines held, cutting down the Japanese attack with machine guns and mortars. The following morning, Lieutenant Colonel Lenard Creswell's 1st Battalion, 1st Marines crossed the Tenaru and attacked Ichiki as Pollock's battalion moved to trap him against the sea and Colonel Pedro del Valle's artillery pounded the retreating brigade. Colonel Ichiki, trapped between the sea and two Marine battalions and bombarded by artillery, burned his unit's flag and committed *seppuku*, ritual suicide.

The Marines suffered 35 men killed and 75 wounded. The Japanese suffered 777 killed. But the nature of the war in the Pacific was soon revealed to the Marines. Wounded Japanese soldiers often feigned death, lying among their dead comrades, until an American approached to check the body, at which point the "dead" man would rise up to shoot the Marine or detonate a hand grenade, killing them both. The fierce dedication and loyalty of the Japanese troops indicated that the Pacific war would be a war without mercy. Only 15 of Ichiki's men were taken prisoner.

During the day on August 20, MAG-23 arrived at Henderson Field. Captain John Smith had at his command 19 brand-new Grumman F4F-4 Wildcats, and Major Richard Mangrum had at his command 12 Douglas SBD-3 Dauntless dive bombers. The "Cactus Air Force"—a name the group adopted from the code name for Guadalcanal—quickly developed new aerial tactics. In a straight aerial dogfight, the faster and more maneuverable Japanese Zero had the advantage. The Cactus Air Force, however, adopted the tactic of swooping down at the backs of the Zeros from an altitude of 30,000 feet, attacking, then continuing downward as rapidly as possible. These hit-and-run tactics proved effective.

GRUMMAN F4F-4 WILDCAT AND DOUGLAS SBD-3 DAUNTLESS

The Grumman F4F-4 was the primary fighter plane flown by the Navy and Marine Corps during the first years of the Second World War. Although the Wildcat was slower and less maneuverable than the Mitsubishi Zeros flown by Japanese pilots, the new F4F-4 model had several improvements over earlier Navy and Marine planes such as the Brewster Buffalo. Equipped with the 1,200 horsepower Pratt and Whitney R-1830-86, the F4F-4 could achieve air speeds of 320 miles per hour. The plane was also rugged, having heavier armor—one of the reasons it remained slower than the Zero—and self-sealing gas tanks. It also had impressive firepower: six .50-caliber Browning machine guns and two 100-pound bombs. Finally, the Wildcat was equipped with folding wings, allowing for easier storage on board aircraft carriers.

The Grumman F4F-4 Wildcat proved to be a deadly weapon at Guadalcanal and the Solomon Islands. The planes were really designed for launch from an aircraft carrier and so were not well suited for the muddy landing strip of Henderson Field, and the Japanese planes could outfly the cumbrous Wildcats. Nevertheless, the improved armor often proved resistant to the lighter Japanese weapons. Furthermore, the Wildcats proved deadly weapons in the hands of talented and experienced pilots: Joseph Foss shot down 26 enemy planes, John Smith shot down 19 planes, and Marion Carl shot down 18 while flying Wildcats.

While the Grumman F4F-4 Wildcat became the principal fighter plane for the Navy and Marine Corps during the first years of the Second World War, the Douglas SBD-3 Dauntless became the principal dive bomber. Like the Wildcat, the Dauntless proved slow but rugged, earning the nickname "Slow But Deadly." Equipped with a 1,000-horsepower Wright-Cyclone R-1820-52 engine, the plane could achieve air speeds of up to 250 miles per hour and a range of 1,580 miles. Armed with only two .50-caliber machine guns in the nose and two .30-caliber in the rear, the Dauntless could haul 1,000 pounds of bombs and could sustain a dive angle of up to 70 degrees. The Dauntless saw combat throughout the Pacific campaign but especially at the Battle of Midway, the Battle of Coral Sea, and in the Solomon Islands campaign.

On August 21, Captain John Smith downed his first Zero, and on August 24, Smith's squadron intercepted a Japanese raid, shooting down 16 of the 27 enemy planes. Thirteen planes were shot down on August 26, eight on August 28, and fourteen on August 30. Captain Smith accounted for seven of the enemy planes, and Captain Marion Carl, a veteran of Midway, accounted for eight.

Major Mangrum also had success with his bomber squadron. On August 28, they caught four destroyers, only one of which escaped undamaged.

Brigadier General Roy Geiger took command of the Cactus Air Force on September 3. Geiger studied Japanese aerial combat tactics and improved the operations of the Cactus Air Force, freeing Vandegrift to conduct the ground battle. Additional fighter and bomber squadrons arrived early in October, including Major Leonard Davis's VMF-121. Among the pilots of Davis's squadron was Joseph Foss. Foss flew almost daily for the next month and shot down 23 enemy airplanes. By January 1943, Foss had shot down a total of 26 enemy planes, the highest number of confirmed planes shot down by a Marine.

Edson was given command of a combined Raider-parachute unit and led them from Tulagi, Gavutu, and Tanambongo over to Guadalcanal on August 31. One week later, Edson led his unit in an amphibious raid near Tasimboko behind Japanese lines. Supported by MAG-23 and the USS *Manley,* the Raiders and the parachute battalion were able to overrun the enemy position, and the Japanese decided to withdraw. Captured Japanese documents revealed that the force Edson had attacked was part of Kiyotaki Kawaguchi's 36th Brigade, which had landed undetected at Taivu Point earlier in September. The documents also revealed that Kawaguchi was planning an assault on Henderson field.

Edson surmised that Kawaguchi's attack would come through the foothills of Mount Austen, and on September 12, he deployed the Raider-parachute battalion along a ridge overlooking the Lunga Plain. Edson was right. Kawaguchi launched a series of attacks against the Marine perimeter from September 12 to 14, but Edson's Marines held. One of Edson's officers, Major Kenneth Bailey, led Raider Company C during 10 hours of fierce hand-to-hand combat along the ridge on the night of September 12. Bailey, who was killed in a later battle on Guadalcanal, was awarded the Medal of Honor posthumously. By morning on September 14, the Marines had lost 69 men dead and 194 wounded. The Japanese had lost 800 men dead. The position where Edson had held Kawaguchi was called "Bloody Ridge" after that, though some preferred "Edson's Ridge." Edson was awarded the Medal of Honor for the defense of the ridge.

Intelligence reports soon revealed that the Japanese intended to reinforce their effort to take Guadalcanal. President Roosevelt determined to hold the island, and ordered the Joint Chiefs of Staff to support the defense of Guadalcanal with "every possible weapon." In response to this commitment, Admiral Turner returned to Guadalcanal with reinforcements in the form of the 7th Marines, which had been stationed in Samoa until then, and much needed supplies.

Fearing Japanese reinforcements, Vandegrift decided to extend the Marine perimeter to the Matanikau River. Lieutenant Colonel Chesty Puller's 1st Battalion, 7th Marines was ordered to reconnoiter the Mount Austen area. On September 25, Puller ran into stiff resistance. The 2nd Battalion, 5th Marines reinforced Puller, and Colonel Edson, now commanding the 5th Marines, took over command of the operation. Unfortunately, confused orders and friendly fire resulted in the death of 60 Marines and another 100 wounded. The Marines withdrew.

Vandegrift knew that he couldn't allow the Japanese to control the Matanikau River. From there, artillery would be able to bombard the entire Marine perimeter. So on October 7, Edson led five battalions in an attempt to push beyond the Matanikau. While two battalions moved along the coast, three others crossed the river farther inland and then descended on the enemy's flank. The Marines caught Colonel Tadamasu Nakaguma's 4th Infantry Regiment by surprise and shattered it. Having lost 700 men, Nakaguma broke off the engagement after 2 days. Edson's 5th Marines dug in on the east bank of the Matanikau.

The Japanese would soon retaliate. Early in the morning on October 14, the Japanese battleships *Kongo* and *Haruna* bombarded Henderson Field while the 2nd Sendai Division, reinforced to 20,000 men, landed west of Koli Point. Henderson Field was torn apart. Of the 90 planes on the airfield, 48 were destroyed, and 41 Marines were killed. The remaining planes took to the air as soon as possible and attacked the Japanese transports.

On October 21, Maruyama attacked the American position on the Matanikau, but del Valle's artillery obliterated the advance and Edson's Marines drove off the remnant. More than 650 Japanese were killed in the assault.

Three nights later, Maruyama launched 6,000 troops against Bloody Ridge, defended by Chesty Puller's 1st Battalion, 7th Marines and Herman Hanneken's 2nd Battalion, 7th Marines. The 3rd Battalion, 164th Infantry, which had arrived on October 13, scrambled to reinforce Puller's left.

Despite the fierce and confused hand-to-hand combat in the drenching rain, the Marines held.

Sergeant "Manila John" Basilone, commanding two machine gun crews in Puller's battalion, refused to give way before the Japanese assault. Under constant mortar fire, Basilone kept his crew blasting away at the Japanese assault. At one point, he repaired one of the weapons and manned it himself. Sergeant Mitchell Paige in Hanneken's battalion likewise kept firing at the enemy until all of his men had been killed or wounded and then kept firing on his own until reinforcements arrived and then led a charge that drove the enemy back. Basilone was awarded a battlefield commission for his valor, which he turned down, and the Medal of Honor, the first enlisted Marine to receive that honor during the Second World War. Paige was awarded a battlefield commission, which he accepted, and the Medal of Honor. All told, the Japanese had lost an estimated 1,000 men.

BROWNING MODEL 1917 .30-CALIBER MACHINE GUN

During World War I, the American forces needed weapons that required a minimum of maintenance and training for the troops in the field. The Browning 1917 .30-caliber water-cooled machine gun was perfect for the armed forces. Tripod mounted, the Browning had a cyclic rate of 500 to 600 rounds per minute, and a range of 2,800 yards, making it an excellent support weapon. When machine guns were needed for tanks and other vehicles, the Browning was mounted on various vehicles in an air-cooled model, which basically was the water-cooled model without the jacket. Despite this change, the gun performed just fine.

The Browning 1917 saw action in World War II, Korea, and into the 1960s, when it was phased out in favor of the M-60 machine gun.

Maruyama launched another attack that night, but Puller's and Hanneken's Marines held once more. By October 26, the Japanese had lost more than 3,500 men, and Maruyama withdrew into the jungle.

On October 28, I Marine Amphibious Corps was created and headquartered at Noumea to coordinate all Fleet Marine Forces in the Pacific theater, and reinforcements, including the 8th Marines and Carlson's 2nd Marine Raider Battalion, were soon sent to Guadalcanal. On November 4, Brigadier General Louis Woods replaced Brigadier General Roy Geiger as commander of the Cactus Air Force. Geiger was awarded a Navy Cross—his second, the first having been earned during the First World War—for his leadership of the Cactus Air Force, which shot down 268 enemy planes between September 3 and November 4.

General Vandegrift determined to push west beyond the Matanikau River. He ordered Edson to lead the 5th and 2nd Marines to initiate the attack on November 1 and sent Hanneken on a reconnaissance mission to the east, specifically to Koli Point. By the time Hanneken arrived, the Japanese 230th Imperial Infantry was in the process of landing. Vandegrift cancelled the westward push and assigned the 7th Marines and the 164th Infantry to assist Hanneken at Koli Point. Lieutenant Colonel Carlson's Raiders were ordered to cut off the Japanese retreat.

The envelopment at Koli Point was successful but failed to tie a noose around the Japanese, many of whom managed to squeeze through the American lines. Carlson led the 2nd Raider Battalion in pursuit of the enemy on November 6, initiating the Long Patrol, 30 days behind enemy lines. The Raiders began encountering Japanese soldiers on November 11 and continued to harass them until December 4. In that time, Carlson's Raiders fought a dozen battles and killed 488 Japanese soldiers. Carlson's Raiders lost 16 men dead and another 18 wounded. However, another 225 Raiders had to be evacuated over the course of Carlson's patrol due to malaria and ringworm. Upon their return, General Vandegrift commended the Raiders for their skill and fortitude.

GUNG HO

Carlson had enlisted in the Marine Corps in 1922—by which time he had already served in the Army for 10 years—and in 1923 he was commissioned as a second lieutenant. He served several tours in Nicaragua and China, and in 1937, he returned to China as a military observer, spending several months with Mao Tse-tung's Eighth Route Army learning guerilla warfare tactics. In 1939, Carlson resigned his commission in order to lecture on the dangers of Japanese aggression, but when those dangers were realized, he was recommissioned and given command of the 2nd Marine Raider Battalion.

Lieutenant Colonel Evans Carlson's combat philosophy, developed during his tour as a military observer in China, may be summed up in the phrase *gung ho,* which translated from the Chinese means "work together," but perhaps "spirit of cooperation" comes closer to explaining its essence. Carlson had adopted the phrase from the 600 Communist Chinese fighters he had observed in 1937. He realized that these men were capable of enduring incredible hardships to accomplish their goals because they understood that their accomplishments were absolutely necessary for the success of their mission.

Carlson instituted a system of radical egalitarianism within the 2nd Raider Battalion. Officers and men alike shared the same accommodations and rations and frequently sang patriotic songs together. Carlson took the time to instruct his Marines in the importance of the war to ensure that they understood why they were fighting, and every man was allowed to ask questions and state his opinions. Carlson was able to engender in his men an incredible willingness to make sacrifices.

Gung ho would become the motto for the Raider battalions and many other Marines.

On November 10, Vandegrift resumed his westward push with the 8th Marines and the 164th Infantry, but again felt compelled to delay the attack when he learned that a substantial portion of the Japanese 38th Division, approximately 10,000 men, were embarked on transports and headed toward Guadalcanal. On November 12, Rear Admiral Daniel Callaghan landed the 182nd U.S. Infantry on Guadalcanal and then set out with five cruisers and eight destroyers to intercept the Japanese task force bearing down on Guadalcanal. The naval battle began the next morning, and although Callaghan was killed, the Japanese were badly damaged and forced to withdraw. The Cactus Air Force caught one of the limping Japanese battleships, the *Hiei*, and damaged it so badly that it had to be scuttled.

On November 14, Navy and Marine airplanes sank seven of the transports carrying the Japanese 38th Division. The remaining four transports under guard of the badly damaged Japanese task force continued to limp toward Guadalcanal, where another naval battle was fought in the channel. The Japanese cruiser *Kirishima* was sunk, but the 4 transports were able to beach themselves on the island, and approximately 4,000 soldiers joined Hyakutake on the west end of the island.

Vandegrift began a third push west with the 8th Marines, the 164th Infantry, and two battalions from the 182nd Infantry. The Americans encountered Hyakutake advancing on Henderson Field on the night of November 19 and engaged his forces in a two-day battle that was ultimately inconclusive.

By this time, "starvation island" had taken its toll on the 1st Marine Division. Exhausted, malnourished, and suffering from malaria, at least one third of the division was medically unfit for service. Vandegrift demanded that the unit be relieved and moved to a better climate. The Japanese, too, were beginning to suffer similar problems. In the desperate hope of supplying their forces by sea, eight Japanese destroyers attacked the American ships in the channel on November 29 and managed to sink the *Northhampton* and badly damage three other cruisers, but it was too little too late. By early December, the Japanese were beginning to realize that Guadalcanal was lost.

The 132nd U.S. Infantry landed on Guadalcanal on December 8, and command passed from Vandegrift to Army Major General Alexander Patch. Shortly thereafter, the 1st, 5th, and 7th Marines left the 'Canal bound for Australia. The 2nd Marines and the 8th Marine Division left for New Zealand in January 1943.

Patch had at his command the XIV Corps, nearly three full divisions, including the 6th Marines, which had landed on Guadalcanal in January 1943. Patch launched the final assault against the remaining Japanese forces on January 10. The fighting was fierce, but, recalling the Marine spirit of Dan Daly at Belleau Wood, Captain Henry "Jim" Crowe of the 8th Marines strode forward on January 13 and yelled at his men, "Goddamn it, you'll never get the Purple Heart hiding in a foxhole! Follow me!" By February 9, the Marines and GIs had chased Hyakutake's forces into the western end of Guadalcanal only to find that they had slipped off the island in the middle of the night.

Over a span of 6 months, the Marines suffered 1,044 dead, 2,894 wounded, 55 missing, and 8,580 cases of malaria. The Cactus Air Force lost 55 dead, 127 wounded, and 85 missing. The U.S. Army lost 446 dead and 1,910 wounded. Approximately 25,000 of the 31,000 Japanese soldiers deployed to Guadalcanal had been killed. General Alexander Vandegrift and Colonel Red Mike Edson were awarded the Medal of Honor for their leadership on Guadalcanal.

★★★

Despite the loss of Guadalcanal, the Japanese had a strong hold in the Solomon Islands. They had been hard at work on a well-camouflaged airfield at Munda on the northern end of New Georgia, they had completed another airfield on Kolombangara, and they had four operational airfields on Buka and Bougainville and five around Rabaul on New Britain. Having secured Guadalcanal, the Joint Chiefs of Staff determined to capture or neutralize the strong Japanese position at Rabaul. Neither General Douglas MacArthur, Supreme Allied Commander in the Pacific, nor Admiral Chester Nimitz, commanding the 3rd and 7th Fleets, believed they had adequate ground or air forces to capture New Britain. They decided on a cautious, island-by-island approach.

While MacArthur's forces advanced toward Rabaul from Port Moresby in New Guinea, Vice Admiral William Halsey, commanding the 3rd Fleet, would advance from Guadalcanal, converging on Rabaul. Halsey's first was to leap from Guadalcanal 55 miles "up the slot" to the Russell Islands, a small island group within the Solomons. On February 21, Colonel Harry "the Horse" Liversedge led the newly formed 3rd Marine Raider Battalion in an unopposed landing at Pavuvu Island in the Russell Islands group.

Brigadier General Francis Mulcahy, one of the few Marines who had a confirmed German aircraft kill during the First World War, relieved General Woods as commander of the Cactus Air Force on December 26, 1942. In mid-February, the Army, Marine, Navy, and New Zealand air forces were combined under a single commander, ComAirSols—Commander, Aircraft, Solomons. In February 1943, a Marine fighter squadron arrived at Henderson Field with 12 new Vought Corsair F4Us. By August 1943, all Marine fighter squadrons would be equipped with the new Corsairs. An airstrip was built on the island of Banika in the Russell Islands group, and by March 14, MAG-21, with three squadrons of Wildcats, had landed there and began flying missions.

VOUGHT F4U CORSAIR

A revolutionary plane in several ways, the F4U "Corsair" series filled the much-needed role of a fast interceptor aircraft that could also serve as a bomber if necessary.

The Corsair had to conquer several problems in its design alone. Because of the huge Pratt and Whitney R-2800 18-cylinder engine (that could put out 2,000 horsepower) powering the craft, a larger propeller was needed, which required longer landing gear. However, because the aircraft was designed to land on carriers, the gear had to be short and strong to absorb the punishing impact of a deck landing. The engineers at United Aircraft Corporation solved the problem by creating the famed "bent-wing" design, in which the wings sloped down from the fuselage, then angled back up in an inverted gull-wing layout. This gave the airplane the prop clearance it needed while allowing for the short landing gear required for a carrier aircraft.

The Corsair was designed to be the sleekest plane in the air at that time. It was the first naval aircraft that could fly more than 400 miles per hour. The F4U-1, the first production model, was armed with six .50-caliber machine guns in the wings. The last model used in the Pacific theater, the F4U-4, was a fighter-bomber carrying the machine guns along with either two 1,000-pound bombs or eight 5-inch rockets.

Initially the F4U series ran into problems involving landing gear and tail-hooks during carrier landing tests. The resulting accidents earned the plane the nickname of "Ensign Eliminator." The British solved the landing problem by approaching their carriers from downwind in a long curve to watch the LSO until the last second. The Japanese named the aircraft "Whistling Death," due to the unusual noise produced by its wing-mounted air intakes.

The F4U series also served in the Korean War as a ground attack model, the AU-1, armed with 10 rockets or 4,000 pounds of bombs. A later model, the F4U-7, which was a revamped version of the AU-1, was sold to the French Navy in 1952. With that production run, the operational life of the F4U series came to an end.

The assault on New Georgia, the next island in the advance toward Rabaul, began in June 1943. Two companies of the 4th Marine Raider Battalion under Lieutenant Colonel Michael Currin landed at Segi Point on the southeastern end of New Georgia on June 21, marched through jungle and mangrove swamps for four days, and captured Viru Harbor. The 103rd U.S. Infantry and the 9th Marine Defense Battalion landed on Rendova, an island off the west coast of New Georgia, on June 30. There was little fighting on the ground, but in the air American planes shot down 101 Japanese aircraft, 53 of which were shot down by Marine pilots.

While the 9th Marine Defense Battalion and Army artillery bombarded the Munda airfield across the channel on New Georgia, Liversedge, now commanding the 1st Marine Raider Regiment, led his headquarters, the 1st Raider Battalion, and two battalions of the 37th Division on shore at Rice Anchorage on the eastern side of the island. From there, he marched to Enogai Inlet, an important barge landing, and captured it after a three-day battle on July 10.

On July 18, Currin's 4th Raider Battalion joined Liversedge at Enogai, and two days later the two Marine battalions and the two Army battalions marched toward Bairoko, another important barge terminal. At Bairoko, however, Liversedge found his units pinned down by well-placed machine guns and mortars. Suffering heavy casualties, Liversedge pulled back to Enogai to await reinforcement. Meanwhile, the 37th and 25th Divisions secured Munda, and Marine Fighter Squadrons 214 and 221 took over the airfield on August 14.

The Japanese still had a force of around 10,000 men defending a good airfield on Kolombangara, an island just north of New Georgia. On August 15, however, the Army's 35th Regimental Combat Team and the 4th Marine Defense Battalion secured Vella Lavella farther to the north. Doing this bypassed Kolombangara and gave the Allies control of New Georgia, despite the substantial Japanese forces still on Kolombangara, as the Allies now had control of supply routes and communications.

A MARINE'S BEST FRIEND

In 1942, the Marine Corps initiated a war dog training program. Dogs had been used in warfare for centuries, and the other branches of the U.S. military had begun dog programs much earlier than the Marine Corps. Those branches often used their dogs for security, however. True to General Lejeune's vision of the Marine Corps as a primarily offensive weapon, any dogs used by the Marine Corps would have to be trained for combat.

Two types of training were conducted at the War Dog Training Company, Camp Lejeune: messenger dog training and scout dog training. The dogs most commonly used by the Corps were the Doberman Pinscher and the German Shepherd, although other breeds were sometimes trained. The dogs had to be between 1 and 5 years old, weigh at least 50 pounds, and stand at least 25 inches high.

Two Marines were assigned to work with each dog. Training consisted primarily of teaching the dogs commands using praise. Scout dogs, for example, were chained or leashed next to their trainer and commanded to "watch." When the dog reacted aggressively to the approach of a threatening stranger, the dog was praised and rewarded. Likewise, messenger dogs were trained by having one of their attending Marines move away from the trainer and the dog. The trainer attached a message to the dog's collar and commanded the dog to "report." The second Marine called the dog, and when the dog reported to the Marine, the dog was praised and rewarded. Gradually, the distance between the Marines was increased.

War dog platoons included 1 officer, 65 Marines, and 36 dogs—18 scouts and 18 messengers. One man was assigned to each scout dog and two men to each messenger dog. The 1st Marine War Dog Platoon was attached to the 2nd Marine Raider Regiment and served on Bougainville Island in November 1943. The commanding officer of the 2nd Raider Regiment reported that the war dogs were an unqualified success.

One of the dogs, Caesar, had carried vital messages and captured papers between Company M and the battalion command post. Because phone lines had been cut, Caesar proved to be the only means of communication. Another dog, Otto, alerted his reconnaissance patrol of a machine gun nest, and the Marines were able to take cover without any casualties. A third dog, Jack, managed to carry a message that his company had been attacked even though he had been shot in the back. As a result of Jack's message, help arrived in time to save his handler and many other Marines.

Marine dogs went on to serve on Guam, Peleliu, Iwo Jima, and Okinawa. Many of the dogs were awarded citations for their invaluable service.

With New Georgia under allied control, Admiral Halsey planned to take Bougainville next. This island was as big as Guadalcanal and it was believed that some 35,000 Japanese soldiers were now on the island. The initial plan of attack on Bougainville was to secure a beachhead at Empress Augusta Bay along Cape Toronika, where there were two miles of good beach. This would allow the Marines to set up an airfield behind the front line.

The date of the attack was set for November 1, 1943. Vandegrift, who had been promoted to lieutenant general, commanded the attack. He would have at his command I Marine Amphibious Corps headquarters, the 3rd Marine Division commanded by Major General Allen Turnage, and the Army's 37th Division. In addition, the Allied Solomon Air Force stood ready with 52 squadrons, 14 of which were Marine Corps squadrons.

A brilliant diversion was set up to deceive the Japanese and hide the true objective of the allied assault. The 2nd Marine Parachute Battalion under Lieutenant Colonel Victor "Brute" Krulak landed on Choiseul, a nearby island, on the night of October 27 and pretended to be the 3rd Marine Division, storming across the island for the next nine days. The deception worked beautifully, and the Japanese wildly overestimated the number of

Americans that had landed on Choiseul—Krulak had 725 men in his battalion. Hyakutake ordered troops from Bougainville to reinforce Choiseul. Early in the morning on November 1, the 3rd Marine Division began landing at Empress Augusta Bay.

Despite the important deception carried out by Krulak's battalion, resistance was stiff. On the left flank the 9th Marines ran into rough surf, swamping 86 of their landing craft. They had to abandon the left flank and come in behind the 3rd Marines on the right. The 3rd Marines, reinforced by the 2nd Raider Battalion, landed at Cape Toronika, but the 1st Battalion was soon pinned down by a deadly crossfire. A Japanese air raid from Rabaul slowed the assault further. Nevertheless, the Marines pushed ahead and managed to land 14,000 men on the beach by nightfall. On November 4, when General Vandegrift returned to Washington to assume the office of Marine Corps commandant, General Roy Geiger took over command of I Marine Amphibious Corps.

General Hyakutake, in command of the Japanese defense from Rabaul, had at his command the surviving units from his assault on Guadalcanal as well as the 6th Division and the Kure 7th Special Naval Landing Force. He ordered the 23rd Infantry Regiment, under the command of Colonel Kawano, to reinforce the Cape Toronika defense while he sent part of the 17th Division from Rabaul to outflank the American beachhead. Only 4 of the destroyers carrying these reinforcements made it to Bougainville, however, where they were able to land some 475 soldiers to the left of the Marine beachhead on November 6 and 7. This meager unit of soldiers dug in at the Koromokina River and fought bravely for two days against three Marine battalions before they were defeated.

The 2nd Marine Raider Battalion set out along the Piva Trail on November 5 and set up a stronghold at the Numa Numa Trail, forcing a Japanese battalion to withdraw to Piva Village. Aided by a carpet of 100-pound bombs laid in front of them, 2 battalions of the 9th Marines passed through the Raider Battalion on November 10 and attacked Piva Village. On the same day, the 21st Marines and the 37th Infantry came ashore at Empress Augusta Bay, and the 37th Infantry secured the left flank while the 21st Marines advanced toward a ridge the Marines called Hellzapoppin Ridge. The 3rd Marines advanced to Piva Village on November 19 and, in what came to be known as the Battle of Piva Forks, fought six battles with Japanese troops, eventually securing the village on November 24.

General Hyakutake continued to send air raids against Cape Toronika throughout November, but the 3rd Marine Defense Battalion had set up a battery of 90mm guns to defend the beach. On November 29, the 1st Marine Parachute Battalion launched a raid against Koiari, where they encountered more than 1,000 Japanese soldiers. The firefight turned against the Marines, and they were forced to withdraw under covering fire from Navy destroyers at Cape Toronika. On December 12, however, the 21st Marines found the remnant of the 23rd Japanese Imperial Infantry and fought a series of battles with them that lasted until December 23. With the defeat of the 23rd Imperial Infantry, Bougainville was essentially secured. The Army's Americal Division arrived to relieve the 3rd Marine Division, and the Army's XXIV Corps took over command from I Marine Amphibious Corps, although the 3rd Marine Defense Battalion would remain on Bougainville into the new year. The battle for Bougainville cost the Marine Corps 423 dead and 1,418 wounded.

With the capture of Bougainville, Halsey's advance met MacArthur's drive through the South Pacific. The attack on Rabaul, now only about 200 miles away, would be initiated with an aerial assault. Major General Ralph Mitchell, ComAirSols, began bombarding Rabaul with heavy Army bombers and Marine fighter sweeps. In February, the Japanese withdrew what fighters remained in Rabaul, and Marine SBD aircraft bombed Japanese shipping. Marine bombing was so efficient that by March most fighting ships had been sunk or driven off and so many transport barges had been destroyed that the Japanese were not even receiving mail at Rabaul.

★★★

One of the most famous Marines of the Second World War was the flamboyant Major Gregory "Pappy" Boyington. In 1941, Boyington had resigned his Marine commission to join the Flying Tigers, an American volunteer unit, in China. He claimed six kills, two of which were confirmed. When the United States entered the war, he rejoined the Corps, and in the summer of 1943 he was assigned to Marine Fighter Squadron 121 flying missions over Guadalcanal. In September, Boyington was given command of VMF-214, a fighter squadron composed of pilots left from other squadrons. They took the name "Black Sheep."

The much younger Marines of Black Sheep Squadron often viewed the 31-year-old Boyington as an antique and took to calling him "Pappy." Despite his age, Pappy led by example. Boyington led his squadron on aggressive fighter sweeps over enemy airfields, tuning into Japanese radio frequencies to challenge the Japanese pilots to fight. Boyington recorded the Black Sheep's first kill and added another four kills by the end of their first week.

On October 17, 1943, Boyington led a daring raid on Kahili. The Black Sheep circled over the airbase, taunting the vastly superior Japanese force still on the ground until some 60 Zeros rose to meet them. The Black Sheep shot down 20 enemy planes and then returned to base without a single loss.

By the end of 1943, Boyington had claimed 25 air-to-air kills, including the 6 he had claimed with the Flying Tigers. On January 3, 1944, he led his last raid against Rabaul, where he claimed 3 of the 50 Japanese Zeros that rose to meet his challenge before he himself was shot down off the coast of New Ireland. He was picked up by a Japanese submarine several hours later and spent the next 20 months at the Omori Prison Camp in Tokyo. Pappy Boyington claimed 28 air-to-air kills, although only 22 of those kills had been claimed as a Marine. Nevertheless, the Marine Corps still recognizes Boyington as their top ace. He was awarded the Medal of Honor.

★★★

While the Allied air force pounded Rabaul, MacArthur launched an attack at Cape Gloucester on the western end of New Britain. The 1st Marine Division, now under the command of Major General William Rupertus assisted by Brigadier General Lemuel Shepherd, was chosen for the assault. The 1st Marine Division, the "Old Breed," had been recuperating in Australia since Guadalcanal but had recently been given an excellent rating for combat readiness and was equipped with new M-1 Garand rifles. The defense of New Britain was under the command of Major General Iwao Matsuda, who had at his command the 65th Brigade and the 53rd and 141st Regiments.

GARAND M-1 .30-CALIBER RIFLE

The Garand series of rifles were chosen by the U.S. Army to gradually replace the Springfield Model 1903, which had been adopted in the first years of the twentieth century. The first model, the M-1 .30-caliber, was chosen in 1936, and was the first self-loading rifle adopted by any army in the world. Weighing 9.5 pounds, it carried an 8-round internal clip. When the last round was fired, the clip automatically ejected and the breech remained open, ready for reloading.

Produced primarily by Springfield Armory and Winchester Repeating Arms Company, some 5.5 million Garands were delivered. There was also an M-1 carbine that used a 15- to 30-round box magazine, but fired a different type of .30-caliber ammunition than the standard rifle.

The 1st Marine Division embarked on Christmas Eve for the assault and spent Christmas day at sea. At approximately 7:45 A.M. on December 26, after a traditional breakfast of steak and eggs, the Marine transports passed through breaks in the reef surrounding Cape Gloucester and the 1st Marine Division began landing. The 7th Marines landed seven miles east of the cape and were followed by most of the 1st Marines. The 2nd Battalion, 1st Marines landed at Tauali to the west of the cape, in position to cut off escape or reinforcements. The initial landing met little resistance, and within the hour, the 7th Marines had established a strong beachhead. The 1st Marines moved past them and advanced toward the nearby airfield.

As the monsoon rains struck on the night of December 26, however, the 2nd Battalion, 53rd Japanese Imperial Infantry counterattacked, striking at the center of the Marine perimeter. In the morning, the 1st and 3rd Battalions, 1st Marines pushed through the swamp and up the coastal road. They encountered the 1st Battalion, 53rd Japanese Imperial Infantry in a line of defenses that the Marines soon dubbed "Hell's Point." By December 28, however, the Marines had managed to dislodge the Japanese and push them back. The 5th Marines, held in reserve up until this point, landed and moved up to support the 1st Marines, and by the end of December 28, the 1st and 5th Marines had captured the nearby airfield.

On the next day, Rupertus ordered Shepherd to lead the 7th Marines and the 3rd Battalion, 5th Marines against General Matsuda, then believed to be well established in high jungle terrain to the south. As the Marines advanced through the rain-soaked jungles, they intercepted an order indicating that the Japanese planned to hold Aogiri Ridge at any cost. The Marines reached Aogiri on January 8, 1944. Lieutenant Colonel Lewis Walt dragged a 37mm gun, the only heavy field piece the 7th Marines had, into position and blasted the ridge with anti-personnel canister. Walt reloaded the gun, pushed it farther up hill, and blasted the ridge again. His Marines jumped to help him, and inch by inch, the 3rd Battalion, 5th Marines struggled up the ridge, capturing it by nightfall. Walt's Marines held the ridge against five wild banzai attacks on the night of January 9, and Aogiri Ridge was dubbed "Walt's Ridge."

The last height remaining in Japanese hands after Walt's assault on Aogiri ridge was Hill 660. Lieutenant Colonel Henry Buse led the 3rd Battalion, 7th Marines around behind the hill while another battalion distracted the enemy. The 3rd Battalion hauled itself up the hill, surprised the few remaining defenders, and captured Hill 660. Matsuda launched a weak counterattack that was easily repulsed on January 16 and then retreated along the north coast, leaving dead and dying soldiers along the trail. Although Matsuda's straggling forces managed to elude the Marines, the Japanese had lost most of their desire to fight.

The 40th U.S. Infantry Division relieved the 1st Marine Division on April 28, 1944. New Britain had cost the Old Breed 310 dead and another 1,083 wounded. With Rabaul neutralized, however, the Allied campaign in the Pacific could begin its advance toward the Japanese home islands.

CHAPTER 10

UNCOMMON VALOR: THE SECOND WORLD WAR, 1943–1945

The Battle of Guadalcanal was the turning point in the Pacific theater of the Second World War. Initially put on the defensive by Japan's surprise attack at the end of 1941, the Battles of Midway and Coral Sea proved to be essentially defensive actions, stopping the Japanese advance. Operation Watchtower marked the first offensive move made by Allied forces in the Pacific, and the capture of Guadalcanal prevented a renewed Japanese offensive.

The question now was, which way do we go from here? Two strategies were proposed. General Douglas MacArthur, obsessed with returning to the Philippines, argued that the Allied advance should continue in the southwest Pacific toward the Philippines, which could provide important air bases. Admiral Ernest King, the Chief of Naval Operations, argued that the strategic plans prepared during the interwar years, which called for an amphibious campaign through the central Pacific, should be followed, driving a wedge in Japan's far-flung empire.

In the end, both strategies were followed, and MacArthur began his march toward the Philippines while Admiral Chester Nimitz, commander in chief of the Pacific Fleet, launched a campaign through the central Pacific. Nimitz's campaign would begin in the Gilbert Islands, which would provide important bases for aerial support, and continue through the Marshall Islands, the Mariana Islands, the Caroline Islands, then on to Japan itself. The Marine Corps would make up the majority of his expeditionary forces.

Major General Holland "Howlin' Mad" Smith was given command of V Amphibious Corps, composed of the Army's 27th Infantry Division under the command of Major General Ralph Smith and the 2nd Marine Division under the command of Major General Julian Smith, for Operation Galvanic in the Gilbert Islands. Smith had enlisted in the Marine Corps in 1905 and served in Santo Domingo and in France during the First World War. During the 1920s and 1930s, Smith had become heavily involved in the development of amphibious warfare doctrines. Nimitz had selected Smith specifically to command the expeditionary forces.

The assault on the Gilbert Islands would consist of the 2nd Marine Division attacking the Tarawa Atoll while the 165th Infantry, 27th Division attacked the Makin Atoll. On November 20, the 165th Infantry landed on Butaritari Island in the Makin Atoll. There were only some 800 Japanese on the island, but it took the 6,470 men of the 165th Infantry, led by old officers employing First World War tactics unsuitable for island warfare, 4 days to clear the island.

Betio Island was selected as the key island in the Tarawa Atoll because the Japanese had built three airfields on it. The island had been fortified with more than 500 artillery pieces and pillboxes and was defended by some 2,600 Japanese sailors under the command of Rear Admiral Keichi Shibasaki. Another 2,600 airfield specialists and laborers were on the island as well.

In addition, the island was ringed by a coral reef, promising great difficulty in landing on its beaches. Major Henry Drewes's 2nd Amphibian Tractor Battalion began tinkering with amphibian tractors and converting them into assault landing craft. His men added some armor and machine gun turrets and modified the exhaust system and bilge pump for an extended ship-to-shore amphibious landing. They managed to convert the 75 vehicles immediately available, and Howlin' Mad Smith demanded another 50 before the assault began.

THE ALLIGATOR

In 1926, and again in 1928 and 1932, Florida was hit by a series of disastrous hurricanes. In 1933, engineer and inventor Donald Roebling began work on a vehicle that could operate in the area where a boat would be beached and a car or truck would be flooded. By 1935, Roebling had built a prototype vehicle made of aluminum. Dubbed the "Alligator," the vehicle was propelled by its tracks both in water and on land.

Life magazine published an article on the Alligator in the October 4, 1937, issue, which was brought to the attention of Major General Louis Little, commander of the Fleet Marine Force. Intrigued, General Little forwarded the article to Commandant Holcomb, who in 1938 directed the Marine Corps Equipment Board to investigate its possible use for amphibious warfare. Although the Equipment Board returned a favorable report recommending further investigations, the Alligator wasn't immediately adopted due to a lack of funding. A few months later, however, the Equipment Board convinced Roebling, using his own resources as the Marines had none to spare, to make a number of modifications to the Alligator. Roebling's new model was completed and tested at Quantico and in the Caribbean in 1940. It was adopted and designated the Landing Vehicle, Tracked (LVT).

The first LVT, built of steel instead of aluminum and equipped with .50-caliber and .30-caliber machine guns, weighed in at 16,900 pounds and could achieve speeds of only about 4 knots on water and 15 miles per hour on land. However, it was an amphibious vehicle capable of carrying up to 20 troops and their equipment, or up to 4,500 pounds of equipment. The first LVTs would be ready for the assault on Tarawa.

Variants on the Alligator soon followed. Larger LVTs, weighing up to 28,000 pounds, could carry 24 troops or 8,000 pounds of cargo, and could achieve speeds of 5.2 knots on water and 25 miles per hour on land. Another model, the LVT(a), was equipped with heavier armor and weapons. The third variation of this model weighed 38,000 pounds, was equipped with a 75mm howitzer, and could still achieve speeds of 5.2 knots on water and 25 miles per hour on land. LVTs were used extensively during the Pacific island-hopping campaign of the Second World War.

On November 20, the Marines launched their attack on Betio. The assault began with a naval bombardment that was supposed to knock out the island's guns. As the 2nd Marine Division began its assault, however, it came under heavy fire. Nevertheless, Lieutenant William Hawkins led his party of scout-snipers and combat engineers onto the beach and began burning out the maze of gun emplacements with flamethrowers. Hawkins himself was wounded twice but still destroyed six machine gun nests. His heroic efforts would earn him the Medal of Honor. Following Hawkins's men, the 2nd battalion, 8th Marines and the 2nd and 3rd Battalions, 2nd Marines landed on Betio as well. Without sufficient LVTs, however, the 1st Battalion, 2nd Marines and the 3rd Battalion, 8th Marines were forced to wade across the reef and suffered heavy casualties as they struggled toward the beach.

The assault on Betio was plagued by difficulty. The 2nd Battalion, 2nd Marines suffered heavy casualties from gun emplacements that Hawkins's scout-snipers had been unable to reach. The 1st Battalion, 2nd Marines followed the 2nd Battalion, 2nd Marines, but the 3rd Battalion, 8th Marines, was shelled as it unloaded its landing craft. Colonel David Shoup, commanding the 2nd Marines, found himself defending a perimeter around the pier with parts of four different battalions.

Major Michael Ryan, a company commander in the 3rd Battalion, 2nd Marines, found himself leading the entire 3rd Battalion, which had become separated from its command group, onto the far western shore. The remnants of four different landing parties eventually joined Ryan's battalion and were dubbed "Ryan's Orphans." Behind Ryan, two Sherman tanks stumbled up the beach. Colonel Shoup had expected the 14 Sherman tanks attached to the division to perform well during the assault, but the 2 that scrambled on to the beach behind Ryan were the only ones to survive the landing. Some 5,000 Marines had made it to shore, but another 1,500 had been killed or wounded. Shoup and Ryan began to advance across the island. Using the two Sherman tanks to his best advantage, Ryan was able to secure the western end of the island by noon. Shoup led four battalions across the middle of the island, and by nightfall, he had reached the southern shore. General Julian Smith realized that the situation was desperate and requested the 6th Marines be brought out of reserve. Late in the afternoon on November 21, Major William Jones led the 1st Battalion, 6th Marines on shore, and the next morning launched an attack that helped secure the western two thirds of the island.

The Japanese counterattacked that night but with little effect, and the next morning the 3rd Battalion, 6th Marines passed through the Marine line to capture the eastern end of the island. By early afternoon, after more than three days of combat, General Julian Smith declared the island secure.

Approximately 4,690 Japanese had been killed on Betio, and 17 Japanese soldiers and 129 Korean laborers had been taken prisoner. The 2nd Marine Division lost 984 dead, 2,072 wounded, and 88 missing in action, a casualty rate of 19 percent. Colonel Shoup was awarded the Medal of Honor for his leadership on Tarawa.

★★★

Commandant Thomas Holcomb retired on January 1, 1944, and was awarded a fourth star for his service, making him the first Marine to hold the rank of full general. General Alexander Vandegrift, who had returned to Washington from the Pacific campaign in November, assumed the office of Marine Corps commandant.

The Allied campaign continued its advance toward Japan by attacking the Marshall Islands, which the Japanese had controlled in trust since the end of the First World War. Howlin' Mad Smith objected to an attack in the Marshall Islands, however. The assault on Tarawa had been extremely costly, and Smith believed it had been a terrible mistake; the Marshall Islands seemed to offer no better prospects than had Tarawa. Admiral Turner overruled Smith, however, and Operation Flintlock would be carried out as planned.

Nevertheless, the lessons learned at Tarawa proved invaluable in taking the Marshall Islands. Howlin' Mad Smith had at his command the V Amphibious Corps. The Army's 7th Division was assigned to take Kwajalein Atoll at the southern end of the islands, while the newly created 4th Marine Division would take the islands of Roi-Namur in the north. In a second operation, Operation Catchpole, the 22nd Marines and the 106th Infantry would seize Eniwetok Atoll.

The western half of Roi-Namur was dominated by an X-shape airfield. Most of the quarters and supply depots were on the eastern half. The island itself boasted a sizeable Japanese base of approximately 3,000 soldiers, but it wasn't very well defended. For 2 days prior to the assault, the Navy dropped more than 36,000 shells on the island—more than 4 times the number used at Tarawa—and aircraft squadrons managed to destroy all the Japanese planes in the Marshall Islands. On January 31, the 25th Marines secured numerous islets around Roi-Namur, and the 14th Marines, the

4th Marine Division's artillery regiment, prepared to provide covering fire for the next day's assault. At 11 A.M. on February 1, equipped with three times the number of LVTs as at Tarawa, Colonel Louis Jones's 23rd Marines landed on Roi, and Colonel Franklin Hart's 24th Marines landed on Namur.

There was little opposition on Roi, and the regiment charged over the island rather chaotically, killing the few confused Japanese soldiers who had survived the naval bombardment. The 24th Marines found greater resistance on Namur, but by evening they had control of approximately two thirds of the island, and by February 2, they had secured the rest of the island. The Japanese lost 3,563 dead. The 4th Marine Division lost 313 dead and another 502 wounded.

The same day the Marines landed on Roi-Namur, the 7th Infantry Division began its assault on Kwajalein Atoll and secured it by February 5. They lost 173 GIs killed and 793 wounded and killed some 4,800 Japanese soldiers.

Due to the success on Roi-Namur and Kwajalein, Operation Catchpole—the amphibious assault on Eniwetok Atoll—was accelerated from May 1 to February 17. The V Amphibious Corps reserve unit, the 22nd Marines and the 106th Infantry, under the command of Brigadier General Thomas "Terrible Tommy" Watson, would make the assault. Three islands in the atoll were targeted: Engebi, where there was an airfield; Eniwetok itself; and Parry.

As at Kwajalein, elements of the 22nd Marines landed on several small islands surrounding Engebi to secure supporting artillery positions for the main assault. On February 18, following an impressive naval bombardment, the 22nd Marines stormed onto the shore of Engebi. By February 19, Engebi was secure, and the American flag was raised as a Marine played "To the Colors" on a captured Japanese bugle.

Eniwetok Island proved more difficult. The 106th Infantry landed there on the morning of February 19 but made little progress. The 3rd Battalion, 22nd Marines joined the 106th Infantry that afternoon. Two days of fierce combat followed, but by February 21, Eniwetok was secured as well. Somewhat disappointed by the performance of the 106th Infantry on Eniwetok, and worried that the Army would be unable to secure Parry Island, which had even more defenders than Eniwetok, General Watson assigned the capture of Parry Island to the 22nd Marines.

In preparation, Navy ships bombarded Parry while Marine artillery blasted it from nearby Japtan. On February 22, the 22nd Marines went ashore. Despite the heavy bombardment, fighting was fierce. One band of 50 Japanese soldiers launched a desperate counterattack but was cut down by machine guns. By February 23, Parry Island was secure. Approximately 3,400 Japanese were killed and 66 were taken prisoner. The Marines lost 254 dead and another 555 wounded. The Marshall Islands had been captured with relative ease compared to Tarawa Atoll.

There were other islands in the Marshall Islands group but most of them were small and lightly defended. Furthermore, with the capture of Eniwetok Atoll, the Allies could control supply and reinforcement of the Marshalls. To ensure that the other islands remained quiet, the 4th Marine Base Defense Aircraft Wing established its headquarters at Kwajalein on March 9, MAG-31 moved up to Roi on March 15, and MAG-13 moved to Majuro on March 21. Frequent bombardment and fighter sweeps pacified the bypassed islands. The Allies had effectively reclaimed nearly 60,000 square miles in the central Pacific.

NAVAJO CODE TALKERS

Communications proved crucial during the Second World War. The interception of a significant code at the appropriate moment could save the day, as it had at Midway. The reverse was true as well, and the U.S. Marine Corps initiated a program to safeguard its own communications.

Philip Johnston, a First World War veteran and missionary to the Navajo for 24 years who spoke their language fluently, knew of the military need for communication codes. In February 1942, Johnston met with Major General Clayton Vogel, the commanding general of Amphibious Corps, Pacific Fleet, at Camp Elliot, California, and convinced him that Navajo could be used as a code for communications. Johnston demonstrated that military orders could be translated into Navajo, transmitted, and translated back into English flawlessly. In fact, Johnston's demonstration proved that reports and orders could be transmitted faster than conventional cryptographic methods. Vogel passed the idea on to Marine Commandant Thomas Holcomb.

In September 1942, the Marine Corps began recruiting 200 Navajo into a highly classified program. The first recruits were trained at Camp Pendleton, where they received basic training and communications training and helped devise the code language to be used before being assigned to the Pacific. In May 1943, the Code Talkers were given high praise for their performance in combat. By August 1943, 191 Navajo had joined the program and served throughout the Pacific theater, including at Guadalcanal, Tarawa, Saipan, Peleliu, Iwo Jima, and the Philippines. Although Navajo messages were undoubtedly intercepted, no evidence exists that they were ever deciphered.

★★★

The third link in the drive toward Japan was the Mariana Islands. The Marianas were to be an important strategic move. An attack there, the Navy hoped, would draw out the Japanese fleet for a final battle. More important, perhaps, the capture of the Marianas would provide an important base from which the Air Force could begin launching aerial attacks against Japan itself.

The U.S. military gathered a massive force in the Marshall Islands: 800 ships and 162,000 men forming Admiral Raymond Spruance's Fifth Fleet. Rear Admiral Richmond Turner commanded the amphibious forces while Lieutenant General Holland Smith commanded the expeditionary forces, which were divided into a northern force and a southern force. The Northern Troops and Landing Force, which Howlin' Mad Smith also commanded, included General Watson's 2nd Marine Division and General Schmidt's 4th Marine Division. The Southern Troops and Landing Force, commanded by Major General Roy Geiger, included the 3rd Marine Division under Major General Allen Turnage, the 1st Provisional Marine Brigade under Brigadier General Lemuel Shepherd, and the 9th and 14th Marine Defense Battalions. The Army's 27th Infantry Division under General Ralph Smith was held in floating reserve while the 77th Infantry Division was in strategic reserve in Hawaii.

Three islands in particular were targeted. Saipan would be attacked first on June 15, 1944, followed by Guam three days later, and then Tinian. Unfortunately, these islands would prove much more difficult and costly to capture than had the Marshall Islands. Saipan was 14 miles of mountainous, wooded terrain surrounded by coral reef. Nearly 30,000 Japanese troops were stationed on the island, including the 31st Army under the command of Lieutenant General Yoshitsugo Saito. In addition, the Japanese Central Pacific Fleet under Admiral Chiuchi Nagumo was headquartered at Saipan.

The Marines were well equipped for the assault on the Marianas with a variety of LVTs and LVT(a)s, Sherman tanks, mortars, and flamethrowers. From June 11 through 14, the Navy bombarded Saipan, and early on the morning of June 15 the 24th Marines and the 1st Battalion, 29th Marines launched a feint at Tanapag Harbor. Neither preparation was successful, however. The 6th and 8th Marines, 2nd Division led the assault on the north end of the beach while the 23rd and 25th Marines, 4th Division led the assault farther south. In 20 minutes, 700 LVTs carried some 8,000 Marines over the reef and onto the beach, where they immediately encountered heavy mortar and artillery fire. The Marines suffered more than 2,000 casualties during the initial assault and lost several battalion commanders.

Almost immediately, however, the assault on Saipan had the desired effect of drawing out the main Japanese battle fleet. On June 16, Admiral Spruance assigned Task Force 58 under the command of Vice Admiral Marc Mitscher to deal with the Japanese fleet. On June 19, during the so-called Marianas Turkey Shoot, Mitscher's Task Force shot down 346 Japanese planes and on the following day launched an attack on the Japanese fleet that sank an aircraft carrier. One hundred American planes were lost during the Battle of the Philippine Sea.

Holland Smith met with Turner and decided to postpone the assault on Guam. Furthermore, they decided to land the 27th Infantry Division on Saipan and bring the 77th Division forward from Hawaii. The fighting was rough, but by noon on June 16 the 2nd Division had managed to capture Charan-Kanoa, and the 4th Division was struggling forward to give the 165th Infantry enough room to come ashore. On the morning of June 17, the Japanese 9th Tank Division counterattacked against the 2nd Division and roared through its ranks, nearly reaching the command post of the 6th Marines before it was stopped. Later that morning, the Marines renewed their slow advance. The 4th Division struggled across the island, reaching Magicienne Bay, and the 165th and the 105th Infantry moved south to capture Aslito airfield and push a Japanese battalion into Nafutan Point at the southern tip of the island.

For three days, the three American divisions on the southern end of Saipan maneuvered in preparation for a northward push. The 2nd Division held its ground while the 4th Division began a move to the north. The 27th

Infantry, leaving one battalion behind to deal with Nafutan Point, moved up between the 2nd and the 4th Marine Divisions.

On June 23, 18 batteries of artillery laid down a covering screen as the three divisions began the push to the north. The 2nd Marines captured the now deserted town of Garapan on June 24 while the 8th Marines began climbing Mount Tapotchau and the 4th Marine Division captured Hill 600, "Hot Potato Hill," at the northern end of Magicienne Bay. The 27th Infantry, however, following General Ralph Smith's outdated tactics, lagged behind in the middle.

General Holland Smith had come to doubt the efficiency of General Ralph Smith's leadership throughout the entire campaign in the central Pacific and now felt compelled to relieve him of command. Admiral Spruance and Admiral Turner supported his decision. The decision had unfortunate consequences for interservice relations, however. The Army resented the fact that one of its officers had been relieved of command by a Marine and determined never to allow another Marine to command Army forces. Despite Spruance's and Turner's initial support, the Navy failed to support General Holland Smith's decision. Relations between the Army and the Marines remained poor throughout the end of the Second World War and into the Korean War.

On June 25, Lieutenant Colonel Rathvon Tompkins, leading the 1st Battalion, 29th Marines, outflanked the Japanese and captured Mount Tapotchau. On June 26, the Japanese punched through the 2nd Battalion, 105th Infantry and broke out of Nafutan Point. The Japanese battalion managed to make it as far as Aslito airfield before the 25th and the 14th Marines stopped them. In the north, the 4th Marine Division and the 27th Infantry pressed the assault.

By early July, the Japanese commanders had come to realize that it was just a matter of time before the Americans defeated their troops. On July 6, General Saito committed *seppuku* and was ceremoniously shot by his executive officer, and Admiral Nagumo shot himself. The Japanese made one final counterattack on July 7. Some 3,000 Japanese soldiers led by officers waving samurai swords launched a banzai attack and exploded into the 105th Infantry. They were stopped by the artillery of the 3rd Battalion, 10th Marines, firing their howitzers at an enemy only 55 yards distant.

The 2nd Marine Division relieved the 27th Infantry, and the two Marine divisions pressed on toward the northern tip of the island. The few remaining Japanese soldiers and civilians fled before the Marines to the 220-foot cliff at Marpi Point on the north end of the island where, to the distress of even battle-hardened Marines, soldiers and civilians alike committed mass suicide by throwing themselves off the cliff or exploding hand grenades. Such suicidal determination indicated just how hard it would be to defeat the Japanese. After 24 days of combat, Saipan was declared secure on July 9.

The death toll on Saipan was horrendous. More than 28,800 Japanese were killed on Saipan while only 736 prisoners were captured, most of whom were Korean laborers. American casualties numbered 3,225 killed, 13,099 wounded, and 326 missing in action. Two thirds of the casualties were Marines.

★★★

Guam was similar to Saipan but larger. Approximately 225 square miles in area, the southern half of the island was mountainous and wooded, while the northern half was flatter but just as densely covered. Lieutenant General Takeshi Takashina, a veteran of the Japanese invasion of Manchuria, commanded the defense of the island. Under his command were approximately 13,000 army soldiers, with another 5,500 naval troops led by Captain Yutaka Sugimoto.

General Roy Geiger's Southern Troops and Landing Force was given the task of invading Guam. The invasion had originally been planned for June 18, 1944, but the difficulty in taking Saipan required that the invasion date be postponed until July 21, 1944. In the meantime, the Marines waited in the sweltering heat.

The Japanese had been overly confident at the beginning of the Allied campaign in the Pacific and had believed several of the islands and atolls they controlled, such as Tarawa, to be impregnable. As a result, Takashina had not begun fortifying Guam until after the Marshall Islands had fallen. He concentrated his defenses at Tumon Bay, an ideal landing site on the west coast of the island just north of the capital, where he expected the Americans to strike. Geiger had other plans, however.

After a 13-day aerial and naval bombardment, Geiger struck at the beach between Adelup Point and Asan Point and at Gaan Point along the southwest coast. On July 21, LVTs carrying the 3rd Division crawled over the coral reef surrounding the island as LVT(a)s armed with 37mm and 75mm cannons provided some cover for the scrambling Marines. As soon as the Marines came across the reef the Japanese began bombarding them with artillery fire, and as they scrambled onto the beach they found themselves caught in a deadly crossfire from machine guns carefully concealed in the cliffs surrounding the beach.

Farther south at Gaan Point, the 1st Provisional Marine Brigade encountered two 75mm guns in the hollowed-out rock of the point. The Japanese guns managed to destroy some two dozen LVTs, but the Marines scrambled onto the beach, wading ashore from their wrecked LVTs. The 77th Division came ashore the next day.

The stiff resistance slowed the Marine advance, but they held their positions on the beach and continued to press inland. At about midnight on July 25, Takashina's troops stormed out of the jungles and attacked the Marines. Lieutenant Colonel Robert Cushman's 2nd Battalion, 9th Marines fought off seven attacks, losing half his men that night. Despite having been wounded three times earlier in the day, Captain Louis Wilson, commanding Company F of Cushman's battalion, led his company through 10 hours of fierce hand-to-hand combat. At one point, Wilson bravely ran out into the open to rescue one of his wounded Marines, and at another, he led a small patrol that knocked out a Japanese machine gun. Captain Wilson was awarded the Medal of Honor.

By July 27, Takashina had lost nearly 3,500 men, and the Marines had resumed their offensive. On July 28, the 1st Provisional Marine Brigade cleared Orote Peninsula, and the 22nd Marines reached the burned-out husk of the old Marine barrack there. A few days later, MAG-21 began flying missions from the airfield on the peninsula.

The 3rd Marine Division and the 77th Infantry Division began a sweep through the rest of the island. Struggling through the hot jungle and the pouring rain, the Marines crushed the remaining Japanese resistance and drove them onto the northern cliffs of the island, where they, too, committed mass suicide. Geiger declared Guam secure on August 10.

The Marines lost 1,919 dead and 7,122 wounded. Another 70 Marines were reported missing in action. Approximately 485 Japanese were taken prisoner and 17,300 killed. Incredibly, one Japanese soldier managed to escape the American advance: Sergeant Shoichi Yokoi hid in the jungles of Guam, living in a cave and surviving on berries, nuts, snails, and rats. He was discovered in 1972, 26 years later.

★★★

Three days after the invasion of Guam began, the Allies invaded Tinian, a small island just south of Saipan. In contrast to Saipan and Guam, Tinian is a relatively flat plateau and was widely planted with sugar cane. This was the attraction of Tinian—relatively flat land largely cleared of brush and jungle would make an excellent airfield from which B-29 bombers could launch attacks on Japan. The defense of the island was led by the conservative Colonel Keishi Ogata, who had at his disposal 4,700 soldiers and 4,110 sailors.

All the artillery on Saipan was massed at the southern tip of that island to facilitate the bombardment of the northern tip of Tinian, only 2.5 miles away. Navy ships and Army and Marine squadrons flying bombing missions from Saipan supplied additional bombardment. On July 24, the 2nd Marine Division under General Watson executed a convincing amphibious feint against Tinian Town on the southwest coast of the island while the 4th Marine Division under Colonel Clifton Cates made a shore-to-shore amphibious assault from Saipan in LVTs. The Marines encountered only light resistance, and the 23rd Marines came ashore later in the day.

Colonel Ogata hoped to stop the invasion on the beaches and launched an immediate counterattack on July 25, but to no effect. General Watson led the 2nd Marine Division on shore the next morning and captured Ushi airfield. The two divisions turned south and, riding on tanks, chased the fleeing Japanese soldiers through sugar cane fields. On August 1, the Marines had reached the southern coast of the island, and Tinian was declared secure.

The Marines captured 255 Japanese soldiers and sailors and killed 6,050. Marine casualties numbered 290 dead and 1,515 wounded; 24 Marines were missing in action. The Marianas campaign had consumed some 30,000 Japanese troops and another 27,000 Japanese civilians in total. American casualties numbered more than 27,000. Ten Marines were awarded Medals of Honor for the Marianas campaign, eight of which were awarded post-humously.

★★★

For the next stage of the war in the Pacific, the Marines were ordered to take the island of Peleliu. General MacArthur, obsessed with returning to the Philippines, believed that the elimination of the Japanese airfields on Peleliu were necessary to protect the Army's advance, and Admiral Chester Nimitz had promised MacArthur that the Navy and the Marines would assist him in this endeavor.

Peleliu was the southernmost island of the Palau island group, which in turn was the westernmost extremity of the Caroline Islands. It was a relatively small island, perhaps six miles long and two miles wide, but it was riddled with natural and man-made caves in the coral cliffs, especially in Umurobrogal Ridge in the center of the island, and sweltering mangrove swamps. There was an airfield on the southern end of the island, which was somewhat flatter than the rest of the island. Colonel Kunio Nakagawa was in charge of the defense of Peleliu and had at his command some 6,000 soldiers and another 4,100 sailors.

Operation Stalemate II, the invasion of Peleliu, was given to Major General Roy Geiger. The expeditionary force would be composed of the Major General William Rupertus's 1st Marine Division, the "Old Breed," reinforced to a strength of 28,484 men, and the 81st U.S. Division fresh out of Hawaii. The plan of attack was very similar to the attack on Tinian. While the 81st Division demonstrated off Babelthuap, the largest island in the Palaus, the 1st Marine Division would launch an assault on Peleliu, landing near the airfield on the southernmost beaches of the island.

The assault was set for September 15, 1944, and military planners believed that the island would be secured in only four days. As at Tinian, a naval bombardment preceded the assault on Peleliu beginning on September 12, 1944. On the morning of September 15, the 1st Marine Division—led by some of the most experienced officers in the Corps, including Colonel Herman Hanneken, Colonel Harold "Bucky" Harris, and Colonel Chesty Puller—began its landing on the island. Private First Class Eugene "Sledgehammer" Sledge, a 19-year-old raw recruit facing his first battle, described how the beaches seemed to burn with fire from the naval bombardment. White with terror, Sledge and his fellow Marines stumbled out of their LVT into a web of machine gun fire.

The Japanese Imperial Army had become distressed by the apparent ease with which the American Navy and Marines had conquered their supposedly impregnable islands. An investigation of the amphibious assaults carried out by the Americans led to a reevaluation of Japanese defensive tactics. Instead of trying to oppose the landing at the water's edge, as Colonel Ogata had attempted on Tinian, the defenders were to disrupt the landing, retreat to a "honeycomb" of defensive positions, and then launch small, stinging counterattacks in an attempt to "bleed" the invaders. These new tactics proved effective.

For the most part, the naval bombardment had been ineffectual; Nakagawa's troops had hunkered down inside Umurbrogol Ridge. As the amphibious landing vehicles crossed the reef, Nakagawa pounded the landing force with machine guns, mortars, and 47mm antiboat guns hidden in the caves along the beaches. Some 60 LVTs were wrecked. Once the Marines had waded ashore, Chesty Puller led the 1st Marines north against Umurbrogol Ridge while Hanneken led the 7th Marines into the southern end of the island and Bucky Harris struck out toward the airfield. That afternoon, Nakagawa attacked the Marines with tanks and infantry. Harris's 5th Marines shattered the assault, but the Marine advance had ground to a halt. Some 200 Marines had been killed and another 900 wounded during the first day of battle.

The next morning, the 7th Marines made significant progress in the south, and the 5th Marines scrambled across the airfield. As they crossed the airfield, the 5th Marines came under heavy artillery fire from Umurbrogol Ridge. Chesty Puller's 1st Marines ran up against Umurbrogol Ridge itself. Rupertus expected the Japanese to come storming out of the ridge in a wild banzai attack as they had done in every previous battle, but they didn't. Nakagawa sat in his fortified caves and continued to pound the Marines. For six days, Puller's 1st Marines tried to storm "Bloody Nose Ridge." By September 20, the 1st Marines had suffered nearly 60 percent casualties, and Geiger ordered the 7th Marines to relieve Puller's battalion.

While Hanneken attacked the ridge, Colonel Harris led the 5th Marines up along the coast to the northern end of the island. By September 26,

Harris had secured the northern tip, but mortar fire rained down on the 5th Marines from nearby Ngesebus Island. On September 28, preceded by a naval bombardment and supported by 16 Sherman tanks and Marine Fighter Squadron 114, the 3rd Battalion, 5th Marines made a shore-to-shore amphibious assault on Ngesebus and secured it.

This left just Umurbrogol itself, which Nakagawa still controlled, and Harris's Marines moved up to take a turn at the ridge. Eugene Sledge could only describe the experience as surreal nightmare. Sledge's company suffered 65 percent causalities on Peleliu. By October 1, however, MAG-11 and Marine Fighter Squadrons 114 and 122 were on Peleliu and ready to use the airfield, which had been repaired by the Seabees, the Navy's industrious construction unit. Their targets were so close to the airfield that the pilots made their attack run 15 seconds after take-off. This allowed them to use a few new weapons, including rockets and napalm.

The bombardment took its toll on Nakagawa. In the end, having withstood the American assault for nearly a month, Nakagawa burned his regimental colors and committed suicide. The Japanese government promoted him to lieutenant general posthumously for his defense of the island. By October 15, Peleliu was essentially secure, and the 81st Infantry took over mopping up operations.

The fighting on Peleliu had been savage. American casualties numbered 1,794 killed, of whom 1,241 were Marines, and 7,800 wounded, of whom 5,024 were Marines. Another 117 Marines were reported missing in action. Eight Marines were awarded Medals of Honor; 6 of them were awarded posthumously. The Japanese suffered 10,695 men killed; only 302 Japanese soldiers were taken prisoner.

Eugene Sledge had been horrified as he waded ashore and his comrades were cut down helplessly. The Japanese, he later commented, killed without hope or higher purpose. They seemed to know that they could not stop the Americans and that no reinforcements were coming to their aid. Driven by an ancient code of honor, the Japanese refused to surrender even if it meant death. Faced with such mad fanaticism, the Marines turned savage as well. Enduring filth, fatigue, terror, and death, the Marines fought for survival and developed a brutish hatred for the Japanese. Sledge recounted stories of Marines collecting gold teeth from dead Japanese soldiers, and even more horrifying, his own desire to collect the same. In the brutish

Pacific war, civilization wore thin and life lost meaning. The experience of Peleliu proved to be in vain, however: The airfields on the island were never used to support MacArthur's return to the Philippines.

★★★

The reoccupation of the Philippines, which began on October 20, 1944, was primarily an Army affair involving the X and XXIV Corps. However, the artillery of the Army's XXIV Corps was moved to support the Marine assault on the Mariana Islands, and MacArthur suddenly found that he didn't have sufficient artillery support for an invasion of the Philippines. Marine Brigadier General Thomas Bourke led elements of the Marine V Amphibious Corps Artillery onto Leyte Island, supporting the Army's XXIV Corps during the landing. True to the Marine spirit, Privates First Class Walter Dangerfield, Shelby Heimback, and Frank Pinciotti hung a sign over their 155mm "Long Tom" Howitzer that read, "By the Grace of God and the Help of the Marines MacArthur Has Returned to the Philippines." The Marines were ordered to take down the sign lest MacArthur happen to see it, but the phrase soon spread throughout the islands.

The V Amphibious Corps artillery continued to support the Army's assault on Leyte Island into December, when it was relieved by return of the Army's XXIV Corps artillery. But Marine activities did not end with the departure of Bourke's artillery. Japanese air superiority continued in the Philippines, allowing the Japanese to significantly reinforce their position on Leyte, nearly doubling their forces to 48,000 men. The Japanese were equipped with Nakajima Ki-43 Hayabusa planes, fast night fighter-bombers that simply outclassed the P-61 Northrop Black Widow fighters with which the Army Air Force was equipped. Marine Major General Ralph Mitchell, commander of the 1st Marine Aircraft Wing still stationed in the Solomon Islands, offered MacArthur Marine air support, and MacArthur opted to take advantage of the vast experience of the Marine pilots. By December 3, Marine Night-Fighter Squadron 541 had arrived at Tacloban airfield on Leyte and began flying missions in support of the Army's campaign on the island.

Four squadrons of Corsairs, forming MAG-12, soon followed. Initially, Marine aviation offered protection to U.S. Navy convoys and attacked

Japanese shipping in an effort to stifle the flow of Japanese reinforcements into western ports on Leyte Island. By the end of December, MAG-12, flying as a component of the Fifth Army Air Force, had suffered the loss of 34 planes and 9 pilots but had flown 264 missions, destroyed 40 planes, sunk 7 destroyers, 9 cargo ships, and 3 troop transports, and damaged another 11 ships. In addition, VMF(N)-541 had shot down 22 enemy planes and destroyed another 5 on the ground. The Army later awarded VMF(N)-541 its Distinguished Unit Citation.

By the end of December, the Army effectively controlled Leyte Island. In preparation for the continued invasion of the Philippines, more Marine Aircraft Groups were brought forward. Seven Marine Scout-Bomber Squadrons (VMSB) comprising MAG-24 and MAG-32 had arrived on Leyte by January 1945 and began flying missions in support of the Army's invasion of Luzon on January 25. Flying Douglass Dauntless SBDs, the Marines had dumped more than 200,000 pounds of bombs on Luzon by the end of February. In addition, the four Corsair fighter squadrons of MAG-14 were flying missions from Samar.

Beginning with the assault on Luzon and continuing through the rest of the campaign in the Philippines, Marine pilots provided close air support for the Army's ground forces, the mission for which Marine aviation had been created. Diving at angles approaching 70 degrees, the pilots dove at their targets, holding their target in their sights, and releasing their bombs at an elevation of 2,000 feet. The planes' momentum continued to carry them down to treetop level before the pilots were able to pull them out of their dive. Lieutenant Colonel Keith McCutcheon, the operations officer of MAG-24, described Marine aviation as "aerial artillery," but the audacity of the Marine pilots soon earned them the nickname "The Diving Devildogs of Luzon."

The Marines provided close air support throughout the Philippines campaign, including the 1st Cavalry Division's advance to Manila, the capital of the islands, and guerilla forces in northern Luzon. Between January 27 and April 14, MAG-24 and MAG-32 flew 8,842 combat missions, nearly half of all the missions flown on Luzon, even though the Marine planes accounted for only 13 percent of the aircraft on the island, and dropped 19,167 bombs. After Luzon, MAG-14 flew missions in support of various operations on Basilan, Panay, Cebu, and Negros. By May 15, when the

Group's operations ended, it had flown 7,396 sorties and destroyed 28 planes on the ground. MAG-12, MAG-24, and MAG-32 flew missions in support of the 41st Infantry on Mindano. Army Major General Jens Doe, commanding officer of the 41st Infantry, presented to the Marine aviators a plaque bearing a Japanese machine gun, a Japanese battle flag, and the inscription, "In Appreciation—41st Infantry Division." Mindano was declared secure on June 30. Between March 3, 1 week before the actual assault began, and June 30, Marines flew more than 20,000 sorties in 10,046 missions, dropped 4,800 tons of bombs, and launched 1,300 rockets.

★★★

Iwo Jima is a small volcanic island in the Volcano-Bonin Archipelago almost midway between the Mariana Islands and Japan. The island is perhaps five miles long and two and a half miles wide, maybe eight square miles in all. At its southern tip stands the island's volcano, Mount Suribachi. The rest of the island is made up of volcanic rock and loose black sand, and at the time the extinct volcano still radiated some heat and released noxious fumes, earning the island its name, "sulfur island." The loose volcanic sand was perfect for mixing with cement, and the Japanese had already built two airfields on the island and were building a third as well.

Lieutenant General Tadamichi Kuribayashi was in command of the defense of Iwo Jima. With some 14,000 soldiers and 7,000 sailors. Kuribayashi had heavily fortified the island with a line of fortifications crossing the island between the first and second airfields and a second line just constructed north of the second airfield. Kuribayashi had built more than 600 concrete bunkers and fortified machine gun and anti-tank gun emplacements on the small island.

Major General Harry Schmidt and the V Amphibious Corps would assault Iwo Jima. At Schmidt's command were the 3rd Marine Division under General Graves Erskine, the 4th Marine Division under Major General Clifton Cates, and the new 5th Marine Division under Major General Keller Rockey. The assault was originally planned for January 20, 1945, but the campaign in the Philippines delayed it until February 19. For 74 days before the assault, Army and Navy aircraft bombed the island, and shelling intensified for the 3 days prior to the assault. It was the most intense bombardment of the Pacific campaign, but the Japanese defenders hunkered down in their bunkers and waited it out.

Although there were no coral reefs to impede the landing on Iwo Jima, as there had been at Tarawa, Saipan, Guam, and Tinian, Kuribayashi had placed his guns to cover every beach. The Marines would be able to reach the island's beaches quickly, but they would come under immediate fire. General Holland Smith estimated than an assault on the bleak island would cost more than 15,000 American lives, but there seemed little alternative except a direct assault. The 4th and 5th Marine Divisions landed on the east coast of the island on February 19, the 5th Division on the southernmost beaches and the 4th Division farther north, while the 3rd Division remained in floating reserve. The Marines encountered only small arms fire as they landed.

By 10 A.M., 9,000 Marines were ashore, and Kuribayashi unleashed his artillery. Few landing vehicles were able to make it to the beaches after the formidable barrage began. Those that did found it difficult to move in the wet sand, and the few tanks on shore soon found themselves the targets of 47mm antitank guns. Sergeant Manila John Basilone, one of the heroes of Guadalcanal, urged his platoon to move off the beach as quickly as possible. He was killed by a mortar round. Basilone was awarded a Navy Cross posthumously for his heroism.

The Marines had made little progress on the first day of the assault, but more than 30,000 Marines had come ashore. On February 20, the 4th Division turned northward while the 27th Marines cut across the island just south of the first airfield and then began moving north in coordination with the 4th Division. The Lieutenant Colonel Harry Liversedge's 28th Marines began an assault on Mount Suribachi.

Approximately 1,600 Japanese defended Mount Suribachi, and by evening the 28th Marines had only progressed 200 yards. The following day, the Japanese launched a counterattack, but the Marines continued to crawl up the slopes. After four days of intense fighting, however, the Marines finally secured Mount Suribachi. A small American flag was attached to a pole on top of the mountain, and shortly thereafter a larger American flag replaced it. The Marines had difficulty setting the flag's pole in the volcanic rock, however, and another Marine and a hospital corpsman lent them a hand. Correspondent Joe Rosenthal captured the moment on film. Secretary of the Navy James Forrestal, who spotted the flag from offshore, remarked, "The raising of that flag on Suribachi means a Marine Corps for the next 500 years."

(Photo courtesy of AP Wide World Photos)

U.S. Marines of the 28th Regiment of the Fifth Division raise the American flag atop Mount Suribachi, Iwo Jima, on February 23, 1945. Strategically located only 660 miles from Tokyo, the Pacific island became the site of the bloodiest, most famous battles of World War II.

Meanwhile, the 4th Division and the 27th Marines continued to push north but ran into stiff resistance as they reached Kuribayashi's fortifications. Schmidt decided to lead the assault against the second airfield with the 21st Marines. Naval gunfire, carrier launched aircraft, and artillery provided a thunderous bombardment of the Japanese defenses, and on February 24, supported by as many tanks as could be found, the 21st Marines pushed a half mile to the north. General Erskine came ashore with elements of the 3rd Marines, and General Schmidt directed him to relieve the 21st Marines in the center. For three more days, the 9th Marines fought forward and took two small hills north of the second airfield. On February 28, the 21st Marines captured what remained of Motoyama Village and advanced into the hills near the third airfield.

The 3rd Division had made important progress, but the 5th Division had been stopped short of Hill 362A, and the 4th Division was struggling to take Hill 382, the "Meatgrinder." Schmidt brought the 28th Marines up from Suribachi to attack Hill 362A on March 1. By evening, they had secured it. The 26th Marines captured Hill 362B two days later. The 3rd Division pressed forward but was stopped by the dismounted Japanese 26th Tank Regiment at Hill 362C. The Japanese tank jockeys fought hard, but on March 7, with no artillery preparation, Erskine led a silent predawn assault on the hill and took them by surprise. By March 9, the 3rd Division had broken through to the northern shore of Iwo Jima.

The 9th Marines swung west while the 21st Marines swung east, and both regiments began marching south, pushing the remaining Japanese defenders before them and catching them against the 5th Division in the west and the 4th Division in the east. In the east, the Japanese made a desperate counter-attack on March 8, but with little effect, and by March 10 the last of the defenders had been killed. In the west, Rockey's 5th Division was facing Kuribayashi himself, who held out for another two weeks. The 5th and 3rd Divisions finally combined to trap Kuribayashi at Kintano Point. On the night of March 26, the Japanese made one last spasmodic counterattack. The 5th Pioneer Battalion killed 223 Japanese soldiers that night, among them many officers and probably Kuribayashi himself. The island was secure.

More than 22,000 Japanese soldiers were killed on Iwo Jima, and of the 71,245 Marines who landed on Iwo Jima, 5,931 were killed and 17,372 of them were wounded. Twenty-two Marines were awarded the Medal of Honor. Regarding the incredible achievement of the Marines, Fleet Admiral Chester Nimitz remarked, "Among the men who fought on Iwo Jima, uncommon valor was a common virtue."

★★★

Finally, the Allied forces prepared to assault Japan itself: Okinawa. Okinawa is approximately 60 miles long and varies between 2 and 18 miles wide. The northern half of the island, above its narrow waist, was rugged and mountainous but sparsely populated. The southern end of the island was heavily cultivated but still hilly, and several ridges cut across the island offering ideal defensive positions.

The island's defenses were under the command of Lieutenant General Mitsuru Ushijima. Under his command was the 32nd Army composed of two divisions, a brigade, a tank regiment, and lots of artillery. Rear Admiral Ota Minoru's naval base was situated at the southern end of the island as well. More than 155,000 defenders were estimated to be on the island. Taking advantage of the island's geography, Ushijima concentrated his defensive positions in the southern half of the island in three lines along the Kakazu Ridge, in front of Shuri Castle and the capital city of Naha, and along the Kunishi Ridge in the south. His command was centered at Shuri Castle. Ushijima had adopted the same plan of defense that had proven so deadly at Tinian and Iwo Jima: Allow the invaders to land, draw them into the open and hold them in place with a maze of defenses, then strike back hard.

Admiral Raymond Spruance was given overall command of Operation Iceberg, the invasion of Okinawa, while Admiral Richmond Turner commanded the amphibious forces. On shore, the expeditionary forces would be under the command of Army Lieutenant General Simon Buckner Jr., commander of the Tenth Army. There were two units. The northern force was composed of the General Roy Geiger's III Amphibious Corps, which included Major General Pedro del Valle's 1st Marine Division and General Lemuel Shepherd's 6th Marine Division. The southern force was composed of Major General John Hodge's XXIV Army Corps, including the 7th, 77th, and 96th Infantry Divisions. Major General LeRoy Hunt's 2nd Marine Division would stage a diversion for the southern landing force, and the 27th Infantry Division was held in reserve. All together, there were 182,112 men in the Tenth Army; 81,165 of them were Marines.

The assault was scheduled for Sunday, April 1, 1945. For one week before the assault, naval gunfire and aerial bombardment blasted the island in preparation for the landing. On April 1, General Hunt prepared to launch a feint attack with the 2nd Marine Division against the extreme southern tip of Okinawa. Before the feint could be launched, however, a kamikaze strike destroyed a transport and a landing ship, but the division made its run against the southern beaches anyway and then veered off at the last moment.

Meanwhile, the III Amphibious Corps and the XXIV Army Corps made their landing at the Tagushi beaches along the western coast of the island. The III Amphibious Corps landed near Yontan airfield just below Okinawa's narrow waist, and the XXIV Army Corps landed just south of the III Amphibious Corps.

The III Amphibious Corps was assigned to cut across the island and then turn north and secure the northern half of the island. By noon, Shepherd's 6th Division had raced across the island and secured the Yontan airfield, and by April 4, del Valle's 1st Marine Division had secured the Katchin Peninsula, effectively cutting the island in half.

The XXIV Army Corps was likewise assigned to cut across the island and then turn south and secure the southern half of the island. By April 2, the Army had captured Kadena airfield, and then turned south, spreading four regiments across the narrow island. So far, resistance had been negligible.

Immediately after Yontan and Kadena airfields had been secured, the light-observation aircraft squadrons attached to the III Amphibious Corps moved in and set up base. Shortly thereafter, MAG-31 began operating out of Yontan and MAG-33 out of Kadena. Within 10 days of the initial landing, more than 200 aircraft had been brought on shore, and by the end of operations in June, there would be 22 Marine squadrons on shore and flying missions in support of the Marine and Army advance.

In addition, four Marine squadrons aboard the *Bunker Hill* and the *Bennington* flew missions in support of the Okinawa operation. On May 11, however, a kamikaze strike crippled the *Bunker Hill*, leaving only the two squadrons aboard the *Bennington*. Nevertheless, the Marine squadrons proved valuable. In 5 months of combat missions between February 16 and June 8, the *Bennington*'s 2 squadrons shot down 82 Japanese planes and destroyed another 149 on the ground. They dropped more than 100 tons of bombs and fired more than 4,000 rockets. These two Marine squadrons lost 48 planes and 18 pilots. In addition, missions flown by squadrons aboard the *Block Island* and the *Gilbert Islands* neutralized Japanese airfields at Sakishima Gunto, an island between Okinawa and Formosa, preventing Japanese aerial support of Okinawa.

Shepherd's 6th Division moved northward, and on April 12 attacked Motobu Peninsula. The 29th Marines led the attack against Mount Yaetake, the central piece of terrain on the peninsula. The young regiment found it too difficult to take alone, however, and the 4th Marines moved in to support them. Corporal Richard Bush led his squad through a storm of steel up the face of the hill and over the ridge to drive the defenders backward. Once wounded, Corporal Bush was evacuated from the front, but when a grenade landed nearby, he clutched it to himself, absorbing the blast and saving several wounded Marines and medical corpsmen. Amazingly, Corporal Bush survived the blast. President Truman later presented him with the Medal of Honor. Mount Yaetake was secure by April 16. Three days later, Motobu peninsula was secure, and the 22nd Marines had reached the northern end of Okinawa.

The XXIV Army Corps found the southern half of the island more difficult, running into Ushijima's first defensive line along Kakazu Ridge on April 12. The advance came to a dead stop. Three divisions were brought into line along the ridge, the 7th on the left, the 96th in the center, and the 27th on the right, and a massed attack was launched on April 19. After eight days of difficult fighting, the Army took Kakazu Ridge.

The battle for the southern half of Okinawa looked to be a long and difficult one. General Geiger recommended an amphibious assault using the 2nd Marine Corps to turn the Japanese line of defense, but General Buckner decided to continue the frontal assault. The 1st Marine Division was reassigned to the XXIV Corps, and on May 1 relieved the 27th Infantry Division. The 77th Infantry Division relieved the 96th Infantry Division.

On May 4, however, Ushijima launched a counterattack all along the line. A heavy artillery bombardment led off the counterattack, which was followed closely by tanks and infantry. The American line was broken between the 7th and 77th Divisions, and Buckner ordered Geiger to bring up the rest of the III Amphibious Corps to support the advance. The 27th Infantry Division took over control of the northern half of Okinawa, and Shepherd's 6th Division moved up to the right flank of the American line. The majority of the III Amphibious Corps and the XXIV Army Corps were now devoted to the southern advance. On May 11, the two corps began an advance southward.

On May 13, the 22nd Marines began an assault on "Sugar Loaf," a collection of low hills northwest of Shuri Castle. Assisted by the 29th Marines, they broke through the Shuri defensive line five days later. The 4th Marines, relieving the 29th Marines, took over the lead and continued to advance.

By May 23, Shepherd's 6th Division was on the outskirts of the capital, Naha. On the left, the 96th Infantry Division continued to advance as well, taking Conical Hill, and the 77th Infantry Division and the 1st Marine Division were advancing toward Shuri Castle.

The 1st and 5th Marines were within striking distance of the castle by May 21. Ushijima withdrew south under heavy fire but managed to make it behind his final line of defense along the Kunishi Ridge. On May 29, Company A of the 5th Marines secured Shuri Castle.

Shepherd's 6th Division was ordered to secure Oroku Peninsula, still defended by a naval garrison under the command of Rear Admiral Minoru Ota. On June 4, the 22nd Marines attacked the base of the peninsula while the 4th and 29th Marines made a shore-to-shore amphibious landing on the peninsula itself. The Japanese defenders were pressed back into Oroku Village by the Marines, where they died "gloriously," according to Admiral Ota's last message from the peninsula, and were eliminated by June 14. Farther south, del Valle's 1st Marine Division led the attack against the Kunishi Ridge and captured it by June 15. Three days later, the 8th Marines landed on Okinawa to relieve the 7th Marines, who had led the assault on Kunishi Ridge.

Watching the 8th Marines land, General Buckner was struck and killed by a fragment of Japanese artillery shell. General Roy Geiger, then senior officer in the field, took over command of the Tenth Army and became the first Marine to command a field army. Army general Joseph Stilwell would succeed him on June 23, but on June 21, General Geiger announced that organized resistance had ceased, and the American flag was raised at the Tenth Army headquarters. Later that day, Lieutenant General Ushijima and his chief of staff, Lieutenant General Cho, committed ritual *seppuku*.

Okinawa had been the largest amphibious landing and island battle in history. The Japanese lost 7,830 planes during the battle while the United States lost only 768 planes. The Tenth Army captured 7,401 Japanese and Okinawans and killed a staggering 107,539. Total American battle casualties were 49,151. The Army lost 4,582 killed, and 18,066 wounded, and 93 missing in action. The Navy lost 4,907 killed or missing and 4,824 wounded and lost 36 ships sunk and 368 damaged—most of these casualties due to Japanese kamikaze attacks. The Marines lost 2,938 killed and missing and

13,708 wounded. Another 15,613 soldiers and 10,598 Marines were lost as nonbattle casualties during the campaign.

★★★

During the campaign on Okinawa, the Navy had erected a blockade of Japan itself. Several Marine squadrons aboard the *Bennington, Bunker Hill, Essex, Wasp,* and *Franklin* participated in some of the raids against the Japanese islands. Marine and Navy air raids were devastating—one such air raid on the night of March 9 killed some 80,000 Japanese citizens in Tokyo—but Japan appeared unwilling to surrender. This was distressing. The battles for Iwo Jima and Okinawa had proven incredibly bloody, and the prospect of having to invade the Japanese islands themselves seemed a daunting task. Nevertheless, President Truman, who had become president after Roosevelt's death on April 12, planned an invasion of Kyushu—Operation Olympic—to take place late in 1945 and an invasion of Honshu—Operation Coronet—for early 1946. These invasions were unnecessary, however, because the successful detonation of the atomic bomb at Alamogordo, New Mexico, on July 16, 1945, gave the new president an alternative solution.

On July 25, while meeting with Joseph Stalin at Potsdam, Germany, President Truman issued an order that the atomic bomb be used against Japan if she did not surrender unconditionally by August 3. Japan rejected Truman's ultimatum. On August 6, the *Enola Gay* took off from Tinian and dropped the first atomic bomb on Hiroshima. Nearly 80,000 people died instantly in a flash of heat and light. A second atomic bomb was dropped on Nagasaki three days later. Most of the city was annihilated, and nearly 40,000 people were incinerated in the blast. Shaken, the Japanese government agreed to the terms of surrender, and on September 2, 1945, General MacArthur received the Japanese surrender aboard the USS *Missouri.* Standing nearby, lost in the crowd, was Lieutenant General Roy Geiger, Commanding General, Fleet Marine Force, Pacific.

The Second World War was over. The U.S. Marine Corps had suffered 19,733 men killed in action and 67,207 men wounded.

CHAPTER 11

ACROSS THE 38TH PARALLEL: KOREA AND THE COLD WAR

With the surrender of the Japanese and the end of the Second World War, Task Force 31 was created for the initial occupation of the Japanese islands. The 4th Marines joined Admiral Halsey's 3rd Fleet for this purpose. There was understandable apprehension as the 3rd Fleet sailed into Tokyo Bay. The Japanese had proven themselves fanatical fighters in their kamikaze raids, banzai attacks, and mass suicides. However, when the 1st and 3rd Battalions, 4th Marines went ashore on August 28, 1945, they were met with white flags.

The original 4th Marines, captured at Corregidor, were liberated. The "old" 4th Regiment of Marines, the regiment captured at Corregidor and imprisoned during the Second World War, was granted the colors of the "new" regiment, the 4th Regiment of Marines created from the Raider battalions during the war. By the end of December 1945, however, most of the regiment had been reassigned. The last battalion remaining in Japan was redesignated the 2nd Separate Guard Battalion and assigned to guard the Yokosuka naval base. Harry Schmidt's V Amphibious Corps was given the responsibility of occupying the island of Kyushu. The 5th Marine Division, which occupied Sasebo, remained on duty until December 1945. It was deactivated in January 1946. The 2nd Marine Division, which occupied Nagasaki, remained until June 1946. Neither division had any difficulties during the occupation of Japan.

★★★

The III Amphibious Corps under the command of Major General Keller Rockey was assigned to disarm the 630,000 Japanese who had occupied China, but an important second purpose of the assignment was to establish an American presence in northern China before the arrival of Russian Communist forces. As promised at the Tehran conference in 1943, Stalin had declared war on Japan on August 8, 1945, two days after the dropping of the first atomic bomb on Hiroshima and three months to the day after the surrender of Germany. With the end of the war, the former allies resumed their mutual suspicions of one another. Many Americans feared that the Soviet Army would flood into Asia, as it had in Eastern Europe, and hoped to prevent the same thing from occurring in Asia. The Cold War had begun.

Most of the 1st Marine Division occupied the Tientsin area, while the 5th Marines continued on to Peking and established its headquarters at the old Legation Guard barracks there. On October 6, 1945, General Rockey formally accepted the surrender of 50,000 Japanese troops in Tientsin, and on October 10, another 50,000 surrendered in Peking. The 6th Marine Division under the command of Major General Lemuel Shepherd landed at Tsingtao at the base of the Shantung Peninsula on October 10, and two weeks later accepted the surrender of the Japanese garrison there. The division took over control of the city, roads, and railway but controlled nothing beyond the city limits: Chinese Nationalist forces tended to control the cities while Chinese Communists controlled the countryside.

Growing fears of the spread of communism led the United States to support Chiang Kai-shek's Nationalists, and Chinese Nationalist armies were brought into Peking and Chinwangtao. In addition, the 1st Marine Aircraft Wing, under Major General Louis Woods, set up its base outside

Tientsin while MAG-12 and MAG-24 went to Peking, and MAG-32 went to Tsingtao.

As tensions mounted between the Nationalists and the Communists in China, Marines frequently had to deal with problems caused by the civil war, including railroad derailments, blown-up bridges, and even ambushes. On July 29, 1946, for example, a supply convoy escorted by a platoon of Marines was ambushed at An Ping. The platoon's lieutenant and 2 other Marines were killed, and 12 others were wounded. Likewise, the supply depot at Hsin Ho was raided during the night on April 4, 1947. Five Marines were killed and another sixteen wounded.

Throughout this period, however, the numbers of Marines in China were reduced as combat veterans mustered out, and the Marine Corps began to shrink. The 6th Marine Division was deactivated on April 1, 1946, although the 4th Marines was eventually reassigned to the 1st Marine Division. In December 1946, the 7th Marines, 4th Marine Division returned to the United States while the 11th Marines, 4th Marine Division went to Guam.

In 1947, the 5th Marines, the 1st Marine Division Headquarters, and the 1st Marine Aircraft Wing left China as well. By September, there were only two Marine infantry battalions concentrated at Tsingtao. Their responsibilities included defending the base of the Seventh Fleet and American nationals in Shanghai, Nanking, and Tientsin. Tsingtao was virtually the only Nationalist stronghold left on mainland China by mid-1948, and it was clear that the Communists would be victorious. An understrength 9th Marines came forward from Guam to evacuate Americans from Shanghai in December 1948, and by June 1949 the last Marines had left China. The "loss" of China came as a blow to many westerners as it seemed that suddenly communism was spreading rapidly throughout the world. During the late 1940s, however, the United States wasn't yet prepared to support a major offensive against the advance of communism in Asia; it was more concerned with Eastern Europe, especially Germany. Nevertheless, the success of the Communists in China would lead to the famed "containment" policy put forth in George F. Kennan's "X Article" and to the equally famous "domino theory," which suggested that if one country fell to communism, neighboring countries, like dominos in a row, would fall as well. These policies and theories would lead the United States to intervene increasingly in Asia over the next 25 years.

★★★

The Marine Corps had reached peak strength of 485,000 men and women during the Second World War. This number had been reduced to 155,000 by the summer of 1946. The Marine Corps determined to establish its size at approximately 107,000 men and women on active duty—less than a quarter of its wartime strength but still 6 times larger than before the war. Four of the divisions that had been active during the war, the 3rd, 4th, 5th, and 6th, were deactivated after its conclusion. The 1st Marine Division was established at Camp Pendleton while the 1st Marine Aircraft Wing was based at El Toro. The 2nd Division was established at Camp Lejeune while the 2nd Marine Aircraft Wing was based at Cherry Point.

Marine units in addition to the 1st and 2nd Marine Divisions and the 1st and 2nd Marine Aircraft Wings were established for specific duties. A Marine brigade was based on Guam, for example, and Marines came to be the standard security guards at U.S. Embassies throughout the world. Furthermore, when the U.S. Mediterranean Squadron—later known as the Sixth Fleet—was reestablished in late 1946, a battalion from the 2nd Marine Division was assigned to it as a landing force on a rotating basis.

Despite its terrific sacrifices and achievements during the Second World War, however, the U.S. Marine Corps soon found its existence in question. The U.S. Army, with the support of President Harry S Truman, suggested far-reaching changes in the structure of the U.S. Armed Services. The Army Air Forces would become a separate branch of service, and the Army, the Navy, and the Air Force would be unified under a single overarching department, the Department of Defense. The Marine Corps—perhaps fuelled by residual resentment over Holland Smith's relief of Ralph Smith at Saipan—reduced to a strength of 60,000, would supply a few light infantry units and would lose its aviation branch. This would eliminate the Marine Corps as an effective force, as Admiral Chester Nimitz pointed out. Army general Omar Bradley countered that the need for amphibious warfare had been obviated by the atomic bomb; an enemy armed with nuclear weapons could obliterate a massed force well before it could make an assault.

The Army's suggested reforms were introduced in Senate Bill S.2044 in January 1946. Brigadier General Merritt Edson and Brigadier General

Gerald Thomas led two groups of Marine officers in lobbying for the defeat of the bill. Among those officers were Lieutenant Colonel Victor "Brute" Krulak and Lieutenant Colonel Merrill Twining. On May 6, 1946, Commandant Vandegrift read a statement drafted by Krulak and Twining:

> The bended knee is not a tradition of our Corps. If the Marine as a fighting man has not made a case for himself after 170 years of service, he must go. But he has earned the right to depart with dignity and honor, not by subjugation to the status of uselessness and servility ....

The bill failed.

Nevertheless, a second bill was introduced the following year. The Marine Corps's political action team proved very effective, and it soon became apparent that the "unification" of the armed services could not be accomplished without the support of the Marine Corps. A third bill, this time with Marine Corps participation, was introduced and passed as the National Security Act of 1947. It created the Department of Defense, the Joint Chiefs of Staff, the National Security Council, and the Central Intelligence Agency. It also created the U.S. Air Force as an independent branch of military service. And in a section drafted by Krulak, Twining, and Lieutenant Colonel James Hittle, it defined the U.S. Marine Corps as an independent branch of service within the Navy Department with the responsibility to develop amphibious warfare doctrines and to provide fleet Marine forces capable of establishing advance bases and conducting such land operations as required by a naval campaign.

The Army's criticism of amphibious warfare remained, however. General Roy Geiger, who had witnessed the atomic bomb tests on the island of Bikini, recommended to Commandant Vandegrift that the Marine Corps develop specific protocols for amphibious landings during the atomic age, and Vandegrift appointed General Lemuel Shepherd, then assistant commandant, to investigate. Shepherd's study concluded that amphibious landings as had been carried out during the Second World War were impossible in the atomic age. However, Shepherd suggested that new doctrines be developed that would allow amphibious landings without presenting massed targets to the enemy. In particular, Shepherd suggested the use of helicopters as a solution. Commandant Vandegrift approved Shepherd's conclusions on December 19, 1946, three days after Shepherd submitted them.

The strategy of using carrier-based helicopter squadrons that could deploy rapidly from ship to shore would come to be known as "vertical envelopment." The first Marine Helicopter Experimental Squadron, HMX-1, was organized in December 1947, and the first helicopter exercises were held at Camp Lejeune in May 1948. In November, Quantico released *Employment of Helicopters (Tentative)—PHIB 31*, the manual that became the basis of the vertical envelopment assault doctrine.

General Vandegrift resigned as Marine Corps commandant on December 31, 1947, at the end of his term, and President Truman selected Major General Clifton Cates as the nineteenth commandant. Cates's tenure as commandant would witness further changes and challenges for the Marine Corps. In June 1948, for example, the Women's Armed Forces Integration Act was passed, requiring all military branches to integrate women into regular as well as Reserve services, and in July 1948 President Truman abolished racial segregation in the armed services.

AFRICAN AMERICAN MARINES

A few African Americans had served during the American Revolutionary War, but when the U.S. Marine Corps was officially created in 1798, measures were taken to ensure that no African Americans—and no Native Americans and few foreigners—were allowed to join the Corps. The people pushing for these measures justified them with the argument that the loyalty of the Marines must be guaranteed and that non-Caucasians could not be relied upon. Undoubtedly, simple racism played a role as well.

During the Second World War, however, the Marine Corps was ordered to recruit African Americans, and Commandant Holcomb appointed Colonel Samuel Woods Jr. to run a segregated training camp at Montford Point. The first recruits arrived in August 1942. Initially, all instruction was conducted by Caucasians, but African Americans were promoted to NCO ranks as soon as possible. African Americans served in segregated units throughout the Second World War in ammunition companies, depot labor companies, and in the 51st and 52nd Defense Battalions. Some of these men saw action in the Pacific theater. African Americans in service companies landed with the assault waves at Saipan and came under fire; several were killed and many wounded. At one point, 12 African Americans stepped in to the line to help repel a Japanese counterattack against the 4th Marine Division; they were commended by their white officers.

By the end of the war, more than 19,000 African Americans had served in the Marine Corps. One African American had been commissioned as a second lieutenant on November 10, 1945—the birthday of the Corps—as well, but he was immediately put on an inactive list as the war had come to an end by then. In 1949, the Secretary of the Navy declared that no distinctions were to be made between individuals in uniform, and the segregated camp at Montford Point was closed. In 1950, there were approximately 1,500 African Americans in a Marine Corps of 74,000. During the Korean War, 15,000 African Americans would serve in the Corps in integrated units. In 1967, Private First Class James Anderson Jr. became the first African American Marine to be awarded the Medal of Honor for heroism during the Vietnam War. In 1979, Frank Petersen became the first African American selected for brigadier general.

Race relations in the Corps have not always been easy, especially during the late 1960s and early 1970s, but African Americans have come to serve throughout the U.S. Marine Corps. More than 26,000 African American men and women now serve in the U.S. Marine Corps.

In addition, Commandant Cates was faced with the difficult political battle of keeping the Marine Corps alive. The National Security Act's definition of the Marine Corps as a separate branch within the Navy Department allowed President Truman and the first Secretary of Defense, James Forrestal, to view it as subordinate to the Navy and the Chief of Naval Operation. As a result, Commandant Cates was not considered a member of the Joint Chiefs of Staff. Secretary Forrestal later informed the press that the Marines would not be allowed to constitute a second land army, that no Marine would be allowed to command a unit higher than Corps level, and that the Marine Corps itself would be limited to four divisions during wartime.

The second Secretary of Defense, Louis Johnson, drastically cut the Fleet Marine Force from 35,000 to 29,400 in 1949 and then to 23,900 in 1950. Johnson went so far as to ban the celebration of the traditional birthday of the U.S. Marine Corps, November 10, though Marines continued to celebrate that day privately. Commandant Cates protested such treatment of the Marine Corps to Congress, pointing out that the Marine Corps had no voice in decisions made by the Joint Chiefs of Staff regarding the Corps's status. In January 1950, sympathetic congressmen proposed bills to make the Marine Corps commandant a member of the Joint Chiefs of Staff and to guarantee Corps strength sufficient to man the Fleet Marine Forces, but they did not pass.

By 1950, the U.S. Marine Corps had reached its lowest level since before the Second World War. Japan had occupied and exploited Korea as early as 1910. At the end of the Second World War, however, the United States and the Soviet Union divided Korea along the 38th Parallel for the purpose of disarming the Japanese forces in Korea and reconstructing the Korean nation. Korea was supposed to have been reunited into one country, but with the development of the Cold War, as happened in Germany, two separate states were organized: the Democratic People's Republic of Korea in the North, sponsored by the Soviet Union, and the Republic of Korea in the South, sponsored by the United States. On June 25, 1950, however, the North Korean People's Army (NKPA) crossed the 38th Parallel and invaded South Korea. Seoul fell on June 28. The United States intervened immediately and soon had the support of the United Nations. Great Britain, Australia, and other countries would soon send troops to support the American and Republic of Korea forces.

Commandant Cates was ignored during the first hours of the crisis, President Truman assuming that the Chief of Naval Operations, Admiral Forrest Sherman, commanded both the Navy and the Marines. Left out of the planning sessions, Cates sought out Sherman and offered him the use of a Marine regiment and aircraft group. Initially, Sherman expressed little interest in the possibility of using the Marines, but at Cates's continued urging, Sherman sent Commander in Chief, Far East General Douglas MacArthur a message offering the use of a Marine air-ground brigade. MacArthur, who had witnessed their ability during the war in the Pacific, placed an immediate request to the Joint Chiefs of Staff for the use of the Marines. The Fleet Marine Force was approved for use in Korea on July 3, 1950.

The 1st Provisional Marine Brigade, intended to be an air-ground brigade, was created from the 1st Marine Division and the 1st Marine Aircraft Wing on July 7. Brigadier General Edward Craig was given command. The 5th Marines under Lieutenant Colonel Raymond Murray formed the basis of the brigade's ground forces while Marine Aircraft Group 33 under Brigadier General Thomas Cushman formed the basis of the brigade's air element, which consisted of three carrier-qualified fighter-bomber F4U Corsair squadrons and an observation squadron composed of eight light airplanes and two H03S-1 Sikorsky helicopters. The 6,534-man brigade sailed from San Diego on July 12.

Meanwhile, Lieutenant General Lemuel Shepherd, commander of Fleet Marine Force, Pacific, and Colonel Victor "Brute" Krulak, his operations officer, met with MacArthur in Tokyo. MacArthur promised not to interfere with the Marines air-ground organization or coordination, stating, for example, that he would not give control of the Marine Aircraft Groups to the Air Force. As he considered a map of the Korean Peninsula, he is supposed to have commented to Shepherd that if he had the 1st Marine Division under his command, he would land them at Inchon, march to Seoul, isolate the NKPA, and trap them against the 8th Army. Shepherd enthusiastically promised MacArthur that the 1st Marine Division could be ready by September 1. MacArthur sent several messages to the Joint Chiefs of Staff requesting the 1st Marine Division for use in Korea, which they approved.

The NKPA had pushed well into South Korea in only about two weeks time, however. The U.S. Eighth Army and Republic of Korea (ROK) forces, combined as a United Nations Command (UNC), could not stop the NKPA's advance and were pushed back to the southern end of the Korean peninsula. By the end of August, 4 American infantry divisions and 5 ROK divisions were facing off against 13 NKPA divisions along a weak 50-mile perimeter around Pusan, the last port controlled by the UNC, and the Joint Chiefs of Staff briefly considered the possibility of simply evacuating Korea. MacArthur had hoped to use the 1st Provisional Marine Brigade as the basis for his envelopment of Inchon, but all of Korea seemed to be collapsing. The brigade's first duty would have to be to secure Pusan.

The brigade landed at Pusan on August 2, 1950, and on the following day Lieutenant Colonel Raymond Murray's 5th Marines moved to Changwon. Their first objective was Sachon, which they were to capture as part of the 25th Infantry Division's counterattack against the NKPA. With precision air support delivered by two of Cushman's Corsair fighter-bomber squadrons launched from the carriers *Sicily* and *Badoeng Strait*, the 5th Marines began their assault on August 7. Night-fighter squadron VMF(N)-513 began launching night raids from Itazuke in Japan.

By August 13, the 5th Marines had reached the outskirts of Sachon. Suddenly, the 4th NKPA Division crossed the Naktong River, creating a bulge near Obong-ni. General Craig was ordered to disengage the 5th Marines from its assault on Sachon and move north to help contain the "Naktong Bulge." On August 15, the Marines launched a series of assaults on "No-Name Ridge," which they eventually secured. The NKPA launched a counterattack that night led by Russian-built T-34 tanks, but the Marines repulsed it easily, and on the following day, the badly beaten 4th NKPA Division withdrew back across the Naktong.

The 9th NKPA Division crossed the Naktong on September 3 and attacked the 9th U.S. Infantry, 2nd Division. The 5th Marines again came to the assistance of the beleaguered Army. The 5th Marines launched a counterattack and pushed the 9th NKPA Division back six miles. The North Korean offensive against the Pusan perimeter came to a halt. In just over a month's time, the 5th Marines had launched 4 counterattacks, inflicted some 10,000 casualties against the North Koreans, and sustained 172 deaths and 730 wounded; no Marines were captured. On September 5, the brigade went into reserve for some much-deserved rest before MacArthur's attack on Inchon. The Corps had proven itself once again.

Meanwhile, on July 19, President Truman authorized the mobilization of the Marine Corps Reserve, and cadre units were established at Camp Lejeune for the development of the 1st Marines. Colonel Chesty Puller, then commanding officer of the Marine Barracks at Pearl Harbor, was reinstated as commander of his old unit. The 1st Marines, cobbled together in 10 days, sailed from San Diego in August with the 1st Marine Division Headquarters. The 1st Marine Aircraft Wing Headquarters under the command of Major General Field Harris sailed by the beginning of September.

"HORRIBLE HARRY'S POLICE FORCE"

President Harry S Truman didn't share MacArthur's appreciation of the U.S. Marine Corps. A veteran U.S. Army artillery officer, Truman clearly favored the U.S. Army and other main military branches. Witnessing a simulated vertical envelopment assault landing on June 10, 1950, 10 days before the North Korean invasion of South Korea, he indicated his preference for a nearby 75mm howitzer.

On August 21, as the 5th Marines were securing the Pusan perimeter and the 1st Marines were rapidly reassembled, California Congressman Gordon MacDonough wrote to the president suggesting that the Marine Corps commandant be given a voice on the Joint Chiefs of Staff. Truman, displaying his resentment of the Corps, replied to MacDonough, "For your information, the Marine Corps is the Navy's police force and as long as I am president that is what it will remain. They have a propaganda machine that is almost equal to Stalin's ...."

Truman's comment was published on September 5 and was greeted with outrage from the public. On the following day, Truman grudgingly apologized to Commandant Cates over his choice of language. The Marines on the other side of the world, who learned of Truman's comments through *Stars and Stripes,* chalked "Horrible Harry's Police Force" on their vehicles before they launched for Inchon.

★★★

MacArthur had planned from the beginning of the campaign to use the Marines in a daring amphibious assault at Inchon. The general believed an attack at Inchon, behind the North Korean lines, would cut off the supply lines of North Korean troops at the Pusan perimeter. He also felt the liberation of Seoul, 25 miles from Inchon, would open an important airfield at Kimpo.

The assault would be extremely difficult, however. The approach to the port city was through a narrow channel partially blocked by the island of Wolmi-do. In addition, the extreme range of the tides, which roared in and out at 8 knots, bringing with them high tides more than 30 feet high or leaving behind them a vast mud flat, meant there was only 1 day in September when the assault could be carried off: September 15. Due to these extreme tides, the island of Wolmi-do would have to be secured in the morning, and the actual assault on Inchon would have to wait until the evening tide came in. The element of surprise would be lost. Finally, there was a high seawall that would have to be scaled. Only 2,200 North Korean troops were in the city itself, but another 21,500 troops were a short distance inland.

The assault was assigned to X Corps under the command of Army Major General Edward Almond, MacArthur's Chief of Staff. The actual landing force, composed of the 1st and 5th Marines and the 7th Infantry Division, would be lifted to Inchon by Amphibious Group 1 under the command of Admiral James Doyle. The 3rd Battalion, 5th Marines would land on Wolmi-do in the morning, with the remainder of the 5th Marines and the 1st Marines landing on the mainland in the evening.

Aerial and naval gunfire bombed Inchon beginning on September 10. On September 15, the 3rd Battalion, 5th Marines led by Lieutenant Colonel

Robert Taplett landed on Wolmi-do and raised the flag over Radio Hill in 25 minutes. The Marines had killed 180 North Koreans—and probably another 100 had been buried in burned-out bunkers—and captured 136. Only 18 Marines were wounded; none were killed.

Twelve restless hours ticked by as the assault force awaited the evening tide. When the Marines finally stormed ashore late in the afternoon, there was virtually no resistance—most of the North Koreans in the city surrendered—and by the following morning the Marines were on the outskirts of Inchon. Allied casualties numbered only 25 men dead and 196 wounded. Craig, Murray, and Puller were awarded Silver Stars for the assault.

On September 16, the Marines moved inland and began advancing along the road to Seoul. Lieutenant H. J. Smith's Company D, 5th Marines surprised a column of T-34 tanks and some 200 infantry and destroyed them in seconds. VMF-214 burned another column with napalm. Murray's 5th Marines captured Kimpo airfield on September 17, and MAG-33 began flying missions there two days later.

The 1st Marines fought their way through Sosa arriving at Yongdong-po, just across the Han River from Seoul, on September 19, and the next day the 2nd and 3rd Battalions, 5th Marines crossed the Han River, placing them just north of Seoul. On September 21, the 1st Marines attacked Yongdong-po. After an entire night of fighting—Captain Robert Barrow's Company A fought off five attacks by five T-34 tanks and North Korean infantry—the city was secured. Puller's 1st Marines crossed the Han on September 24.

On September 25, the 1st and 5th Marines attacked Seoul simultaneously. There was a large civilian population in the city, so supporting artillery was used sparingly, and the Marines relied primarily on their small arms and grenades throughout a day of house-to-house fighting. The North Koreans launched a counterattack that night, but it failed. Seoul was secure by September 27, and on September 29 General MacArthur escorted Syngman Rhee, the president of the Republic of Korea, back into the capital and up Ma Po Boulevard to Ducksoo Palace, the traditional seat of the Korean government.

Colonel Homer Litzenberg's 7th Marines, which had landed at Inchon on September 21, joined the 1st and 5th Marines in Seoul on September 30, reestablishing the 1st Marine Division. On that same day, Litzenberg's Marines marched out along the Seoul-Pyonyang road to Uijongbu 10 miles away, which it captured after a bloody 3-day fight. By then, the Eighth Army had broken out of the Pusan perimeter, and by October 5, the 1st Cavalry Division was in Seoul.

The Marines had accomplished an amazing landing, coming together from all over the world on short notice to land under extreme conditions and achieve their mission objectives in 12 days. Not bad for a "police force." The "Old Breed" 1st Marine Division lost 421 killed and 2,029 wounded, more than half of them during the bloody street fighting in Seoul. Eleven Marine planes were shot down by enemy fire.

★★★

American policy-makers were encouraged by the success of the Inchon landing. Instead of simply defending South Korea against North Korea, many now thought Korean reunification was possible, and on October 1, a ROK division, with authorization from President Truman, crossed the 38th Parallel into North Korea. Chinese Premier Chou En-lai immediately announced that China would not tolerate the invasion of North Korea by imperialists. MacArthur ignored the Chinese threats, however, and prepared to launch a campaign into North Korea.

The 1st Marine Division returned to Inchon and prepared for a second amphibious assault, this time at the North Korean port of Wonsan on the eastern side of the Korean Peninsula. By the time the 1st Marine Division reached Wonsan, however, it had been secured by the advance of ROK forces. The Marines landed with no resistance to find Marine Fighter Squadron 312 already established and flying missions from Wonsan airfield.

Nevertheless, the 1st Marines were given a 300-mile zone around Wonsan to control, and the 5th and 7th Marines marched north toward Hamhung in preparation for an advance on the Yalu River. From there, the Marines would advance through the mountains to the Chosin Reservoir. From Chosin, the two regiments would advance to the Yalu River, marking the boundary between North Korea and China.

Rumors had begun to circulate that Communist Chinese forces had already crossed the Yalu and entered North Korea. General MacArthur, at his headquarters in Tokyo, played down the strength of any Chinese forces in Korea, commenting that even if there were a few Chinese forces in Korea, it was much too late for them to have any impact on the campaign.

On November 2, Litzenberg's 7th Marines set out from Hungnam toward Chosin Reservoir, and by midnight they had engaged the 124th Chinese Division at Sudong-ni. Litzenberg's Marines fought their way up into the Funchilin Pass until the Chinese broke contact on November 7. Many Chinese soldiers had been captured during the battle, but MacArthur dismissed them as mere volunteers, refusing to believe that the Chinese were effectively aiding the North Koreans.

By November 10, the 7th Marines had reached Hagaru-ri at the southern tip of Chosin Reservoir. Marine engineers began construction of an airfield that would be completed by Army engineers when General Almond's X Corps Headquarters moved up. The 7th Marines stayed in Hagaru-ri for two weeks, and the temperature began to drop. On November 24, Litzenberg's 7th Marines marched out of Hagaru-ri through the Toktong Pass to Yudam-ni, where Murray's 5th Marines joined them two days later. Puller's 1st Marines, having been relieved by the 3rd Infantry Division, began moving up to join the rest of the 1st Marine Division but were strung out through the Funchilin Pass, with the 1st Battalion at Chinhung-ni, the 2nd Battalion at Koto-ri, and the 3rd Battalion at Hagaru-ri, to maintain the lines of communication.

From its position near Chosin Reservoir, the 1st Marine Division was ordered to form the northern arm of a coordinated pincer attack with the Eighth Army on November 27. Before they could attack, however, disaster struck. The Chinese suddenly counterattacked on November 25, then deliberately retreated, drawing the American and the Republic of Korea forces into a trap. The right flank of the Eighth Army, composed of the II ROK Corps, was struck hard by the Chinese assault and collapsed, bringing the advance to a halt.

Unfortunately, orders were never modified to take this situation into account, and Major General Oliver Smith ordered the 5th Marines to launch an attack from Yudam-ni to the west. They were stopped after advancing only one mile. It started to snow, the temperature dropped to –20 degrees, and General Sung Shih-lun appeared with 8 Chinese divisions. Three divisions attacked the 5th and 7th Marines at Yudam-ni. Another division attacked Hagaru-ri, defended by the 3rd Battalion, 1st Marines. A fifth division attacked Koto-ri.

The Chinese attack was successful, cutting off lines of communication both between Yudam-ni and Hagaru-ri and between Hagaru-ri and Koto-ri, and severely threatening Captain William Barber's F Company, 7th Marines assigned to hold Toktong Pass. On November 28, a Chinese battalion attacked that pass. Although he was wounded, Barber continued to command his troops for two more days, and Company F held. The company lost 20 men killed and 54 wounded, but they killed 450 Chinese. Barber was awarded the Medal of Honor.

At Hagaru-ri, the Chinese made serious inroads into the town itself, capturing East Hill, which dominated much of the town, the southern exit to Koto-ri, and threatening the airfield. General Smith managed to fly into Hagaru-ri on November 28 and ordered Murray's 5th Marines to hold Yudam-ni and the 7th Marines to strike out south to clear the pass between Yudam-ni and Hagaru-ri. Chesty Puller put together a relief force including Lieutenant Colonel Douglas Drysdale's 41st Independent Commando, British Royal Marines—Drysdale had reported to the 1st Marine Division at Hungnam on November 20—Company G, 1st Marines, Company B, 31st Infantry, and two Marine tank companies. The column set out on November 29 and was ambushed twice as it climbed through Funchilin Pass. Drysdale, ordered to push on at all costs, scrambled into Hagaru-ri with the 41 Commando, G Company, and one of the tank companies by midnight. The truck column was carved up in the mountain pass, and with few exceptions, everyone else had been killed or captured by the next morning.

General Almond, who flew into Hagaru-ri to speak to General Smith, ordered X Corps to fall back to Hungnam, abandoning equipment and vehicles as necessary. One journalist, flown in to report on the beleaguered Marines at Hagaru-ri, asked Smith if the Marines, surrounded by Chinese divisions, were retreating. Echoing Belleau Wood, the Marine general replied, "Retreat, hell! We're attacking in another direction."

Lieutenant Colonel Raymond Davis led the 1st Battalion, 7th Marines out of Yudam-ni and across the barren mountain landscape to relieve Company F, still desperately holding Toktong Pass. By the time Davis arrived on December 2, Company F was just barely holding on. Of the 200 men in the company, 26 had been killed, 89 had been wounded, 3 were missing, and many others were suffering from frostbite and unable to fight. Davis was awarded the Medal of Honor for heroism in leading his battalion across the frozen mountains to relieve Barber's company.

The rest of the 5th and 7th Marines set out along the road to Hagaru-ri under the watchful eye of Marine aircraft. They fought the entire 14-mile, 79-hour trek, finally arriving in Hagaru-ri on December 3. By then, Marine R4D transport planes had begun landing at the Hagaru-ri airfield, bringing in supplies and relief troops and taking out the wounded. The 5th and 7th Marines, the 3rd Battalion, 1st Marines, and Drysdale's 41 Commando left Hagaru-ri for Koto-ri on December 6. The column of 10,000 men and 1,000 vehicles stretched for 11 miles.

The division's path to Hungnam was blocked by Funchilin Pass, now held by the Chinese, however. In a howling snowstorm in which the temperature dropped from –14°F to –24°F, Captain Robert Barrow led Company A, 1st Marines out of Chinhung-ni to clear Hill 1081 at the southern end of the pass. Despite the frigid temperatures, the snowstorm worked to Barrow's advantage, obscuring the movements of the Marines and allowing them to surprise the Chinese on Hill 1081. The Chinese knew that Hill 1081 was their last opportunity to hold and destroy the 1st Marine Division; they counterattacked furiously.

A bloody battle raged throughout the night of December 8. Eventually, the storm passed, and General Harris's Corsairs flew in low over the mountains, strafing, bombing, and dropping napalm on the Chinese. The unique nature of combined Marine arms served to win the day, and the Chinese failed to hold Funchilin Pass. The 1st Marine Division reached Hungnam by December 12.

The 1st Division was transported to Pusan and spent Christmas at Masan. It had suffered 718 men killed and 3,700 wounded as well as thousands of cases of frostbite and pneumonia. The Chinese 9th Army suffered 25,000 men killed. Marine aviation accounted for approximately 40 percent of those casualties. Chesty Puller was awarded a fifth Navy Cross for the Chosin campaign, the most ever awarded to an individual.

★★★

The situation was brought under control at the beginning of 1951. The Eighth Army, now under the command of Lieutenant General Matthew Ridgway, had established a line just south of Seoul. The 1st Marine Division was given an area between Pohang and Andong to patrol and spent the period between January 12 and February 15 in antiguerilla operations, further developing vertical envelopment tactics with helicopter reconnaissance squads.

General Ridgway was a much different commander who preferred organized close-order advances rather than the disorganized operations that had characterized the Korean War to that point. Operation Killer was to be a shoulder-to-shoulder UN advance northward with IX Corps, including the 1st Marine Division, in the center of the line. The Marines's objective in this operation was the town of Hoengsong, 8 miles to the north.

The advance began on February 21, and the 1st and 5th Marines captured Hoengsong three days later. The IX Corps commander died of a heart attack that same day, however, and General Oliver Smith took command of IX Corps until the Army could replace him with one of their own. Chesty Puller, recently promoted to brigadier general, temporarily took command of the 1st Marine Division. Operation Ripper followed Operation Killer on March 7, and by April the Eighth Army had advanced its line north of the 38th Parallel.

On April 21, the Chinese launched a counteroffensive. Striking just to the right of the 1st Marine Division, the Chinese quickly knocked out the 6th ROK Division and opened a 10-mile gap in the Eighth Army's line. The 1st Marines, now under the command of Colonel Francis MacAlister, leapt into the gap. The 27th British Commonwealth Brigade moved up to join the 1st Marine Division, and after five days of fighting, the two units had managed to close the gap. On April 27, Major General Gerald Thomas, a veteran of both Belleau Wood and Guadalcanal, took over command of the 1st Marine Division. At the end of the month, the 1st Marine Division was given a defensive position at Hongchon as part of General Almond's X Corps.

A second Chinese counteroffensive was launched two weeks later, again striking to the right of the 1st Marine Division, breaking several ROK divisions and penetrating 30 miles into the flank. The Marines bent with the attack but refused to break, holding the line and allowing the 2nd Infantry Division to retake land lost as the ROK divisions had collapsed. The Chinese offensive lost force, and the Eighth Army, now under the command of Lieutenant General James Van Fleet, resumed its northward advance.

At the beginning of June, the 1st Marine Division found itself at Hwachon Reservoir, just north of the 38th Parallel. The Marines advanced across the rugged mountain terrain fighting their way through tenacious North Korean troops, and by late June, they had secured a series of ridges overlooking a circular valley dubbed the "Punchbowl."

★★★

The UN advance was put on hold during the summer of 1951 as truce negotiations began. MacArthur was sacked as Commander in Chief, Far East on April 10 for blatant disobedience—Truman wished to hold the line in Korea; MacArthur, who couldn't stand the idea of a stalemate, declared that "[i]n war, there is no substitute for victory," and publicly criticized the administration.

Ridgway moved up to become Commander in Chief, Far East, but MacArthur's removal also meant the end of his promise not to interfere with the Marines "aerial artillery." The 1st Marine Aircraft Wing, now under Major General Christian Schilt, was put under operational control of the 5th Air Force. On June 5, the 5th Air Force began Operation Strangle, an interdiction directed against North Korean and Chinese supply lines with the intent of limiting their supplies and thus their ability to fight.

In September, the UN advance resumed, and the 1st Marine Division was ordered to take the Punchbowl. The assault began on September 5, and 18 days of hard fighting followed. The main problem the Marines encountered was lack of air support, as the 5th Air Force held to a doctrine of a single operational command to provide aerial support across the front. The entire front probably received better aerial support under this doctrine, but the loss of control of the 1st Marine Aircraft Wing seriously hindered Marine operations. The Marines were able to call for impressive 25-mile bombardments from the battleship *New Jersey*, but these weren't really a satisfactory substitute for the precision bombing and strafing of Marine pilots.

The fighting over the Punchbowl was costly. The 1st and 7th Marines lost 800 casualties in just 4 days of fighting. With peace negotiations underway and growing antiwar protest at home, General Van Fleet was ordered to cease such high-intensity attacks. The 1st Marine Division held the northern side of the Punchbowl throughout the winter, but in March 1952, the 1st Marine Division was transferred 180 miles west to a position overlooking Panmunjom on the historic invasion route to Seoul.

The war of movement was over. There were no more offensives, only patrols and raids and the occasional capture of an outpost. The Marines engaged in several of these smaller battles, including "Bunker Hill" in August 1952, "Berlin" and "East Berlin" early in 1953, and "Reno," "Carson," and "Vegas" in March 1953.

★★★

Despite Air Force control, Marine aviation did have its successes. In September 1951, while the 1st Division was standing over the Punchbowl, the first Helicopter Transport Squadron, (HMR)-161, arrived equipped with new Sikorsky HRS-1 helicopters. (HMR)-161 quickly justified the Marine Corps's interest in the use of helicopters for vertical envelopment. In September, the squadron transported nearly 19,000 pounds of supplies to the front and evacuated wounded soldiers. The squadron was also successful in transporting a reconnaissance company.

The Marines also entered the jet age during the Korean War, exchanging their F4U Corsairs for Grumman F9F-2 Panthers or F-86 Sabrejets. There were only a few fights between Marine and Korean or Chinese aviators, however. Major John Bolt was the only Marine ace of the war, shooting down six MiG-15s while on exchange with the U.S. Air Force. Other Marines who flew missions in Korea included future baseball star Captain Theodore "Ted" Williams and future astronaut Major John Glenn.

Major John H. Glenn in front of his unidentified plane (most likely a Grumman F9F-2 Panther) during the Korean War. Glenn would go on to achieve fame in the U.S. space program.

The Korean War came to an end on July 27, 1953, with the signing of a truce at Panmunjom. Korea was divided along the 38th Parallel, its prewar dividing line, and arrangements were made for the repatriation of prisoners of war.

During the Korean War, 60 percent of the U.S. Marine Corps had seen action. The Corps suffered 4,267 killed and 23,744 wounded. Only 221 Marines had been taken prisoner, however, and 194 of them survived. The 1st Marine Aircraft Wing flew 127,496 sorties and lost 436 aircraft. Forty-two Marines were awarded the Medal of Honor; twenty-six of them were presented posthumously.

The 1st Marine Division stayed in Korea until 1955, when it returned stateside and took up residence at Camp Pendleton. The 1st Marine Aircraft Wing moved to Japan, where it joined the 3rd Marine Division, which had been reactivated in January 1952. The 4th Marines, 3rd Division eventually returned to Hawaii in 1955, but the remainder of the regiment remained on Okinawa.

★★★

In the meantime, the political battle over the status of the Marine Corps finally seemed to be coming to an end. Senator Paul Douglas and Congressman Mike Mansfield, both former Marines, introduced a bill to Congress in January 1951. The Douglas-Mansfield Bill recommended that four Marine divisions and four Marine aircraft wings be kept on active duty, emphasizing that the Marine Corps was a "force-in-readiness," well prepared to serve anywhere, anytime. Furthermore, the House Armed Services Committee commented that the Marine Corps had always been a separate and distinct military service. The Douglas-Mansfield Bill was modified somewhat in various committees and debates such that three Marine divisions and three Marine aircraft wings were to remain on active duty, but it was eventually passed and signed into law by President Truman. The new law also gave the Marine Corps commandant equal status with the other Joint Chiefs of Staff in matters concerning the Marine Corps.

The U.S. Marine Corps also underwent some reorganization during the 1950s. General Lemuel Shepherd became commandant on January 1, 1952. Shepherd did a great deal to reorganize the structure of the Corps. The Marine Corps Headquarters general staff was streamlined so that it consisted of Personnel (G-1), Intelligence (G-2), Operations and Training (G-3), and Logistics (G-4) officers.

Shepherd also helped reorganize the structure of Marine expeditionary forces. The Marine force sent to Korea in 1950 had been named the 1st Provisional Marine Brigade and had been conceived as an air-ground task force. The effectiveness of such a combined arms brigade was proven during the early stages of the Korean Conflict and became an organizational principal afterward. The 1st Provisional Air-Ground Task Force was created at Kaneohe Bay, Oahu, in January 1953, and three years after its activation, the Task Force became simply the 1st Marine Brigade, Fleet Marine Force, regularizing the air-ground task force as the organizational principal.

Having served his four years as commandant, General Shepherd retired on December 31, 1955. President Eisenhower appointed General Randolph Pate as his successor. The 57-year-old Pate had served in the Army during World War I. Afterward, he attended the Virginia Military Institute, graduating in 1921, and was commissioned as a second lieutenant in the Marine Corps. He served in Santo Domingo and China during the 1920s, as the logistics officer at Guadalcanal, and as commander of the 1st Marine Division at the end of the Korean War.

The Marines remained active throughout the mid-1950s with several small actions. When an earthquake struck Greece in August 1953, elements of the Fleet Marine Force serving with the Sixth Fleet in the Mediterranean provided relief services. Likewise, when a flood ravaged Tampico, Mexico, Marine pilots flew in emergency supplies and engineers.

Elements of the 1st Marine Aircraft Wing provided support for the beleaguered French troops at Dien Bien Phu in Indo-China in 1954. When the Chinese Communists seized the island of Ichiang in February 1955, the 3rd Marine Division assisted the U.S. Navy in the evacuation of some 26,000 Chinese Nationalist soldiers and civilians from the Tachen Islands to Taiwan. As the Suez Crisis deepened in 1956, the 3rd Battalion, 2nd Marines, embarked with the Sixth Fleet, helped evacuate some 1,500 refugees from Alexandria, Egypt, during the Anglo-French invasion.

In January 1958, Venezuelan dictator Perez Jimenez was overthrown and chaos reigned in Caracas. The USS *Des Moines*, embarked with a company of Marines, cruised the Venezuelan coast ready to intervene should American lives or property be threatened, but the crisis subsided and no landing was necessary. Marines aboard the USS *Boston* returned to the Venezuelan coast in May 1958 when Vice President Richard Nixon's goodwill tour was suddenly interrupted by rioting, but once again, the Venezuelan authorities were able to subdue the rioters before a Marine landing became necessary.

DISASTER AT RIBBON CREEK

On April 8, 1956, Staff Sergeant Matthew McKeon an inexperienced drill instructor at Parris Island, led his platoon of 74 recruits on an unauthorized night march into the swampy Ribbon Creek. Six of his men drowned. The tragedy brought both public and congressional attention to the Marine Corps. Major General David Shoup was ordered to conduct an investigation of Marine Corps training procedures, and several hundred drill instructors were relieved of duty. Furthermore, it became clear that training procedures had to be altered. Although training would remain challenging, it reinforced the idea that all Marines are brothers and sisters, and that their safety and dignity should be respected. The idea that Marines take care of their own, which had been developing for 175 years, took on a new dimension after Ribbon Creek.

★★★

The largest Marine landing of the late 1950s occurred in Lebanon. The spread of Arab nationalism threatened western interests in the Middle East, which had been dramatically demonstrated by the Suez Crisis in 1956. Lebanese President Camille Chamoun had adopted a pro-Western position, but as Arab nationalism and opposition to western imperialism spread, opposition to Chamoun's government grew rapidly, and Chamoun was suddenly faced with open rebellion supported by Syria. General Fuad Chehab, the commander of the Lebanese army with political ambitions of his own, did little to suppress the rebellion, and Chamoun requested British and American help. With the collapse of the Iraqi government, which had traditionally supported Lebanon, Chamoun's situation became desperate, and President Eisenhower approved American intervention in Lebanon.

The 2nd Battalion, 2nd Marines landed just south of Beirut at 3 P.M. on July 15 and waded ashore among bikini-clad sunbathers. By evening, the 2nd Battalion had taken control of the nearby International Airport. The following morning, the 3rd Battalion, 6th Marines landed on the same beach, and after several false starts as Chamoun and Chehab argued over what role the Americans should play in Lebanon, the 2nd Battalion, 2nd Marines advanced toward Beirut. By 7 that evening, the battalion had control of the docks and several important bridges and was guarding the U.S. Embassy. A few shots were fired, but there were no casualties. On July 17, the 1st Battalion, 8th Marines landed on a beach just north of Beirut, and the 2nd Battalion, 8th Marines was flown into the International Airport from Camp Lejeune.

Elections were held in Lebanon on July 31. General Chehab won the election and took office on September 23, forming a Coalition government including the leaders of the rebels. Nevertheless, all four Marine battalions were withdrawn from Lebanon by mid-October in a demonstration of good faith on the part of the United States. Despite the outcome of the election, the presence of the Marines had prevented the outbreak of violence.

In January 1960, President Eisenhower named General David Shoup commandant of the U.S. Marine Corps. Shoup respected Marine Corps traditions, but at the same time he was committed to the modernization of the Marine Corps. Under Shoup's direction, the Corps adopted the M-14 rifle, which replaced the reliable but now obsolete M-1 Garand as well as the BAR, and the M-60 machine gun, which replaced the Browning machine gun.

M-14 7.62MM RIFLE

During World War II, the Army began examining a selective-fire weapon for its soldiers. The logical choice was an extension of the M-1 Garand, the M-14, which used the NATO-approved 7.62mm (.30-caliber) cartridge. The gun was redesigned, with the 8-round internal magazine replaced by a 20-round external box magazine. Capable of firing single-shot or burst fire, the majority of issued weapons were set for single-fire only. While a number were assigned for use as light machine guns, sustained fire caused the barrel to overheat. The otherwise heavy-duty rifle served the Army and Marines, including an excellent sniper model. About 1.5 million M-14 rifles were produced before the weapon was gradually replaced by the M-16A1.

For several years the M-14 was the primary rifle of the Marine Corps, but is now used only for drill and ceremonial occasions.

Budget constraints during the early 1960s limited Corps strength to 175,000 men. Fleet Marine Forces were therefore smaller than their authorized strength, but during these years technology allowed the realization of the doctrine of vertical envelopment. Under Pate's leadership, the Corps had been reorganized so that heavy support units such as artillery and tank battalions were no longer attached to divisions but rather to larger force troops. This meant that divisions were to a large extent transportable by helicopter, allowing quick and flexible deployment. To supply close-range aerial support for expeditionary forces, the Short Airfield for Tactical Support (SATS) was developed in the late 1950s based on aircraft carrier technology. Employing new aluminum matting, expeditionary forces could build an expeditionary airfield relatively quickly.

Furthermore, by the early 1960s, the Corps had a large number of helicopters and had gained access to platforms from which to launch them. The USS *Boxer* and the USS *Princeton* were recommissioned under a new configuration as Landing Platform Helicopter Carriers (LPH), and the USS *Iwo Jima*, appropriately, was the first purpose-built LPH.

M-60 7.62MM MACHINE GUN

The U.S. military had needed a new infantry machine gun since Korea. The M-60 7.62mm machine gun was created for this purpose.

The Army lifted several innovations from the excellent German machine guns of World War II, notably the ammunition feed, taken from the MG42, and the bolt assembly, copied from the FG42. Constructed of steel stampings and plastics, the M-60 first saw combat in the 1960s and is best known for its service in Vietnam.

Early models of the M-60 had an alarming tendency to "run away." The gas blowback system would keep the gun firing even after the trigger was no longer depressed, and could only be stopped by preventing the ammunition belt from feeding into the receiver. The so-called carrying handle on the top of the gun was also placed poorly for balance, and gunners often slung the weapon from one shoulder while carrying it.

An unloaded M-60 weighs 23 pounds, which necessitated a crew of 3 to carry the weapon: 1 with the gun and ammunition, a second man with spare parts, including at least 3 barrels (the barrel could sometimes reach 500°F during sustained firing), and more ammunition, and a third man who carried the 6.7-pound tripod—which was rarely used—and even more ammunition. (It wasn't called the "pig" by American soldiers in Vietnam for nothing.) When ready to fire, the second man made sure that the ammunition being fed into the gun wasn't twisted or snagged, and also kept replacement belts nearby for quick reloads.

When the gun fired, though, it got people's attention. With a cyclic rate of 600 rounds per minute, and a range of 1,000 yards, the M-60 could lay down a devastating curtain of fire quickly. Often used by the infantry as well as on helicopters, the M-60, despite its tendency to jam and overheat, was used throughout the Vietnam Conflict and into the 1970s, eventually phased out in the late 1980s by the Squad Automatic Weapon M-249.

Finally, the Marine Air-Ground Task Force (MAGTF or "Mag-taf") was formalized in 1962 by Marine Corps Order 3120.3. This order established the modern organization of the U.S. Marine Corps and defined four kinds of MAGTF: the Marine Expeditionary Unit (MEU), consisting of an infantry battalion and a helicopter squadron; the Marine Expeditionary Brigade (MEB), consisting of an infantry regiment and an aircraft group; the Marine Expeditionary Force (MEF), consisting of a division and an aircraft wing; and the Marine Expeditionary Corps (MEC), which often acted as headquarters for two MEFs. Each of these units consisted of a command unit, a ground combat unit, an air combat unit, and a support unit.

USS *IWO JIMA* LANDING PLATFORM HELICOPTER CARRIER (LPH 2)

The primary mission of the new amphibious assault ships, Landing Platform Helicopter Carrier (LPH), was to transport Marine forces anywhere, anytime. The first purpose-built LPH commissioned was the USS *Iwo Jima*. At 598 feet long and 84 feet wide and displacing 19,395 tons, the *Iwo Jima* could achieve speeds of up to 23 knots (26.5 miles per hour). It was crewed by 80 officers and 638 sailors and carried a Marine complement of 1,750 officers and men and 24 helicopters. Although the main purpose of the *Iwo Jima* was the transport of its Marine complement, the ship was flexible and could perform a number of different missions, including mine countermeasures, search and rescue, and evacuation operations. The *Iwo Jima* was also equipped with a large onboard hospital and operating room.

The *Iwo Jima* was commissioned from August 26, 1961, until July 14, 1993. In that time, she engaged in a number of different operations. She served in the Caribbean during the Cuban Missile Crisis of 1962. She was deployed six times to the western Pacific where she engaged in more than 30 amphibious landing operations during the 1960s. The *Iwo Jima* recovered astronauts Lovell, Haise, and Sweigert after Apollo 13 returned to earth. She also supplied command and logistical support for the multinational peacekeeping force in Beirut, Lebanon, in 1983, and had the sad task of caring for the Marines wounded when the Marine compound was destroyed by a terrorist attack. The *Iwo Jima* was the first amphibious assault ship deployed to the Persian Gulf during Operations Desert Shield and Desert Storm, where she engaged in numerous Marine landings and mine countermeasure operations.

★★★

In October 1962, aerial photographs revealed that the Soviet Union had been working to place nuclear missiles in Cuba, which had undergone a revolution led by Fidel Castro in 1959. President Kennedy issued an ultimatum to the Soviet Union ordering them to remove the missiles from Cuba, and for 13 days the United States and the Soviet Union stood "eyeball to eyeball," as Secretary of State Dean Rusk put it. Privately, Commandant Shoup was critical of the government's policies toward Cuba—as he was of growing American involvement in Vietnam—but the Marine Corps responded appropriately to the threat posed by Khrushchev's missiles. The Marine garrison at Guantanamo Bay was reinforced, the majority of the 2nd Marine Division embarked on Navy ships in preparation for an invasion of the island, the 5th Marine Expeditionary Brigade sailed from California through the Panama Canal and likewise stood ready for an invasion of the island, and the majority of the 2nd Marine Aircraft Wing was deployed to Florida and Puerto Rico.

Fortunately, Khrushchev backed down and withdrew the missiles from Cuba, but for two weeks the world had stood on the brink of nuclear holocaust. In 1992, after the collapse of the Communist Soviet regime, Russia revealed that there had been 36 nuclear warheads for 24 intermediate-range missiles and an additional 9 tactical nuclear weapons on the island. President Kennedy and his advisors hadn't known about the nuclear weapons or their intended use. Speaking in 1992, Robert McNamara, who had been Kennedy's Secretary of Defense in 1962, commented that had nuclear weapons been used against the Marines during an invasion of Cuba, there is no doubt that the United States would have responded in kind.

Shoup stepped down as commandant on December 31, 1963, and President Johnson named General Wallace Greene as his successor. Greene had graduated from the Naval Academy in 1930 and served in a wide variety of duties at sea, in China, and at Guantanamo Bay. During the Second World War, he served as operations officer in the Marshalls and on Saipan and Tinian. After the Ribbon Creek tragedy, Greene took command of the recruiting depot at Parris Island, and Shoup made him chief of staff upon becoming commandant in 1960.

Unlike Shoup, however, Greene was an internationalist, committed to building international contacts. Operation Steel Spike, for example, conducted in the fall 1964, was a joint American and Spanish Marine Corps amphibious exercise, the largest since the end of the Second World War.

★★★

In the spring of 1965, trouble erupted once again in the Dominican Republic. The small island republic had witnessed a great number of troubles over the course of the twentieth century, stretching back to the earlier Marine interventions at the beginning of the century and during the 1920s. After the latter intervention, Raphael Trujillo, who had risen through the *Guardia Nacional Dominicana*, had come to dominate the republic and instituted a repressive regime. In 1961, he was assassinated. For the next four years, an occasional American presence had helped to maintain order in the struggling republic, but in April 1965 the threat of a Communist coup led to a large-scale intervention.

Captain James Dare, USN, commander of the Caribbean Task Group, including the 3rd Battalion, 6th Marine Expeditionary Unit (MEU) and Medium Helicopter Squadron 264, stationed at Vieques, Puerto Rico, received word that a coup to overthrow Dominican President Donald Reid Cabral was in progress on April 24. He was ordered to station his task force off the southern coast of the island and prepare to evacuate some 1,200 American citizens should the need arise. The task force arrived off the coast near Haina at 2 A.M. on April 25. By then, the rebels controlled much of Santo Domingo and President Cabral had resigned his presidency and gone into hiding.

On April 27, the USS *Ruchamkin* and the USS *Wood County* put into port at Haina and began evacuating American citizens and foreign nationals; 620 individuals were evacuated from the Embajador Hotel to the 2 American ships by car, and another 556 were lifted out by Marine helicopters to the USS *Boxer* and the USS *Raleigh*. Meanwhile, the U.S. Embassy was receiving occasional gunfire, and on the following day the Dominican police informed American officials that they would be unable to protect the evacuees.

Ambassador W. Tapley Bennett Jr. requested Marine assistance in the evacuation efforts and for additional protection at the Embassy. One Marine platoon was lifted by helicopter to the Embajador Hotel and another to the embassy. At 6:53 P.M., 526 Marines in full battle gear were flown into the grounds of the Embajador Hotel. The Marine helicopters returned to the *Boxer* and the *Raleigh* with evacuees, but refugees continued to flow into the Embajador Hotel. Later in the day, Colonel Pedro Bartolome Benoit, the head of the military junta at San Isidro Airbase some eight miles east of the capital, requested Marine assistance in restoring order. The situation continued to grow worse.

By the morning of April 29, the American Embassy was under relatively heavy fire from small arms. Asked if the situation warranted a full intervention, Ambassador Bennett said, "Yes," and by that afternoon, more than 1,500 Marines had landed at Santo Domingo.

The next day, the 2nd Brigade, 82nd Airborne Division arrived at San Isidro Airbase. The 3rd Battalion, 6th Marines pushed forward from the Embajador Hotel to a line just past the U.S. Embassy, and the 2nd Brigade, 82nd Airborne pushed out of San Isidro to the Duarte Bridge on the Rio Ozama in the hopes of separating the warring factions and establishing an International Safety Zone.

On May 1, Army lieutenant general Bruce Palmer took command of the American ground forces. On that same day, Marine brigadier general John Bouker, commander of the 4th Marine Expeditionary Brigade, arrived with 1st Battalion, 6th Marines, as did the peace committee from the Organization of American States (OAS). Shortly after midnight on May 3, the Army and the Marines linked, creating a kind of safety zone. The 2nd Battalion, 8th Marines were flown into San Isidro and the 1st Battalion, 2nd Marines arrived embarked on LPH *Okinawa*.

After three days of negotiation, the OAS agreed to the American proposal to create an Inter-American Peace Force to restore order to the beleaguered government. Brazilian General Hugo Panasco Alvim was named commander of the Peace Force, and General Palmer was named his deputy. The first Brazilian units began arriving on May 25 and were soon joined by units from Paraguay, Honduras, Nicaragua, and Costa Rica. In the meantime, the U.S. Army and the Marine Corps continued to engage rebels in occasional firefights. The Marines finally began to withdraw from the Dominican Republic on May 26, with the last units leaving on June 6.

Nine Marines were killed and another thirty were wounded during the 1965 intervention in the Dominican Republic. At the peak of the intervention, there were more than 8,000 Marines ashore, not to mention 2 Army airborne brigades and a Navy task force. Such a large force invited criticism of President Johnson's administration. Some critics simply stated that the threat of a Communist coup in the Dominican Republic had never been all that great and that the president had clearly used overkill in this situation. Others speculated about the types of troops sent into the Dominican Republic and wondered if this had not been a test of the relative merits of Marine amphibious operations and Army airborne operations. The high-profile intervention in the Dominican Republic was soon overshadowed, however, by a much higher-profile intervention on the other side of the world.

CHAPTER 12

TOUR OF DUTY: 'NAM

American involvement in Vietnam began rather ambiguously. Mao Tse-tung's triumph in China in 1949 combined with the Korean Conflict invigorated American interest in Southeast Asia, which now seemed an important arena in the Cold War. In Vietnam, the Nationalist Vietminh led by the Communist Ho Chi Minh were struggling for independence against the French, who were trying to reestablish their colonies in Southeast Asia after the defeat of Japan. Fearing a Communist takeover of Vietnam, and hoping to bring the French into the North Atlantic Treaty Organization (NATO)—which the United States had organized for the defense of Europe at the onset of the Cold War—the Truman administration had begun supplying the French with military assistance, mainly in the form of weapons and equipment, to combat the Vietminh. America provided nearly three quarters of French expenditures for the struggle by 1954.

The French were losing the battle, however. In 1954, the Vietminh trapped 12,000 French troops at Dien Bien Phu. The French appealed to the United States for assistance, and several of President Eisenhower's advisors urged him to intervene, even suggesting the use of nuclear weapons. Eisenhower declined, however, unwilling to involve American forces in a "hot" war in Southeast

Asia. The French surrendered on May 7, 1954, and French public opinion demanded the withdrawal of French forces from Vietnam. An international conference held in Geneva, Switzerland, in July 1954 negotiated a cease-fire, temporarily divided the country along the 17th Parallel, and arranged for national elections to reunify the country. In the meantime, the Vietnminh controlled the North while the French controlled the South.

Nevertheless, Eisenhower feared the consequences of a Communist victory in Vietnam. Giving voice to what came to be known as the "domino theory," he warned that if Vietnam fell, neighboring countries such as Thailand and Laos, like dominos in a row, would topple, too. Eisenhower therefore moved to block the election scheduled for 1956, which, he was advised, would almost certainly result in a landslide victory for Ho Chi Minh, and instructed the CIA to install Ngo Dinh Diem, a French-educated aristocrat and fierce anti-Communist Catholic, as president of an independent South Vietnam. In addition, the Eisenhower administration promised economic assistance and military training to Diem's government. Arriving on August 2, 1954, Marine Lieutenant Colonel Victor Croizant was one of the first military advisors sent to Vietnam. By 1960, the Military Assistance and Advisory Group (MAAG) had grown to include 685 American military advisors.

Diem was a poor choice, however. His Catholicism alienated the majority Buddhist populace, his refusal to institute land reform alienated the peasantry, and his government was corrupt and repressive. By 1957, the Vietminh were making guerilla attacks against the South Vietnamese government, and by 1960, opposition to Diem's oppressive policies led to the formation of the National Liberation Front of South Vietnam (NLF), organized by the Vietminh and supported by North Vietnam. The United States urged Diem to institute reforms, but he refused. Apparently lacking alternatives, the administration decided to "sink or swim with Ngo Dinh Diem."

★★★

President Kennedy, even more committed to preventing the expansion of communism than Eisenhower had been, increased American commitments. Weapon shipments to Diem's government increased, as did the American forces in Vietnam, which rose from 700 in 1961 to more than 16,000 by the end of 1963. The first Marines arrived in Vietnam on April 15, 1962.

Medium Helicopter Squadron 362, codenamed "Shu-fly," was initially stationed at Soc Trang just south of Saigon. Marine helicopter squadrons provided electronic intelligence and tactical mobility to the Army of the Republic of Vietnam (ARVN)—the South Vietnamese Army. Shu-fly moved to Da Nang in September, and eventually a Hawk missile battalion was stationed on Monkey Mountain overlooking the port and the airfield there. Over the next three years, half of the Marine Corps's helicopter squadrons rotated through the operation.

(Photo courtesy of Robert F. Dorr)

A Marine H-34 helicopter from the Vietnam Conflict era.

Diem's ARVN troops proved to be inept, however, and on November 1, 1963, South Vietnamese military leaders, with American support, assassinated Ngo Dinh Diem and his brother and seized power. The United States quickly recognized the new government, which proved to be little better than Diem's. The morass that was Vietnam was thus passed on to President Lyndon Johnson.

★★★

Johnson, too, was uncertain what to do about the "raggedy-ass fourth-rate country" that he felt didn't deserve American money and blood, and he feared that American military intervention would provoke the Chinese and the Soviet Union, possibly leading to a third world war. He knew, too, that involvement in "that bitch of a war" would strangle his plans for the Great Society in the United States. However, he also feared appearing weak to the American public and the international community. Insisting that he would not be another "Chamberlain umbrella man"—a reference to the British policy of appeasement and the 1938 Munich agreement that had allowed Hitler to invade Czechoslovakia—and invoking the domino theory like Eisenhower and Kennedy before him, Johnson declared, "I am not going to lose Vietnam. I am not going to be the president who saw Southeast Asia go the way China went."

Johnson increased the American commitment to Vietnam in 1964. In August of that year, North Vietnamese patrol boats allegedly attacked two American destroyers, which were assisting South Vietnamese raids against North Vietnam, in the Gulf of Tonkin. Evidence for the attack was thin, but Johnson asked Congress for the authority to take "all necessary means" to prevent further aggression against American troops, and Congress approved the so-called Gulf of Tonkin Resolution. Johnson had been given "the functional equivalent of a declaration of war," as his attorney general described it, and Johnson interpreted the approval of the resolution as a mandate to commit more American troops to Vietnam.

Johnson ordered more American forces to Vietnam, and by early 1965 there were some 23,000 American troops in the country. Nevertheless, the Viet Cong (Vietnamese Communists) launched a series of attacks against American bases and personnel in late 1964 and early 1965, and in March 1965 Johnson ordered a bombing offensive against North Vietnam, Operation Rolling Thunder. The bombardment failed to turn the tide of battle, however, and Johnson decided to commit American ground forces to the undeclared war in Vietnam. The Marines were the first combat ground forces deployed to South Vietnam.

★★★

General William Westmoreland, commander of the U.S. Military Assistance Command, Vietnam (MACV, a renamed MAAG), requested a Marine unit to secure the Da Nang airfield, which housed the headquarters for Military Region I as well as providing an important base for the U.S. Air Force and the Vietnamese air force. The 9th Marine Expeditionary Brigade under Brigadier General Frederick Karch landed at Da Nang just south of the Demilitarized Zone on March 8, 1965, the 3rd Battalion, 9th Marines landing in full battle gear to be greeted by an official South Vietnamese welcoming committee, flowers, and speeches. The 1st Battalion, 3rd Marines was flown into Da Nang air base. By then there were already 1,300 Marines in helicopter squadrons and antiaircraft battalions stationed in Vietnam.

The 9th MEB had the assignment of securing the air base and other installations around Da Nang. The 1st Battalion, 3rd Marines secured the air base, one of only three very busy jet airfields in South Vietnam. The 3rd Battalion, 9th Marines moved to Hill 327 and a ridgeline west of the air base. On April 11, the 2nd Battalion, 3rd Marines landed at Da Nang, and VMFA-531, a Marine fixed-wing aircraft squadron with F-4B Phantom II jets, arrived at Da Nang air base. On April 14, the 3rd Battalion, 4th Marines landed at Phu Bai and moved up the Perfume River to the ancient capital of Hue, the third largest city in South Vietnam.

Vietnam was divided at the 17th Parallel by a Demilitarized Zone. Immediately south of the DMZ was the I Corps—"Eye Corps"—Tactical Zone. I Corps comprised South Vietnam's five northernmost provinces, Quang Tri, Thua Thien, Quang Nam, Quang Tin, and Quang Ngai, and was home to some 2.5 million Vietnamese, most of whom resided in the cities of Da Nang, Hue, and Quang Tri. The South Vietnamese government controlled the cities; the Viet Cong (VC) controlled the countryside. Republic of Vietnam Major General Nguyen Chanh Thi was given command of I Corps.

At the beginning of May, the Marine forces underwent reorganization and became the III Marine Expeditionary Force. The 9th Marine Expeditionary Brigade was assimilated into the 3rd Marine Division under Major General William "Rip" Collins. Marine aircraft were grouped into Marine

Aircraft Group 16 under Major General Paul Fontana in the headquarters of the 1st Marine Aircraft Wing. All three units—Force, Division, and Wing—had their headquarters at Da Nang. The III Marine Expeditionary Force designation, however, was soon changed to "III Marine Amphibious Force" in an effort to avoid uncomfortable associations of words such as *Expeditionary* or *Corps* to recent Vietnamese experiences with imperialism under the French Expeditionary Corps.

At the beginning of June, command of the Marine forces was transferred to Major General Lewis "Uncle Lew" Walt—who took command of the 3rd Division as well as III MAF—and Brigadier General Keith McCutcheon—who took command of MAG-16—in an understated ceremony intended to avoid the display of American colors.

Marine units continued to land in Vietnam during the summer of 1965. On May 6, the 3rd Marine Amphibious Brigade under Brigadier General Marion Carl, one of Guadalcanal's Cactus Air Force aces, landed 55 miles south of Da Nang at "Chu Lai"—a geographic designation apparently created by General Victor "Brute" Krulak, commander of Fleet Marine Force Pacific, using his own name spelled in Mandarin Chinese. The Marines began construction of an 8,000-foot expeditionary airfield using the new Short Airfield for Tactical Support (SATS) aluminum matting developed during the late 1950s. Eight Douglas A4 Sky Hawks began flying missions from Chu Lai on June 1. On July 1, the 3rd Battalion, 7th Marines established a beachhead at Qui Nohn in preparation for the 1st Air Cavalry Division. They were relieved shortly thereafter by the 1st Battalion, 7th Marines.

The 9th Marines arrived at Da Nang on July 6, and the rest of the 7th Marines landed at Chu Lai on August 14. By the end of the summer, there were four Marine regiments in Vietnam—the 3rd, 4th, 7th, and 9th—and four Marine aircraft groups—MAG-12 (Chu Lai), MAG-11 (Da Nang), MAG-16 (Da Nang), MAG-36 (Chu Lai).

Marines engaged the black-clad Viet Cong in numerous small-scale firefights throughout this period, and after 90 days the Corps had already suffered 29 men killed and another 180 wounded. On July 12, First Lieutenant Frank Reasoner of Company A, 3rd Reconnaissance Battalion was killed defending his wounded radio operator while on patrol. He was the first Marine awarded the Medal of Honor in Vietnam.

CAM DO

Media coverage of war grew tremendously over the course of the twentieth century, reaching the surreal point where warfare was reported on CNN as it happened during the Persian Gulf War. Frequently, the U.S. Marine Corps had benefited from such journalism, from Stephen Crane's report on Cuzco Well to Floyd Gibbons's report on Belleau Wood to Joe Rosenthal's picture of the raising of the American flag over Mount Suribachi on Iwo Jima. Occasionally, the Corps had been hurt by such journalism, as in the condemnation of Major Waller as the "Butcher of Samar" or the tragedy at Ribbon Creek. Cam Do was of the latter variety.

A company of the 9th Marines marched into a small village along the Cam Do River on August 3, 1965, where they came under fire from small arms. The Marines responded with rifles and machine guns and then swept into the village. The regiment had been lured into a trap, however. The village had been set up with rigged guns, bombs, and *punji* sticks (wooden stakes covered in excrement). Surprised, the Marines suffered many casualties and, in reprisal, torched the village.

Morley Safer reported the incident for CBS news, condemning the Marine attack on civilians, and from the very beginning, American involvement in Vietnam would always be tainted by such atrocities and their reportage. Cam Do also reflected the nature of the war, however. The Marines had acted as if there was an easily identifiable enemy. Instead, they found an elusive enemy who attacked from nowhere and then disappeared again. It was impossible to identify the true enemy. The reaction of the Marines to the ambush was certainly reprehensible, but it also indicated just how frustrating this war would be.

★★★

Operation Starlite was the first major Marine operation of the Vietnam War. The 1st Viet Cong Regiment had been found just south of Chu Lai on the Van Tuong Peninsula, and intelligence suggested that the regiment planned to attack the airfield there. On August 18, the 7th Marines, under Colonel Oscar Peatross, a veteran of Evans Carlson's 2nd Raider Battalion, launched an attack on the Van Tuong Peninsula, which had been fortified with caves, "spider holes," and punji traps by the 1st Viet Cong Regiment.

In a beautiful example of vertical envelopment, one battalion attacked over land while a second made an amphibious landing from the sea and a third was brought in from the west via helicopters. Supported by the USS *Orleck* off the coast and Phantoms and Sky Hawks from Da Nang and Chu Lai, the Marines eventually dislodged the VC regiment. After 6 days of combat, 964 VC guerillas had been killed, and the Marines had lost 51 men killed and 203 wounded. Two Marines, Corporal Robert O'Malley and Lance Corporal Joe Paul, were awarded the Medal of Honor. It seemed the Marines were well on their way to victory.

As summer gave way to fall, the monsoon season settled in, and by November an average of one inch of rain fell per day. The monsoon season brought with it changes to the VC strategy. Operation Starlite clearly demonstrated that the VC were no match for Marines in open battles. The VC quickly turned to classic guerilla tactics, surprising and striking small units, squads, platoons, the occasional company, and then melting back into the jungle, or small teams of saboteurs and sappers would infiltrate district capitals, towns, or bases in an attempt to destroy weapons and equipment.

On October 7, VC sappers, supported by mortar teams, infiltrated the Marine air bases at Marble Mountain (Da Nang) and Chu Lai. At Marble Mountain, 6 of the sappers managed to reach the helicopters and destroyed 24 of them and damaged another 23 with satchel charges. At Chu Lai, two A4s were destroyed and six were damaged. The damage done by the VC set the tone for much of the rest of the conflict in Vietnam: No defense was absolute against such infiltration, as would be proven by the Tet Offensive in 1968.

Although the VC avoided direct confrontation with the U.S. military, they had no such reservations about engaging with the ARVN. During the night of November 16, VC forces overran the city of Hiep Duc, a district headquarters some 25 miles west of Tam Ky. Marine helicopters flew two battalions of ARVN troops through the rain and across a ridge lined with machine guns into the valley around Hiep Duc. The ARVN retook the town but had to abandon it because there were too few troops to establish a garrison.

The VC soon struck at another district headquarters, Que Son. On December 8, American Marines and ARVN troops launched Operation Harvest Moon in an effort to relieve the besieged district, which was pretty well dominated by VC. Two battalions of the ARVN 5th Regiment set out from Thang Binh but came under heavy fire in the early afternoon. Marine helicopters flew in another ARVN battalion, but on December 9, the commander of the 5th Regiment was killed and the whole unit was driven south and east.

The 2nd Battalion, 7th Marines landed west of the ARVN regiment while the 3rd Battalion, 3rd Marines landed southeast of the battle to shore up the collapsing situation, and on December 10, the 2nd Battalion, 1st Marines, designated a Special Landing Force, landed between the other two Marine battalions. The ARVN regiment, now under Major General Hoang Xuan Lam, commander of the 2nd ARVN Division, returned to the valley. After four bombing runs by B-52s, Lam's regiment pushed north while Task Force Delta—the three Marine battalions—pushed south and into the hills. Resistance disappeared by December 16.

★★★

Early in 1966, the VC and the North Vietnamese army returned to the Que Son valley. Task Force Delta, now composed of four battalions, returned to the valley in January 1966 for Operation Double Eagle, a coordinated operation with the 1st Air Cavalry Division. For several months, a number of battalions fought under the rubric of Task Force Delta against the 36th NVA Regiment and the 1st VC Regiment.

Traditional military tactics, however, were difficult to apply to the Vietnam War, and confusing, almost surreal events sometimes took place. One example was the political rivalry between the Republic of Vietnam Premier, Air Marshal Ngyuen Cao Ky, and the Commander of I Corps, General Thi. On March 10, 1966, Ky removed Thi from his command and ordered him out of South Vietnam. Protest erupted in Da Nang, Hue, and Saigon over Thi's removal, and the 1st ARVN Division began demanding the overthrow of the Saigon government.

At Ky's command, three battalions of Vietnamese marines landed at Da Nang on April 4. Five days later, the "Struggle Force," as the protesters called themselves, began marching from Hoi An toward Da Nang. Company F, 9th Marines intercepted the column at the Thanh Quit bridge some 12 miles south of the Marine air base. A tense standoff ensued as

South Vietnam stood on the brink of civil war. General Walt was able to negotiate a truce between the rival factions until the middle of May, but on May 15, four battalions loyal to Ky landed at the Da Nang airfield and secured Thi's old headquarters. After a week of chaotic fighting, Ky's forces secured Da Nang and then marched north to Hue and Quang Tri. By June 22, the revolt was over, and Thi went into exile.

In the meantime, the entire 1st Marine Division had landed in Vietnam, and the 5th Division had been reactivated. With five divisions active, however, the Marine Corps was spread thin. In order to avoid political opposition to the rapidly escalating war, President Johnson refused to call up the Marine Corps Reserve. Unable to rely on that reserve strength, regular Marines were forced to serve two or three tours of combat duty, and units often were replenished with draftees rather than trained reservists.

By the end of 1965, 454 Marines had been killed and 2,093 had been wounded. By the end of 1966, more than 67,000 Marines were "in country," and casualties had quadrupled.

★★★

In 1967, combat turned north toward the DMZ. The North Vietnamese Army crossed the 17th Parallel in division strength, and NVA artillery frequently bombarded Marine outposts at Gio Linh, Con Thien, and the "Rock Pile." For some time, combat along the DMZ returned to large-scale battles. Operation Hastings, for example, involved 11 battalions supported by B-52 bombers launching from Guam. Hastings was succeeded by a series of operations named Prairie, which accomplished little except ever-higher body counts.

The Marines did manage to capture Khe Sanh farther west along the DMZ but only after bitter fighting around Hills 561 and 881. By the end of 1967, the Marine Corps had suffered 5,479 men dead and 37,784 wounded. On January 1, 1968, Lieutenant General Leonard Chapman Jr. replaced Wallace Greene as commandant of the U.S. Marine Corps. And the battle was only just beginning.

M-16/M-16A2 5.56MM ASSAULT RIFLE

After World War II, it was obvious that automatic weapons were staying on the battlefield, and submachine and machine guns would play an even more pivotal role in ground combat. While the rest of the world embraced this concept, the U.S. military lagged behind in adopting an automatic rifle, putting their faith in the semiautomatic M-14. Meanwhile, the Russian Kalashnikov AK-47 heralded a new age in automatic weaponry. In the United States, engineer Eugene Stoner was creating his own automatic weapon, the groundbreaking Armalite AR-15 5.56mm rifle. In 1961 the U.S. Army adopted the AR-15 and designated it the M-16, the basic rifle that is still used today in America's armed forces and around the world.

The M-16 is a gas-operated automatic rifle that can fire 800 rounds per minute. It can be loaded with a 20- or 30-round box magazine, and there have been carbine variants (the CAR-15, for example, as well as a light machine gun model with a longer barrel and a bipod for stable firing).

First introduced into combat in Vietnam in 1967, the M-16 suffered from a low-grade powder used in the 5.56mm cartridges as well as a strange message that circulated among the troops stating that the weapon was "self-cleaning." It wasn't, of course, and that led to hundreds of instances of jammed and fouled rifles. The Army eventually fixed the powder problem and retooled the M-16 into the M-16A1 model, adding a bolt closure device to ensure that a jammed round could be cleared without having to shove a cleaning rod down the barrel, which was the only way to clear a jam on the M-16 model.

The M-16 has been referred to as the NATO equivalent of the AK-47, known and used all over the world. The latest model, the M-16A2, has a heavier barrel to take advantage of the SS109 bullet, a three-round burst limiter, meaning the weapon can only fire single shots or three rounds at a time, and a muzzle compensator to limit barrel rise during firing. The handgrip and buttstock were also redesigned to be lighter and tougher, and the rear sight deck was improved. The weapon also has a fitting for a combat bayonet, and can be outfitted with the M-203 40mm underbarrel grenade launcher. The one problem it seemed to have, that of underpowered ammunition, has apparently been fixed with the adoption of the SS109 5.56mm round in the 1990s.

The battle for Hill 561 and Hill 881 had been bitter indeed, and the North Vietnamese Army wasn't willing to let the hill go easily. Early in 1968, it became evident that the NVA was building up its forces near Khe Sanh. The NVA found it relatively easy to maneuver through neighboring

Laos along the famous Ho Chi Minh Trail, infiltrating South Vietnam, supplying Viet Cong guerillas, and setting up heavy 130mm and 152mm artillery inside Laos itself to effect a bombardment of Khe Sanh. In January, the NVA maneuvered two divisions around Khe Sanh and cut off its only overland supply route. North Vietnamese General Vo Nguyen Giap obviously hoped to repeat his 1954 victory against the French at Dien Bien Phu.

"I don't want any damn Dinbinfoos!" President Johnson is supposed to have told General Westmoreland. The situation at Khe Sanh was much different from Dien Bien Phu, however. The French outpost had been located in a valley surrounded by mountains and could be supplied only by airdrop. At Khe Sanh, the Marines controlled the high ground and a well-defended airstrip. Furthermore, Khe Sanh was within range of Army artillery at Camp Carroll and the Rock Pile. In addition, Westmoreland believed there to be two very good reasons to hold on to the combat base. First, it was important to hold the western sector of the DMZ to prevent a flanking attack against Dong Ha or Quang Tri City. Second, the Khe Sanh plateau promised a "target-rich environment" that the Marines could exploit to whittle down NVA troops.

For the Marines themselves, of course, Khe Sanh became hell on earth. So many men had been killed taking Hill 561 and Hill 881 at the end of 1967 that the Marines were engulfed by the noxious odor of the dead every time a foxhole was dug, and so much ordnance had exploded around those two hills that the trees were saturated with shrapnel; it was too dangerous even to cut down trees for bunkers.

The siege of Khe Sanh began on January 20, 1968, when two companies of the 26th Marines under Captain William Dabney went out on patrol between Hills 881-North and 881-South. The patrol ran into an NVA battalion, an unusual sight during the daytime, and attacked aggressively. Suddenly, Colonel David Lownds, commander of the 26th Marines, ordered Dabney to withdraw to his position on Hill 881-South before night fell. An NVA defector, a lieutenant, had been found by the 26th Marines and revealed incredible intelligence: The NVA was in the area in strength and planned to launch an attack that very night.

Fortunately, Dabney's patrol had stumbled upon the advance forces supposed to attack Hill 881-South and so had prevented it. Nevertheless, an NVA battalion attacked Hill 861 shortly after midnight. Marine machine gunners cut down the NVA troops who materialized out of the darkness, but not nearly enough, and the enemy swarmed over Hill 861. The Marines on Hill 881-South fired on Hill 861 with their mortars, launching more than 700 shells so rapidly that tubes glowed red with heat. Company K, which had been driven back by the relentless assault, pushed the NVA back beyond the perimeter and held on to Hill 861.

Before dawn, however, the NVA unleashed a hellish bombardment on Khe Sanh with everything from mortars to heavy artillery. One of the shells from the first barrage hit the main ammo dump and set off a chain reaction that destroyed 90 percent of the Marine supplies. Nevertheless, the Marines managed to hold the perimeter and even defend Khe Sanh Village against a heavy attack. After repelling the initial assault on the wooded hills surrounding Khe Sanh combat base, the Marines settled in for 77 days of bombardment.

The defense of Khe Sanh was costly. More than half of Captain Dabney's Marines defending Hill 881-South would be killed during the siege. Nevertheless, the Marines never allowed their spirit to falter. Every morning, "To the Colors" was sounded, the Marines raised the American flag, and dove back into their foxholes as mortar shells rained down on top of them. When the barrage tapered off, a Marine invariably waved a red tie-dyed shirt above his foxhole, the rifle range symbol indicating that the shooter has completely missed his target.

The 26th Marines, now reinforced by the 1st Battalion, 9th Marines and an ARVN ranger unit, sat tight at Khe Sanh as the annual Tet holiday drew near. General Westmoreland and President Johnson were convinced that a major NVA assault would come through Khe Sanh. Vo Nguyen Giap, the commander of the North Vietnamese forces, would later claim that the assault on Khe Sanh had been a remarkable feint that drew American and South Vietnamese forces away from the cities in preparation for the real attack, the Tet Offensive.

(Photo courtesy of Robert F. Dorr)

An F-8E Crusader jet of Marine All-Weather Fighter Squadron 235 returned to the Da Nang Air Base after a mission in support of Marines pinned down by enemy fire in April 1967.

★★★

On January 30, 1968, NVA and VC units struck suddenly and simultaneously throughout South Vietnam, seeming to materialize from thin air. More than 100 villages, towns, and cities in 36 of South Vietnam's 48 provinces experienced large-scale attacks on that day. In Saigon, VC sappers attacked the American Embassy and killed several Americans, including two Marines. The VC dragged artillery hundreds of miles by hand and bombarded Tan Son Nhut. Viet Cong even infiltrated Da Nang and launched an assault on I Corps headquarters, but Marines, Vietnamese rangers, and CAP eventually broke the assault. And from An Hoa, reconnaissance reports came in that the 2nd NVA Division was headed toward Da Nang.

From a helicopter circling Da Nang, Lieutenant General Robert Cushman, who had taken over command of III MAF on June 1, 1967, spotted some 200 NVA soldiers moving toward the city in broad daylight and directed 2 infantry battalions to intercept them and break the attack on Da Nang. Farther south, Cushman directed ARVN troops in holding off two enemy attacks on Hoi An.

Eventually, all of the NVA and VC attacks in South Vietnam were broken—except at Hue. The ancient imperial capital and cultural center of South Vietnam had been occupied by more than 3,000 NVA and VC troops who had managed to secure the old but still impressive citadel built by Emperor Gia Long in 1802. By the time Marine forces arrived from Phu Bai, the VC and NVA seemed to control nearly the entire city. American forces were spread thin by the Tet Offensive, and as they worked to fight off the simultaneous assaults, they couldn't immediately reinforce Hue. Two companies from the 1st Battalion, 1st Marines entered the city on January 31, and on February 1 they began securing the southern half of the city. The 2nd Battalion, 5th Marines joined them three days later. ARVN units led by Lieutenant General Huang Lam began securing the northern half of the city.

The campaign to retake Hue wasn't easy, however. The NVA and VC forces were entrenched in the citadel and throughout the rest of the city, and the allies were reluctant to use artillery against the historic city and its citizenry. Even so, most of the combat involved brutal street-to-street and house-to-house fighting and much of the city was eventually destroyed.

The Marines captured the southeast wall of the old fortress on February 22 and then allowed the ARVN troops to make the final assault on the old Imperial Palace. On February 24, the flag of South Vietnam flew once more over the battered fortress. Marine and ARVN forces might have eliminated as many as 11 NVA battalions during the battle for Hue. The Marines suffered 142 dead and another 858 wounded during the fighting there.

Ultimately, the Tet Offensive was a defeat for NVA and VC forces. Hue suffered through the siege, an estimated 15,000 VC and NVA troops were killed, and the Communists won few converts among the people. Nevertheless, the Tet Offensive shocked America. For several years, the Johnson administration had been telling the public that the United States was winning the Vietnam War. Then, suddenly, an almost defeated enemy had sprung up everywhere, threatened the U.S. Embassy, and held off the Marines in Hue. And all this in addition to the siege at Khe Sanh. Johnson had suffered his "Dinbinfoo," and public opinion rapidly turned against his war in a faraway land.

★★★

General Westmoreland quickly claimed that Tet had been an elaborate feint to draw troops away from Khe Sanh, where an offensive was imminent, and requested reinforcements for the combat post. The Joint Chiefs of Staff assigned the 27th Marines and an Army paratrooper brigade. Westmoreland believed these units to be insufficient, however, and requested an additional 206,000 troops, which were not authorized. The draft had just called up an additional 48,000 young men, and the weekly death toll had reached an average of 500. Vietnam was straining both the Johnson administration and the American public.

Westmoreland's predictions of a major assault at Khe Sanh were never realized, though war did return to Khe Sanh on February 5, 1968, when electronic sensors warned of approaching enemy units. Colonel Lownds ordered an area along the enemy's approach saturated with artillery and mortar fire. More than 500 shells were dropped, and for a brief moment it seemed as if the enemy had been stopped.

Unfortunately, NVA sappers had sneaked through the wire and launched a surprise attack on Hill 861, defended by Captain Earle Breeding's Company E, 2nd Battalion, 26th Marines. "Echo" Company withdrew to secondary positions and quickly donned gas masks. While Hill 861 was saturated with tear gas, Breeding launched a counterattack, and the Marines caught the NVA troops by surprise while they were looting foxholes. Savage hand-to-hand fighting ensued as the Marines drove the NVA back beyond the wire. In the morning, Captain Dabney, on Hill 881-South, began firing on the retreating NVA. Company E killed 109 NVA soldiers but lost 40 of their own that night.

At midnight on February 7, 1968, NVA PT-76 tanks and assault troops armed with flamethrowers and explosives attacked a Special Forces camp at Lang Vei, 5 miles west of Khe Sanh. They overran the camp in 13 minutes, and the few survivors of the assault were scattered. The Marines at Khe Sanh responded with artillery, firing variable-time-fused shells that could be set to explode in midair, spraying the overrun camp with shrapnel. It was the most Colonel Lownds could do for the beleaguered Green Berets only a few miles away. Given his primary orders to defend Khe Sanh, he didn't feel that he could send relief troops or reinforcements, which were certain to be ambushed, to Lang Vei. Only 15 Special Forces and a few dozen South Vietnamese troops were extracted the next morning.

Sudden sapper attacks such as those on Hill 861 or at Lang Vei were frightening, but the real threat at Khe Sanh was the constant artillery bombardment. Day and night, the NVA pounded the Khe Sanh combat base with mortar shells, rockets launched from Hill 881-North, and heavy artillery from Laos. Shrapnel flew through the air constantly, hitting 1 in 10 Marines.

Supplying the combat base and evacuating the wounded was difficult at best. The NVA had cut off the overland supply routes to Khe Sanh, leaving only the airstrip for supply and evacuation. Nevertheless, the Marines at Khe Sanh were supplied with impressive airlifts. The skies above Khe Sanh were constantly filled with aircraft, sometimes spiraling as high as 35,000 feet awaiting their turn to land on the airstrip to deliver one portion of the 185 tons of daily supplies needed to support the Marines or evacuate the wounded. The Lockheed C-130 Hercules supply planes could deliver up to 18 tons of supplies in one landing, but they were so large and ponderous that the NVA could knock them out of the air easily. Smaller C-123 Providers proved somewhat more efficient overall. The Marine helicopters of MAG-16 and MAG-36 did most of the work, however.

Supplying hill outposts was even more problematic, and despite the greater maneuverability of the helicopters, the NVA was able to pick off undefended helicopters with relative ease. The commander of the 1st Marine Aircraft Wing, Major General Norman Anderson, developed a tactic called the "super gaggle" to protect the helicopters resupplying the hill outposts. The supply mission was preceded by a dozen A-4 Skyhawks flying out of Chu Lai that would lay down a wall of bombs, napalm, gas, and smoke. A dozen CH-46 Sea Knight helicopters from Quang Tri followed closely, carrying some 4,000 pounds of supplies in cargo nets. As the countryside exploded, burned, and smoked from the bombardment, the Sea Knights would deliver their supplies to the outpost.

In addition, a variety of jet aircraft flew over Khe Sanh to deliver incredible payloads of bombs and rockets against the NVA. None of these was more impressive than the "arc light" missions. B-52s flying from Thailand or Guam dropped an incredible 27 tons of ordnance from 30,000 feet in the air. From that distance, the NVA could neither see the plane nor hear the bombs drop until it was too late. And 27 tons of ordnance would ruin anyone's day. The ground shook. Hills and ridgelines disappeared. Human beings were shredded.

The NVA, however, demonstrated impressive fortitude in the face of such technological devastation. They continued to bombard Khe Sanh combat base, dig siege trenches ever closer to the airstrip, and send prob-ing attacks against the Marines. The heaviest attack since the beginning of the siege occurred on February 29. Colonel Lownds believed this attack to be the long expected major offensive and called in as much ordnance as he could muster. B-52s dropped their arc light payloads along the anticipated path of advance as Marine and Army artillery coordinated with devastating impact. The bombardment decimated the NVA action.

As monsoon season ended in March, NVA activity around Khe Sanh tapered off. The bombardment would continue for several more weeks, but the NVA made no further large-scale assaults against the combat base. Electronic sensors, scouts, and aerial observers all indicated that NVA activity outside the perimeter had dropped off sharply, and intelligence estimated that there were fewer than 6,000 NVA troops left in the area. At the order of Colonel Lownds, the Marines went back on the offensive, patrolling outside of the perimeter, looking for the NVA. Frequent ambushes and firefights ensued, but the tension eased somewhat.

Khe Sanh continued to draw media attention, however, and, somewhat ironically, a "relief mission," Operation Pegasus, was now organized. None were more amused by this turn of events than the 26th Marines, who had spent two and a half months bearing the brunt of the storm of steel un-leashed against them. True to the Marine character, and despite the extreme deprivations they had faced so far, the Marines were confident that as long as the supplies could be flown in, they could hold Khe Sanh. Furthermore, if Khe Sanh did need to be abandoned, they had no doubt that they would be able to fight their way out as the 1st Marine Division had fought its way out of the Chosin Reservoir in Korea. Nevertheless, a relief force—"rescue" was anathema in the context of Operation Pegasus—composed of the 1st Marines, the 1st Air Cavalry Division, and three ARVN divisions set out on April 1 and reached Khe Sanh one week later.

The siege of Khe Sanh ended the following week when the Marines in turn besieged the last NVA stronghold, Hill 881-North, on April 14, 1968. The NVA had dug a complex of caves and tunnels into the hill, but it did them little good in the end. Marine units and artillery surrounding the hill concentrated a barrage on the hill before the 3rd Battalion, 26th Marines stormed up the slope. Many NVA soldiers were buried alive, trapped as their own tunnels collapsed around them. Those who struggled free of the earth were cut down with bayonets. A cheer went up around Khe Sanh as the American flag was tied to a denuded tree on the hill. The siege of Khe Sanh was over.

The siege had cost the Marines 205 dead and 1,668 wounded. Estimates suggest, however, that the NVA lost an incredible 10,000 men and quite possibly more. The 26th Marines was presented the Presidential Unit Citation for its defense of Khe Sanh.

Khe Sanh and the Tet Offensive proved to be the turning point of the Vietnam War and may be seen as apt symbols for it. Khe Sanh represented the dedication of the American Marines to their perceived duty to prevent the spread of communism. Holding the line under extreme circumstances, they would not budge. But the Tet Offensive demonstrated that such dedication seemed to have little impact on the war itself. Despite the massive casualties inflicted on the enemy, the NVA and VC seemed to be able to strike anywhere they wished.

Khe Sanh and the Tet Offensive also reflected the destruction inflicted on Vietnam. In 1965, the ancient capital city of Hue had been a charming city; three years later it lay in ruin. The beautifully forested hills at Khe Sanh had been turned into a moonscape, cratered and burnt. The ancient and beautiful country of Vietnam had been devastated.

Khe Sanh and Tet had important repercussions for the Johnson administration as well. Secretary of Defense Robert McNamara resigned. President Johnson relieved General Westmoreland of his command of Military Assistance Command, Vietnam and replaced him with General Creighton Abrams. And on March 31, President Johnson announced that he would not seek reelection in 1968.

★★★

After working so hard to hold Khe Sanh, the U.S. military soon abandoned it. Uncomfortable with the static defense exemplified by the siege of Khe Sanh, General Cushman wished to conduct a mobile war throughout I Corps, taking the battle to the enemy instead of waiting for the enemy to attack. Thus began a second kind of war in Vietnam. The war along the DMZ was characterized by heavy shelling and sapper attacks. The war farther south in I Corps was principally one of counterinsurgency.

While the 3rd Marine Division at the DMZ had faced artillery, rockets, mortars, and satchel charges, the 1st Division headquartered at Da Nang had to deal with mines, snipers, ambushes, and booby traps. Quang Nam province was filled with a variety of booby traps, ranging from simple trip-wires to hand grenades to rearmed American artillery shells. Such traps maimed their targets as frequently—if not more so—as they killed them. Mines could be even worse, detonated by contact or set off by a nearby Viet Cong sympathizer.

Pacification, Khe Sanh, and counterinsurgency measures all proved exceedingly frustrating. The U.S. Marine Corps had been trained and equipped, and had proven itself, to be an efficient offensive weapon. It was best when striking suddenly and striking hard. The NVA and the VC had known this since Operation Starlite and had turned to typical guerilla tactics of ambush and fade away. The Marines may have preferred to meet the enemy in open combat.

After Khe Sanh and Tet, the Marines did make an effort to take the fight to the enemy. In May 1968, the 7th Marines swept over Go Noi Island in a delta south of Hoi An that served as a VC base camp. In Operation Pipestone Canyon, the Marines brought huge bulldozers borrowed from the Army Corps of Engineers and plowed over the whole island. The VC, however, simply moved to a new location.

★★★

U.S. forces engaged in more conventional combat in what the Marines called the "Arizona Territory" west of An Hoa. In addition to conventional battles, Marines frequently went on recon missions throughout "Arizona" and the Que Son mountains. In a sense turning the tables on the NVA, six-man "sting ray" units were inserted into the mountains to establish observation posts and direct Marine units to intercept the NVA units.

Along the DMZ, the 3rd Marine Division, led by Major General Raymond Davis, likewise left behind static operations in favor of more mobile and offensive operations. Beginning on January 22, 1969, Colonel Robert Barrow led the 9th Marines on Operation Dewey Canyon. The operation struck into the Da Krong Valley in the western mountains along the Laotian border, an area controlled by the NVA, filled with NVA artillery, and supplied by the infamous Ho Chi Minh Trail.

Barrow ordered a quick strike to establish artillery posts deep within enemy-held territory. Light forces were transported by helicopter to two hilltops, which were quickly cleared of jungle by Marines armed with chainsaws, and 155mm howitzer batteries were flown in, establishing bases "Razor" and "Cunningham." The 9th Marines then traveled overland through thick jungle and over mountains and cliffs. One company encountered an NVA patrol and a bloody firefight erupted. The Marines drove off the patrol but not before sustaining 18 casualties.

The jungle was so thick that it was impossible for helicopters to evacuate the wounded, and the Marines had to carry the wounded the rest of the way, a journey that dragged on for 48 hours. As if that wasn't bad enough, it was also monsoon season. Rain and cloud cover was so thick that it became nearly impossible to supply Razor and Cunningham. Supply helicopters were kept on constant alert for those brief moments when the clouds cleared and the Marines could be resupplied.

Barrow's Marines captured Tiger Mountain, which had an extensive NVA headquarters and stockpile carved inside it, and knocked out a powerful 122mm artillery battery placed there. Combat in the mountains, however, could be even more brutal and surreal than the siege at Khe Sanh or more nerve-wracking than counterinsurgency missions in Quang Nam.

On February 22, Company A, 1st Battalion, 9th Marines stumbled upon a well-placed NVA company in the nearby A Shau Valley. The two units blasted away at each other at such close quarters that it was impossible to call in air or artillery support. In savage point-blank fighting, the Marines eventually took the field, but 11 were killed and 72 were wounded, including the company's commander, Lieutenant Wesley Fox, who was wounded 3 times. He received the Medal of Honor.

The 9th Marines also found themselves near the Laotian border. Maddeningly, they could follow the NVA supply columns as they moved along Route 922 across the border, but since the trail was actually in Laos, they were forbidden from interfering with the traffic. Barrow requested permission to interdict the traffic along Route 922. Commander MACV Creighton Abrams agreed with Barrow and granted permission for a strike at Route 922. Captain David Winecoff led Company H across the border and ambushed an NVA column.

Barrow's 9th Marines fought for a while longer in the mountainous border country before coming out. In support of Operation Dewey Canyon, Marine aircraft flew 461 missions and dropped more than 2,000 tons of ordnance, helicopters had flown more than 1,200 sorties, and Barrow's artillery had fired more than 134,000 rounds. The Marines lost 130 dead during the operation and another 920 wounded. Approximately 1,600 NVA were killed.

Fears of a major NVA offensive continued into 1969, however. In January, the 7th Marines captured NVA soldiers who claimed to belong to the 21st NVA Regiment in Quang Nam Province. Not long after that, an ARVN unit fought an NVA battalion, killing 49 NVA soldiers; prisoners captured claimed they belonged to the 36th NVA Regiment. Captain Paul Van Riper's Company M, 3rd Battalion, 7th Marines spotted a sizeable NVA unit heading toward Da Nang. Van Riper's Marines ambushed the NVA and found themselves engaged in desperate hand-to-hand combat in thick bamboo and elephant grass.

Lieutenant Colonel Francis Quinn led the remainder of the 3rd Battalion into the battle, which turned into some of the most brutal combat the war had seen. When Lance Corporal Lester Weber's platoon was attacked, he charged the enemy, killing one and driving off several more NVA soldiers. He overwhelmed a second NVA soldier, and then dove at two more firing on his men. Grabbing one soldier's rifle, Weber beat the two NVA soldiers to death. He was mortally wounded when he attacked yet a fifth NVA soldier. Weber was awarded the Medal of Honor.

During the battle, Company K took several prisoners, including an NVA regimental commander. The NVA had hoped to hurt the 7th Marines so badly that it would draw the entire 1st Marine Division west of Da Nang, where two NVA regiments waited in ambush. The 3rd Battalion, 7th Marines went on the offensive and decimated the lurking NVA regiments.

★★★

By 1969 the Vietnam War had become "routine." III MAF headquarters at Da Nang were air-conditioned. Mess halls offered decent meals and beer and soda. Marines were given an opportunity for rest and relaxation at White Beach on the Pacific coast or liberty at some exotic Asian city. It was a very different kind of war from the Second World War or Korea.

It was clear, too, however, that the Marines themselves were exhausted. Men turned to drugs and prostitutes for a few moments of escape from the horror of war. The anti-Communist fervor present during the middle of the decade had given way to cynicism. South Vietnam appeared horribly corrupt and incapable of ruling its own people, let alone defending itself against the North, and racial slurs crept into the vocabulary of the Marines. Some men even took it upon themselves to deal with a particularly difficult commander by tossing a fragmentation grenade into his tent at night— "fragging," it was called.

Public pressure in the States and general exhaustion led to a new strategy: Vietnamization, which would place the burden of the war on South Vietnamese rather than American troops. A general withdrawal of troops from Vietnam began in mid-1969, and by the end of the year, the 3rd Marine Division had left the country. In September 1970, the 7th Marines returned to Camp Pendleton, and in February 1971, the 5th Marines did likewise. By the spring 1971, the last elements of the 1st Marine Division and the 1st Marine Aircraft Wing had left as well, leaving only some 500 Marine advisers with the South Vietnamese marines.

With the American forces out of the country, North Vietnam attempted a major offensive against South Vietnam at Easter 1972. A mass of tanks and infantry swept across the border, driving toward Saigon. A Marine adviser at Dong Ha single-handedly stalled the NVA advance, however. Captain John Ripley, under constant fire for 3 hours, rigged more than 500 pounds of explosive to the bridge over the Cua Viet River.

The explosion dropped a 100-foot span of bridge. The smoke could be seen for miles, and 30,000 NVA troops had been stopped in their tracks. Stunned by this sudden development, and pummeled by U.S. warships still in the South China Sea, the NVA offensive stalled. President Nixon threatened the resumption of hostilities and renewed the bombing campaign against North Vietnam. General Vo Nguyen Giap, the commander of the NVA who had been the mastermind behind the siege at Khe Sanh and the Tet Offensive, was relieved of his command, and Captain Ripley was awarded the Navy Cross.

On January 27, 1973, the Paris Peace Accords ended American involvement in Vietnam. Two years later, the NVA stormed south once more with even greater force. The few Marines left in South Vietnam were instrumental in organizing the mass evacuation of Americans and South Vietnamese nationals via helicopter. Master Sergeant Juan Valdez, commander of the U.S. Embassy's Marine Guard, was the last man to board the final helicopter on April 30, 1975.

The Marines lost 13,067 men killed and 88,633 wounded in Vietnam between 1965 and 1972. More Marines were killed during the Second World War, but the number of wounded in Vietnam, and the total number of casualties, far exceeded those of the Second World War. This stunning epitaph reflected the nature of the war for those Marines who served in Vietnam. Only 38 Marines were captured during the war. Eight of them died; the others were eventually released. Forty-nine Marines remain missing in action. The Medal of Honor was awarded to 57 Marines, 46 of them posthumously.

CHAPTER 13

THE NEW CORPS: DESERT STORM AND THE NEW WORLD ORDER

The fall of Saigon represented a low point for U.S. foreign and military policy. Although the Marine Corps had withdrawn from Vietnam in good order, the withdrawal ushered in two decades of troubles for the Marine Corps with few bright spots. Indeed, for a moment it seemed that American fears about the spread of communism had proven correct. At the same time that the North Vietnamese invaded South Vietnam, Pol Pot's Khmer Rouge—Cambodian Communists—were encircling the Cambodian capital of Phnom Penh. American airlifts into the city delivered tons of medical supplies and food to the city, but Pol Pot's forces continued to pressure the city.

On April 1, 1975, the legitimate president of Cambodia, Lon Nol, left Phnom Penh for Indonesia, essentially entering exile; his government collapsed shortly thereafter. On April 12, President Gerald Ford authorized Operation Eagle Pull, and the 31st Marine Amphibious Unit—embarked with the Seventh Fleet in the Gulf of Siam—flew into Phnom Penh, erected a perimeter around a soccer field near the U.S. Embassy, and evacuated 276 Americans, Cambodian officials, and foreign nationals from the city. As in Saigon, the Embassy Guard took down the American flag and left in the last helicopter out of Phnom Penh.

Trouble with the Khmer Rouge government didn't end there, however. One month later, in an event that might be emblematic of American problems, a Cambodian gunboat fired a warning shot at the container ship *Mayaguez* on its way to Thailand. The *Mayaguez* stopped and allowed the Khmer Rouge to come on board and then followed the gunboat to the island of Koh Tang. The crew of the *Mayaguez* was transferred to the port city Kompong Som 34 miles away. President Ford ordered the crew of the *Mayaguez* rescued, and the 2nd Battalion, 9th Marines, reinforced with Company D, 1st Battalion, 4th Marines, boarded Air Force transports at Okinawa and flew to Utapao, Thailand. No amphibious assault ships or Marine helicopter squadrons were available, so the Air Force lifted Company D to the destroyer *Harold E. Holt* off Koh Tang, and the Marines scrambled aboard the *Mayaguez* on May 15 only to find it deserted.

(Photo courtesy of Robert F. Dorr)

U.S. Marines return to the escort ship USS Harold E. Holt *after storming the merchant freighter SS* Mayaguez *to recover the ship, which had been taken over by elements of the Khmer Rouge. The ship was deserted (the crew had been moved to a nearby island), and the* Mayaguez *was taken into tow by the* Harold E. Holt.

The Khmer Rouge regime in Cambodia realized that it was in over its head and released the crew of the *Mayaguez*. By then, however, Lieutenant Colonel Randall Austin's 2nd Battalion had begun its assault on Koh Tang. The Khmer Rouge defended the island tenaciously, shooting down the first two helicopters to approach Koh Tang and killing seven Marines, two Navy corpsmen, and the Air Force copilot. Three more Marines died trying to reach the shore. The few survivors of a third helicopter that just barely made it to the island with its tail rotor shot off took up defensive positions and managed to hold off Cambodian assaults throughout the day.

On the other side of the island, Cambodian fire damaged another helicopter, which was forced to return to Thailand, but five helicopters landed successfully. Eventually, air strikes and mortar fire drove the Cambodians into the jungle, and more Marines began to come ashore. With news that the crew of the *Mayaguez* had been released, the Marines began to withdraw, and by 8 P.M., the last of the Marines had been lifted off the island.

In all, the Air Force had supplied 15 helicopters for the rescue mission. Three of them had been shot down and another 10 had been damaged. Forty-one Americans died during the assault, including eleven Marines, and another three Marines were reported missing in action. Another 41 Marines were injured, as were 2 sailors and 7 airmen. The "rescue" had been a fiasco.

The fall of Saigon and Phnom Penh and the *Mayaguez* incident aroused criticism of U.S. foreign and military policy, and critics suggested that the amphibious assault had serious limitations in modern warfare. In addition, the Vietnam War had a profound effect on the Marine Corps. It became very difficult to recruit young men and women, and the strength of the Marine Corps soon dropped below 200,000. Those men and women who were recruited were often found to have little of the character that the Corps had come to expect from its Marines; many of them lacked the skills or the drive desired by the Corps, and many officers and NCOs despaired over the future of the service.

★★★

In an effort to attract better recruits, Congress authorized the establishment of higher-quality living quarters, replacing barracks with a kind of "military motel," but such developments did little to improve the quality of the recruits, and officers frequently found it harder to keep their troops under control. Theft, racism, drug abuse, and alcoholism all increased during the 1970s. The Marine Corps qualities of discipline and fortitude seemed to have disappeared. Indeed, one might suggest that the general decline in the morale and quality of the average Marine contributed to such tragedies as the *Mayaguez* incident. General Robert Cushman Jr., Marine Corps commandant, summarized the situation best when he commented, "I still need Marines who can shoot and salute. But I need Marines who can fix jet engines and man sophisticated radar sets as well."

Cushman became Marine Corps commandant on January 1, 1972, and was faced with severe criticism in the wake of the Vietnam War. The Defense Department, members of Congress, and the Brookings Institute, all declared that the Corps was in need of restructuring to meet the needs of modern warfare. As after the First World War and after the Second World War, the Marine Corps was criticized as an anachronism, ill suited to meet American security concerns, which now focused heavily on Western Europe and NATO. Amphibious warfare, the specialty of the Marine Corps, seemed to have no value for a defense strategy based on tanks and missiles. Cushman, however, as had his predecessors, adeptly declared that the Marine Corps would "pull its head out of the jungle" and focus its attention on its partnership with the Navy. And the Navy supported the renewed focus of the Corps, building two amphibious assault ships (LHA), the *Tarawa* and the *Saipan*. Seven more such ships were planned, but the number of ships was eventually cut in half.

Unfortunately, the Corps again came under serious scrutiny at home. On December 6, 1975, recruits beat their fellow Marine recruit Private Lynn McClure unconscious during a training exercise; McClure later died of head injuries sustained during the drill. Not long after McClure's death, a drill instructor at Parris Island accidentally shot and killed a recruit during an exercise. Inquiries into the incidents led to criticism of the Marine Corps training, but Wilson and Barrow were able to defend the traditional Marine Corps boot camp.

General Lewis Wilson, who had succeeded Cushman as commandant on July 1, 1975, appointed Lieutenant General Robert Barrow to institute corrections to the Marine recruiting and training program. Barrow encouraged recruiters to target high school graduates hoping to improve the quality of the Marines. Furthermore, Barrow required the new recruit to actually complete basic training before the recruiter would be awarded credit for the recruit, thus providing an incentive for the recruitment of better quality candidates.

Marine Corps training was reorganized as well. The Marine Corps base at Twentynine Palms, California, became an all-purpose training base, and Battalion Landing Teams (BLT) began combined arms exercises (CAX) there. Commanding officers soon noted an improvement in the quality of the Marines.

On July 1, 1979, Barrow succeeded Wilson as commandant and continued Wilson's efforts to improve Corps efficiency. He granted field officers authority to offer substantial reenlistment incentives. He instituted random drug testing within the Corps, and drug use declined significantly. He instituted a policy of "uniformity, quality, and availability" in 1981; emphasizing the need to look like a Marine, he instituted dress codes in order to project the appropriate Marine "posture."

The strategy of "prepositioning" was adopted under Commandant Barrow's tenure as well. Working with President Jimmy Carter's secretary of defense, Harold Brown, Barrow adopted the idea that supplies could be prepositioned at a depot—an idea Wilson had adopted earlier, establishing a depot in Norway—or on board a ship. The Marines themselves would be transported to the depot or ship, where they would arm before initiating an operation. This would improve the speed and efficiency of deployment. Furthermore, Barrow appointed Lieutenant General Paul Kelley to explore the possibility of developing a Rapid Deployment Joint Task Force (RDJTF or RDF). An all-service force was established at MacDill Air Force Base on March 1, 1980, and Gallant Eagle joint-service exercises involving thousands of troops from various branches of the military were initiated at Twentynine Palms in 1982. Prepositioning, Rapid Deployment, and the Gallant Eagle exercises would provide the basis for Operation Desert Storm in 1991.

Finally, working with the Reagan administration, Barrow was able to improve Marine Corps equipment. F/A-18 Hornets replaced obsolete F-4 Phantoms, for example, and the new M-198 155mm artillery piece replaced the M-109 155mm gun and the 105mm howitzer.

★★★

Despite improvements in recruit training and efficiency, difficulties continued to plague the Marine Corps. Since the end of the Second World War, Marines had supplied Embassy Guards. However, in November 1979, Iranian revolutionaries seized the U.S. Embassy in Teheran, including a number of Marine Guards.

President Jimmy Carter at first decided not to respond to the crisis militarily, but he eventually authorized Operation Blue Light, an attempt to rescue the hostages. On April 24, 1980, eight Marine RH-53D helicopters were launched from the USS *Nimitz*. Three of the helicopters suffered mechanical failures, however, and the mission was aborted. On departure from the Desert One staging area, unfortunately, one of the helicopters collided with one of the transports. Five airmen and three Marines were killed in the accident. This accident, like the unfortunate assault on Koh Tang in Cambodia, aroused criticism of the Marine Corps and once again called into question the feasibility of amphibious warfare in the modern world. The hostages were eventually released on January 20, 1981, after 444 days of confinement.

The next year wasn't much better for the Corps. In 1982, the 32nd Marine Amphibious Unit aboard Amphibious Squadron Four was assigned to the Sixth Fleet in the Mediterranean. The assignment was supposed to have been relatively routine, but the deteriorating political situation in the Middle East led to the MAU's reassignment to Beirut shortly after it had arrived in Rota, Spain. On June 6, 1982, the Israeli Defense Force invaded southern Lebanon with the intention of rooting out the Palestinian Liberation Organization (PLO) on the Israeli-Lebanese border. The Lebanese government requested assistance evacuating foreign nationals and the PLO.

Refugees were gathered at Juniyah, a small port city just north of Beirut. On August 25, in a moment that recalled the surreal landing made by the 2nd Battalion, 2nd Marines 24 years earlier, the 32nd MAU came ashore at Juniyah amid sunbathers and windsurfers and began to evacuate the assembled foreign nationals to merchant ships off the coast. Some 6,400 refugees were evacuated from Juniyah. PLO leader Yasir Arafat was evacuated on August 30, and two days later the last of the PLO had been evacuated from Lebanon. The 32nd MAU left Lebanon and returned to the Sixth Fleet on September 10.

Unfortunately, the situation continued to deteriorate. On September 4, Lebanese president-elect Bashir Gemayel was assassinated, and on September 12, Christian militants massacred 800 Palestinians at the Sabra and Shatilla refugee camps. Lebanese President Amin Gemayel again requested assistance, and the 32nd MAU returned to Lebanon, joining an international peacekeeping force of some 2,200 French and Italian troops and taking up positions around the international airport at Beirut. The 24th MAU relieved the 32nd MAU on November 3, 1982, and for the remainder of 1982, the Marines provided a "presence" in Lebanon. The Marines were also issued "Rules of Engagement" (ROE) cards outlining what they could and could not do. Despite the fact that the Marines were obviously deployed in a combat zone, they were essentially instructed to use their weapons only in self-defense. Indeed, they were not even supposed to chamber a round in their weapons unless they had been fired upon. For the most part, Marines participated in motorized patrols of east Beirut, despite the limitations of their mission. In February 1983, however, American Marines and French and Italian units worked to rescue Christians and Muslims during a blizzard in the mountains outside the city.

There were a few tense moments, however. In February, three Israeli tanks tried to pass a checkpoint near Beirut University. Captain Charles Johnson drew his pistol and blocked their path. In March, five Marines were wounded by a grenade thrown at them from a second story window, probably by a supporter of Hizbullah, a Lebanese resistance movement. On April 18, a van carrying 2,000 pounds of explosives crashed into the U.S. Embassy in Beiruit, killing 63 people, including 17 Americans, one of whom was Corporal Robert McMaugh, an Embassy Marine Guard. Islamic Jihad, a Palestinian terrorist organization, claimed responsibility for the bombing. In the wake of these confrontations and attacks, security measures were rapidly increased. Concrete barriers and barbed wire were erected around the bases and additional Marines were added to the Embassy security force. Marine guards were given orders to admit no one without specific clearance.

(Photo courtesy of Robert F. Dorr)

Two U.S. Marines patrol the city streets during the multi-national peace-keeping operation in Beirut, Lebanon.

For a time, as the 24th MAU was relieved in February by the 22nd MAU (formerly the 32nd MAU) and then returned once more at the end of May, the Marine "presence" in the "Root," as they called Beirut, returned to a peaceful routine; tensions abated and the Marines relaxed. Unfortunately, a false sense of security seemed to permeate the Marine compound in Beirut. Early in the fall of 1983, the 24th MAU issued warnings regarding the possible breach of security by car bombers, but bombings were far from most Marines' mind as they planned a picnic for Sunday, October 23. At 6:22 A.M., shortly before reveille was to be sounded on that Sunday, a yellow Mercedes truck suddenly accelerated, crashed through the barricade around the compound, and drove into the Marine BLT building, where it exploded, releasing the equivalent force of six tons of TNT. Of the 300 Americans in the building, 241 were killed in the explosion, including 220 Marines.

U.S. foreign and military policy in Lebanon was again criticized, and critics demanded that the negligent commanders responsible for the tragedy be disciplined. Retired Navy Admiral Robert Long was appointed to head an investigation into the terrorist attack. The Long Commission concluded that senior military commanders were at fault for failing to provide an adequate definition of the mission of "presence" to which these Marines had been assigned. Furthermore, the commission concluded that no specific guidelines for countering terrorist attacks had been prepared despite the obvious threat of such attacks. Finally, Long's commission criticized MAU commanders for failing to provide sufficient protection for their men. The Marines were finally withdrawn from Lebanon in February 1984.

Recently appointed 28th Marine Corps commandant General Paul Kelley, who had served as a battalion and a regiment commander in Vietnam, rejected the criticism directed at the Corps. He argued that reasonable precautions had been taken, but given the attack on the Marine compound, the existence of ROE orders undermined such assertions.

★★★

Although the Marine Corps seemed to be plagued by problems during the late 1970s and early 1980s, there were positive moments as well. On October 19, a military coup led by army chief General Hudson Austin overthrew Grenadian prime minister Maurice Bishop. This presented the Reagan administration with two problems: First, there were many American citizens on the small Caribbean island, most of whom were students at St. George Medical University; and second, Cuba had begun construction of an airfield on Grenada at Point Salines on the southern end of the island. President Reagan and his advisors decided that intervention in Grenada to safeguard American lives and to subvert any possible Cuban designs on the island was of paramount importance.

The 22nd Marine Amphibious Unit under Colonel James Faulkner had left North Carolina on October 17 headed for Lebanon to relieve the 24th MAU. Amphibious Squadron 4 received orders on October 22 to divert to the Caribbean for intervention on Grenada. In addition to a Marine amphibious landing on Grenada, Army General John Vesey, chairman of the Joint Chiefs of Staff, suggested the deployment of one the Army's new Ranger battalions. The Air Force sided with the Army regarding the plan, and a complicated joint-service operation developed. The amphibious task force was given the assignment of securing Pearls Airport and Grenville on the Atlantic side of the island, while the 82nd Airborne Division and Army Rangers would secure the airfield at Point Salines on the southern end of the island.

Lieutenant Colonel Ray Smith's 2nd Battalion, 8th Marines began its landing on Grenada early in the morning on October 25. Twenty-one AH-1 Cobra gunships and CH-46 transport helicopters launched from the USS *Guam* and landed two companies of Marines just south of Pearls airport. There was some scattered but ineffective resistance. Company F was lifted to a soccer field in Grenville and secured the town.

The Rangers who landed at Point Salines encountered much stiffer resistance from well-armed Cuban troops. Two battalions from the 82nd Airborne Division reinforced the Rangers, and the soldiers were able to secure the airfield. The American medical students on the island were evacuated.

Company G, 2nd Battalion, 8th Marines advanced into Grenville and secured a racetrack as a convenient base for the MAU's tanks. Company F rescued Governor-General Sir Paul Scoon and his family; they were evacuated to the *Guam*. Shortly thereafter, Colonel Faulkner was informed that there were more American students on the southeastern coast of Grenada. The 22nd MAU provided 13 helicopters to transport a unit of Army Rangers into position and evacuate the remaining Americans.

By October 28, American troops controlled most of the island. The joint-service forces had evacuated 590 U.S. citizens and 80 foreign nationals. U.S. forces suffered 18 men dead, including 3 Marines, and 116 wounded, including 15 Marines. Twenty-four Cubans were killed, fifty-nine were wounded, and six hundred twenty-four were captured. Forty-five Grenadian soldiers were also killed. In addition, captured plans revealed that the Reagan administration's concerns about Cuban designs on Grenada were justified: A garrison of 6,800 Cuban soldiers was to be established on the island. By November 2, the last of the Marines had left Grenada, and the 22nd MAU resumed its journey to the Mediterranean.

The intervention in Grenada was a small success in a decade of scandals for the U.S. Marine Corps. Unfortunately, the scandals continued to accumulate throughout the last years of the 1980s. In particular, seven Marines assigned as guards at the U.S. Embassy in Moscow were accused of allowing KGB agents access to sensitive areas of the embassy in return for sexual favors. The investigations were poorly conducted, little hard evidence was found, and most of the charges were dismissed. Another Marine, however, Sergeant Clayton Lonetree, who had become entangled in an affair with a Russian woman, was blackmailed into spying for the KGB even after he was transferred to the U.S. Embassy in Vienna. He eventually turned himself in to the CIA. Lonetree was court-martialed for espionage and sentenced to 30 years in prison, although he was released in 1996.

There's no question that Paul Kelley's tenure as commandant was a troubled one. Yet Kelley must be credited with improving the general quality of the average Marine. His policies led to a Marine Corps composed almost entirely of high school graduates, a significant improvement over the mid-1970s, and the officer corps had become better educated as well. Furthermore, the average Marine was better equipped than he had been at the beginning of Kelley's term of office, and the Corps had adopted new aircraft and an eight-wheeled, light-armored vehicle with multiple configurations, offering greater flexibility and mobility on the battlefield. In addition, Marine amphibious brigade operations stations had been established in Diego Garcia and Guam, as had an equipment and supply depot in Norway, and by 1986 the Corps had 13 ships at their disposal.

M-249 5.56MM SQUAD AUTOMATIC WEAPON (SAW)

During the 1970s, the U.S. military saw a need for a light machine gun that would be more portable than the M-60. The M-249, based on the FN 5.56mm Minimi machine gun from Belgium, has replaced the M-60 since the mid-1980s.

Fully loaded with 200 rounds of belted ammunition, the M-249 weighs just 22 pounds with bipod, sling, and cleaning kit—1 pound less than an unloaded M-60! About the size of an M-16, but twice as heavy, the 5.56mm ammunition used in the M-249 means that a four-man team can all use each other's rounds if necessary. The SAW has a rate of fire of about 750 rounds per minute, and an effective range of 400 yards.

Although the machine gun can be fired on full automatic, Marine training encourages the use of controlled short bursts to prevent jamming.

A heavier version of the M-249, the M-240G, was also adopted for a vehicle-mounted weapon platform, replacing the long-outdated M-60E3. The M-240 is virtually identical to the SAW, but is longer and heavier, and fires the 7.62mm round.

The scandals that wracked the Corps throughout the 1980s, from Iran to Beirut to Moscow, brought a great deal of scrutiny upon the Corps. Even those sympathetic to the Marines felt it was time for a change. Secretary of the Navy James Webb Jr. was himself a former Marine. He had graduated from the Naval Academy in 1968 and spent a tour as a platoon commander in Vietnam, earning the Navy Cross before receiving a medical discharge for wounds he sustained there. After his discharge, he entered government service while writing on the side, but he retained a great deal of pride in the Corps—after all, once a Marine, always a Marine.

Webb believed that Commandant Kelley and other leading Marine officers had become little more than military bureaucrats; the "warrior" spirit needed to be returned to the Corps. At the end of Kelley's term in office, Webb recommended Lieutenant General Alfred Gray as his successor, and on July 1, 1987, Gray became the 29th commandant of the U.S. Marine Corps.

Gray had served more than 30 years in the Marine Corps, beginning with the Korean War. Al Gray, a tough, tobacco-chewing soldier, soon became the champion of enlisted Marines. Here was an officer who understood what it meant to be a Marine. Gray set about restoring the lost "warrior" spirit: Jogging was replaced by traditional forced marches, and camouflage became the uniform of the day under his leadership.

In addition, Commandant Gray focused on training his Marines in the art of war. In November 1987, Quantico's schools were redesignated the Marine Corps Combat Development Command (MCCDC). Five interrelated school centers were established: MAGTF Warfighting, Training and Education, Intelligence, Wargaming and Assessment, and Information Technology. In addition, Gray established the Marine Corps University in August 1989. Brigadier General Paul Van Riper was its first president, and its purpose was to foster an academic atmosphere in which Marines of all ranks could learn the "philosophical underpinnings of warfare." The university consisted of the Command and Staff College, the Amphibious Warfare School, Staff NCO School, Communications Officer School, and the Basic School. There was also a Marine Corps Research Center. In addition to these educational developments, Gray established the Marine Corps Research, Development, and Acquisition Command at Quantico to facilitate the adoption of new weapons and technologies.

SHOULDER LAUNCHED MULTIPURPOSE ASSAULT WEAPON (SMAW)

The Marine standard antiarmor weapon is the SMAW, a portable rocket launcher carried only by the Marines because they needed something with more power than the standard Army M72 LAW rocket. Based on the Israeli B-300 model, the SMAW can disable a tank or bust a bunker with equal ease. Its 83mm rocket can carry two kinds of warheads, a High Explosive Dual Purpose (HEDP) for use against light-armored vehicles or buildings or a High Explosive Anti-Tank (HEAT) for use against heavily armored vehicles. The maximum range for a SMAW is 550 yards, but it is designed to be a relatively close-range weapon.

The SMAW is fired with the aid of a spotting rifle, which is used to acquire the target by hitting it with a special tracer round, which the rocket then homes in on. The SMAW system worked so well that the Army found itself borrowing 150 launchers and 5,000 rockets from the Marines during Operation Desert Storm.

★★★

In 1991, the Marine Corps had a chance to demonstrate just how much it had improved. On August 2, 1990, three Iraqi divisions invaded the small, oil-producing sheikdom of Kuwait. A fourth division was transported by helicopter to Kuwait City, and by August 3, Kuwait City had been captured and Iraqi forces seemed on the verge of invading Saudi Arabia. On August 7, Secretary of Defense Dick Cheney instructed General Colin Powell, the chairman of the Joint Chiefs of Staff, to prepare military personnel for possible deployment to the Persian Gulf. Commandant Gray readied the 4th Marine Expeditionary Brigade on the East Coast—Marine unit designations having resumed the use of "expeditionary" in place of "amphibious"—the 7th MEB on the West Coast, and the 1st MEB in Hawaii.

Commander in Chief, Central Command (CENTCOM), General "Stormin'" Norman Schwarzkopf requested three Marine MEBs for deployment in the Persian Gulf as part of Operation Desert Shield, the defense of Saudi Arabia. The 7th MEB arrived at Al Jubayl, Saudi Arabia, on August 14, followed closely by the 1st MEB. Maritime Prepositioning Shipping Squadron 2 sailed from Diego Garcia in the Indian Ocean to join the 7th MEB, and Maritime Prepositioning Shipping Squadron 3 from Guam joined the 1st MEB on August 26. The 4th MEB sailed for the Persian Gulf from North Carolina on August 17.

The I Marine Expeditionary Force was organized and assumed command of all Marine forces in the Persian Gulf on September 2, and by September 6, I MEF under Lieutenant General Walter Boomer consisted of the 1st Marine Division, the 3rd Marine Aircraft Wing, and the 1st Force Service Support Group. By November, 42,000 Marines were in the Persian Gulf region, 31,000 of whom had landed on shore; the 4th MEB and the 13th Marine Expeditionary Unit (Special Operations Capable) remained in floating reserve. Marine forces in the Gulf region represented more than one quarter of all Marine forces available, and they made up one fifth of all U.S. forces in the region.

President George Bush announced on November 8 that more than 200,000 additional troops would be sent to the Persian Gulf, and forces continued to build up through November and December. The II MEF and the 5th MEB were selected to go to the Persian Gulf, effectively doubling the number of Marines in the region. In addition, on November 13, 80 Marine Reserve units from the 4th Marine Division and the 4th Marine Aircraft Wing, some 31,000 men and women, were activated. With the exception of the 3rd Civil Affairs Group, which had volunteered to handle relations with the civilian populations in Saudi Arabia and Kuwait, these units were the first Reserve units activated since the Korean War.

The 5th MEB arrived in the Gulf from California on December 1. The II MEF, consisting of the 2nd Marine Division, the 2nd Marine Aircraft Wing, and the 2nd Force Service Support Group, was airlifted from the East Coast to the Gulf at a rate of 1,000 Marines per day between December 9, 1990, and January 15, 1991. The headquarters of the II MEF remained in North Carolina, it having been decided that it was not required in the region. The 2nd MAW joined the 3rd MAW, which had deployed to the

Persian Gulf previously. By January 15, 1991, half the U.S. Marine Corps, 84,000 Marines, had been deployed to the Persian Gulf; 66,000 of these Marines served on shore with I MEF while the remaining 18,000 Marines remained afloat with the 4th MEB, the 5th MEB, and the 13th MEU(SOC).

The United States didn't act alone to check Saddam Hussein's aggression, of course. In contrast to the mistakes made by Lyndon Johnson 25 years earlier, President Bush sought support in Congress and the United Nations, which he received by articulating a clearly defined military objective: the withdrawal of Iraqi forces from Kuwait. In addition to supporting the American military buildup, the United Nations passed a number of resolutions imposing economic sanctions against Iraq and insisted that Saddam Hussein withdraw from Kuwait by January 15, 1991. Saddam Hussein ignored the impact of the economic embargo on his people and discounted the overwhelming coalition arrayed against him; he continued to stand his ground.

On January 12, 1991, three days before the UN deadline, the U.S. Congress authorized the use of military force against Saddam Hussein by a vote of 52 to 47 in the Senate and 250 to 183 in the House of Representatives. Although not an overwhelming mandate—most Democrats voted for continued economic sanctions—President Bush had been given the authority to use force in the Persian Gulf.

Saddam Hussein didn't withdraw his troops from Kuwait by the January 15 deadline, and on the following day the air campaign of Operation Desert Storm commenced. Marine Corps F/A-18 Hornets and AV-8 Harriers joined Air Force stealth bombers, Army Apache helicopters, and Navy Tomahawk missiles to target strategic objectives in the opening days of the campaign. Iraqi command and control systems were destroyed, communications and transportation were disrupted, Scud missile launch sites were targeted, and Iraqi Republican Guard units were attacked. In the first day of the air campaign, Coalition air forces flew more than 2,000 missions and dropped some 2,500 tons of ordnance on Iraqi positions. Only four aircraft were reported lost. The air campaign would continue for nearly 6 weeks with Coalition aircraft flying as many as 3,000 sorties per day.

The 3rd Marine Aircraft Wing under the command of Major General Royal Moore constituted approximately one fourth of all U.S. fixed-wing aircraft in the region and played an important role during the campaign. Marine aircraft launched their first sorties on the morning of January 17 when 48 F/A-18 Hornets and A-6 Intruders from MAG-11 struck at targets in southern Iraq. AV-8 Harriers and OV-10 Broncos from MAG-13 launched attacks against targets in southern Kuwait later that same morning. By the end of the air campaign, the 3rd MAW would fly more than 18,000 missions, dropping nearly 15,000 tons of ordnance.

Marine aircraft also played a significant role in isolating the theater of operations by striking at Iraqi ground forces to cut off reinforcement or retreat and in preparation for the commencement of the ground campaign. As the end of January approached, Marine and Coalition aircraft shifted their targets to the armored and infantry divisions in Kuwait itself. General Schwarzkopf estimated that the air campaign eliminated approximately 50 percent of Iraqi frontline forces and as much as 75 percent of Iraqi second-line forces.

In response to this massive bombing campaign, Saddam Hussein elected to launch deadly Scud missile attacks against Tel Aviv and other Israeli cities as well as Riyadh in Saudi Arabia—at least in part because Coalition air forces had gained air supremacy almost immediately, limiting the ability of Iraq to respond in kind. U.S. and Coalition forces had placed Patriot ground-to-air interceptor missiles specifically to counter this threat. Few of the Scud missiles struck their targets or did much damage, but audiences around the world watched the video game–like scenes as Patriots intercepted the Scuds.

On January 29, Iraqi forces attempted a preemptive strike against Coalition forces in Saudi Arabia. The Iraqi 5th Mechanized Division struck along the coast toward the town of Ra's al Khafji, and the 3rd Armored Division struck at the Coalition front between I MEF and Pan-Arabic units, hoping to break through the two forces and then strike at the port of Al Mish'ab some 20 miles south of Khafji. The 1st Mechanized Division struck at Marine units near Umm Hujul. A Marine reconnaissance team sighted the Iraqi 3rd Armored Division and called in air strikes to eliminate it. Marine ground and air units repulsed the 1st Mechanized Division, suffering 11 Marine deaths, all, sadly, from friendly fire. The

Iraqi 5th Mechanized Division, however, achieved its objective by capturing Khafji.

Two Marine reconnaissance teams were caught in Khafji when the Iraqis overran the town. Corporal Charles Ingraham decided to stay in the town, where his team remained hidden on a rooftop for two days. When Saudi Arabian units counterattacked, Ingraham's Marines directed supporting Marine artillery and air strikes that helped secure the recapture of the town on January 31.

Simultaneously with the Saudi Arabian counterattack on Khafji, the 13th MEU(SOC) conducted Operation Sting, an amphibious raid that secured the abandoned island of Maradim and seized numerous supplies. Marine units afloat also participated in the blockade of Iraq, boarding and searching six ships in the Persian Gulf.

★★★

The ground campaign of Operation Desert Storm commenced in mid-February. For the offensive, the XVIII Airborne Corps would strike across Iraq and then move along the Euphrates River, cutting off Iraqi reinforcement or retreat, while the VII Corps would strike at and destroy Iraqi units in Kuwait. General Boomer suggested that I MEF strike at Kuwait City, and General Schwarzkopf agreed to his plan. Many planners in CENTCOM viewed the Marine thrust at Kuwait City as a diversionary tactic, distracting Iraqi units while the Army Airborne and Armored units destroyed them. Boomer believed his Marines could reach Kuwait City in three days.

The I MEF would drive into Kuwait around Umm Hujul, Major General James Myatt's 1st Division to the right of the town and Major General William Keys's 2nd Division to the left of it. The Marines would be supported on the left by the Army's 2nd Armored Division's Tiger Brigade, which had been attached to I MEF for the campaign, and in the air by the 3rd MAW. The 5th MEB's 5th Regimental Combat Team would land to act as a reserve unit.

In preparation for the assault, Brigadier General Charles Krulak, the son of retired Lieutenant General Brute Krulak, commanding the 2nd Force Service Command, an element of Brigadier General James Brabham's

1st Force Service Group, began construction of a forward supply base some 20 miles southwest of Umm Hujul on February 6. It was completed 2 weeks later and covered some 11,280 acres, much of it underground. Krulak called it *Al Khanjar*, "the dagger." Brabham's "Baghdad Express" filled the massive depot in 10 days with 5 million gallons of fuel, 1 million gallons of water, and 780 acres filled with ammunition. General Boomer moved his command center forward near *Al Khanjar* on February 14.

There was some apprehension on the eve of the ground campaign. Although Iraqi air forces had been neutralized easily, and the Coalition air campaign had pummeled Iraqi ground forces, there was concern that Iraq had stockpiled chemical and biological weapons. Coalition air forces had attempted to strike what were believed to be weapon stockpiles, but no one was sure if these depots had contained chemical or biological weapons, if the weapons had been destroyed, or if all of the depots had been targeted. All Marines engaged in the assault were equipped with Mission Oriented Protective Posture (MOPP) chemical protective suits in the event the Iraqis actually used chemical or biological weapons against them.

MISSION ORIENTED PROTECTIVE POSTURE (MOPP) CHEMICAL PROTECTIVE SUITS

One hazard the Marines, and indeed all the armed forces, have to contend with is a weapon they can't even see. Biological and chemical agents in the wrong hands can prove deadlier than missiles, planes, and tanks, because the weapons are often invisible to the eye and difficult to detect until actual contact—or later.

The latest version of the chemical protection suit is the Joint Service Lightweight Integrated Suite Technology, or JSLIST, designed to replace the older Chemical Protection Overgarment as well as reduce strain on the soldier wearing it. The new suit provides more protection with a hood that fits over the head and neck, as well as increased charcoal liner protection, which also allows better mobility as well as letting the suit actually be washed once a week. (However, if the suit is contaminated with a chemical or biological agent, it can only be reused once.)

The JSLIST suits can be worn over battle dress uniform (BDU) or the Multi-purpose Rain-Snow-Chemical Biological Overboot (MULO) and provides 45 days of protection—15 days more than its predecessor. Currently used by both the Air Force and the Navy, the JSLISTs will not be integrated into the Marines until the older suits (the "Saratoga") have been used up.

At 4 A.M. on February 24, 1991, the I MEF launched its attack into Kuwait, opening the ground campaign. By dawn both Marine divisions had overcome the various obstacles placed by the Iraqis and were moving toward their objectives. Myatt's 1st Division captured Al Jaber airfield, an Iraqi command center, and made it to the Al Burqan oil field. The 1st Division suffered 10 casualties, 1 Marine killed and 9 wounded. It captured 21 Iraqi tanks and 4,000 Iraqi soldiers.

Keys's 2nd Division drove forward into Kuwait as the Tiger Brigade's psychological warfare unit blasted "The Marine Hymn" at full volume. "From the Halls of Montezuma to the shores of Tripoli ..." sounded across the desert. Keys's Marines captured an entire Iraqi tank battalion, 35 tanks, 5,000 soldiers, and the brigade commander. The 2nd Division suffered nine casualties, one killed and eight wounded.

The 3rd MAW flew 671 missions, destroying 40 tanks, 121 other vehicles, 3 antiaircraft sites, and 4 missile sites. The 5th RCT, 5th MEB came ashore at Mish'ab.

By the end of the day, Boomer's I MEF was halfway to Kuwait City. The unanticipated success of I MEF caused some concern that the Marines' flank had been exposed to an Iraqi counterattack. Boomer suggested that the main assault begin immediately, and Schwarzkopf ordered the VII Armored Corps to launch its assault on the afternoon of February 24, one day earlier than planned.

The next morning, the Marines awakened outside Al Burqan oil field to see thick clouds of smoke clogging the air as Saddam Hussein's troops burned the oil wells, part of his "scorched earth" plan. Out of this smoke roared two Iraqi mechanized brigades. Myatt's 1st Division was pushed back briefly by the counterattack, which came within 400 yards of Myatt's command post, but the Marines had resumed their offensive by midday and finished clearing Al Jaber airfield. Some 80 Iraqi tanks were destroyed and another 2,000 Iraqi soldiers were captured. The 2nd Division attacked fortified areas dubbed the "Ice Tray" and the "Ice Cube" and destroyed another 248 tanks and captured 4,500 soldiers. Iraqi soldiers were surrendering in droves or fleeing back across the desert into Iraq. The 3rd MAW continued its support, flying another 460 missions.

On February 26, the third day of the ground campaign, the 4th MEB demonstrated a series of feint amphibious landings against Bubiyan and

Faylaka Islands, distracting an Iraqi division. Meanwhile, the 1st Marine Division launched an assault against the international airport outside Kuwait City. The 2nd Division raced across the Kuwaiti desert to secure positions near Al Jahra overlooking the main highway north into Iraq. On February 27, the 1st Division secured the international airport and allowed an Egyptian-Syrian force to enter Kuwait City. General Boomer entered the city later that afternoon.

President Bush ordered a cease-fire on February 28, only four days after commencement of the ground campaign. Concerns over Iraqi resistance and the use of chemical or biological weapons proved unnecessary. Although there was some evidence that a few chemical weapons had been deployed— although no evidence of biological weapons—at the time, no units seemed affected by them. (Subsequently, many who served in the Gulf War have claimed to suffer from what has been called Gulf War Syndrome. Whether this was the result of chemical or biological weapons or some other cause such as psychological stress is still unclear.) The I MEF had suffered very few casualties. Only 5 Marines had been killed in action and another 48 wounded in 4 days of combat. On the other hand, Marines killed more than 1,500 Iraqi soldiers and captured 22,308 POWs! The I MEF destroyed more than 1,000 Iraqi tanks, more than 600 other vehicles, more than 400 artillery pieces, and 5 missile sites. The 3rd MAW had lost only two fixed-wing aircraft and three helicopters as of February 24 when the ground campaign began and only two more aircraft were lost in the four days that followed. Total Marine casualties during the Gulf War numbered 24 killed and 92 wounded.

★★★

In the wake of the Gulf War, General Carl Mundy succeeded Al Gray as commandant of the U.S. Marine Corps. Mundy was successful in limiting the traditional downsizing of the Marine Corps during peacetime, justifying the maintenance of a peacetime strength of 174,000 Marines. He was less successful in his recruiting policies. Mundy was openly critical of the Clinton administration's liberal policies toward homosexuals and women in the armed forces and at one point announced that married recruits no longer would be accepted in the Corps. Secretary of Defense Les Aspin overruled him, however, commenting that such a policy was "antifamily." On several occasions, Mundy came close to being dismissed from his post for his position on these issues, but his commitment to "jointness," joint service operations, kept him in office until 1995.

Mundy was able to reestablish the Marine Corps's traditional relationship with the Navy. After the collapse of the Soviet Union, the Navy's long-held need to match the Soviet Union's deep-sea fleet seemed less important, and a revision of strategic thinking seemed in order. In 1992, the Navy and Marine Corps issued a joint paper titled *From the Sea: A New Direction for the Naval Services* that defined new naval strategies. Focusing on regional threats rather than global conflict, U.S. naval forces, the Navy and the Marine Corps, came to emphasize the importance of joint operations, offering naval expeditionary forces operating from the sea to control littoral, or coastal, areas of the world.

★★★

In the 1990s, the new orientation in naval strategy was reflected in the missions conducted by the Marine Corps. In the wake of the Gulf War, ethnic Kurds within Iraq rebelled against Hussein's rule. The Iraqis responded brutally. Operation Desert Storm became Operation Provide Comfort, and the 24th MEU under Colonel James L. Jones established a forward support base at Silopi, Turkey, before moving farther inland and delivering much-needed supplies. Some one million pounds of supplies were transported by Lieutenant Colonel Joseph Byrtus Jr.'s helicopter squadron, HMM-264.

On April 20, Lieutenant Colonel Tony Corwin led the 2nd BLT, 8th Marines into Iraq itself and established a resettlement camp at Zakhu. Iraqi forces were ordered to leave the city, and Coalition forces came up to secure it. In May, the 24th MEU with the support of the 3rd Battalion 325th Airborne Combat Team (ACT) cleared the city of Dahuk, the Iraqis withdrawing without resistance, and began evacuating some 55,000 refugees from various camps in the area. Coalition forces left Iraq in July, 2nd BLT, 8th Marines and the 3rd Battalion 325th Airborne Combat Team leaving last on July 15, 1991.

In the wake of a terrible cyclone that swept through the Bay of Bengal, Marines assisted the U.S. Army, Navy, and Air Force in providing relief to Bangladesh during Operation Sea Angel. Supplies poured in from all over the world, but Bangladesh's infrastructure was insufficient to move the supplies to where they could best be used. Brigadier General Peter Rowe's 5th Marine Expeditionary Brigade and Lieutenant Colonel Larry Johnson's Contingency Marine Air-Ground Task Force 2-91 (CMAGTF 2-91) engaged in the full-scale relief effort, using their helicopters and landing craft to move water-purification units and Medical Civic Action Program teams on shore. In addition, Marines assisted in rebuilding roads, ferries, and local transportation services.

Marines engaged in relief efforts in Somalia as well. Unfortunately, the situation in Somalia degenerated into a disastrous peacekeeping effort as the nation tore itself apart in civil war. Marine Brigadier General Frank Libutti organized and directed Joint Task Force "Provide Relief" to deliver supplies to Somalia. Lieutenant General Robert Johnston was placed in charge of the Joint Task Force, which was assigned to establish a safe environment in which to deliver supplies. Major General Charles Wilhem, commander of the 1st Marine Division, commanded the Coalition Marine Forces, Somalia. Colonel Gregory Newbold's 15th MEU(SOC) engaged in a number of actions during Operation Restore Hope, including securing Mogadishu, Baidoa, the "City of Death," and Kismayo.

At Baidoa, weapons were confiscated and raids against urban guerillas were carried out. In addition, Newbold initiated the training of the Somali civic police force and promoted civic action programs, and the Marines helped rebuild the road between Baidoa and Bardera. Marines began pulling out of Somalia in January 1993, the last leaving on May 4. U.S. Army forces remained stationed in Somalia as a peacekeeping force and, unfortunately, suffered a tragic event when an Army Blackhawk helicopter was shot down in Mogadishu on October 3. Rescue efforts resulted in tragedy: 18 men were killed and 75 wounded. President Clinton ordered 15,000 troops to the country, including the 13th and 22nd MEUs, which stayed on until March 25, 1994. One Marine security platoon remained to guard the U.S. diplomatic mission to Somalia until March 3, 1995. Two Marines were killed and 15 were wounded in Somalia.

★★★

Marines likewise participated in Operation Uphold/Support Democracy, which sought to maintain a democratic government in Haiti. In September 1991, Lieutenant General Raoul Cedras had overthrown President Jean-Bertrand Aristide. The military government erected by Cedras was oppressive, and Haitians sought escape the only way available to them, climbing in small wooden boats and trusting the tides to get them to Florida. Thousands of Haitians left the country, some of them washing up on the shore in Florida, others arriving in Cuba, where they were placed in a refugee camp at Guantanamo Bay. The United States had been working for the return of Aristide, and on July 31, 1994, the UN Security Council approved a U.S. invasion of the Caribbean country.

Special Purpose Marine Air-Ground Task Force Caribbean (SPMAGTF Carib) was placed under the command of Colonel Thomas Jones, a veteran of Vietnam and the Gulf. Working in combination with the U.S. Army, Jones's Marines would land on the northern coast of the island while the Army's XVIII Airborne Corps secured Port-au-Prince. The invasion was scheduled for September 19, but in an effort to avoid actual conflict, former President Jimmy Carter led a peace commission including retired General Colin Powell and Senator Sam Nunn to Port-au-Prince. The commission was able to convince Cedras to stand down and allow the American troops to land, and Cedras further agreed to leave the island in October. The Army landed unopposed at Port-au-Prince on September 19, and the Marines landed one day later at Amphibious Objective Area Hanneken, named after the Marine who had killed the *caco* chieftain Charlemagne 75 years earlier.

Jones's Marines secured the port of Cap-Haitien and the nearby airport without difficulty, and Jones reported his objective to the Haitian district commander. The Marines now turned to aiding the people of Haiti, supplying medicine, food, fuel, and sanitation; the airport was operational by September 22. Unfortunately, oppressive policies were continued after the landing, and Jones initiated patrols of the nearby villages. On September 24, First Lieutenant Virgil Palumbo's squad approached a group of Haitian military police, one of whom drew on the Marines and fired. Palumbo shot him with his M-16 as a general melee broke out. In the end, 10 Haitians were killed and 1 was seriously wounded.

In the aftermath of the firefight, Cedras demanded the court-martial of the Marines involved, but his regime fell apart almost immediately as soldiers and policemen defected from his cause. Company G confiscated weapons and helped restore order. On October 2, the Army's 2nd Brigade, 10th Mountain Division relieved SPMAGTF Carib, which reembarked on the USS *Wasp* and USS *Nashville* until Aristide returned to Haiti on October 15, when it returned to Camp Lejeune.

★★★

General Charles Krulak became the thirty-first commandant of the U.S. Marine Corps in 1995. Like his predecessor, Krulak embraced "jointness" and continued to advocate joint/combined operations between the military branches. Krulak even moved the Marine Corps headquarters to the Pentagon.

Also like his predecessor, Krulak was critical of the general movement toward gender-integration evident in both the Navy and the Army. Unlike Mundy, however, this criticism seemed to have been motivated by a concern for proper training rather than any kind of bigotry. In the wake of a wave of sexual harassment accusations in the Army and the Navy, Krulak's decision not to integrate men and women during basic training seemed justified.

Nevertheless, the importance of human relations and the awareness of gender and ethnic status has increased within the Corps, and women and minorities have risen to positions of acceptance and respect. Frank Peterson, for example, a Marine aviator, became the first African American promoted to general rank on April 27, 1979. In 1978, Margaret Brewer became the first woman to hold the rank of brigadier general when she was appointed director of information, and Gail Reals became the first woman selected for brigadier general on May 15, 1985. In addition, women were deployed to the Persian Gulf region during Operations Desert Shield and Storm.

In 1992, Brigadier General Carol Mutter became the first woman to command a Fleet Marine Force unit when she assumed command of the 3rd Force Service Support Group, Okinawa. She was promoted to major general in 1994 and to lieutenant general in 1996, becoming the first woman Marine and only the second woman in the armed services to hold that rank. In 1993, Second Lieutenant Sarah Deal became the first woman Marine accepted for Navy aviation training.

Krulak was committed to preparing the Marine Corps for the twenty-first century. To his mind, and to many military analysts, the twenty-first century promised a violent era of ethnic and religious conflict and chemical and biological weapons. Krulak believed that each Marine had to be properly trained in order to operate in such a world and instituted grueling new training procedures intended to instill confidence, courage, and commitment in new recruits.

In order to properly equip the new Marine, Krulak set up a Warfighting Laboratory at Quantico to investigate the potential of new technologies, such as the Dragon Drone Unmanned Aerial Vehicle (UAV), the V-22 Osprey, and advanced assault amphibian vehicles. Throughout the process, however, Krulak emphasized the importance of preparing the Marine and not simply building new weapons.

(Photo courtesy of Robert F. Dorr)

General John J. Sheehan, the Supreme Allied Commander, Atlantic, until his retirement in 2002.

General James L. Jones, the thirty-second commandant of the U.S. Marines Corps, assumed the position in 1999.

Marines continued engaging in a wide variety of operations throughout the end of the 1990s. On June 8, 1995, the 24th MEU(SOC)'s Tactical Recovery of Aircraft and Personnel (TRAP) rescued Captain Scott O'Grady, who had been shot down over Bosnia, and evacuated him to the USS *Kearsarge*. In 1997, the 26th MEU provided relief services to Bosnian refugees in Slovenia, the 11th MEU assisted in training the Kuwaiti national guard in urban warfare, and the 22nd MEU evacuated 530 Americans from Albania.

President Clinton announced the selection of Lieutenant General James L. Jones as the thirty-second commandant of the Marine Corps on July 1, 1999. The Marine Corps that Commandant Jones inherited was vastly different from what it had been a few decades earlier. The Marines of the "New Corps" were better educated, better equipped, and more diverse, reflecting the vast political, social, cultural, and technological changes that the Corps had witnessed in its 225-year history. But no matter how much it changed, the Corps remained The Few. The Proud. The Marines!

BIBLIOGRAPHY

BOOKS AND PERIODICALS

Alexander, Joseph H. *The Battle History of the United States Marine Corps: A Fellowship of Valor.* New York: HarperCollins, 1999.

———. *Closing In: Marines in the Seizure of Iwo Jima.* Washington, DC: History and Museums Division, Headquarters, U.S. Marine Corps, 1994.

———. *U.S. Marines in the Recapture of Seoul: Battle of the Barricades.* Washington, DC: History and Museums Division, Headquarters, U.S. Marine Corps, 2000.

Bartlett, Merrill L., and Jack Sweetman. *The U.S. Marine Corps: An Illustrated History.* Annapolis: Naval Institute Press, 2001.

Brown, Ronald J. *Counteroffensive: U.S. Marines from Pohang to No Name Line.* Washington, DC: History and Museums Division, Headquarters, U.S. Marine Corps, 2001.

———. *Humanitarian Operations in Northern Iraq, 1991: With Marines in Operations Provide Comfort.* Washington, DC: History and Museums Division, Headquarters, U.S. Marine Corps, 1995.

Butler, Smedley D. "In Time of Peace." *Common Sense*, 4, no. 11 (November, 1935), pp. 8–12.

Caputo, Philip. *A Rumor of War.* New York: Holt, Rinehart and Winston, 1977.

Chapin, John C. *And a Few Marines: Marines in the Liberation of the Philippines*. Washington, DC: History and Museums Division, Headquarters, U.S. Marine Corps, 1997.

———. *U.S. Marines in the Pusan Perimeter: Fire Brigade*. Washington, DC: History and Museums Division, Headquarters, U.S. Marine Corps, 2000.

Clancy, Tom. *Marine: A Guided Tour of a Marine Expeditionary Unit*. New York: Berkley Pub Group, 2000.

Cosmas, Graham A., ed. *Marine Corps Aviation: The Early Years, 1912–1940*. Washington, DC: History and Museums Division, Headquarters, U.S. Marine Corps, 1977.

Cureton, Charles H. *U.S. Marines in the Persian Gulf, 1990–1991: With the 1st Marine Division in Desert Shield and Desert Storm*. Washington, DC: History and Museums Division, Headquarters, U.S. Marine Corps, 1993.

Cushman, R. E. Jr. *A Brief History of the Marine Corps Recruit Depot Parris Island, South Carolina, 1891–1962*. Washington, DC: Historical Branch, Headquarters, U.S. Marine Corps, 1962.

Davis, Alphonse G. *Pride, Progress, and Prospects: The Marine Corps' Efforts to Increase the Presence of African-American Officers (1970–1995)*. Washington, DC: History and Museums Division, Headquarters, U.S. Marine Corps, 2000.

Edwards, Harry W. *A Different War: Marines in Europe and North Africa*. Washington, DC: History and Museums Division, Headquarters, U.S. Marine Corps, 1994.

Fortitudine: Bulletin of the Marine Corps Historical Program 15–29 (Summer 1985–Summer 2002). Washington, DC: History and Museums Division, Headquarters, U.S. Marine Corps.

Frank, Benis M. *U.S. Marines in Lebanon, 1982–1984*. Washington, DC: History and Museums Division, Headquarters, U.S. Marine Corps, 1987.

Fuller, Stephen M., and Graham A. Cosmas. *Marines in the Dominican Republic, 1916–1924*. Washington, DC: History and Museums Division, Headquarters, U.S. Marine Corps, 1974.

BIBLIOGRAPHY

Fussell, Paul. *Wartime, Understanding and Behavior in the Second World War*. New York: Oxford University Press, 1989.

Heinl, Robert D. *Soldiers of the Sea: The United States Marine Corps, 1775–1962*. Annapolis: U.S. Naval Institute, 1962.

A History of the Women Marines, 1946–1977. Washington, DC: History and Museums Division, Headquarters, U.S. Marine Corps, 1986.

Hoffman, Jon T. *From Makin to Bougainville: Marine Raiders in the Pacific War*. Washington, DC: History and Museums Division, Headquarters, U.S. Marine Corps, 1995.

Krulak, Victor H. *First to Fight: An Inside View of the U.S. Marine Corps*. Annapolis: Naval Institute Press, 1984.

The Marines in Vietnam, 1954–1973: An Anthology and Annotated Bibliography. Washington, DC: History and Museums Division, Headquarters, U.S. Marine Corps, 1985.

Melson, Charles D. *Condition Red: Marine Defense Battalions in World War II*. Washington, DC: History and Museums Division, Headquarters, U.S. Marine Corps, 1996.

Mersky, Peter B. *Time of the Aces: Marine Pilots in the Solomons, 1942–1944*. Washington, DC: History and Museums Division, Headquarters, U.S. Marine Corps, 1993.

Millet, Allen R. *U.S. Marines at the Punch Bowl: Drive North*. Washington, DC: History and Museums Division, Headquarters, U.S. Marine Corps, 2001.

———. *Semper Fidelis: The History of the United States Marine Corps*. New York: Macmillan, 1980.

———. *Semper Fidelis: The History of the United States Marine Corps*. New York: Maxwell Macmillan International, 1991.

Mroczkowski, Dennis P. *U.S. Marines in the Persian Gulf, 1990–1991: With the 2d Marine Division in Desert Shield and Desert Storm*. Washington, DC: History and Museums Division, Headquarters, U.S. Marine Corps, 1993.

Nalty, Bernard C. *Cape Gloucester: The Green Inferno*. Washington, DC: History and Museums Division, Headquarters, U.S. Marine Corps, 1994.

———. *The Right to Fight: African-American Marines in World War II.* Washington, DC: History and Museums Division, Headquarters, U.S. Marine Corps, 1995.

———. *The United States Marines in the Civil War.* Washington, DC: History and Museums Division, Headquarters, U.S. Marine Corps, 1983.

———. *The United States Marines in Nicaragua.* Washington, DC: History and Museums Division, Headquarters, U.S. Marine Corps, 1962.

Parker, William D. *A Concise History of the United States Marine Corps, 1775–1969.* Washington, DC: History and Museums Division, Headquarters, U.S. Marine Corps, 1970.

Quilter, Charles J. II. *U.S. Marines in the Persian Gulf, 1990–1991: With the I Marine Expeditionary Force in Desert Shield and Desert Storm.* Washington, DC: History and Museums Division, Headquarters, U.S. Marine Corps, 1993.

Ressler, D. Michael. *Historical Perspective on The President's Own U.S. Marine Band.* Washington, DC: History and Museums Division, Headquarters, U.S. Marine Corps, 1998.

Shaw, Henry I. Jr. *First Offensive: The Marine Campaign for Guadalcanal.* Washington, DC: History and Museums Division, Headquarters, U.S. Marine Corps, 1992.

Shaw, Henry I. Jr., and Ralph W. Donnelly. *Blacks in the Marine Corps.* Washington, DC: History and Museums Division, Headquarters, U.S. Marine Corps, 1988.

Shulimson, Jack. *U.S. Marines in Vietnam: The Defining Year, 1968.* Washington, DC: History and Museums Division, Headquarters, U.S. Marine Corps, 1997.

Shulimson, Jack et. al. *Marines in the Spanish-American War, 1895–1899: Anthology and Annotated Bibliography.* Washington, DC: History and Museums Division, Headquarters, U.S. Marine Corps, 1998.

Simmons, Edwin H. *The United States Marines: A History.* Annapolis: Naval Institute Press, 1998.

———. *U.S. Marines at Inchon: Over the Seawall.* Washington, DC: History and Museums Division, Headquarters, U.S. Marine Corps, 2000.

———. *U.S. Marines at the Changjin Reservoir: Frozen Chosin.* Washington, DC: History and Museums Division, Headquarters, U.S. Marine Corps, 2002.

———. "With Lincoln at Gettysburg." *Fortitudine,* XVIII, no. 2 (Fall 1988): pp. 3–6.

Sledge, Eugene. *With the Old Breed: At Peleliu and Okinawa.* New York: Oxford University Press, 1990.

Smith, Charles R. *Marines in the Revolution: A History of the Continental Marines in the American Revolution, 1775–1783.* Washington, DC: History and Museums Division, Headquarters, U.S. Marine Corps, 1975.

———. *U.S. Marines in Humanitarian Operations: Angels from the Sea: Relief Operations in Bangladesh, 1991.* Washington, DC: History and Museums Division, Headquarters, U.S. Marine Corps, 1995.

Smith, Holland M. *The Development of Amphibious Tactics in the U.S. Navy.* Washington, DC: History and Museums Division, Headquarters, U.S. Marine Corps, 1992.

Spector, Ronald H. *U.S. Marines in Grenada, 1983.* Washington, DC: History and Museums Division, Headquarters, U.S. Marine Corps, 1987.

Stolfi, Russel H. *U.S. Marine Corps Civic Action Effort in Vietnam, March 1965–March 1966.* Washington, DC: History and Museums Division, Headquarters, U.S. Marine Corps, 1968.

Stremlow, Mary V. *Free a Marine to Fight: Women Marines in World War II.* Washington, DC: History and Museums Division, Headquarters, U.S. Marine Corps, 1994.

Thompson, John W. *Fix Bayonets!* New York: C. Scribner's Sons, 1926.

Updegraph, Charles L. Jr. *Special Marine Corps Units of World War II.* Washington, DC: History and Museums Division, Headquarters, U.S. Marine Corps, 1972.

WEBSITES

www.usmc.mil

U.S. Marine Corps website

hqinet001.hqmc.usmc.mil/HD/Home_Page.htm

U.S. Marine Corps History and Museums Division website

INDEX